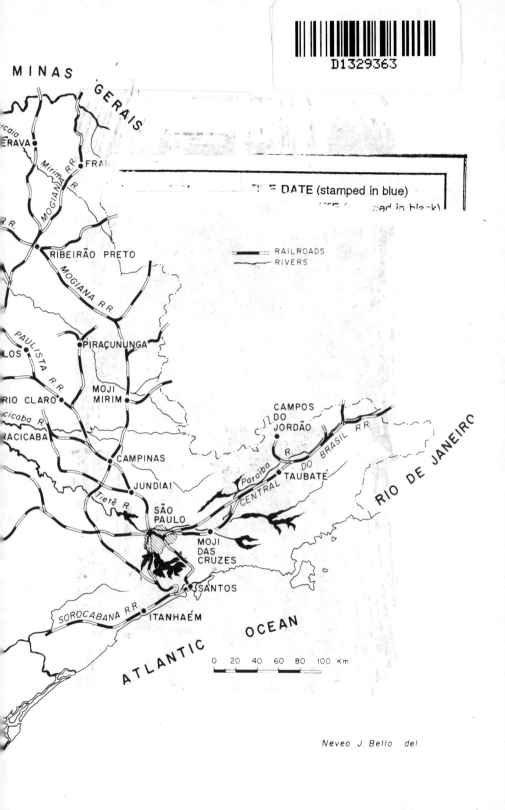

MINAS

GERAIS

rcaia
ERAVA

Mirim R.R.

FRAN

MOGIANA R.R.

R.R.

RIBEIRÃO PRETO

MOGIANA R.R.

RAILROADS
RIVERS

PAULISTA R.R.

LOS

PIRAÇUNUNGA

RIO CLARO

MOJI
MIRIM

CAMPOS
DO
JORDÃO

cicaba R.

RACICABA

CAMPINAS

Paraíba R.

CENTRAL DO BRASIL R.R.

TAUBATÉ

RIO DE JANEIRO

JUNDIAI

Tietê R.

SÃO
PAULO

MOJI
DAS
CRUZES

SANTOS

SOROCABANA R.R.

ITANHAÉM

ATLANTIC

OCEAN

0   20   40   60   80   100 Km

Neveo J. Bello   del.

From Community to Metropolis

A biography of
São Paulo, Brazil

THE CITY OF SÃO PAULO

0 2 4 6 8 10 km

THE CITY
IN 1840

CITY GROWTH
1840-1890

CITY GROWTH
1890-1925

CITY GROWTH
1925-1950

RIO DE JANEIRO

CENTRAL DO BRASIL

SANTOS

PENHA

CANTAREIRA

BRAZ

MOOCA

IPIRANGA

SÉ

TIETÊ R.

JARDIM AMÉRICA

LAPA

PINHEIROS R.

BUTANTÃ

SANTO AMARO

"SANTOS A JUNDIAI"

JUNDIAI

SOROCABANA

TIETÊ R.

SOROCABA

RICHARD M. MORSE

From Community to Metropolis

A biography of
São Paulo, Brazil

New and enlarged edition

OCTAGON BOOKS

A DIVISION OF FARRAR, STRAUS AND GIROUX

New York   1974

For Emerante

Reprinted 1974
by special arrangement with the University of Florida Press

OCTAGON BOOKS
A DIVISION OF FARRAR, STRAUS & GIROUX, INC.
19 Union Square West
New York, N. Y. 10003

LIBRARY OF CONGRESS CATALOG CARD NUMBER: 75-159248
ISBN 0-374-95914-5

Printed in USA by
Thomson-Shore, Inc.
Dexter, Michigan

Preface

THE RESEARCH upon which this history is based was made possible by a travel and maintenance grant from the United States Department of State that enabled me to spend over a year in Brazil, from September, 1947, to December, 1948. Preparation and publication of the manuscript were assisted by two grants from the Council for Research in the Social Sciences, Columbia University, and by a grant from the Dunning Fund of the Department of History, Columbia University. In addition to expressing my gratitude for these sources of help, I extend thanks to the Comissão do IV Centenário de São Paulo, which published a somewhat different version of this study, translated into Portuguese by Maria Apparecida Madeira Kerbeg, in connection with the fourth centennial of São Paulo city, celebrated in 1954.

It is difficult to name all the persons, both Brazilians and Americans, who freely shared their time and knowledge with me during the period of my research. The list which follows, moreover, contains the names of many who became warm friends, and whose contributions cannot be assessed in any calculus of "acknowledgments." Among those whose help and kindness I remember with gratitude are: Guilherme de Almeida, Décio and Ruth de Almeida Prado, Jan F. de Almeida Prado, Jorge Americano, Rone Amorim, Alceu Amoroso Lima, Oswald de Andrade Filho, Oscar Egydio de Araújo, Aury Avillez, Fernando de Azevedo, Rivadavia de Barros, Sérgio Buarque de Holanda, Antônio and Gilda Cândido de Mello e Souza, Alice P. Cannabrava, Guiomar de Carvalho Franco, João Cruz Costa, Francisco Dias de Andrade, Paulo Duarte, Florestan

Fernandes, Maria Antonieta Ferraz, Gilberto Freyre, Lourival and Lourdes Gomes Machado, the late Lucila Herrmann, Edgard Leuenroth, Rino Levi, Anita Malfatti, Sérgio Milliet, Maria Luisa Monteiro da Cunha, Donald Pierson, Caio Prado Junior, Francisco Prestes Maia, Joseph and Betty Privitera, Luís Saia, Afonso Schmidt, Carlos Borges Schmidt, the late Lasar Segall, Monsenhor Paulo Florêncio da Silveira Camargo, Carleton Sprague Smith, Ernesto de Souza Campos, and Mário Wagner Vieira da Cunha. I wish also to record my appreciation for the year of generous Brazilian hospitality which I enjoyed in the home of D. Alice and the late Dr. José Avelino Chaves.

The following institutions were constant sources of help and cooperation. In São Paulo: the Arquivo do Estado de São Paulo; the Associação Brasileira Cimento Portland; the Biblioteca Municipal; the Companhia Geral de Engenharia, S.A.; the Departamento de Cultura da Prefeitura do Município de São Paulo; the Departamento Estadual de Estatística; the Escola de Sociologia e Política de São Paulo; the Instituto Histórico e Geográfico de São Paulo; the Museu Paulista; the newspaper O Estado de São Paulo; the Secretaria da Agricultura, Indústria e Comércio do Estado de São Paulo; the Secretaria de Obras da Prefeitura do Município de São Paulo; the Sociedade Amigos da Cidade; the União Cultural Brasil-Estados Unidos; and the Universidade de São Paulo (in particular the Faculdade de Direito, the Faculdade de Filosofia, Ciências e Letras, and the Instituto de Administração). In Rio de Janeiro: the Arquivo Nacional, the Biblioteca Nacional, and the Instituto Histórico e Geográfico Brasileiro.

At an early stage of the writing, Dwight C. Miner offered some most useful suggestions regarding the organization of subject matter. Manoel Cardozo and Benjamin N. Nelson gave the manuscript a painstaking reading when it was near completion and made penetrating comments on style, details, and interpretation. I have also benefited from the observations of Robert Redfield, who was kind enough to read a large portion of the study. My debt is especially heavy to my teacher and colleague Frank Tannenbaum and to his large vision of Latin America in its human terms. Armando Piñol gave freely of his time in drawing maps, and Gladys Susman, now Gladys Topkis, prepared the typescript with much efficiency. The editors of the University of Florida Press have been extremely observant readers of the final version.

In the interest of the less-specialized reader, bibliographical footnotes are not used in this book. Many references, however, generally identifying quoted material, are incorporated into the text in a shorthand form that is keyed to the alphabetized bibliography at the end of the book. In addition, each section closes with a bibliographical note which reviews the more general sources that may not have been cited in the text. Preceding the bibliography is a note containing references that are relevant to the study as a whole. The bibliography is a selective one; and although I have made an effort to keep abreast of new publications since my departure from Brazil at the end of 1948, this attempt has of necessity been only partially successful. Except for the bibliography and references thereto, modern orthography has been used for Portuguese words.

Mention needs to be made about Brazilian monetary values, which appear throughout the study. Until October, 1942, the unit of currency was the *milréis* (that is, 1,000 reals, or *réis*), written as 1$000. Since then the equivalent unit has been the *cruzeiro*, written as 1$00 and made up of a hundred *centavos*. A *conto* is 1,000 milréis (1:000$000) or cruzeiros (1:000$00). During much of the nineteenth century the value of the milréis remained near fifty American cents. In the 1890's, the early years of the republic, this value declined by almost three-quarters; it recovered somewhat before World War I, only to fall again in the 1920's. A third, more drastic wave of inflation set in during the depression which lowered the cruzeiro to about five and a half cents by the 1940's and to well under one cent at the time of writing.

Acknowledgment is hereby made for permission to quote from the following books and articles: *An Approach to Urban Planning,* edited by Gerald Breese and Dorothy E. Whiteman: Princeton University Press; *Brazil, Portrait of Half a Continent,* edited by T. Lynn Smith and Alexander Marchant: The Dryden Press, Inc.; *Cities of Latin America,* by Francis Violich: Reinhold Publishing Corporation; "City of Enterprise": *Time,* LIX, 3 (January 21, 1952); *On the Limits of Poetry: Selected Essays,* by Allen Tate: The Swallow Press; *Proceedings of the International Colloquium on Luso-Brazilian Studies:* Vanderbilt University Press; "Sears, Roebuck in

Rio": *Fortune* (February, 1950); *The Decline of the West* (Vol. II), by Oswald Spengler: Alfred A. Knopf, Inc.; *The Life of Joaquim Nabuco,* by Carolina Nabuco: Stanford University Press; *The Pocket History of American Painting,* by James Thomas Flexner: Pocket Books, Inc.

R. M. M.

New York City

Note to the Second Edition

The text of the first edition is reprinted here without change. To it I have appended a new section which attempts to summarize urban developments and research thereon from 1955 to 1970. An earlier version of this section appeared in Volume I of *Latin American Urban Research;* I am grateful to the editors, Francine P. Rabinovitz and Felicity M. Trueblood, and to Sage Publications, Inc., for their kindness in allowing reuse of this material. The Center for Advanced Study in the Behavioral Sciences gave me time to revise the chapter; Irene Bickenbach typed it with great precision, and Ralph della Cava, Joseph L. Love, Stanley J. Stein, and John D. Wirth offered constructive comments. During my five short visits to São Paulo between 1965 and 1971 old friends of twenty-five years' standing who are mentioned in the Preface and many newer ones were unfailingly gracious and helpful. The Centro Brasileiro de Análise e Planejamento made available unpublished research. Neveo J. Bello of the Instituto de Geografia, Universidade de São Paulo, redrew the endpaper and frontispiece maps.

R. M. M.

Woodbridge, Connecticut

Contents

ix

Illustrations

Introduction

S ÃO PAULO, BRAZIL, with a reported population in 1957 of 3,069,626 inhabitants, is today the fastest-growing city and leading industrial center of Latin America. In 1955 the Council for Inter-American Cooperation called it, in fact, the fastest-growing city in the world, and estimated that it will have a population of 4,700,000 by 1964. Travelers who have visited São Paulo in recent decades almost invariably refer to its "dynamism" and "spirit of Yankee enterprise," and characterize it as a "boom town" or as "the Chicago of South America." That such a metropolis should, in less than a century, have erupted within a plantation economy, within a Roman Catholic, patriarchal, and tradition-bound culture, and in a country indifferently blessed with the resources for industrial development often seems, to the traveler's eye, anachronistic. To explore if not wholly to explain this anachronism is the purpose of this book. In the course of the study it will become clear that São Paulo is not a replica of Chicago, that the mesh and action of its society are influenced by traditions of the Brazilian hinterland, and that what there exists of the "ethos of capitalism" crystallizes in forms often unfamiliar to North Americans.

At the outset, however, it should be stressed that there does appear to be an environment common to Latin and to "Anglo-Saxon" America which imparts special traits to the cities of the New World. The analogy between the Brazilian and the United States city is a suggestive one, the important implications of which are revealed in the genetic view of how cities were brought forth in the New World rather than in casual impressions of present-day city life. This genetic view calls for some prior generalizations about city growth in the European mother continent.

The town or city of western Europe in about 1500, in the era of the discovery of America, was by and large a product of the Middle Ages. There is little continuity, that is, between the urban history of the Roman Empire and that of early modern Europe. The towns established by the Romans had appeared, so to speak, in a moment of time. Their typical town, laid out on a strategically chosen site, was rectilinear and camplike in appearance, and surrounding lands were distributed by lot among soldier-farmers; if it served as a commercial entrepôt, it did so only fortuitously. Local government was modeled after that of the city of Rome. In short, the town was an outpost of the imperial metropolis, rather than a nucleus of settlement which had grown in answer to the needs of an adjacent society and economy.

The third century A.D. witnessed a decline in city life throughout Roman Europe. A salient cause was the tendency of the imperial government, as it entered its phase of autocratic "state socialism," to exploit the conveniently concentrated wealth of the cities instead of subsidizing them in the name of Roman grandeur. As the cities' energies and the size of their population dwindled, it was in the rural villa that the activities for maintaining life came to center. The proprietor moved from the city to make his residence there permanently, and around him clustered the laborers and artisans who, in diverse relations of subordination, carried on the harvesting and manufacturing that made survival possible on a relatively self-sufficient basis.

According to the thesis of the Belgian historian Henri Pirenne (which has been qualified by other scholars in ways that need not here concern us), it was the seventh and eighth centuries, when Islam acquired control of the Mediterranean Sea, that marked the final stage of Roman Europe. As the Frankish, Carolingian Empire succeeded the Roman, the Rhine River succeeded the Mediterranean as the core of European unity, to the extent that such unity existed. The new empire, lacking foreign markets and economically turned in upon itself, was a predominantly agrarian one. This meant, for one thing, that it had no populous and wealthy cities, living off extensive foreign commerce and the surplus production of lands adjacent to them. For another, it meant that the old Roman villa system, which had been essentially a projection of urban social forms and economic demands upon the countryside, was replaced by medieval demesnial organization.

When at length in the twelfth century the meager trade of the post-Roman era began to quicken, the revived activities of commerce and manufacture found their own points of crystallization. Customarily, according to Pirenne, such points were fortified towns that served as diocesan centers. The cities of Europe took form as these favorably situated towns, or "burgs," acquired commercial suburbs, or *faubourgs*. This process led to a differentiation of function between city and country; and it created commercial and manufacturing middle classes that had no counterpart either in the village-communities which had developed upon and often superseded the old Roman villas, or in those burgs which had been bypassed by the revival of trade and which persisted as semirural market towns. The differentiation of city and country, however, did not signify sharp discontinuity between them. Late-medieval cities were created, not by rationally elaborated, imperial design, but by spontaneous growth which articulated them with the regional economy and with the arteries of the continental one. To this external articulation corresponded a slow, internal sedimentation of functions.

That the Europeans who colonized the New World after 1492 should re-create in it the villages and towns of their homelands was hardly to be expected. In the first place, the long-evolved functionalism of the European town, which by the late Middle Ages was sustained by a certain balance between man and nature as well as by forces of tradition, could scarcely be reproduced by a few handfuls of settlers in the vast, untamed, unknown Americas, where trade routes and regional economies were unlikely to achieve permanent features for generations, even centuries. On the plateau of southern Brazil where São Paulo was founded, for example, the routine functions of many a town government were paralyzed for long intervals throughout the colonial period when the town fathers decamped on slave- or gold-hunting expeditions, or when they gave precedence to the job of clearing and working outlying plantations. It was particularly in such regions as this, where "primary accumulations" of wealth (to use the Marxist phrase) were not easily come by, that municipal affairs were imperfectly and intermittently administered and that town nuclei showed a frequently centrifugal character.

In the second place, many of those who emigrated to the Americas had little intention of transplanting Old World communities to it. American settlements received numbers of persons from restless and marginal walks of life who, by the very act of emigrating, revealed impatience with the tradition-bound order. They came — and for centuries continued to come — not from isolated, conservative regions, where the ties of the past and of the primary group were vigorous, but from regions or sectors of society which, although shaken by contact with the outside world, had not been reorganized sufficiently to allow the individual to become absorbed into a larger entity, such as the nation. To the extent that a New World community received persons of this description — and they were perhaps representative of those who came to southern Brazil — its binding force was contingent largely upon needs of the moment.

Lastly, it remains to point out that the colonization of the Americas got under way at a time when the European was beginning to speculate on the possibilities of imparting rational order to the communities in which he lived. The urgency with which the New World was explored and the speed with which it was settled were in fact indices of man's newborn confidence that he might fashion his environment for social ends. Untrammeled by the usages, communities, and delicate ecological balance of Europe, the New World became an inevitable proving ground for schemes of rational social organization that ranged from Father Bartolomé de Las Casas' land of "True Peace" in sixteenth-century Guatemala to Robert Owen's "New Harmony" in nineteenth-century Indiana. It is significant that Sir Thomas More's *Utopia*, although visionary for the country in which he lived, served as a practical handbook for the missionary labors of Father Vasco de Quiroga among the Indians of Mexico.

The incipient outlook of modern "planning," then, served to counteract, or perhaps to camouflage, the unsteadying effects which the protean hinterland economy and the restless nature of the emigrants had upon New World communities. One may generalize by saying, as William I. Thomas and Florian Znaniecki did in their study of Polish emigration to the United States, that whereas in post-Roman Europe territorial vicinity has been the foundation of community life, in the Americas rationalized social organization became the main factor of territorial concentration.

The regulations for the founding of towns set forth in the

Spanish "Laws of the Indies" indicate how the rationalist attitude might shape city growth in the New World. These laws stipulated the economic and geographic factors to be weighed in choosing the site; they specified the orientation and measurements for a rectilinear street plan, centering on a spacious plaza, which contrasted with the cramped and jumbled plan of cities in Spain; and they minutely codified the procedures of municipal administration. As the historian Sérgio Buarque de HOLANDA (1948, p. 134) has observed, this use of Renaissance geometrism in the Americas sprang from "the idea that man can arbitrarily and successfully intervene in the sequence of things and that history not only 'happens' but can also be directed and even fabricated."

In Portuguese Brazil, as in the United States, it was not until the nineteenth-century occupation of the hinterland that the proliferation of geometric, or gridiron, cities occurred. Yet the larger towns of colonial Brazil, to whatever degree their physical plan was improvised in response to local conditions and topography, represented, as did their Spanish American counterparts, the intrusion of a ready-made metropolitan order. Salvador, Bahia, for example, the Brazilian capital until 1763, was founded in 1549 as the seat of an urban bureaucracy — judiciary, administrative, and military; in later years it overflowed with such metropolitan types as clerics, magistrates, doctors, and students. Even had it been domiciled within a neatly rectilinear city, however, one could scarcely have looked for this transplanted segment of the imperial bureaucracy to diffuse order and coherence to the sprawling, unexploited backlands. As an outpost rather than a radiating center of the metropolitan order, Salvador in a sense turned in upon itself, and the urban hierarchy took on a largely parasitic character. The job of truly *settling* the new land could be done only through a decentralized reassertion of man's claims upon nature. It involved a "telluric" experience. And those elements of society which undertook the task, which became "functional," that is, as explorers, planters, miners, or graziers, were permanently drawn off from the city nucleus. The very fact that they carried with them the calculative outlook of the city hastened them to slough off the formalities and involutions of urban life.

A parallel now becomes evident between the extension of the Spanish and Portuguese empires to America and the extension, in ancient times, of the Roman Empire to western Europe. In both cases the process was keyed to the outlook, needs, and institutions of a distant metropolis. In both cases the enlargement of the empire was effected by the creation of towns in the image of the metropolis, so far as local conditions permitted, and by subdivision of rural lands on an individual, exploitative basis that mirrored the needs of urban economy and society. In both cases the village-community, whether independent or subordinate to the large private holding, was an occasional remnant or growth in the interstices of the dominant order.

The analogy between the Americas and post-Roman Europe is, of course, by no means a complete one. The institutional history of western Europe during the first millennium and a half of the Christian era appears to exhibit — at least from our distant point of vantage — a sequence of phases during which the Roman towns, the villas, the manors and village-communities, and finally the commercial and industrial towns were the successive centers of importance. The Americas, on the other hand, have at no time, as colonies or as nations, escaped the pressures of the metropolitan motherland. Those outlying New World regions which are left to self-development as subsistence economies may, as they show possibilities for surplus production, be swept into the orbit and processes of the world economy. Concurrently, regions intensely exploited by the metropolis may suddenly be abandoned to self-subsistence and to a larger measure of institutional self-determination. In the history, then, as in the music of the Americas, one discerns, as it were, a "syncopation" that is alien to the European experience.

The plateau in southern Brazil upon which the Jesuits founded São Paulo in 1554 was throughout the colonial period a relatively isolated, impoverished, and self-supplying area. By the time of Brazilian independence in 1822, São Paulo had come into certain commercial and political importance, but it was the coffee boom of some thirty years later that made possible the phenomenal growth of the modern metropolis. Before that time there was no urbanization of the São Paulo region. Starting with the early *sesmarias,* or land grants, made by representatives of the Portuguese crown, the settlement was the story of individuals trying to "strike it rich" through extractive pursuits, agricultural or mineral. Such communities as evolved — the small village, the patriarchal sugar plantation, or the roving *bandeira* which searched the wilderness for Indian slaves or gold — were of a contingent nature. Their binding force, that is, was imposed by the rigors and isolation of the region and by the threat of Indian attack, and was not generated internally by a nuclear sedimentation of usage and function. Although municipal governments came into being from the start, the primary and effective ties among men were those of the extended family; and the criteria for family leadership were in great measure pragmatic ones, imposed by the environment. The Jesuits alone, who founded many missions on the plateau, including São Paulo itself, represented a "universal," rationally nucleated order; but they never won the upper hand with the settlers, and their missions never achieved the dominance that they did in parts of Spanish America, notably Paraguay.

As late as the second half of the eighteenth century, the captain-general of São Paulo found it well-nigh impossible to create village settlements such as he had known in Portugal. The "little" men, he wrote, rebel at village life "because they want to live in liberty, in dissoluteness, in their vices, free from every kind of justice; and the great ones because they want to exploit the former, under the name of wards, and have them as genuine slaves, and from this is born or thought up all the ways possible to impede the establishment of the villages." (SMITH and MARCHANT, 1951, p. 170.) The call of the forests, and the short life of the farms which settlers cleared in them by the wasteful methods of slash-and-burn agriculture, were an important cause for this dispersive pattern of settlement. Of the thirty-eight modest villages which did exist in the captaincy in the 1760's, the majority had so limited a radius of influence that a large part of the rural population did not even attend church, and many were not baptized until they were adults.

The more important villages on the plateau, whose inhabitants often included a high proportion of newly arrived Portuguese, were those which served functions beyond those of an agrarian nucleus. They might be, for example, centers for worship, pilgrimage, or missionary activity; way stations for bandeiras or mule teams; or military garrisons. The purely agrarian villages had often originated upon the land grants and plantations, much as small hamlets once appeared on the lands of, and in subordination to, the Roman villas. Other farm towns that had been founded by the captain-general tended, because of their artificial character, to have a marginal existence or even to dwindle to extinction.

The present study of São Paulo begins with the early nineteenth century, the era of Brazilian independence. The first chapter, however, opens with a brief survey of the city's colonial history, in which São Paulo's role as a religious, commercial, and bureaucratic center is indicated. This role was a fluctuating one, and it failed to give the town an appearance less rustic than that of others in the region. Yet perhaps it did impart an extra measure of coherence and continuity to the municipal center. In fact the sociologist Oliveira VIANNA (1949, I, p. 169) claimed that colonial São Paulo is the exception to the lack of group solidarity in Brazil, and provides "a fine instance of an 'agrarian hamlet' in operation, such as today we still see in the Hispanic *pueblos*, Swiss *Gemeinden*, or Anglo-Saxon townships of the new and old continents." The statement is exaggerated and the analogies misleading; but given the fact that colonial São Paulo was for certain reasons a natural point of settlement, its relative isolation and the modesty of regional resources endowed it with some of the cooperativist traits that we associate with the "face-to-face" community.

It is because this history is concerned with the urbanization of São Paulo that it does not dwell on the colonial centuries. In the view of Oswald SPENGLER (1939, II, pp. 94-97), in fact, it is only for urban civilization that "history" has significance. Rural peoples precede and outlive "every Culture that ensconces itself in the cities. . . . The city is intellect. . . . It is in resistance to the 'feudal' powers of blood and tradition that the burgherdom or bourgeoisie, the intellectual class, begins to be conscious of its own separate existence. It upsets thrones and limits old rights in the name of reason and above all in the name of 'the People,' which henceforward means exclusively the people of the city."

The village, "with its quiet hillocky roofs, its evening smoke, its wells, its hedges, and its beasts," *confirms* the countryside; it lies "fused and embedded in the landscape." The town insists that the countryside *conform* to its own formalized, artificial outlook. "*Extra muros*, chaussées and woods and pastures become a park, mountains become tourists' view-points; and *intra muros* arises an imitation Nature, fountains in lieu of springs, flower-beds, formal pools, and clipped hedges in lieu of meadows and ponds and bushes."

This study deals with the impingement of a metropolitan order upon the hinterland of Brazil. It is a process which in some ways repeats what occurred in parts of Spanish America as early as the sixteenth century, but which in other ways is unique to systems and forces of the nineteenth and twentieth centuries.

The words "community" and "metropolis" appearing in the title merit a note of explanation. "Community" is used to suggest some general qualities of life in the São Paulo of *ca.* 1820: its limited size, its relative isolation and parochialism, the ways in which its physical appearance and the life of its inhabitants reflected the modest subsistence economy of its environs, the high importance of "face-to-face" relationships, and the unity deriving from the faith, ritual, and pageantry of a common religion. Although these traits contributed to a certain "spirit of community" and to certain co-operativist modes of behavior, one need not conclude that the processes of life were knit into an overarching communalist pattern corresponding to the model type which, with varying connotations, is referred to by such sociological terms as folk society, mechanical solidarity, and *Gemeinschaft*. The presence of what Thorstein Veblen called "predatory" economic attitudes, the unstable relations prevailing between man and the largely unexploited hinterland, and the multiplying contacts with the outside world all militated against the achievement of "community" in the somewhat idyllic sense. Indeed, part of what we might identify as "the spirit of community" in the São Paulo of 1820 was less indicative of a vigorous tradition of cooperativism than of the apathy, misoneism, and social introversion that result when individual economic initiative fails of its goals.

For the term "metropolis" the context will sometimes suggest pejorative connotations of overgrowth and chaos, and imply that in modern São Paulo lie the seeds of what Spengler and Lewis Mumford call the "megalopolis." By and large, however, the word is used not as normative, but as descriptive of an urban order which overflows its "city limits" to rearrange the institutions of the whole countryside. With the advent of a metropolis, surrounding settlements become functionally specialized satellites, while the wider hinterland becomes an economic tributary. "Metropolis" conveys a sense of institutional derangement partly because the economic interdependence which a metropolis brings to a region is frequently not accompanied by the requisite social vision and political reorganization.

Of recent years the penetration of the industrial, urban world into the agrarian societies of Latin America has come under scrutiny by sociologists and social anthropologists. The more important studies, however, deal with small rural communities upon which city influences impinge. Moreover, they are contemporary analyses, deficient in historical context. The present study of São Paulo deals with the growth of a large city over a period of nearly a century and a half. Whatever may be gained by this genetic treatment of urbanization is, to be sure, somewhat offset by the diversity and fragmentariness of historical data in comparison with those yielded by an on-the-spot investigation of a small contemporary village. This history, however, does not purport to match the exhaustiveness and precise categorization of a sociological "community study." The themes taken up, it is hoped, will not be found alien to the interests of social scientists; but the principles by which they are ordered perhaps derive more from the humanistic than from the scientific vein of historiography.

In the first place, the various realms of data, including ecological, economic, sociological, institutional, and cultural, have been drawn from with a rather free eclecticism. So that the city, as an entity, will remain fairly consistently in focus, these data have been interwoven rather than compartmentalized; and syntheses suggested by cultural expression have repeatedly been made use of. Secondly, this history is periodized in a fashion intended to indicate the "phrasing" and "rhythms" of the city's development. The historian, indeed, must permit himself license to bring out the shifts and stresses of his story — for the very purpose of telling a "story." As soon, however, as one characterizes the mood and activities of a city for any ten- or twenty-year period, one easily warps the amorphous and recalcitrant substrate of human affairs into false patterns. It will therefore be important to keep in mind that, whatever temper and rhetoric or whatever potentialities for change appear to characterize São Paulo during a given generation, the city's history during the past hundred and fifty years or more has certain steady undercurrents. Perhaps the most significant such current may be expressed in institutional terms as a shift from a dominantly horizontal organization of public life through local familial ties to a dominantly vertical one through public and quasi-public bureaucracies. In relation to western European experience, this development, which occurs throughout the Americas, is a highly telescoped one. It brings serious imbalance and dislocation. At the same time, however, the ways in which the old and new, the parochial and cosmopolitan, the familial and the bureaucratic are still found to coexist in Brazil lead one to speculate how domestic traditions of the community might, in forms that have no precedent, imbue the universalist order of the metropolis with coherence and vitality.

Part 1—Colonialism and New Stimulants

Chapter 1

ANTECEDENTS

*T*HE TOWNS OF COLONIAL BRAZIL, as was pointed out
in the Introduction, showed little of the elegance
and trim geometry which characterized Spanish cities in the New
World. The call of the plantations and of the backlands had a
centrifugal effect on town life. This effect was reinforced by the
inability of the settlers, for two centuries at least, to strike the gold
and precious stones that might have given impetus to urbanization.

The Portuguese, also, were less concerned than the Spaniards
with establishing abroad the metropolitan symbols of imperial prestige. For more than three centuries before the landing of the Portuguese navigator Pedro Alvares Cabral in Brazil in 1500, a class of
merchants and seafarers had been imparting to Portugal's relations
with other lands the wiliness and permissiveness of the commercial
spirit. This is not to say that the country's foreign ventures lacked
any infusion of nationalist or missionary spirit. The great epic of
sixteenth-century Portuguese expansion, the *Lusiads* of Luís de
Camões, proves quite the contrary. Portugal, however, had long
since achieved political unity, and its Moors had long since been
driven out or assimilated. At the time, therefore, when overseas
expansion gathered momentum, the country experienced nothing
quite comparable to the afflatus of nationalist fervor and Catholic
zeal with which the Moorish campaigns of Ferdinand and Isabella
had just imbued neighboring Spain. And, however warmly the
pretensions of Portugal to imperial grandeur may have been kindled,
its population was too small, its resources too limited, and its interests in Africa, the Orient, and America too extensive for it to

2

sustain heavy emigration and the proliferation of metropolitan centers.

Significantly, the name which Cabral first gave to Brazil, "Land of the True Cross," was soon replaced by one which suggested a modest, frankly commercial venture — for "brazilwood" was a valuable dyewood, so named because its redness suggested a live coal (*brasa*). For three decades after 1500 the Portuguese, absorbed in their trade with the fabled Orient, sent merely sporadic expeditions to coastal Brazil for this dyewood. Not until the end of that period did the crown undertake permanent colonization. By then it had become clear that Brazil formed part of an immense new world which, as the Spanish conquistadors were proving, contained important sources of wealth. Already corsairs of other nations, notably France, were making incursions along the Brazilian coast, to which Portugal held title by the Treaty of Tordesillas (1494), and were carrying off cargoes of brazilwood. The Portuguese king, João III, saw that he must make good his claim to Brazil or forever forfeit it.

In December, 1530, under the king's orders, Martim Afonso de Sousa set sail from Lisbon with five ships and four hundred men. His mission was to clear the sea lanes of privateers and to establish communication with a small trading post, or *feitoria,* that existed at Pernambuco toward the north of Brazil. He was then to proceed southward, surveying the coast and exploring possibilities for agricultural colonization and further commercial development. This he did, and from one point he dispatched an eighty-man expedition inland to look for precious metals — the forerunner of hundreds which were for two centuries to penetrate the hinterland in search of minerals or Indian slaves; this one, however, was swallowed up in the wilds and never again heard from. Later, when his flagship ran aground, Martim Afonso sent ahead his brother, Pero Lopes de Sousa, to explore the River Plate, for he had been charged by the king to ascertain whether this "river of silver" lay on the Spanish side of the Tordesillas line — which indeed it did.

After his brother's ship had rejoined, Martim Afonso returned northward in January, 1532, and finally chose the little island of São Vicente, at about 23° south, for the first colony. "Here in this port of São Vicente we beached one of the ships," reads the journal of Pero Lopes de Sousa (1861, p. 66). "We all thought so well of the place that the captain determined to settle it, and he gave each man land for farming....He established conditions for law and order, from which all the people took great comfort, in seeing towns settled, in having laws and the saying of mass, in celebrating marriages and in living in a civilized way; and in being each the master of his own, in having redress for private grievances, and in enjoying all the other goods of a life safe and secure."

Its harbor, fertile coastal plain, and benign, semitropical climate did not, however, solely determine the choice of São Vicente. Another consideration was the presence of a Portuguese castaway, one João Ramalho, who had, presumably, been shipwrecked some twenty years earlier and was living in friendship with the Indians. Although these Indians, the Tupinakins, regularly came down to the ocean to fish, their villages were inland on the plateau which lies behind the abrupt, 2,400-foot coastal range, the *Serra do Mar.* By 1532 Ramalho was headman of one of these upland communities and lived with a daughter of the chieftain Tibiriçá. He, and a scattering of fellow castaways at this and other points of the coast, typified the endurance, fiber, and shrewd acquiescence in the ways of the backlands upon which was to depend the success of the colonists.

Some months after his arrival Martim Afonso accompanied Ramalho to his headquarters on the plateau. Because it was situated by an open plain, the settlement was called Borda do Campo (Edge of the Field). In its straggling huts of thatch and wattle-and-daub lived Indians, a few whites, and the first mestizos, or half-breeds, later known as *mamelucos.* Martim Afonso, concluding that this rude settlement lay in a land of promise, was aware that free traffic between whites of the coast and the Indians would lead to the exploitation and even enslavement of the latter. Accordingly, on his return to São Vicente he ordered that none of the newly arrived Portuguese be allowed access to the plateau without official permission, which was to be given with circumspection and only to persons of good character. Ramalho himself was directed to establish Borda do Campo as an official village.

In 1549 Tomé de Sousa arrived in Salvador, Bahia, as the first governor-general of Brazil, and he bore instructions from the king, similar to the above, which applied to the whole of the coast. It was evident that for the present Portugal must conserve its limited human resources by concentrating its settlements near the ocean and navigable rivers. Colonists who might penetrate the backlands, called the *sertão*, would provoke debilitating strife with the Indians. Those of them who struck roots, moreover, would little benefit the empire, for they would be reluctant to pay the heavy expenses of shipping out their produce over tortuous trails that were subject to Indian attack, only to have the profits absorbed by coastal merchants. Portuguese colonization therefore assumed a gradual, vegetative character. It bore no parallel to the methods of those Spaniards who, attracted by silver mines or by concentrations of sedentary Indian labor, implanted sizable cities far inland, on mountain plateaus.

Before long, however, it became clear that the colonization of São Vicente would be an exception to the Brazilian pattern. Martim Afonso, "donatary" of the captaincy, was one of the few active proprietors, or freeholders, of the twelve whom the king appointed in 1534-1536 to administer segments of the coast. The port of São Vicente soon boasted a stockade, a church, municipal buildings, and adequate residences. Land grants were made to encourage agriculture and stock raising. A water-driven sugar mill, which passed into the hands of the Schetz firm of Antwerp, was erected to process the crop that until the start of the coffee cycle in the nineteenth century was to be Brazil's leading agricultural export. A society of merchants was formed which sent sugar and other produce to Europe and imported commodities for resale to the Indians. The port city of Santos, later to overshadow São Vicente, was founded in 1536 and chartered in 1545.

It was not to be expected that so enterprising a settlement would exist for long without putting forth centers on the adjacent plateau, especially since certain factors favored penetration at this point on the coast. For one thing, the littoral narrows to a few miles at São Vicente, making the coastal range easily accessible. For another, the mountains are less precipitous here than farther north and less sprawling and heavily forested than farther south. This, however, is not to say that there was an easy ascent from São Vicente. According to the seventeenth-century Jesuit chronicler Simão de Vasconcellos (1865, I, p. 87): "Most of the way one cannot walk but must climb with feet and hands, clutching roots of trees, and among such chasms and precipices that I confess when I first ascended it made my flesh tremble to look down."

After ascending the Serra, one is on the edge of a vast plateau of about 180,000 square miles which slopes gradually to the west and south, where its rivers — the largest being the Tietê and Paranapanema — join the Paraná-Plate system. Removed from the thermostatic action of the sea, the plateau near the Serra is of a more varied and less humid climate than the coast; its mean temperature drops from 69° in the summer to 55° in the winter, and Vasconcellos wrote that one was never satiated with the freshness of this "second region of the air." Although the eastern part of the plateau is not excessively fertile, its light forestation was advantageous for colonists concerned with clearing farmlands and with defending them against Indian attack. It provided, moreover, a natural base from which to explore inland in search of rumored mineral deposits.

Together with the plateau's geographical advantages were counted its human resources. Only from the Indians could the settlers expect to draw the labor supply of which Europeans in the New World inevitably stood in need. For this purpose João Ramalho, who had long since taken up Indian ways, and his mestizo progeny would serve as admirable go-betweens. The Jesuit provincial Manuel da Nóbrega wrote of him in 1553: "João Ramalho is well known and venerated among the natives, and has daughters married to the principal men of this Captaincy." His family "goes to war with the Indians, and their ceremonies are those of the Indians, and thus they live, going naked among these same Indians." (S. LEITE, 1940, pp. 52, 46.)

The Tupinakins (sometimes called Guaianases) of São Vicente were the southernmost of the Tupinambá tribes that occupied the Brazilian coast as far north as the Amazon River. These were hunting and farming tribes, their staples being such crops as manioc, maize, and beans; such small game as deer, wild pigs, monkeys, and forest hens; and salt- and fresh-water fish. Though unfamiliar with domestic animals, metal tools, or the wheel and axle, they had the use of fire, pottery, basketry, cotton hammocks, axes, chisels, bows and arrows, and pirogues for coastal and river traffic that carried up to sixty men. Except for their colorful tattooing and ornaments of feathers, shells, and human teeth, the Tupinambá went naked; this absence of clothing, as also the ritual cannibalism by which they disposed of prisoners of war, greatly distressed the Jesuit missionaries. An Indian village consisted of four to eight large communal houses; its site was changed every few years, when the soil became exhausted or the house thatching rotted. A village or group of villages was the largest political unit, and communities lived in such perpetual hostility that they willingly took sides with European invaders against Indian rivals. For European and Indian alike the claims of "tribe" were often stronger than those of race. It must be observed, however, that Tupinambá warfare was highly ceremonial, as was the treatment of captives before they were killed and eaten. Among members of a tribe, gentle manners, control of passions, generosity, and cooperative work were the norm. The Tupinakins of São Vicente were of especially mild behavior and, according to Father Manuel da NÓBREGA (1931, pp. 144-45), were the ones readiest for conversion to Christianity: "For many generations they have not eaten human flesh; their women go about clothed; they are not cruel in their wars like those of the coast, for they only defend themselves; some have a single chieftain and other customs very congenial to natural law."

Because of its natural and human resources, therefore, the plateau held strong attractions for the Portuguese on the coast. Before many years they were given license to go inland. In 1544 Dona Ana Pimentel, who had succeeded her husband Martim Afonso as donatary of the captaincy, authorized them to mingle and trade with the Tupinakins. Immediately Portuguese began departing for João Ramalho's base of operation in Borda do Campo. So many were living there by 1553 that the governor-general, on a visit to the captaincy, ordered that the settlement be erected into a town (vila), thenceforth to be called Santo André da Borda do Campo.[1]

Instead of establishing an outpost of the empire on the plateau, however, whites who went there adopted Indian ways and, like their mettlesome leader Ramalho, a defiant attitude toward their countrymen on the coast. A German named Ulrich Schmidel, or Schmidt, who in 1553 traveled overland from Paraguay to São Vicente, wrote after passing through Santo André that João Ramalho had "fortunately" not been at home, "for this place certainly appeared to me to be a robber's nest.... This said Reinmelle [sic] can, in one single day, gather around him five thousand Indians, whereas the king is not able to bring two thousand together, so much power and consideration has he got in the country." A son of Ramalho

1. Present-day Santo André, an industrial suburb of the city of São Paulo, is at some distance from the site of the first town of that name, which is today believed to be occupied by the suburb of São Bernardo.

"received us very well, though we had to look closer after him than after the Indians." (DOMINGUEZ, 1891, p. 84.)

It was a religious rather than an imperial or commercial interest that brought about the effective colonization of the plateau. In 1549 Father Nóbrega, who had just arrived in Bahia with the governor-general, received disturbing accounts of the paganism of the Portuguese in São Vicente and of their maltreatment of the Indians. He sent three Jesuit colleagues to the scene, who founded a mission, or *colégio*, for the Indians in the town of São Vicente. One of these emissaries reported in August, 1550, that the whites of the plateau were scattered about living "a life of savages." Since some of them had gone without mass or confession for a year, he had ministered to their spiritual needs for "two or three days" and urged them to build a chapel and live together in a single Christian settlement. When he visited an Indian village the house of its chieftain would not hold all who came to hear him preach the faith; they were so sad at his departure that he promised to return again. (SAMPAIO, 1904, pp. 5-6.)

Nóbrega himself visited São Vicente in 1553 with the governor-general. The new colégio had already become such a source of contention between Jesuit and colonist that it could no longer properly catechize the Indians and mestizos. With the enthusiasm characteristic of the young Jesuit order, Nóbrega resolved to undertake the arduous task of founding another mission inland, on the plateau. It was the location that he selected — namely, the plain of Piratininga, several miles from Santo André and some forty-five miles from Santos — that became the site of the city of São Paulo. From here the Jesuits planned to proselyte among many Indian villages, serving as agents of the cross and of the crown and as counterweights to Ramalho and his refractory followers. Here, too, they hoped to find a fresher climate and more possibilities for agriculture than on the coast.

In January, 1554, thirteen or fourteen Jesuits made their toilsome ascent of the Serra to found the colégio. The site chosen was a hill at the confluence of two small rivers, the Tamanduateí and the Anhangabaú. The hilltop, accessible from only one side, promised a good defense against Indian attack. Here a rude shelter and chapel were soon built, and as the first mass was said on January 25, the anniversary of the conversion of St. Paul, the settlement was called São Paulo do Campo de Piratininga.

Pre-eminent among the founders of São Paulo were the Jesuit superior, Manuel de Paiva, and the tireless young José de Anchieta, who at age nineteen had just arrived from Portugal and who ranks with Nóbrega as one of the two great early missionaries of Brazil. With incredible diligence Anchieta began learning the Indian tongue; he later composed its first dictionary and grammar, translated Christian works for the Indians, and even composed religious *autos*, or dramatic representations, in their language. He frequently went without sleep to copy out lessons for his pupils, in spite of strenuous physical tasks which each day held in store for his frail constitution. In a letter of 1554, ANCHIETA (1933, p. 43) described São Paulo's first dwelling, a rude hut, fourteen paces by ten, which served as "school, infirmary, dormitory, refectory, kitchen, storeroom." So suffocating was the smoke within this building that the Jesuits sometimes preferred to give lessons in the open, even when exposed to sharp winter winds. They served not only as teachers and preachers but as barbers, phlebotomists, blacksmiths, and architects. Anchieta himself became skilled at making sandals of wild thistle.

Within a few years the original structure was replaced by a small cluster of buildings, including a church and a school, surrounded by a stockade. Indians were attracted to the settlement by its promise of protection, by the products of its handicrafts, and, most important, by the inspiring leadership and dedication of the Jesuits. Anchieta wrote in 1560 of how his colleagues ceaselessly visited outlying villages to relieve the sick, "paying no heed to heat, rain, and great floods of the rivers, and many times at night through very dark woods." They made of São Paulo a communal society, receiving from the Indians a regulated amount of labor in return for physical security, objects of utility, and the comfort of the church. In the school, Indian children mingled with orphans sent from Portugal. The former embraced the faith readily, being more impressionable than their parents and unexposed to the worldliness of the Portuguese at Santo André. Some children even came to despise their parents and would speak to them only at the Jesuits' insistence.

The Jesuits, no less than Ramalho, showed great adaptiveness in confronting the hinterland and its Indian inhabitants. They achieved leadership, however, by suasion and compassion, rather than by defiance and ferocity, while their abiding purpose was to transform the sertão into a Christian community, rather than merely to dominate it by a day-to-day assertion of wiles and physical endurance.

As might be expected, São Paulo and Santo André were uneasy neighbors. During the first year ANCHIETA (1933, p. 46) wrote that the "Christians" of Santo André were making "continual efforts to destroy the work which, with the aid of God's grace, we are trying to advance. With assiduous and evil counsel they persuade the very catechumens to desert us, to believe only in them, who like the Indians use the bow and arrow, and to place not the slightest faith in us, who were sent here because of our perversity."

Yet, although missionary and colonist might be at cross-purposes in their policy toward friendly Indians, they were at one in putting up a defense against hostile ones. Ramalho could not but admire the Jesuits' soldierly discipline and their sturdy stockade — which, indeed, he and his father-in-law Tibiriçá had helped to build. The Jesuits, in turn, saw in the mamelucos a valuable reserve of man power and frontier experience. They also recognized that, in this part of the continent at least, the success of their missionary activities would depend in the long run upon the extent to which the mestizos became agents of civilization and of the faith. Anchieta wrote to his superior requesting that, in the absence of any information about Ramalho's Portuguese wife, he be authorized to marry Ramalho and his Indian consort, for "we hope to find in him, in her, and in their children a great means for converting these heathen." (S. LEITE, 1933-1934, pp. 249-62.) Relations between Jesuit and colonist were for two centuries to exhibit this ambivalent character.

It was not long before the two communities were thrown together by the mounting hostility of adjacent Indian tribes. Prominent among these were the Tamóios from the northeast, incited by French colonists under Nicolas Durand de Villegaignon, who in 1555 had begun to establish an ill-fated "Antarctic France" at Rio de Janeiro. As the tempo of Tamóio raids increased, the settlers of Santo André petitioned the governor of Brazil, Mem de Sá, that their town be incorporated into better-defended São Paulo. To this the governor acceded in a decree of 1560, and in the next year São Paulo was raised to a vila. In 1562 occurred a fierce assault which consolidated the transfer. The Tamóios, with some disaffected Tupinakin allies, destroyed every farm outside the stockade and carried off the cattle; but São Paulo, fighting under its newly appointed captain, João Ramalho, beat off the enemy after two days of siege and inflicted decisive losses. This assault set a seal upon the union of Portuguese, Indian, and Jesuit.

In spite of their defeat in 1562, the Tamóios' attacks continued for another three decades. And, after 1580, foreign freebooters along the coast were another source of danger. Since these raiders, of whom Thomas Cavendish was the most notable, were enemies of Spain, their attacks are often attributed to the accession of Philip II of Spain to the Portuguese throne in 1580. Raids upon Santos occasionally suspended São Paulo's tenuous connection with the outside world, and made necessary the dispatch of armed bands from the plateau. Not until the end of the sixteenth century did the threats of Indians and freebooters abate; and Brazil's first inland settlement, having struck roots, was left free to expand and to put forth offshoots.

By 1600 the town of São Paulo had some 150 white and mameluco households, perhaps 1,500 free citizens, and many more Indians in a servile status. Of the Europeans almost three-quarters were from Portugal and from the Azores and Madeira; others were Spaniards, partly explainable by the Spanish accession of 1580; and a scattering were of Germanic and Italian origin. Some were petty aristocrats, the rest commoners, and many of the immigrants came from straitened, marginal walks of life that had tempered them for this new hardship and adventure.

Society was patriarchal. The family head might have a dozen children, often including illegitimate ones by his Indian women. The patriarchs, each the undisputed master of his large family and retinue, were the effective source of public authority. If a feud broke out between two families and their respective allies, such as that which smoldered for decades between the houses of Pires and Camargo, it dominated the life of the community. The family heads comprised the town's *homens bons* — "good men," or "respectable citizens" — who elected the *Câmara Municipal* (Town Council) and who were eligible as its officers. Of these the most important were the magistrates *(juizes)*, who had criminal jurisdiction and administered the police; the aldermen *(vereadores)*, who advised the magistrates and supervised municipal finances, commerce, price control, food rationing, and public works; the attorneys *(procuradores)*; and the clerks of the market *(almotacéis)*, who enforced standards for artisans and tradesmen and for municipal hygiene. In emergencies the whole electorate of homens bons met in open assembly with the Câmara.

This form of town government, which allowed a high degree of local independence and citizen participation, was reminiscent of medieval Portugal. The conditions of frontier life on the plateau, in fact, were in some ways comparable to those which prevailed during the medieval reconquest of Portugal from the Moors and which had favored the establishment of hardy, self-governing townships. By 1600 municipal autonomy was being supplanted in most of the empire by centralized, bureaucratic control from Lisbon. Isolated São Paulo, however, maintained the earlier tradition until the eighteenth century. Its spirit of localism was most clearly manifested in 1641, just after the restoration of the Portuguese monarchy; the townsmen, incited by Spaniards among them, protested by acclaiming Amador Bueno, one of their number, as king of São Paulo, and only the prudence of their candidate in declining the offer kept the incident from assuming importance.

Life on the plateau was a spare one. Although the soil and climate favored stock raising and diversified agriculture, virtually nothing could profitably be shipped to Europe. Even the coastal sugar industry soon lost its hegemony to the more accessible regions of northern Brazil. São Paulo's meager exports of quince marmalade, wheat, flour, and salt meat paid for only such essential imports as iron utensils, firearms, salt, and a trickle of semiluxuries for the few well to do. Of four hundred seventeenth-century wills and testaments studied by José de Alcântara MACHADO (1930, p. 19), only twenty reveal even modest wealth.

From these documents it is clear that gold and silver coins were a rarity and that cotton cloth, wax, hides, sugar, and salt pork were the usual media of exchange. Items of common use and dress were plainly fashioned of leather, wood, and coarse cotton. Families ate with their fingers and spoons and drank from a common gourd. It is recorded that a leading citizen once excused himself from appearing before the Câmara because he had no boots to wear. Couple after couple used the same wedding clothes for the marriage ceremony. In 1620 the Câmara requisitioned the town's only presentable bed for a visiting official for whom the usual cot or hammock was not deemed fitting. If a last will itemized such a luxury as a silk and velvet dress, it was valued at more than a whole farm with its buildings, while two cotton shirts were worth a horse, and a musket was worth eight head of cattle. Given the modesty of São Paulo's nearby resources, given the hardiness and enterprise of its citizens, and given the trails and rivers which led off into the unexplored sertão, it was natural that the settlement should be a centrifugal one. As the hostile Indians were driven away, the homens bons began to clear farms around the town and to divide their time between municipal and rural pursuits — often to the detriment of efficient government. Soon other towns began to appear on the plateau, some of which rivaled São Paulo in size and wealth throughout the colonial period and even later. The Jesuits, anxious to bypass secular authorities in their missionary efforts, founded additional settlements of their own. It was not, however, by vegetatively expanding colonization, but rather by the penetrations of organized expeditions that the ultimate secrets of the backlands were revealed.

The sixteenth century saw a few deep *entradas*, or excursions, into the interior from São Paulo — such as the three-hundred-league journey of Braz Cubas, the founder of Santos, in 1560 — and many lesser forays for Indian slaves. It was the formally organized bandeiras of the seventeenth century, however, which gave São Paulo and its audacious settlers their fame and which were responsible for extending Brazil's borders far beyond the Tordesillas line, eventually to make it the largest country on the continent.

How the term "bandeira" came to be used in this connection is not clear. Possibly its meaning of "flag," or the "standard" which armed men rallied around, is relevant; also, the word had been used in medieval Portugal to designate a "militia." In any case, as applied to the *paulistas*[2] it signifies a band of men, sometimes accompanied by their women, organized to search for Indian slaves or gold. In a given bandeira one might expect to find any of the ethnic and national elements of the plateau: Portuguese, Spaniards, Flemings, Italians, mamelucos, free and enslaved Indians, an occasional Negro. Yet despite this heterogeneity, organization was along strict patriarchal lines, and command was accorded to a leader eminent for his family ties, experience, and valor. A bandeira, that is, was a community become mobile. It might be gone years at a

2. The paulistas were the inhabitants of the plateau, and later of the captaincy, province, and state of São Paulo. *Paulistanos* are the inhabitants of São Paulo city.

time, emptying the contributing towns of nearly all their able-bodied men. During the course of the century, bandeiras penetrated the whole heartland of the continent, north to the Amazon, west to the Andes, south to the River Plate. Protected against insects, snakes, and spiny undergrowth by stout leather clothing and shields, expedition members — the *bandeirantes* — constantly faced, and often succumbed to, the harshest perils of heat and cold, disease and hunger, jungle and savanna, hostile savages and wild creatures of nature. In accommodating to the sertão they learned and adopted much from the Indian. They used his hammock, bow and arrow, many of his foods. When they broke a march they used the methods of his slash-and-burn agriculture in planting and harvesting crops. They fashioned pirogues from tree trunks to navigate rivers. They even used his Tupi language as a *lingua franca* (as did the towns of the plateau until the eighteenth century).

For the first few decades bandeiras were organized primarily to capture Indian slaves. Unable, because of the colonists' insatiable need for labor, to make good its attempt to accord all Indians the rights of free men, the crown in 1611 condoned the enslavement of prisoners of war and of any Indians rescued from death at the hands of their fellows. For the paulistas this statute was an ample pretext for their slave-hunting forays; indeed, so inaccessible were they to royal authority that they scarcely troubled themselves with the formalities of legal justification.

In 1628 a force of nearly three thousand paulistas and Indians under Antônio Raposo set out toward the southwest to initiate a long series of raids upon the populous missions — known as "reductions" — of the Spanish Jesuits in Guairá (modern Paraná). The disciplined and docile Indian proselytes suited the paulistas' needs admirably, and at length the Jesuits were forced to transfer their reductions west to Paraguay and to obtain permission from Spain to arm their converts for resistance. The Jesuits of São Paulo sharply denounced the raids, and feelings ran so high in the town that a citizens' uprising in 1640 forced them to leave the captaincy.[3] Despite severe restrictions imposed upon them when they were allowed to return thirteen years later, they vigorously resumed their criticism of the bandeirantes. Finally, after decades more of alter-

3. By then, however, there were other orders — the Carmelites, Benedictines, and Franciscans — which, together with the secular clergy, were left to administer spiritual affairs.

cation, when the Jesuits threatened in 1684 to decamp again, the Câmara evinced the town's mixed sentiments by pleading with them to remain and assuring them of the people's devotion. Not until 1759, when it was banished from the whole empire, did the order again leave São Paulo.

The Jesuits claimed, with probable exaggeration, that the paulistas captured 300,000 Indians between 1614 and 1639. Over two-thirds were kept for labor in the captaincy, whose inhabitants could only rarely afford to import African Negroes. The rest were shipped to other parts of Brazil, especially to the prosperous sugar coast in the north, part of which was cut off from its supplies of African slaves during the Dutch occupation (1630-1654).[4] The outside market for Indian slaves being of so contingent a nature, however, the paulista slave trade offered too narrow a base for an economy of plenty; at its height, in fact, the income from it was less than 1 per cent of that accruing to Brazil's major crop, sugar.

As the seventeenth century wore on, precious metals displaced Indian slaves as the paulistas' object of search, and eventually the large, offensive bandeira gave way to a smaller, more maneuverable unit, armed only for self-protection, many of which could set out in a single year. For decades bandeirantes pursued rumors of gold, silver, and gems, particularly through the wilderness that was to be known as Minas Gerais, or "General Mines." Of these the most famous was the vigorous old patriarch Fernão Dias Pais, who died in the sertão in 1681. Not until 1695 did the paulistas make their first important gold strike. Immediately the rush began. Thousands of settlers swarmed inland from the central and northern coast, many with slaves from their sugar fields, while still others arrived from Europe to stake claims.

Soon hostilities broke out between the paulistas and the newcomers as the war of the *emboabas*.[5] The paulistas were forced to cede before better organization and leadership, but were compensated by fresh discoveries of gold in Mato Grosso (1720) and Goiás (1726) and of diamonds along tributaries of the São Fran-

4. On several occasions the paulistas sent a kind of modified bandeira to help repel the Dutch invaders, just as later in the century they sent one to subdue Palmares, a "republic" of runaway Negroes in the northern interior. The bandeira could thus serve as a striking force for which the rest of Brazil came to have high respect.

5. The term "emboaba" meant "one who wears boots," or "foreigner"; it had originally been applied to the paulistas themselves by the Indians.

cisco River (1728). These findings ushered in Brazil's great mineral cycle, during which, in seventy years, more gold was produced than in the rest of the Americas between their discovery and 1850, and during which Brazil's economic center of gravity swung south from the sugar lands to the mines. The transfer of the capital in 1763 from Salvador to Rio de Janeiro, which was the natural port for Minas Gerais, was in part a reflection of this economic shift.

The effect of the gold strikes upon São Paulo and the other towns of the plateau was a chastening one. In the first place, many of the more enterprising paulistas settled in the new mining areas, and their towns of origin were left without the tensions, drama, and eternal hopes of the bandeira days. Second, the Portuguese government, concerned with more efficient and centralized management of its gold-producing American possession, introduced administrative changes designed to curb the near-autonomy that outlying towns such as São Paulo had been enjoying. In 1709 the captaincy of São Paulo and Minas do Ouro was created, superseding São Vicente and including territories from Minas Gerais south to Rio Grande and present-day Uruguay, where paulista settlers had taken up stock raising on the broad plains.[6] Then, during the next forty years, the new captaincy was dismembered. First Minas was detached, then Rio Grande, Santa Catarina, Goiás, and Mato Grosso. For seventeen years (1748-1765) the remainder of São Paulo was ignominiously annexed to the captaincy of Rio de Janeiro.

It is common for historians to refer to the "decadence" of eighteenth-century São Paulo city. If one excepts an initial influx of gold, the new economic activities — mining and stock raising — bypassed the plateau, just as dyewood and sugar had before them. The bandeiras had passed into legend, celebrated by an occasional local historian or genealogist, and many citizens could see no economic horizon beyond their time-honored and almost primitive subsistence agriculture. Their town in 1765 had only 400 homes with a population of 6,000 or 7,000, including slaves. The captains-general, who had their seat there, rarely consulted the wishes of the people or their Câmara. Some were frankly tyrannical in their taxation policies, militarism, exercise of the salt monopoly, disregard of municipal prerogatives, and infringements of individual rights.

6. São Paulo had been made the capital of São Vicente captaincy in 1681, and in 1711 the town was raised to the category of "city."

ANTECEDENTS 17

The people had no recourse but to make mild appeals through the Câmara and, since there were no printing presses in colonial São Paulo, to post anonymous protests at the doors of churches. In spite of the material improvements sponsored by some of the captains-general, the later eighteenth century was for São Paulo a quiescent, almost lethargic interlude between the Spartan, fiercely independent days of the bandeiras and the later years of the Law Academy, the coffee boom, and, eventually, industrialization. Yet the term "decadence" is misleading. For this could with equal relevance be called a time of germination. "The paulistas of today," wrote a royal official in 1777, "no longer have the same character and determination as their forbears. They like to live in more orderly fashion and no longer expose themselves to the labors and discomforts of their grandfathers." (P. PRADO, 1934, p. 156.) The eighteenth century, that is, witnessed a sea change in habits and attitudes which set the stage for the forces and circumstances that were to produce the paulista metropolis of the modern age. And, by committing to noble legend the exploits of the bandeiras, this period created a rallying cry which has, down to the present, instilled regional pride, served as an incentive to economic achievement, and been invoked (sometimes spuriously) in time of crisis.

The dominant figure of the rural bandeirante patriarch yielded to that of the shrewd, more urbanized trader. River and land routes were developed between São Paulo and Cuiabá, in the gold district of Mato Grosso; these were traveled by the monções, commercial expeditions which were an eighteenth-century counterpart to the more adventurous bandeiras. There was traffic in mules from Rio Grande do Sul, which were sold locally or in Minas Gerais. From Minas came sugar and cotton cloth. And of course there was trade with Rio de Janeiro. From such commerce São Paulo became, if not a teeming emporium, at least a modest entrepôt. And, if no traders achieved opulence, at least a few of the dwellings began to display an increment of European luxury against their severe walls and austere, massive furniture. Their owners had acquired a stake in orderly administration and in their segment of the imperial system; gradually their horizons of interest and of mind were to amplify, and their descendants, in closer contact with an outside world, would be restless to have São Paulo acquire the endowments, tone, and status of a city.

As the next two chapters indicate, however, the setting, configuration, and life of São Paulo "city" (to use the title bestowed in 1711) in the early nineteenth century showed but slight traces of such new stirrings. It is the concluding chapter of Part I that is reserved for treatment of certain "catalysts" which followed upon the declaration of Brazilian independence in 1822. These catalysts — such as the Law Academy, the public press, and the urban-mindedness of the new provincial presidents — were indeed the hallmarks of a city culture that was entering the travail of self-definition.

Bibliographical Note

A. LEITE (1954, pp. 403-558) is a voluminous listing of books, articles, and periodicals relating to paulista history and not infrequently to the colonial centuries. INSTITUTO DE ADMINISTRAÇÃO (1948) presents critical discussions of primary sources for the settlement and institutions of sixteenth-century São Paulo. The São Paulo state and city governments have published a number of documentary collections; among them are those listed in the bibliography as ACCSP *(Actas da Camara da Cidade de São Paulo)*, DIHCSP *(Documentos Interessantes para a Historia e Costumes de S. Paulo)*, INVENTARIOS E TESTAMENTOS, and RGCMSP *(Registo Geral da Camara Municipal de S. Paulo)*. CATÁLOGO ... (1954) lists documents of colonial São Paulo to be found in the Archive of the Instituto Histórico e Geográfico Brasileiro. The fifty-odd volumes of the *Revista do Instituto Histórico e Geográfico de São Paulo* contain a wealth of articles on colonial São Paulo; to list merely those of primary importance would be impracticable.

MÉTRAUX (1948) and FERNANDES (1949b) are studies of the Tupinambá Indian tribes. Sixteenth-century accounts of the Indians include: M. da NÓBREGA (1931), S. LEITE (1940), ANCHIETA (1933), F. CARDIM (1925), and G. S. de SOUSA (1938). For an excellent critical bibliography in the field of Brazilian ethnography, see BALDUS (1954).

Histories of the captaincy of São Vicente (later São Paulo), written in the eighteenth century by Madre de DEUS (1920) and P. T. de A. P. LEME (n.d.), are authoritative for certain aspects but suffer limitations of perspective. J. J. M. d'OLIVEIRA (1897), written in the last century, is a comprehensive if spotty history of the captaincy to 1822. The patriarch of present-day paulista historians is Afonso d'E. TAUNAY. Those of his works listed in the bibliography include a general account of colonial São Paulo (1922); chronicles of São Paulo city in the sixteenth (1920; 1921), seventeenth (1926-1929), and eighteenth centuries (1923; 1949); an eleven-volume history of the bandeiras (1924-1950), and a two-volume résumé (1954b) of same. Taunay's historiography is prolix and disorganized, but offers a wealth of documentary minutiae. The numerous works on colonial São Paulo by ELLIS JUNIOR, of which two are listed (1937; 1944), are wide-ranging, sociologically oriented syntheses marred by sloppy scholarship and indefensible hypotheses. More succinct and digestible accounts of colonial São Paulo and its bandeiras than those of Taunay and Ellis include J. de A. MACHADO (1930), BELMONTE (1940), P. PRADO (1934), F. de A. C. FRANCO (1944), CIDADE (1954), and

R. de A. e SILVA (1955). R. B. de MORAIS (1935) is an able study of the human geography of paulista colonization.

T. L. FERREIRA (1944), MORSE (1947), and NEMESIO (1954) are studies of the founding and early years of São Paulo city. VASCONCELLOS (1865) and S. LEITE (1938-1950) are seventeenth- and twentieth-century histories, respectively, of the Jesuits in Brazil and devote considerable attention to São Paulo. The genealogist P. T. de A. P. LEME (1953) is a source for the study of paulista family structure, while the seventeenth-century feud between the Pires and Camargo families is analyzed in L. A. C. PINTO (1949, pp. 65-145). F. de A. C. FRANCO (1954) is a biographical dictionary of the bandeirantes. W. L. P. de SOUSA (1938) and A. B. A. de MOURA (1938) are studies in eighteenth-century administration. MILLIET (1946a, pp. 121-41) examines some eighteenth-century censuses of the city. Afonso d'E. TAUNAY (1953a) contains firsthand accounts of the bandeiras which came upon gold in Minas, while a companion volume (1953b) presents accounts of their eighteenth-century commercial counterpart, the monções; a fine history of the monções has been written by HOLANDA (1945). Evidence of the Indian *lingua franca* of colonial São Paulo is furnished in HOLANDA (1948, pp. 179-93). SAIA (1944) is a sensitive study of colonial paulista architecture.

Chapter 2

THE SHAPE OF SÃO PAULO

*. . . incontestablement la plus jolie [ville]
de toutes celles que j'avais visitées depuis
que j'étais au Brésil.*
— SAINT-HILAIRE (1819)

A CARDINAL FACT OF São Paulo's history is its position near the crest of the Serra do Mar as the
distribution point for a wide hinterland. Although a number of
outlets over the Serra have from time to time drawn traffic, all have
been of local or temporary importance save the São Paulo-Santos
route, which, in mule and locomotive eras alike, has been the
jugular of the inland plateau. The modern city, like Chicago in our
own West, merely perpetuates the pattern of routes which, by
converging upon it, so largely contributed to its first growth.

Just as colonial São Paulo scorned Santos for being a nexus
with imperial Lisbon, so modern São Paulo scorns it for being a
mere point of commercial transfer. The highland city has absorbed
the important political, industrial, and cultural functions. Santos
is the stevedore, denied the prestige — such as has accrued to Rio
de Janeiro — of a cosmopolitan Atlantic crossroads. Labeled in
official statistics as a city of the "interior," Santos has never held
in its orbit more than a few generally decadent towns of the coastal
plain, while São Paulo strategically commands the land and water
routes of what came in the nineteenth century to be the rich heartland of the nation.

In 1822, the year of Brazilian independence, one observer en-
visioned this inland destiny. He urged São Paulo to turn its back
upon Santos, which was of difficult access and badly served by
shipping, and to dispatch farm produce west to Paraguay and Peru

20

by the Paraná River system, challenging the commerce of Buenos Aires. This, he felt, would re-establish the erstwhile claim of the bandeiras to the silver of Potosí, and would stimulate local crafts and manufactures. (A. R. V. de OLIVEIRA, 1822, pp. 87-89.)

This disgust with the Santos route was understandable. At the end of the colonial period, transport between São Paulo and its seaport was scarcely more expeditious than in the seventeenth century. It is true that a zigzagging paved highway had in 1790 been constructed across the Serra, hewn in many places through sheer rock and rimming chasms where a misstep meant death; one British traveler found few public works, even in Europe, superior to it. Yet the way was not kept in good repair, and earthslides loosed by the perpetual rains of the crest often blocked passage. Add to this the narrowness of the road, which forced those ascending to stand aside whenever the muleteer's shout and the clatter of hoofs pierced the mists, followed by the animals themselves, ears erect, impelled uncontrolledly downward by their heavy burdens. The tortuousness of the route made it all the easier to reinforce natural with human obstacles. At inspection posts soldiers of the lowest rank were free to examine and detain the persons and property of strangers, and a foreigner might be obliged to show his papers as many as three different times.

The mule teams which traveled this perilous route comprised forty to eighty animals. Their packsaddles were crudely fashioned, the only touch of delicacy being the headstall of the lead, trimmed with its bells, plume, and shells or silver. The muleteers were wanderers who squandered their wages and owned little more than the cotton shirt and trousers, straw hat, belt, and knife that they wore, and the tobacco and flint in their cartridge box. When after a day's journey of three or four leagues they reached a posthouse, they passed the night in a roistering dance accompanied by a cadence beaten out on wooden benches and by voices still fresh after the vigorous songs and oaths of the day's labor.

The highway had grades up to forty-five degrees; animals needed frequent stops for rest, and riders proceeded half the time on foot so as to relieve their mounts. Large shipments were divided among many mules; to convey a church bell or a cannon to São Paulo involved severe expense and labor. In view of these conditions, the yearly traffic was impressive. Three or four mule teams generally arrived at the port and at the capital in a day. They descended with over 8,000 tons of sugar annually (for sugar cane had by the late eighteenth century come to be the leading export crop of the plateau), dried meat, firewater, and other regional produce; they returned with salt, Portuguese wines, glassware, hardware, cloth, and the like. French silks, linens, muslins, and calicos were preferred to English textiles, but the latter found a wider market because of a tax differential and a livelier spirit of enterprise.

The street plan of São Paulo was magnetized by this route, which left the city for Santos in a southerly direction and caused its buildings to gather around a north-south axis. After the mid-nineteenth century, railways were to alter this orientation. By 1890 the urban periphery would be circular, distended eastward along the line to Rio de Janeiro and westward toward the booming coffee frontier. In the twentieth century the east-west axis dominates.

Railroads, however, have merely altered the balance of forces, without changing the traditional pattern of routes. This pattern is determined by a topography which causes five principal arteries to converge upon the city. In any given era, the city's limit of settlement distends along those that are most active. And in the eras of mule teams and railways alike, São Paulo, as the junction of all the arteries, has been a transit point even for traffic on the plateau that is not destined for Santos.

These five highways can be described as fanning out into the interior from São Paulo in the following fashion: (1) Northeast toward Rio de Janeiro along the Paraíba River. This narrow, densely settled valley was the prosperous cradle of the coffee economy in the early nineteenth century. It had occasional lateral exits — south over the Serra do Mar to the coast and north over the Mantiqueira range into Minas Gerais — but Rio de Janeiro at one end and São Paulo at the other were the natural ways of egress. (2) North through Atibáia and Bragança into southern Minas Gerais. This route was developed relatively late in colonial times and was of only local importance. (3) North-northwest via Jundiaí to Campinas, São Paulo's rival throughout the nineteenth century, and into the subsequent coffee empire. The British railway from Santos later followed this axis. (4) West-northwest to Itu and Pôrto Feliz. It was at Pôrto Feliz that eighteenth-century monções which sought the precious minerals of Mato Grosso took to the Tietê River in pirogues. (5) West to Sorocaba, then southwest to the cattle-raising provinces. Each year livestock and donkeys were driven north along this route to be sold at the winter fair in Sorocaba. Many animals were then taken to São Paulo for use or export, a trade from which the city's few fortunes of consequence at this time were derived.

This cinquefoil of routes is a useful reference for describing the shift and intensification of the regional economy around pivotal São Paulo city down to the present time. The sectional demarcations it suggests are not misleading, for railroads were to accentuate the pattern of linear settlement and underdeveloped interstices.

A traveler approaching along one of the converging highroads in about 1820 would have seen the city from a distance, clustered on its hilltop. It presented a comely appearance with the silhouette of its modest churches and the plain white and sometimes pink or straw yellow walls of its two-storey residences. The encircling plain was enhanced by patches of woods, open fields with occasional palms or araucarias, and handsome country houses *(chácaras)*, whose owners challenged the inferior soil with gardens and orchards. The traveler might more than once have choked on the dust raised by a mule team. Along the Tamanduateí that twined below the city to find the smaller Anhangabaú, he would have seen women slaves crouched over their washing and, coming closer, heard their throaty songs and laughter.

The immediate approach to the city of any highroad was determined by topography, which was in turn a function of the rivers and affluents and their age-old erosion of the plateau's clayey soil. Some roads led toward the city center along level river courses. Others, which had to pass over the high ridge interposing between the city and the Pinheiros River to the southwest, followed the crests of watersheds. These features became integral to the ecology of urban expansion and will be discussed later in fuller detail.

Only on ascending the central rise did one tread the streets of the city proper. For a Brazilian town these streets were surprisingly clean, if allowance were made for open sewers, an antisocial shopkeeper who was thoughtless with his rubbish, and the mongrel pup indecorous enough to expire in a gutter. And they were sufficiently wide to accommodate the screeching oxcarts, burdened mules, and loquacious slaves bearing jugs to and from the public fountains. Paving was more distant from the ideal. In places it existed only in front of buildings. And, where continuous, the stones were so haphazardly set and unequally resistant to wear that the clatter of a passing cart roused the neighborhood, and a pedestrian needed equilibristic skill. In fact, the mincing gait of the women was laid by some to this condition of the streets. Since, however, the paving stones were of alluvial formation, transients — as late as the opening years of the century — were compensated after heavy rains by the appearance of gold particles in the interstices.

The core of the city was what is today still called the "triangle," formed by three streets which enclosed the summit of the hill, connecting the Carmelite, Benedictine, and Franciscan monasteries. Long before the arrival of these orders, the legs of the "triangle" had probably been paths used by the early Jesuits and their converts. By 1820 the city center was composed of perhaps a dozen rather haphazard streets, and even they were not lined solidly with houses but sometimes ran for long stretches along walled gardens. Of the public buildings none was sumptuous or exhibited the elegant baroque façade for which Iberian lands are known. Aside from the monasteries mentioned, there were the cramped, small-windowed college of the expelled Jesuits, then used as the government palace; the modest palace of the Câmara, which also housed the jail; the headquarters of the troops, forming a square of low barracks; the humble cathedral, built in 1745 to replace the Jesuits' first church, erected nearly two centuries previous; and the churches of Boa Morte and St. Gonçalo.

In today's kaleidoscopic metropolis one does not distinguish the flow of produce and persons which at every moment enters and leaves the central heart. But in earlier times any stroller knew when a mule-borne consignment of sugar arrived from the interior, while the visit of a foreigner was publicly registered and might even flush a covey of children who would count his fingers to see if he had the same number as they. Highroads and their commerce, in other words, kept their identity within the city; long after 1820 the urban area was informally defined by legislators as extending along the principal routes to the chácaras of public figures.

These surrounding chácaras evinced considerable prosperity. Brigadier Bauman's estate, northwest of the city, boasted trim orchards of peaches, apricots, plums, apples, and pears, as well as chestnut trees, a vineyard, and familiar flowers such as pinks, sweet peas, and poppies. Strawberries as fine as any in Europe abounded near the city, as did many of Europe's vegetables and most of Portugal's flowers. Oranges, pineapples, quinces, bananas, corn, rice, manioc, potatoes, sugar cane, cauliflowers, artichokes, peas, beans, and asparagus were all to be found, along with the sweet and succulent little *jaboticaba* of local renown. "Here," wrote Hercules Florence in 1826, "the land produces much more food than the inhabitants can consume."

. It remains to reconcile this seeming abundance with the poverty of the soil, which is generally clayey, with sandy fluviolacustrine deposits, and makes the region within a radius of dozens of miles from the "triangle" one of the most infertile of the whole tableland. The answer is simply that in the early nineteenth century the land's carrying capacity was not yet overtaxed by the needs of 20,000 people, even after 250 years of use. Moreover, the farmer was not so prodigally blessed as a first glance suggested. Many of his fruits were mediocre, and seasonal cold snaps adversely affected such crops as oranges, sugar, coffee, and manioc. Grapevines, though they took well to the soil, yielded only one harvest a year, as against two or more farther north. And, then as today, wheat had to be imported from abroad:

NOTICE: In the warehouse of Aguiar Viuva Filhos and Co. in Santos, Wheat Flour of superior quality, lately arrived from Philadelphia, is for sale in lots of 30 Barrels upward at 12:000 réis the Barrel of 6 arrobas or at 12:800 in smaller lots; cash transactions.

(*O Farol Paulistano*, March 28, 1827.)

The chácara owners by no means monopolized the adjacent farmland. In fact, according to MAWE (1812, pp. 70-75), the "greatest proportion" of the townsmen consisted of "farmers and inferior husbandmen."[1] Their dwellings of wattle-and-daub were

---

1. In 1818, occupational groups (including beggars but not slaves) were tabulated, doubtless sketchily, as follows:

Military service	566	Skilled workmen	277
Magistrates	1	Laborers	98
Secular clergy	81	Overseers	52
Regular clergy	14	Carpenters	18
Monks and nuns	56	Miners	1
Farmers	1640	Beggars	152
Merchants	220	TOTAL	3176

(J. J. RIBEIRO 1899-1901, II (1), p. 155.)

The proportion of farmers was 52 per cent. In 1940, farmers were only 3 per cent of those economically active within the municipal limits.

little more than wicker frames plastered with mud. "For an idea of the kitchen...the reader may figure to himself a filthy room with an uneven muddy floor, interspersed with pools of slop-water, and in different parts fire-places formed by three round stones to hold the earthen pots that are used for boiling meat; as green wood is the chief fuel, the place is almost always filled with smoke, which, finding no chimney, vents itself through the doors and other apertures, and leaves all within as black as soot."

Despite the Englishman's strictures, however, wattle-and-daub (which at times served to partition upper-class houses) was a practical, environmental solution, and, if construction was not too slipshod, it had durability. As the anonymous poor have always dispensed with the luxury of styles, wattle-and-daub — with the way of life it imposes — is still common in São Paulo and all Brazil.

Farming methods were primitive. Axe, hoe, and sickle were used almost to the exclusion of draft animals. Only a few chácaras had ploughs. When the land was cleared, the trees and brush were fired where they stood. If the work of the flames was completed before wet weather intervened, fine crops were expected. By the 1830's this system was showing its effects. Poorer families were leaving the city's rural outskirts for farther regions where higher yields more than compensated for the new problems of marketing.

The most important crop of the immediate region was tea. It had been introduced by Toledo Rendon, the first director of São Paulo's Law Academy, who favored it over sugar and coffee since its cultivation was less costly and toilsome and was suited for adolescent workers. Tea was also more practicable for the circumscribed lands of suburban chácaras, and by 1833 Rendon had planted 44,000 bushes near what is still known as Tea Hill (Morro do Chá) and has become the city's fashionable shopping center.[2] In 1835 the city and its adjacent parishes accounted for over one-third of the tea produced in the province, but only insignificant fractions of other cash crops. Unlike the later coffee culture, suburban tea farms did not force the proprietor to choose between living in the city or on his distant plantation. A newspaper notice of 1848, putting up a tea-grower's commodious chácara for sale, gives a picture of such an establishment:

2. Even before Rendon set out his bushes, tea — imported from Asia by Portuguese merchants — had been a cheaper and more widely consumed beverage in São Paulo than coffee.

FOR SALE: A fine chácara in the suburbs of this city, situated along the slopes of Pacaembu rivulet, with a very good two-storey house, ample accommodations for a large family, eighteen glass windows, good living-rooms, bedrooms, a very fine veranda with a large oratory and altar; arbors of rose-trees and many other kinds of trees, seventy-odd mulberry trees in good condition for raising silkworms, six to eight thousand coffee trees already in full production, 45,500 very well maintained tea bushes capable of yielding over 3,200 pounds a year; a good house with proper ovens for processing tea; fields and thickets with excellent pasturage and abundant water; very good stone quarries, and paddocks separated by ditches.   (*O Governista*, March 3, 1848.)

Fowl and cattle were plentiful near the city, but as no fodder was laid up, the latter were sleek only in times of good pasture. Sheep were carelessly tended. Cows were irregularly milked, given meager salt rations, and generally considered an encumbrance; their milk was less widely used than goats' milk. Dairying was so slovenly that butter was often rancid and the cheese hardly edible.

The marketing process was direct enough to provide constant interpenetration of city and country at a social as well as economic level. Perishables might be sold through the streets on the trays of black women or on countrymen's mules that came from nearby and from outlying nuclei. Or they might be found piled along the Rua da Quitanda in front of squatting Negresses. Nonperishables were sold in dark, smoky stalls along the Rua das Casinhas. By day this street throbbed with mule traffic, with the shouts and jostle of commerce, with the cries of those who hawked sweets, biscuits, roasted peanuts. At night, illumined fitfully by the flames of black tapers, the farm hands gathered here for their rhythmic dances (*batuques*) and for the strained, disquieting music of their ballads (*modinhas*):

> *Oh lady! You don't know*
> *In what state my heart is,*
> *It is like the black, black night*
> *In the greatest darkness.*[3]

3. The five- or six-string *viola* which was used on such occasions is Brazil's most popular instrument and is most used in rural areas. More typically urban is the Hispano-Moorish *violão*, or guitar, with its "8"-shaped body and six strings (three of metal and three of gut).

And in the shadows harlots waited silently to share in the day's profits of the countryman.

Laws and institutions were effective only when translated into local terms. Formal modern street names (such as 15th of November Street, 7th of April Street, or Volunteers of the Homeland Street), standard for all Brazilian cities, had not yet displaced such intimate designations as Beco da Cachaça (Firewater Alley), Beco do Sapo (Toad's Alley), Rua do Jôgo da Bola (Ninepins Street), and Beco dos Cornos (Alley of the Horns, named for its nearby slaughterhouse). The anonymous, numbered address did not pass into currency for decades after the edict of 1810 which officially prescribed that there be posted "consecutively on the property of each house the numbers, written in figures, from one until all the houses of the respective streets are numbered, beginning again with number one on the next street, exactly as with the first, so that in all of the city there remains no...property of any house without a number." (SANT'ANNA, 1937-1944, IV, p. 50.)

Relations among men were primary and personal; and some of the tasks now done by the myriad specialized agents of the city were carried out spontaneously, in a tradition of mutual aid. Since there was no fire department, fire fighting was a community enterprise. Whenever the church bells rang out in a code designating the location of a blaze, townsmen rallied in a bucket brigade: freemen, slaves, foreigners, officials, even women — and venders with the potable water they had planned to sell in the streets the next day.

In the 1820's and for decades thereafter, the city was periodically insulated by the overflow of its two close-lying rivers. The worst offender was the serpentine Tamanduateí, which inundated Carmo meadow to inflict the townsmen with fog, colds, and rheumatism and deprive them of productive lands. There were as yet no government funds and facilities for channeling the river; and so in 1827, according to O Farol Paulistano (Dec. 19), a group of citizens "voluntarily and with fervor united in the most useful enterprise of draining Carmo meadow. As for the result of the efforts expended, we need add nothing at all to the evidence revealed by a mere glance across the said meadow." A petition to the provincial government three years earlier, requesting action against the stagnant swamps and mosquitoes, had been fruitless; now, as a private citizen, the provincial vice-president donated 10$000. In all, thirty-seven persons contributed 222$540. The church was freer with slaves than with money for the enterprise. Of 366 slaves that were lent, 25 belonged to the Carmelites, 20 to the Benedictines, 6 to the Franciscans, 14 to two convents, and 23 to two priests.

Veloso de Oliveira found other threats to the city's hygiene than stagnant Carmo meadow: an excess of charlatans over trained physicians, the prevalence of measles and of smallpox, and a plethora of ants. Spix and Martius found more inflammatory, liver, and dropsical diseases (though less gastric, goitrous, and cutaneous infection) than elsewhere in Brazil. Saint-Hilaire was shocked by the venereal rate: "*On demandait à une fille publique si elle était atteinte de la syphilis: qui est-ce qui ne l'est pas? répondit-elle.*" To deliver a child, the midwife sat her patient on a five-gallon container, where several people held her until the birth; from time to time the mother was shaken to facilitate delivery.

The official agents for relief of the sick were the military hospital and a physician salaried by the Câmara Municipal to heal the poor. The hospital had a few skilled doctors and an effectual though sometimes depleted store of medical supplies; it lacked nightshirts and chamber pots, however, and had ten beds for four times as many patients. "In general," reported BEYER (1907, p. 287), "the pharmacists serve as doctors and from their storerooms distribute God-knows-what, for horseshoes can be bought from them with the same ease that a smith sells vomitories." Vaccination was regarded as a curiosity and not widely accepted, despite the threat of jail for those who refused to offer slaves and children to be inoculated. Those stricken with smallpox awaited the end resignedly, refusing food or treatment.

The greatest succor was that given by religious orders: the nuns of the Luz Convent; the Franciscans, who distributed food to the poor daily at noon; and, most notably, the Santa Casa da Misericórdia. The latter's infirmary had been the city's first (1715). Among its patients in the early nineteenth century were a number of slaves suffering from the effects of their weeks in a slave ship, their sudden exposure to the chilling winds of São Paulo, or their pernicious living conditions. Owners often delayed paying a slave's keep and, if his ailment threatened to be mortal, would set him free, leaving the expenses of treatment and burial to the Santa Casa. Just north of the city center the Santa Casa maintained a lepers' home. Its dozen or two inmates, neglected and ill clad, were fed beans and meat, a poor diet for their affliction. Most of them were impatient with confinement and disposed to escape to highroad mendicancy.

New problems of disease control were stemming from the growing concentration of people. Through much of the eighteenth century, São Paulo and its rural parishes had only 2,500 to 4,000 inhabitants; in 1790 there were over 8,000; in the 1820's over 20,000. It was coming to be realized that the denser nucleus facilitates contagion, but can also more effectively counteract it. The early newspaper *O Paulista* noticed (July 26, 1832) that cholera morbus struck "principally in those plazas where there is least cleanliness," and that the abattoir, which overlooked the city, scented the breezes abominably. After deploring the stagnancy of Carmo meadow, the paper went on to urge an end to the unwholesome practice of interring bodies within churches. In 1821 the Câmara set fines for persons failing to use the city's seven trash dumps — a needful provision, since the only street-cleaning service was furnished by prisoners, usually Negroes, who on occasion trudged through the city, chains rattling, to dispose of these dung and rubbish heaps. In general, however, refuse continued to be dumped off bridges into the rivers, or else it simply gravitated down from the central rise across sloping backyards or along streets.[4]

The environs of the abattoir were littered with skulls and slough, and it was here that a tributary of the Anhangabaú passed on its way to the small reservoir which supplied the city's three main fountains. Of these only one was central, and demands on it were excessive; even in rainy seasons the flow of its four spouts was far from copious, and during drought quarrels over their mean trickle led to broken jugs and pommeled heads. It was because of the impurity of the fountains and rivers that potable water was sold through the streets in barrels.

From details so far given it appears that at the time of Brazilian independence São Paulo retained certain characteristics of the rural town that subsists largely by its own polyculture. Such features as the street plan, the modes of transportation, building materials, and methods of farming in the outskirts answered to local environment and had changed little over the centuries. The day of the imper-

4. According to Neo-Malthusians such disposal, by whatever fecal nitrogen it returned to the land, was a hallmark of ecological equilibrium.

sonal bureaucracy that provides standard services and exacts standard compliance had not yet come. If the meadow was flooded, an *ad hoc* committee took action, then disbanded; if fire broke out, a spontaneous brigade was formed. Perhaps the slaughterhouse stank or bedridden patients had to use outdoor privies; nonetheless, São Paulo was far from unclean or slovenly in the eyes of the widely traveled. Mawe and Beyer commented on the comparative scarcity of disease, endemic or epidemic. Kidder found the vicinity "remarkably pleasant" and saw "a great degree of neatness and cheerfulness in the external aspect of the houses," as did Saint-Hilaire. To Beyer the inhabitants seemed "another race, more like the Swiss."

As we know, of course, the tight-knit community of São Paulo's early years had partly disintegrated as soon as the Indian menace was lifted. Colonial São Paulo was as much a symbolic as an operational nucleus. Not only did the bandeiras disrupt municipal life, but leading citizens often lived on distant plantations and came to their city residences only for civil and religious ceremonies. In 1823 we find the president of the Câmara complaining to the provincial government that "the Alderman Captain José Mariano Bueno being ill, there remains only the Alderman Captain José de Almeida Ramos, who, for cause well known, cannot appear for sessions twice during the week by reason of the inordinate distance from his whereabouts to this city." (RGCMSP, XVII, p. 309.)

One can generalize by saying that the São Paulo of 1820, in rounding out its colonial experience, exhibited important, if somewhat fragmented, remnants of its communalistic past. The resources of the region still supported little more than a subsistence economy, and thus militated against the city's acquiring the cosmopolitanism of a Rio de Janeiro, Salvador, or Recife. Time-honored processes, however, that had served the village of 400 or 4,000 were beginning to show themselves ineffectual for a town of 20,000. That there loomed a need for rational city management is implicit in the following letter published in *O Farol Paulistano* (Dec. 7, 1827): "There is in this city a house (though not now in a suitable place) for general stowage of gunpowder, whether nationally owned or commercial, but it is so *in voce*, for there appears to exist none there belonging to the merchants, who keep it (I do not implicate all of them) in their houses in the face of all rights, including that of humanity; because if perchance a fire occurred in one of these houses and only he who kept powder in his house were to suffer the damage, it would be all right, but it does not happen like that; because I, you, and the other citizens are liable to lose our properties, our goods, and even our lives."

The São Paulo of 1820 is called a "community" in this study less for its patterns of social action or for its popular culture than for its townspeople's sense of human relationships, and for their collective awareness of the irrefragable fact of life itself. Men of the period still greeted one another on the street even if strangers, while poorer persons tipped the hat to one well clad. Whenever anyone departed from the city, his friends accompanied him on horseback to the Tree of Tears, two leagues distant, where last leave was taken. The hanging of criminals involved all citizens, for the scaffold stood in public on "Gallows Field"; near it believers had set up a wooden cross where candles could be lit and which came to serve as a center for religious ceremonies. And a city ordinance, affecting sextons and their church bells, provided that: "As soon as any man shall die there will be struck three brief and distinct knells, for a woman two, and for children of 7 to 14 years of age there will be struck only one, be it male or female; and for these death knells no payment will be asked." (SANT'ANNA, 1937-1944, IV, p. 143.)

Bibliographical Note

Among the best travel accounts for the early nineteenth century are those of MAWE (1812), SAINT-HILAIRE (1851; 1887), BEYER (1907), and SPIX and MARTIUS (1824). A. R. V. de OLIVEIRA (1822), ALINCOURT (1830), H. FLORENCE (n.d.), and RUGENDAS (1940) are also valuable. Though his visit was somewhat later, many of the observations of KIDDER (1845) are germane to this era. The memoirs of BUENO (1903) are a mine of information, and the early part of his autobiography (1899) is also useful. VAMPRÉ (1936) is a creditable secondary source. MÜLLER (1923) gives an indispensable statistical survey of the province and its capital in the mid-1830's. DEFFONTAINES (1935b) studies the Sorocaba cattle trade; and RENDON (1851) is a manual for local tea planters, first published in 1833, by a pioneer in the field.

Chapter 3

THE LIFE OF SÃO PAULO

*V*IEIRA BUENO (1899, p. 4), born in São Paulo in
1816, recalled the era's leading families in a telling
sentence that shows how sharply the colonial pattern was yet
etched: "The old paulista families of pure blood, even if not
wealthy (and few are numbered as relatively wealthy), were deeply
imbued with a lofty sentiment of self-esteem, which gave them a
certain aristocratic stamp: by the severity and restraint of the customs; by the punctilio of racial puritanism in choosing matrimonial
alliances; by honorableness of character; by probity in business — all
this refined by an absolute sway of religious beliefs."

The strict patriarchal code of behavior, the culture and functions
attaching to inherited class status, were in contrast to the permissiveness and anonymity of modern urban society. The upper class
used the formal *vos* in address, even between brothers or parent
and child. Visitors were received only by the head of the family,
but once a stranger was accepted as a guest the master freely offered
him his house and affection, which was by no means to be taken
as a mere formula. There were few travelers from abroad, few even
from the interior, as roads were bad and the city held few entice-
ments. Hence there were no inns or eating places; the respectable
visitor had letters to insure him private hospitality. Before finding
such hospitality Saint-Hilaire saw himself forced to put up at a
miserable post for mule teams. His room, one of many that opened
on a miry court, was dank, filthy, windowless, and too narrow to
turn about in once it had received his baggage.

Small wonder it was that the foreigner encountered suspicion.

Those known to paulistanos were few and often of low standing. Saint-Hilaire found a reputable Swiss merchant, but the several Englishmen and few Frenchmen were *"d'une classe inférieure."* Florence encountered only two Europeans: a French shopkeeper and an indigent Prussian gunsmith. An ordinance of 1831 bears out the xenophobia of the community: "No one may give lodging or rent a house to a person unknown in this municipality for more then twenty-four hours without his first being presented to the cognizant Justice of the Peace and obtaining from him a declaration of his entry, and only with this document may he be given residence." (SANT'ANNA, 1937-1944, IV, p. 191.)

Foreign sophistry and exploitation encountered native resistance. When J. M. Liotard, a British subject, sought permission in 1820 to set up a new abattoir that would meet the heavy demand for veal, pork, and mutton, the Câmara was skeptical. To slaughter calves for veal, it reasoned, was pointless, since they would feed more people if allowed to grow. As for pork, Liotard might establish a monopoly on pigs and cut off the bacon supply of venders on the Rua das Casinhas. Only in the matter of sheep was there hope for agreement. (RGCMSP, XVI, p. 7.)

Folkways, family codes, architecture, and domestic arts did not yet reflect the passing fashion. Upper-class residences did not display the elegance — the American furniture and French mirrors — of those in Bahia and Pernambuco. More customary were a row of heavy colonial chairs, a modest Nürnberg looking glass, and, instead of a glass lamp and tapers, a castor-oil-burning lamp of brass. Sitting rooms were cheerfully painted — older ones with arabesques — and tastefully furnished. An occasional framed engraving that had been dumped from the European market for its ugliness only emphasized the paulistano's innocence of citified artistic canons.

Florence found that families were hospitable, straightforward, and "sober in the extreme," drank little wine, and kept a "simple but pleasing table." RUGENDAS (1940, p. 99) wrote of the "great simplicity of the paulistas' customs, the absence of luxury — even among the higher classes — especially as regards furniture and kitchen utensils." Cordiality suffused social relations. "Music, the dance, conversation take the place of...gaming, which is one of the chief diversions in most of the other cities of Brazil." Those of the patriarchs who owned outlying sugar plantations were prototypes of the proud but moneyless coffee planters of later years.

SAINT-HILAIRE (1851, I, p. 260) found in 1819 that the "owner of a refinery leaves at his death a certain number of Negroes who are divided among his sons; each of the latter deems it a point of honor to be a sugar planter...as was his father, and he buys slaves on credit. He can doubtless earn enough to pay for them after a certain time; but meanwhile he often loses several, whether by illness or bad treatment or lack of care; he replaces them, buying again on credit, and passes his life ever in debt."

Sobrados, the one- or two-storey patriarchal dwellings, were gathered along the central streets and squares, while humbler *casas térreas* straggled along the steep approaches. The former were of *taipa* construction (the French *pisé*), a European technique but one which had long been peculiarly suited to the life and conditions of the paulista tableland. The taipa wall was made by setting up parallel supports of wicker, planks, or closely driven posts, secured by crosspieces. Between them earth was fed, to be moistened and rammed. As sections were completed, the supports were shifted to contiguous spaces, with room left for beams and frames. The finished falls, pared and painted, might stand for centuries.

The rustic house of taipa was more than a casual intrusion of the countryside. It pointed up both the attitudes of an owner who used his city residence only when attending religious or municipal functions and the character of an agrarian region which was too straitened to support an opulent, worldly-wise community. São Paulo had few houses of brick, while the varieties of stone which gave Rio de Janeiro, Recife, Salvador, and even Santos an urban, European complexion were never employed.

The sobrado was truly functional, if by that term is meant the unpretentious comeliness arising from rational use of local materials and from cognizance of social patterns and tradition. The social function was evident in the way in which the sobrado was accommodated to the patriarchy. It had as one-storey adjuncts slave quarters, stables, and other dependencies. Women's rooms were removed from the street and often deprived of light and air. The *rótula* (a type of jalousie, though with close-laid diagonal strips of wood instead of louvers) and protruding rótula, or *muxarabie,* were Moorish survivals that formalized the flirtations of sequestered daughters. In the early nineteenth century these Moslem vestiges in Brazil came under official bans and shortly disappeared from Rio de Janeiro and elsewhere. Since, however, the rótula in São Paulo answered both climatic and social needs, it defied ordinances for decades, and became a stage prop for mid-century romanticism. The handsomeness of the sobrado was later denied. A Brazilian architectural manual of 1880 considered taipa suitable only for humble dwellings, and Vieira BUENO (1903, p. 27), reminiscing in 1903, recalled the sobrado as having been "without architecture and even ugly." The metropolis has consigned this structure and its way of life to oblivion, but the sobrado's simple dignity may still be confirmed in early photographs and in the more quiescent towns of the interior, such as Itu and those along the Paraíba valley.

At the start of the last century the severity of architectural line and functional division of the taipa house had become somewhat relaxed. The plain quadruple face of the shelving tile roof was breaking up. The strict demarcation between the family's communal room (sala) with its surrounding bedrooms and the more decorative receiving room with its adjoining oratory and guest room was dissolving. The lines of the structure no longer proclaimed its proprietor as the self-sufficient master of the sertão: "owner of the lands, the family and the slaves, dispenser of justice and of religion." (SAIA, 1944, pp. 247-75.) They foretokened, rather, the sociability, parties, and catholic interests of the new bourgeois aristocrat — the gentleman planter, the huntsman, the litterateur.

Broadly speaking, however, the sobrados that the traveler of 1820 might have seen were still in the mainstream of colonial tradition, as was the patriarchy itself. For just as the milieu was working in many ways to preserve a social mold, so the very nature of taipa called for unitary solutions that precluded the anomalous deviation of parts possible with later techniques.

Furnishings, like architecture, reflected the conventions of society. Ladies were expected to occupy the cane-bottomed sofa at one end of the parlor, men taking the chairs that extended in two precise rows from its either end.[1] Often, though, women did not show themselves, even at table, before male guests; they entered the street under vigilance of the family head, and then usually for devotional ends. With few soirées for their distraction, and with no

1. Rural Argentine homes of this period also contained a divan "inherited from the Arabs, a privileged place in which only women were permitted to sit, and in whose spacious precincts, leaning back against the cushions, they received and prattled with their visitors and the lords of the house." The divan "showed that men could not publicly approach young girls or talk freely or mingle with them." (SARMIENTO, 1916, p. 191.)

gusts of foreign fad and fashion blowing through the city, girls married as young as thirteen and fourteen and busied themselves in the house with lacework, embroidery, preparing sweets, and at evening with guitars and singing. Ladies were well-bred and, though ingenuous, had a polished ease of manner and address. A cherished ritual was the gracious exchange of flowers with favored acquaintances.

So constraining an etiquette needed its safety valve, which was provided by such festival occasions as Carnival. One staid Englishman found the Carnival antics with cologne-filled wax fruits "very annoying": ". . . persons of both sexes amuse themselves by throwing these balls at each other; the lady generally begins the game, the gentleman returns it with such spirit that it seldom ceases until several dozens are thrown, and both parties are as wet as if they had been drawn through a river. Sometimes a lady will dexterously drop one into the bosom of a gentleman, which will infallibly oblige him to change his linen, as it usually contains three or four ounces of cold water." (MAWE, 1812, p. 85.)

Dress was unpretentious. Sunday clothes lasted for years: the man's long topcoat and his trousers of Saragossa cloth or of yellow or blue nankeen, the lady's dress of Málaga serge and cashmere mantilla edged with lace. The poor used simple garments of calico and baize, over which women wrapped a black shawl for church. The slow-gaited countryman was identified by his large gray hat, poncho, and coarse cotton breeches. If on the days of religious processions slaves appeared decked in gold and jewels, it sometimes meant that their mistresses were vicariously showing off ornaments that they themselves could display only on rare festive occasions.

This deputizing of the slave is revealing. It suggests that the limbs and joints of the city — its streets, alleys, plazas, all its areas of circulation and congregation — were the domain of slaves (who were over a fourth of its population) and humble freemen: muleteers, venders, husbandmen. The patriarchal families were self-contained in their sobrados. They had no places for daily assembly, no promenades or shopping centers or restaurants, where a display of manners and finery might arouse envy in the peer and restless desire in the masses. Evening brought with it not the jading traffic and dazzle of later years, but a movement as quiet as the gathering dusk. Both sexes were "enveloped in woolen cloaks with high collars behind which half the face was concealed; women wore felt hats on the back of the head, while the men's were pulled down over their eyes.... [Prostitutes] walked slowly or awaited customers along the main streets, but it must be said that they never approached anyone. They were never heard to insult the men or call each other names; they scarcely looked at those who passed." (SAINT-HILAIRE, 1851, I, pp. 269-72.)

In their cultural expression, the townsmen sometimes made up in enthusiasm what they lacked in sophistication. From the Indians they had inherited no advanced arts; moreover, they lacked the wherewithal to import them on any scale from Europe and the outlook or temper to develop them far locally. The strenuous scenes of daily life nevertheless inspired occasional pictorial expression. One artist was intrigued in the first half of the century by the so-called "popular types": inebriate or balmy street-wanderers with their trains of mocking ragamuffins. There was *Chora Vinagre* (Vinegar Tears), a bathetic declaimer in a Spanish cape, said to have thrown his child into the river wailing, "Poor daughter! If you are to grow up to be as luckless as your father, it is better that you die!" The little innocent was rescued, became known as *Chorinha* (Tearlets) and was later famous as a town strumpet. One *Gibóia* (Watersnake), possessed of an ample torso and scrawny legs, used to enter houses and, lifting his cloak, announce, "I come here to show my body so that you may see how well made I am. My navel particularly is a model of perfection — as though it were turned on a lathe." These "popular types" are recorded in the ingenuous yet convincing water colors of Miguel Arcanjo Benício da Assunção Dutra (1810-1875).

Another painter was Father Jesuíno do Monte Carmelo (1764-1819), who did religious canvases and murals for the Carmelites and the Convent of St. Teresa. A strain attributable to much of São Paulo's formal culture of this era is defined in Mário de ANDRADE's (1945, p. 143) appraisal of him: "Jesuíno resides in that uneasy middleground between legitimate folkloric art and legitimate erudite art. There is a touch of irregularity, of — yes, of commonness in his work which has nothing of the forces, forms, and fatalities of folkloric art. But Jesuíno does not reach the erudite. He has popular appeal. He is really very citified. So that we are always obliged to see him as what he claims to be, a cultured painter: and in this context he is cultured without tradition behind him, cultured without having learned enough, cultured without culture." Father Jesuíno's achievements are slight if viewed against the splendid religious baroque of Salvador, Brazil's opulent colonial capital, or against the lyrical creole-baroque sculpture of "Aleijadinho" (1730-1814) which adorns the mining towns of Minas Gerais. His painting showed, however, albeit incidentally, a vitality and relevance to local life that artists of the later metropolis have been at pains to recapture.

Before the opening of São Paulo's Law Academy in 1827, theater was confined to the cramped stage of the "Opera House," a narrow one-storey structure whose décor was less showy than that of some private residences. It had three rows of boxes and, for men only, a parterre. Actors were colored and the actresses women of doubtful virtue whose talent "was in perfect harmony with their morality; one would have called them marionettes moved by wires." Even so, SAINT-HILAIRE (1851, I, p. 283) after a performance of Molière's *L'Avare* found it "impossible not to recognize that some were born with natural proclivities for the stage." And Martius noted that a barber who appeared as the leading character in the French operetta *Le Déserteur* deeply affected his fellow citizens, despite a musical accompaniment resembling a chaos of elementary sounds. Here as with painting it was not the urban European formula that appealed but the popular native spirit which infused and transfigured it: "It is impossible not to smile at the effect produced by white and red make-up on these more or less dark-complexioned faces. The costumes are no less grotesque, and fealty to local color is certainly what least concerns these extempore artists. There is more charm and at the same time more originality in the purely national divertissements." (J. F. DENIS, 1839, p. 191.)

Negro ceremonials having African elements formed an enclave within the prevailing culture. In colonial years the commotion and alleged indecencies attendant upon them had brought interdiction by city authorities. They continued to be held, however, some clandestinely, some conspicuously, at Misericórdia fountain, the slaves' rallying place. The ban was lifted in the early nineteenth century, and dances were allowed on payment of a license fee. Most important of them was that honoring the black man's patroness, Our Lady of the Rosary. After a religious service, the colorfully dressed Negroes assembled in front of her church for a spirited dance. Then the "king" and "queen" went home and offered a sumptuous meal to their "court," each of whom had adopted a famous title of the empire. The musicians received liberal potations as they waited in the street. The meal over, all returned to church for a solemn procession. Children too attended, their rosaries of red and gold beads, amulets, and jaguar teeth fortifying them against the evil genii of two faiths.

The eerie midnight incantations of Negroes performing burials in the churches recalled even more strongly the mysteries of a far continent, and sometimes caused neighbors to seek new residences. To the muffled thud of pestles they would utter their lugubrious chant: "Eye that saw so much. Mouth that spoke so much. Mouth that ate so much and drank so much. Body that worked so much. Leg that walked so much. Foot that trod so much." (A. E. MARTINS, 1911, II, p. 82.)

The emotional surrender evoked by unorthodox rituals of this nature contrasted with the spirit of secularism which was invading the hierarchy and activities of the Brazilian church itself at the time of independence. Monasteries harbored intrigues of a palpably temporal and at times Masonic character. As shown above, the church in São Paulo was in a position to make money and slaves available for the Carmo meadow drainage project; some citizens felt that the clerics would have done well to apply their resources to the ordering of their own house. A letter in *O Farol Paulistano* (March 21, 1827) urged better management of church funds and smarter upkeep of religious establishments. The province's four Carmelite and four Benedictine monasteries, asserted the writer, owned 131 urban buildings, 743 slaves, 24 agricultural farms, 10 stock farms, 2 Bank of Brazil shares, 5 to 6 square leagues of land, 2 kilns, money at interest, and other assets. These holdings represented a probable yearly income of twenty-two to twenty-four contos: "a sum from which, even allowing for *enjoyment of the lamentable life of Epicurus*, there might be left over — since in the eight convents there exist only 13 recluses — enough to preserve their churches with decency." The friars and monks maintained, however, that the total income of seven monasteries came to only three contos and that the eighth (possessed of 71 dwellings, 102 slaves, 4 farms, and a kiln) could barely support its three inmates.

If the piety and diligence of the regular clergy corresponded to that of the priests, they well deserved public rebuke. In synodic examinations held to fill curacies, untutored candidates who could not sign their own names properly were known to score better than serious, well-educated competitors. If under honorable, cultured Dom Mateus de Abreu Pereira (bishop of São Paulo, 1795-1824) the lower clergy were lax, what improvement could one hope for under his successor, who was a worldly politician and strong arm of the conservatives, who owned a plantation and slaves, and who shocked traditionalists by attending the theater? Many padres were conspicuous neither for celibacy, erudition, nor personal dignity. Once, in the cathedral, a canon threatened a colleague with a dagger. There was the obese and wine-loving Portuguese friar whose discordant, stentorian voice provoked open hilarity during Holy Week services. Another report tells of a young sacristan whose superiors suffered him to sit yawningly before the devout in the church of St. Teresa, with crossed legs and attire so slovenly that his chest was almost wholly bare.

The most popular church was that in which mass was unintelligible and soon over with. The sudden appeal at one time of services held in the former Jesuit church was explained by the beauty of the provincial president's twin daughters, who lived next door. SAINT-HILAIRE (1887, p. 587) thus describes the observance of Easter in São Paulo (April, 1822): "These celebrations attract a large number of country people, I attended some of the ceremonies and was offended by the inattention of the faithful. No one enters into the spirit of the occasion. The most distinguished men take part out of habit, and the people do so as if at a pleasure gathering. ... The streets were full of people strolling from church to church, but solely to look at them and without the least semblance of devotion. Women selling candy and sweets were seated on the ground at the church entrances, and the common people bought from them to treat the female companions of their promenade."

"Brazilian patriarchalism," it has been said, "is distinguished from the patriarchalism of classical times in the sense that it had an economic and not a mystic base." (SMITH and MARCHANT, 1951, p. 336.) What accounted for the vitality of the church in São Paulo was not so much its spiritual message as the correspondence between its imagery, rites, and pageants and the secular needs of the various groups in society. Like modern Carnival, which indeed is of religious inception, church processions suffused the citizenry with festive spirit, uniting all classes and institutions. For important festivals, planters came from distant estates to the city, where those of their sobrados which were located along the processional route commanded higher market values. Some wealthy families may not have entered the streets, but they hung damask curtains from their windows and gathered there with the zeal of participants rather than observers.

The popular Corpus Christi procession, heralded on the eve with drums and firecrackers, never failed to spread carnival revelry. The spectacle transformed the somber town: caparisoned steeds; African knights in yellow breeches, scarlet capes, and plumed hats, with trumpets and drums; and St. George, the patron, a horse-borne wooden image, richly dressed, carrying a lance and a shield. To guarantee the proper staging of this procession the Câmara issued such edicts as that of 1820 which required the participation of "all faithful subjects" and ordered citizens to have "their houses and walls whitewashed and their yards clean and swept, and to throw leaves and flowers along the streets where the said procession is to pass, with each resident having his doors and windows decorated as is proper, under penalty of a six-milréis fine . . . and thirty days in prison." (RGCMSP, XVI, p. 60.)

Other processional occasions were more sobering — for example, the processions in time of plague or drought that brought the image of Our Lady of Penha da França from an adjacent parish; or the funeral cortege led by a towering Roman centurion which halted at intervals for the grim intonation: *O vos omnes qui transitis per viam attendite et videte si est dolor sicut dolor meus.* But in these cases, as during festivals, immediacies external to the church lent purpose and cogency.

After national independence the provincial president held a place of honor in the processions; his secretaries and adjutants also figured prominently, as did members of the Câmara, the soldiery, and a military band. A letter of 1825 addressed to the president and signed by four members of the Câmara underscores this interrelation of the civil and the ecclesiastical: "As the Corpus Christi procession is shortly to be held and as it should take place with all due propriety and solemnity, the Câmara of this city begs Your Excellency kindly to send a horse with harness for the equipage of St. George, and here awaits your generosity." (AESP, 1825.) And it was the civil government, the Câmara, that requested the bishop to authorize transferral of the image of Our Lady from Penha to the city in 1819: "The sad situation threatening greater ruin that we see imminent upon us in the current drought moves us to appeal for the never-failing aid of the Most Holy Mother, Lady of Penha, our especial patroness and advocate on such occasions; therefore we beg that Your Most Reverend Excellency kindly assent to our honest plea, giving the necessary orders so that the sacred image of the same Lady may be removed from that parish to the Holy Diocesan Cathedral of the city, that there we may direct our prayers to Her Highest and Sovereign Son, through whose mediation we doubt not that we shall receive the remedy to our needs." (RGCMSP, XV, p. 409.)[2]

Here, then, is the São Paulo of 1820. It was a city articulated with its rural environs, as evidenced in its street plan,[3] architecture, public services, and economy. Human races and nations had been absorbed into the nucleus. Universal institutions were viable only when translated into local terms; and they could, on occasion, be replaced by spontaneous associations. For each social group there were accepted expectancies and etiquette, and the processes of town life recurrently intercalated all groups within a single community. This life was not without the stresses which contribute to criminality or to personality disorder. The gravest threat to public security, however, lay in precisely those acts of vengeance characteristic of a familial society; cases of homicide and battery, for example, were perhaps three or four times as common as those of robbery. (MÜLLER, 1923, pp. 91-93, 198-203.) Although São Paulo had its lunatics and "popular types," its tensions were not those that produce the "free-floating anxiety" of large city populations, just as they were not those which underlie the inexplicable moments of high cultural attainment.

The senses in which the São Paulo of 1820 may be designated a "community" will become clearer in the following chapter, which treats of certain catalysts, more potent than any yet mentioned, that were starting to dissolve the *status quo*.

2. On January 25, 1948, the writer witnessed an important procession in honor of the city's patron saint. As the worshipers followed along their time-honored route, the state governor and the president of the nation, who was on an official visit, left a building half a block from the processional street and drove off with their motorcycle escort in the opposite direction.

3. In 1808 a geometric street pattern was officially prescribed for the municipality, but Versailles-type planning had to await the city's later physical expansion to exact its toll.

Bibliographical Note

The principal sources for this section are the travel accounts and memoirs listed in the previous note. SAIA (1938; 1944), a present-day architect, understandingly analyzes the techniques and esthetics of taipa construction. REIS JUNIOR (1944, pp. 72-75) places the painting of Dutra and Father Jesuíno within the national context, while Mário de ANDRADE (1945) is a penetrating full-length study of the latter's work.

Chapter 4

ENDOWMENTS FROM NATIONAL INDEPENDENCE

> *Honorable paulistanos: The love that I bear for Brazil in general
> and for your province in particular — since yours was the first of
> all to make known before me and the entire world the Machia-
> vellian, disruptive, and factious system of the Cortes of Lisbon —
> obliged me to come among you to consolidate the fraternal union
> and tranquillity that were wavering and threatened by agitators
> and that will soon be yours again once the inquest ordered by
> me has been closed.*
>
> — DOM PEDRO I, September 8, 1822.

*T*HE "CATALYSTS" now to be considered are associated
with Brazilian independence and the events lead-
ing thereto after 1808. In that year the prince regent of Portugal
(who became King João VI upon the death of his demented mother
in 1816), having been driven from his country by Napoleon's invasion of the Iberian peninsula, reached Brazilian shores to establish
his court in Rio de Janeiro. One immediate repercussion of this
hegira was economic. It was obvious that Brazil, suddenly become
the seat of the empire, must be freed of the restrictions to which,
as a colony, the Portuguese mercantile system had subjected it.
Upon arrival João opened Brazilian ports to the commerce of all
friendly nations and lifted a prohibition of 1785 against home industry, which had been feared as competitive with Portuguese
manufacturers.[1]

The royal ban had not, however, been the sole deterrent to domestic manufacture in late colonial times. Brazil's scattered, inaccessible population and the self-sufficiency of its rural plantations

1. These two measures were to an extent contradictive, for a preferential
tariff accorded to England stifled Brazil's nascent industry.

45

would sharply have restricted the market for heavier industries. Aside from adjuncts of husbandry, such as processing farm products, putting up conserves, distilling firewater, or tanning, the principal craft of São Paulo was the hand manufacture of coarse cottons and woolens — with wealthier ladies giving their time to lacework, brightly figured quilts, and netted hammocks. Near the city lived mestizos who produced handsome earthenware. Beaver hats were another local specialty.

São Paulo had no drifting, fluctuating labor supply. Crafts were either domestic or in the hands of artisans. These latter had to pass examinations administered by the notary of each trade before the Câmara authorized them to practice. In 1820 four cobblers, four tailors, two saddlers, one tinker, and one joiner were either qualified as "examined masters" or allowed to "work publicly with an open shop" — one of the cobblers and one tailor being slaves. (RGCMSP, XVI.)

SAINT-HILAIRE (1851, I, pp. 288-91) reported that the city's artisans regarded work as an occasional evil affording long intervals of indolence. The cordwainer was never supplied with leather nor the joiner with wood. When a customer advanced money for the artisan to buy materials, it was soon spent for other ends. Only by placing the same order with many artisans did one run a fair chance of having it filled by some worker who was pressed for cash. This all savors, however, of the general ethos of the hinterland, and since Saint-Hilaire was piqued at not getting some traveler's chests made up promptly, his strictures can be partly discounted insofar as they apply specifically to artisans. What is important is that, although local craftsmen were not the finest, the city could at least generate its own skilled labor and set minimum professional standards. To this vestigial guild system one may attribute a certain stability and occupational pride. In marked contrast to it were the first experiences with factory labor.

Several travelers of the period, impressed by São Paulo's climate and cheap living costs, had recommended the city as the ideal locus for Brazil's future industry. João had a similar notion, for when an arms factory that he had set up in Rio de Janeiro failed to operate properly, he transferred it to São Paulo in 1816. The improvement was not appreciable. By 1822 its ten German masters and their fifty Brazilian workers had produced only 600 guns. The masters, who were paid handsome wages to keep them from returning to their homeland after the Napoleonic debacle, had lost their stamina and acquiesced, as did most non-Iberian European immigrants of that period, in local mores and in the consolations of local firewater. Though the Brazilian apprentices learned passably, their work was fitful. The incentives of promotion and higher wages took little hold upon men whose station in life was predetermined, whose expenses for food, clothing, and alcohol were minimal, whose need for furniture and accessories had not been stimulated. Only by subsidies from the royal treasury was the arms factory maintained.

João also fretted over a small textile plant, set up in 1811 and directed by a Portuguese "Master Fabricant of Silk and Cotton Cloth." In 1820 he asked São Paulo's captain-general to keep "an eye on it specially" and to "take measures so that that factory does not close down" (DIHCSP, XXXVI, p. 115); but four years later it ceased to function. There was still another project that the king urged the captain-general to foster: a São Paulo branch of Brazil's Central Bank, which was to stimulate trade and agriculture and give the captaincy "means to place its capital in active circulation." (DIHCSP, XXXVI, pp. 90-92.) Yet the branch did not outlast João's sojourn in Brazil.

The assessments in a will and testament of 1838 underscore the parochial character of São Paulo's economy:

10,000 square meters of land near the city	100$000
a row of houses in the city with yards extending down to the river	1:000$000
a vast estate (which included what are now several populous metropolitan districts)	2:400$000
slaves, ranging from Maria, sixty years	40$000
to Faustino, thirty-five years, mulatto, tailor	600$000
oxen at: 12$000	to 15$000
heifers	at: 5$000
chair with leather work	$300
double bed	4$000
large dining table	1$250
piano	100$000
plain glass jam dish	1$600
kettle	3$440
copper basin	60$800
doctor's visit	$640
funeral (expenses for coffin, tomb, sexton, priests, chaplains, choir boys, canons, bishop, masses, music, candles, etc.)	666$262

(SOUZA FILHO, 1938.)

The high value of imports (piano, glass dish, kettle, copper basin) and of a skilled slave stands out against the cheapness of land, animals, homemade furniture, and human services (doctor's visit), while the final item points up the role and claims of religion.

In spite of the enervating effect of this milieu upon the first industrial and financial enterprises, however, certain new economic notions and aspirations had begun to instill themselves. In 1822 the provincial government approved statutes for an Economic Society for Favoring the Agriculture and Industry of the Province, which was to have access to "maps, models, and machines" offered by José Bonifácio, a mineralogist educated at the University of Coimbra in Portugal and known to history as the "Patriarch of Brazilian Independence." (DIHCSP, II, p. 55.) Independence itself brought to São Paulo, as capital of the province, a series of provincial presidents after 1824 who, being crown appointees, promulgated the larger vision of a vigorous national economy. In 1836 one of them — fresh from years of study and legislative experience in Portugal and Rio de Janeiro — urged the Provincial Assembly to "promote commerce, enliven agriculture, and stimulate our nascent industry; . . . the capital which is being consumed almost without renewing itself will enter into active circulation, opening new channels for agriculture, shipping, and commerce; it will give birth to great rural and industrial establishments, improving those in existence; and it will thus further the progress and rapid increase of all these sources of public wealth." (AALPSP, 1835-1836, pp. 263-72.)

Mention of the provincial presidents leads to a consideration of the momentous administrative changes that accompanied Brazilian independence. Two themes are to be kept in mind in reviewing the political events of 1821-1828. First, the dying tradition of municipal autonomy was reinvigorated during these years, only to be summarily extinguished. Second, as the seat of a new provincial executive and legislature, São Paulo city became a political as well as administrative center, and thus more fully involved in national affairs. Municipal issues were placed in the hands of provincial officials whose primary concerns were, from a municipal point of view, artificial. The city's organic needs were to pass unperceived by the new leaders, and with later stimuli city growth, unplanned and tumultuous, was to result in the chaos of the metropolis.

The eighteenth century, as was shown earlier, not only had

seen the hardiest paulistas abandon their homeland for the rich gold and diamond country, but had witnessed the yoking of São Paulo's resilient localism under royal bureaucracy and militarism. The crisis of 1821, however, showed the municipal nucleus to be not yet wholly denatured. The crisis stemmed from João's departure in April for Portugal, where the liberals had revolted, promulgated the "Bases" for a new constitution, and were requiring that the king return to the mother country to continue his reign. Conservatives in Brazil denounced this trend toward constitutionalism and opposed allegiance to the new Constituent Assembly *(Cortes)* in Lisbon. At the grass-roots level they immediately encountered resistance. In São Paulo this resistance crystallized in June, 1821, at an open meeting of the Câmara, where, at the citizens' behest, a provisional paulista government was formed, loyal to the "Bases" for the liberal constitution and headed by the *ci-devant* captain-general, João C. A. de Oeynhausen. The intermediate bureaucracy had collapsed. Consonant with an earlier tradition — and one which had reappeared a decade previous in Spanish America, under similar conditions — initiative had returned to the municipality.

The local leaders who now emerged, however, set forces in motion that were to devitalize the very municipal functions which seemed to be taking a new lease. The provisional government was dominated not by the old rural patriarchs but by men of new backgrounds and talents, wider horizons, and cosmopolitan interests. Among them were the famous Andrada brothers, José Bonifácio and Martim Francisco, both trained at Coimbra in the natural sciences and shortly to be imperial ministers; Colonel Daniel P. Müller, German-descended and educated in Portugal, who carried out important statistical and engineering projects in São Paulo (see MÜLLER, 1923); Nicolau Vergueiro, a Portuguese-born, Coimbra-trained lawyer, subsequently minister of the empire, director of the São Paulo Law Academy, and a pioneer in subsidizing immigration to the coffee fields. Among them also were Francisco de Paulo Oliveira, a professor of rational and moral philosophy; J. F. de Oliveira Bueno, an ecclesiastic who had studied at Coimbra; and Manuel Rodrigues Jordão, the son of a merchant who traded in cloth and gold from the interior.

Before long, Brazilian liberals lost faith in the new regime in Lisbon, the intentions of which they interpreted, perhaps mistakenly, as a desire to relegate their country to inferior, colonial status.

Particular animus was aroused by a decree of October, 1821, which ordered the return to Lisbon of the king's son, Dom Pedro, who had remained in Brazil as prince regent and who was now, for his political education, requested to proceed home by way of specified European capitals.

In São Paulo both the Câmara and the *ad hoc* provincial government dispatched fervent appeals to Pedro in Rio de Janeiro. The Câmara's petition, signed by 267 townsmen, said in part: "The Câmara and undersigned citizens, convinced that on the decision of Your Royal Highness depend the destinies of this kingdom, have resolved to send before the august presence of Your Royal Highness a deputation composed of three citizens...whose mission is to represent to Your Royal Highness the terrible consequences which must of necessity derive from your absence and to beg that you postpone your embarkation." (DIHCSP, I, p. 68.)

Largely in response to this and similar petitions from other Brazilian cities, the prince pronounced his famous *Fico* (I remain). In January, 1822, he named a four-man ministry whose salient figure (and the only native Brazilian) was the minister of the interior, justice, and foreign affairs: José Bonifácio. The new national government, like others in Latin America, drew leadership from municipal taproots. Yet there was a more specific way in which the national destiny was linked to events in São Paulo city.

The members of São Paulo's provisional government were by 1822 splitting into two factions, one loyal to the liberal Andrada brothers, the other led by Colonel Francisco Inácio de Sousa Queirós, a well-to-do merchant who had been educated in Portugal and who commanded the local militia. The division was partly ideological, but political orientations were muddled: among the leaders by personal animosities and among the citizenry by the lack of newspapers that might have clarified public issues. When Pedro's new ministry learned of São Paulo's disunion and of the fact that Oeynhausen, head of the provincial government, was wavering in his allegiance, the latter was ordered to Rio de Janeiro immediately. Martim Francisco de Andrada, whose liberalism and whose loyalty to the prince regent were unquestioned, was designated to take over the provincial presidency (May 10, 1822).

This injunction stung the Sousa Queirós adherents into action. On the afternoon of May 23 the city's narrow streets echoed the rataplan of drums. The militia marched up to the Câmara building, followed by townsmen who had been stirred by the insurrectionists, and shouted for the deposition of Martim Francisco. The latter yielded to the threat of public violence and resigned. Oeynhausen continued in office, and liberal opposition was forced into the interior of the province, where a number of towns banded together in a "Confederation of Itu." Such was the coup known thenceforth as the *Bernarda* (Conspiracy) of Francisco Inácio.

On June 25 the prince regent formally deposed the provincial government, substituting for it a triumvirate headed by Bishop Dom Mateus. Within a few weeks a military detachment arrived in the name of the prince, but so menacing was popular opposition that its commander forewent asserting his authority and the troops were withdrawn to Santos. By now leading townsmen were impatient for a quick and certain end to the confusion. Nothing would suffice short of a direct plea requesting the prince's presence in São Paulo, which they dispatched to him on August 5: "Sir. — The inhabitants of the city of São Paulo, astonished in the extreme by the violent and hostile methods that the military executors of the orders of Y. R. H. have inconsiderately hastened to put into practice,...humbly beseech that Y. R. H. deem it worthy to give ear to the inhabitants of this city." (RGCMSP, XVI, pp. 443-49.)

Here was the time-honored Iberian tradition of a city appealing directly to the sovereign to rectify the blunders of intermediaries who were misinterpreting his will. The prince responded. He left Rio de Janeiro on August 14. On the 24th, he advised the paulistanos from Penha, just outside their city, that he wished to be greeted at noon on the morrow by "those aldermen who were legally serving before the disorder of the 23rd day of May." (RGCMSP, XVI, p. 460.)

The prince's arrival was what was needed to pacify the personal and family rivalries which had been fanning the embers of revolt.[2] São Paulo was soon obedient to royal authority, and Dom Pedro left for Santos on September 5 to inspect fortifications and visit the family of José Bonifácio. He returned two days later and by 4:00 in the afternoon had reached a stream called the Ipiranga in the environs of São Paulo. Here he was met by an officer dis-

2. So slight was the prince's irritation with the *bernardistas* that he amnestied them on September 18. In later years, when the liberal Andradas had fallen into disfavor, Oeynhausen and José da Costa Carvalho, another leading conspirator, were made marquises and both became senators. The latter was named president of São Paulo province in 1842.

patched in haste from Rio de Janeiro who carried further humiliating demands from the Portuguese Cortes. The prince read them, then cried histrionically: "The time is come! Independence or death! We are separated from Portugal!" Seizing his sword, he bade his retinue swear fealty to a sovereign Brazil. The nation's independence had been declared, not in its littoral, Europe-conscious capital, but in the paulista plateau near a rivulet that flowed to the sparsely settled hinterland, the direction of Brazil's future destiny.

At a demonstration in São Paulo's Opera House five hours later, Pedro was acclaimed by a priest, Ildefonso Xavier Ferreira, who has left us the narrative: "We met in front of the theater, and the patriots...told me it was necessary that a monarch be declared and a Brazilian dynasty formed....

"I was the one chosen to make this acclamation. Despite these worthy ideas, I made certain reflections....I feared that the prince would not accept, and then I would be imprisoned as a revolutionary. I feared on the other hand the bernardista group, who might shout: Away! Away with him! and in the midst of the confusion stab me.

"Then my two friends and others (armed, as we all were in those days) assured me that it was more than certain that the prince would accept the title of the first Brazilian King, and...that I need have no fear of being stabbed, as the others would be stabbed first.

"I went to box number 11...and then entered the pit and placed myself in the 3rd row, right in front of the prince's box; as soon as he appeared I let out the cry: *Long live the first Brazilian King!*

"The prince bowed, acknowledging my cry. The outbreak was universal, and I found courage to repeat it three times.

"Therefore my acclamation, which was repeated by Rio de Janeiro and by all the provinces, confirmed the form of a constitutional monarchical government and frustrated the hope of the bernardistas." (ALMANACH, 1880, pp. 20-22.)

A feud centering in local personalities had brought the prince to São Paulo. The citizens acclaimed him king (a title shortly changed to "Emperor"). And those same citizens, acting through the Câmara, reaffirmed their sovereignty by a document (October 12, 1822) which made their allegiance contingent upon the ruler's pledge to "swear to, preserve, uphold, and defend the Political

Constitution." (ACCSP, XXII, pp. 650-64.) Yet the very act of independence awakened forces that were to smother this renascent autonomy. Pedro's appearance was the symbol of the city's political subordination to the province and nation. Quite coincidentally, it was also a cultural symbol.

The fame of the prince's extramarital frolics had preceded him in São Paulo. Daniel Müller threatened to punish any of his five attractive daughters who entered the street or appeared at a window while Dom Pedro was in the city. But no one shielded from the prince the charms of Domitila de Castro, an ardent and gorgeous young woman, three times a mother, who had been separated from her dashing soldier husband. Pedro's trip to São Paulo marked the start of a seven-year *affaire de coeur* which made Domitila the "Brazilian Pompadour" and brought her the title marchioness of Santos. After Pedro's abdication she married a leading paulista and, by the 1840's, presided over São Paulo society as its most distinguished matron, her salon being an early cosmopolitanizing agent.

In the half-dozen years after independence, three events posted new directions for the whole of the city's subsequent development. Two were the setting up of a printing press and the founding of the Law Academy. A third, to be discussed now, was the organization of the nation's administrative schema.

The Brazilian Constitution of 1824, which Pedro imposed after having dissolved a constituent assembly, was submitted to the local câmaras for approval as a last gesture toward municipal autonomy. In ratifying, the câmaras signed their own death warrant, although the constitution itself was noncommittal re their authority; it merely stated that câmaras were to be elective and that a future law would specify their functions and the manner in which municipal ordinances were to be drawn up. This covering law was that of October 1, 1828 (given in MEDEIROS, 1946, pp. 204-15). Although stripped of judicial functions, municipal government was seemingly to be active in many realms. The Câmara, elected by direct ballot, was given such traditional duties as maintaining public order and superintending health, sanitation, and safety, along with such new ones as acquiring model machinery for demonstration to farmers and industrialists, improving cattle raising and agriculture with new strains, caring for the indigent sick, and inspecting and assisting primary schools.

Authority granted, however, did not measure up to obligations imposed. The câmaras were now mere administrative agents, closely controlled by provincial "general councils"[3] and by the crown-appointed provincial presidents. They needed sanction from these higher levels for publishing ordinances, undertaking major public works, making extraordinary uses of municipal funds, or disposing of property. Far from having a free hand to carry out the law's broad program, the câmaras often found it arduous to requisition a meager sum to repair a bridge or build a few yards of highroad. In his *Guide for the Municipal Câmaras of Brazil in the Performance of Their Duties*, Father Diogo Antonio FEIJÓ (1830, pp. 22-31) made clear the atrophy of town government: "It behoves the câmaras to be most cautious and circumspect by not executing before confirmation any ordinances except those of extreme necessity. Otherwise the annoyance will ensue of their being rejected by the General Council after their promulgation, and sometimes after their having produced evils involving vexation of the public and discredit of the institution.

"When the câmara sends its ordinances to the General Council, it will be useful to accompany them with an account of the motives it had for proposing each of them, so that the council may approve or emend them with full knowledge of the intention."

The law divested São Paulo's townsmen of their means for answering the city's intimate needs. Members of the Câmara knew those needs because they *lived* them; but authority now passed to persons who did not share in municipal life, who were beholden to the court at Rio de Janeiro and to its symmetry and pomp. Though later, in 1851, Emperor Pedro II asked that "moral force" be restored to the municipalities, the "Versailles" outlook became deeply seated. The derangements attending São Paulo's physical expansion after 1890 were to be the ultimate disclosure of the pernicious effects of the law of 1828.

The first provincial president, Viscount Congonhas do Campo, was an important innovator. He carried out the long-abandoned plan for a Botanical Garden, which as a public promenade later helped to erode barriers of class and sex. Subsequent presidents ingratiated themselves by embellishing the garden at the expense of more needful but less conspicuous reforms. Wrote the traveler Eugenio María de HOSTOS (1939, p. 340) in the 1870's: "A president

3. These bodies were shortly replaced by the provincial legislative assemblies.

of the Province of São Paulo will not conclude his term without having...sought to win the gratitude of the capital with some improvement for its promenade garden."

Under Congonhas do Campo the city was given easier contacts with the outside: commercial ones via a new road over the escarpment to Santos, intellectual ones via the first public library. Fresh solutions were imported for the growing city's problems. A "House of Correction and Labor" was blueprinted for the prison. A turning box for unwanted babies was installed in the Santa Casa. In 1824 the president made an attempt, though without success, to acquire a printing press for the city.

Congonhas do Campo saw that São Paulo's educational needs were ill served by its two most notorious schoolmasters: one a mulatto priest and terrifying martinet, the other a cripple who conducted classes from his bed, brandishing a long quince-tree wand tipped with a ball of wax. A seminary for orphan girls was founded in 1825, and a similar one for boys was opened on a former Jesuit farm north of the city. Each received an annual subsidy from the emperor, and each had rudiments of foreign guidance. The girls were given a Portuguese directress, while the boys were nominally under the Lancastrian, or monitorial, system which was then winning acceptance in Latin America.

But the introduction of higher learning made a much greater impact upon city life than did the extension of primary education. For decades after its doors were opened in March, 1828, the Law Academy was the city's nerve center. From throughout Brazil and from abroad it drew students and professors, and with them attitudes and needs that stirred the community into ferment: worldly-wise customs; chiding student skepticism, ever ready to disjoint the narrow patterns of provincial life; political ideas and passions transcending local issues; and a demand for theater, reviews and newspapers, bookstores, dances, and informal gathering places such as cafés and restaurants.

One may ask why so modest a town as São Paulo was picked as one of the sites for the two academies that were to relieve Brazilians of the need to acquire legal training across the ocean, usually at the venerable University of Coimbra in Portugal. In 1817 the chorographer Ayres de CASAL (1845, I, p. 194) predicted the choice because of the town's cool and healthy climate, cheap and abundant food, vigorous human stock, and scarcity of bibliophagous insects that might threaten a library – a prophecy in which the traveler Luis d'ALINCOURT (1830, p. 18) later concurred. These and other features – such as geographic accessibility, local financial resources, intellectual tone of leading citizens, availability of student lodgings, and the dialectal speech of rural paulistas – were hotly debated by legislators in Rio de Janeiro. The eventual decree of August 11, 1827, created two law faculties – in Olinda and in São Paulo.

Though many of the factors cited weighed in the balance (together with a general desire to establish two schools, north and south of the nation's capital), the underlying consideration behind São Paulo's selection was perhaps the province's tradition of self-reliance and leadership, which was reborn just prior to national independence. This tradition was made clear by a paulista to his fellow deputies in the national chamber in August, 1826: "What was the province which at any time, and principally that of our revolution, had a more influential, more powerful opinion?...Did by chance the Court of the empire, Rio de Janeiro, ever offer an opinion before the city of São Paulo had expressed itself?...The province of São Paulo, sirs, has a very well formed opinion, not only in its men of letters, who are not as few as has been insinuated, but also in the general mass of the people, who have always given exuberant proof of the most heroic virtues....

"If the paulistas – lacking all means of instruction, having to contend with so many difficulties – have always ennobled the roster of Brazil's learned men, will they perchance degenerate when the means of exercising their talents are extended and made available to them?" (ALMANACH, 1876, p. 121.)

The public press in São Paulo, which dates from the year in which the academy was created, came to be a sounding board for both professors and students. With a few ephemeral exceptions, Brazil had had no press until 1808. By 1826 the capital and seven provinces were publishing newspapers. São Paulo still had none, though for a short time in 1823 the expedient had been tried of circulating eight copies of a handwritten news sheet among forty subscribers. The amanuenses were paid by a "patriotic society" that was eager to "disseminate the useful ideas and knowledge so necessary in a free country." (A. A. de FREITAS, 1914, p. 334.)

A printing press earmarked for São Paulo was held in Rio de Janeiro to publish the debates of the Constituent Assembly, and the plea of President Congonhas do Campo in 1824 went unheeded by the central government. Finally, José da Costa Carvalho acquired some machinery; on February 7, 1827, appeared the city's first printed journal, *O Farol Paulistano,* under his editorship. The maiden editorial limned the services to be rendered. The paper was to arouse liberty-loving citizens with "brief, clear, and very simple" articles on the constitutional monarchy, the representative system, and individual guarantees. It would publish more national and foreign news as it obtained facilities, but its main concern was to be provincial interests — particularly the disposition of public funds. Government acts would be published, along with "our impartial reflections" on them. Magistrates were to be kept under surveillance. So too would the activities of the Câmara, the Santa Casa, the foundling home, and the schools, as well as food prices and commercial affairs.

The press was at once effect and cause of a new tension between close knowledge and the distant idea. Over the fabric of local rote and custom it projected a web of universal concerns. Though parts of these two patterns were coincident, other parts were mutually distorting, while still others, being incompatible, were to produce strain and bewilderment. São Paulo's colonial town criers who had read out their advices to the ruffle of drums were no vehicle for the complexities of the entering age — complexities that drew both resolutions and added intricacy from the forces of "public opinion."

Like most innovations of the time, however, the press modified colonial habits only unobtrusively at first. Many early numbers of *O Farol Paulistano* were devoted almost entirely to letters from readers on such time-honored community subjects as the alleged wealth or poverty of religious orders, the bad condition of roads, or the exorbitance of highway tolls.

Moreover, early newspapers received little commercial support. The city's twenty or so stores — the potential advertisers — were nearly all owned by Portuguese and were commonly gathering places for causerie. Proprietors had popular nicknames, such as *Bom Fumo* (Good Tobacco), *Boas Noites* (Good Night), *Domingos Cai-Cai* (Dominic Tumble-down). There were only one hardware and one chinaware store; the single wineshop sold good wines at moderate prices, but many even of its more distinguished patrons preferred *eau de vie* of local brew. Wares were familiar to all and customers staunch in their habits; often, indeed, there was no alternative source of supply for a given article. Under such conditions a facile advertisement might have riven with suspicion the friendly bond between merchant and customer.

The late-colonial city has now been examined, and certain stimulants, infused during the 1820's, have been recognized. We are next to consider the action of these stimulants. To what extent did they shift the beat and flow of city life? To what extent were they neutralized? And to what extent were their metabolic powers withheld in hidden tissues?

Bibliographical Note

BRUNO (1947) briefly surveys the origins of paulista industry. Alfredo d'E. TAUNAY (1914) and JORGE (1946) give information on Oeynhausen and his term as captain-general. J. J. M. d'OLIVEIRA (1897, pp. 229-89) is a careful account of São Paulo's role in the movement for Brazilian independence; for other versions and more detail see VARNHAGEN (1938), M. de O. LIMA (1907), PIZA (1902), and A. A. de FREITAS (1922). Dom Pedro's liaison with the marchioness of Santos is fully treated in RANGEL (1928). For the effect upon municipal government of the law of 1828 see: FEIJÓ (1830), LAXE (1885), J. de A. C. MAIA (1883), NUNES (1920), and SOUZA (1865). L. A. M. de BARROS (1946) contains the innovations proposed by São Paulo's first provincial president. The early years of the city's press are treated in IHGB (n.d.) and A. A. de FREITAS (1914, pp. 323 ff.; 1915; 1927a).

Part 11—Formation of the City Mind

Chapter 5

POST-COLONIAL MALAISE

*T*HE YEARS from, roughly, 1830 to 1845 may be
thought of as a time of suspension, of malaise, of
contingent promise. The catalysts of the 1820's, to be sure, continued acting. The Law Academy carried on, though with declining
enrollment. Newspapers proliferated. Owing to the press and to
the new political structure, national issues percolated closer to the
people. But these forces had as yet found little on which to take
hold; there were no counterforces to set them into adjustment. São
Paulo failed to show the energies and momentum which, in different
forms, characterize the early colonial period, the mid-nineteenth-
century romanticist years, and the era of the metropolis.

No source of wealth yet existed to further cosmopolitan ideals,
for the nation's free-trade policy deterred even modest industrial
development; and the coffee boom was still of the future. The lack
of funds meant, for one thing, that adequate highways could not be
built to diminish the city's inaccessibility and parochialism. For law
students coming from Rio de Janeiro, the overland journey took ten
to twelve days over execrable roads that were served by the most
primitive lodginghouses. The sea trip was no better, for it was made
in coastal vessels that put into every inhabited inlet on the way,
and it was followed by the martyrdom of the road over the Serra.
The task of maintaining and improving both this road and the network of inland highroads vexed every provincial president. Moreover, regulations of the period served to constrict the arteries of
circulation by establishing internal provincial tolls and empowering

soldiers on the Santos road to arrest "doubtful" travelers for questioning, even though their documents might be in order.

In 1834 an imperial "Additional Act" completed the curtailment of the resources and jurisdiction of municipal government in Brazil. The act nominally federalized the nation by substituting provincial assemblies for the general councils and investing them with wider powers. This provincial centralization stripped the municipalities of even those vestiges of authority left them by the 1828 law; they became voiceless creatures of the assemblies, which now definitively controlled municipal offices, salaries, budgets, expenditures, imposts, and borrowings. In São Paulo this control was fortified for three years (1835-1838) by prefects and subprefects who were dispatched to the câmaras like the *corregidores* of the Spanish empire, as agents of the provincial government with executive and investigatory powers; the capital and other cities witnessed sharp animosities between prefect and câmara. The ostensibly democratic trend toward federalization thus had the ironic effect of sapping initiative at democracy's nuclear level, the municipality.

The first provincial assembly convened in February, 1835, with a distinguished roster: Nicolau Vergueiro, already referred to; the indomitably liberal cleric Father Diogo Feijó, unorthodox for his Gallican leanings toward an autonomous national church, who was soon to be regent of the empire; Dr. Amaral Gurgel, later director of the Law Academy; Father Ildefonso Ferreira, who had proclaimed the emperor in 1822; Father Vicente Pires da Mota, later president and many times vice-president of São Paulo and president of several other provinces; Francisco Antônio de Sousa Queirós, subsequently one of São Paulo's farsighted sponsors of European immigration; and others of more than local renown.

The elaborate military exercises and gun salutes that inaugurated the assembly were symbolic of the shift in interest to provincial and national politics. Equally symbolic was the fact that the city had no proper accommodations for the new legislature. It was crowded into the ill-appointed quarters of the old government palace, where, during late sessions, the dim candlelight made it hard to distinguish one legislator from another. Only in 1879 was a suitable building provided and the provincial government physically reconciled with the city that harbored it.

An incident which gave focus to the political partisanship which São Paulo was coming to experience as the provincial capital was the assassination of G. B. Líbero Badaró. Badaró was a kindly, educated, fervently liberal Italian immigrant who in 1829 founded the city's second printed newspaper, *O Observador Constitucional*. He was murdered in November, 1830, during a political imbroglio which had been brought to a head by a spontaneous celebration over the deposition of the autocratic Charles X of France. Political feelings flared high; Badaró's funeral was attended by some five thousand persons, and the repercussions of the crime added fuel to the liberal clamor that forced Emperor Pedro's abdication the next year. Few there were to recognize a certain incongruity in the little city's jubilance over a liberal victory in faraway France, and to realize that passions unleashed in the guise of political affiliation might, in such a community, hang as a curtain between the people and a knowledge of the life and needs which they shared. One such warning, however, did find its way into the pages of *O Novo Farol Paulistano* (Jan. 28, 1835): "The more I contemplate Brazil, the more I am of a mind that it is not prepared for the republic. All recognize that to maintain itself this form of government, where the people is everything, requires that this same people be correspondingly educated, and that it have good moral behavior, much love of work, and finally many virtues. And is the population of Brazil perchance in these conditions?...Let us not ape the Anglo-American states, which had other beginnings, another education, another regime: yes, the United States were settled and educated by philosophers, Brazil by fugitive and degraded criminals....The United States had from their beginning their provincial assemblies and were nursed on the milk of liberty; Brazil was founded under the harshest colonial regime and knew no other rights than the caprices of its viceroys, called captains-general....In the United States work and industry were soon introduced; in Brazil the idleness and wellbeing of the bigwigs."

Such self-denigration was at best a mere clearing of the ground. In later years, however, when it became more common and was still insufficiently attended by constructive analysis and criticism, the danger increased that the complaining party might stifle in self-pity or seize upon perverse formulae.

The amorphous nature of the city's political relation to the nation will become clearer when its role in the Revolution of 1842 is discussed. Meanwhile that episode needs a context of evidence to show how the new leadership and plans and institutions of the

1820's, having come up against the recalcitrant drift of provincial life, had so far failed to impart to it a decisive rubric.

The Law Academy is a case in point. It was established in the Franciscan convent and, like the Provincial Assembly, had to adapt itself to an aged and unsuited building. The churchyard gave entrance to worshiper and student alike, and there were quarrels between the Franciscan superior and the academy director over the schedule and purpose of the church bells. Secular and religious interests hung — symptomatically of the times — in uneasy balance.

The academy comprised nine chairs, eight in the various branches of law and one in political economy. There was a *Curso Anexo*, or preparatory course, attached to the academy where candidates were taught French, Latin, rational and moral philosophy, rhetoric, and geometry. To enter the academy students needed to be at least fifteen years of age; the course, five years in length, led to the degree of *bacharel*, following which one could become a doctor by writing and successfully defending a thesis.

The enrollment of the academy took a spurt in its first years, then entered a long, steady decline. Between 1832 and 1837 the average number of yearly graduates was forty-five; between 1838 and 1845, it was only thirteen. KIDDER (1845, I, p. 258) visited the academy in 1839 to find its education "formal and exact" in the Coimbra tradition and unfitted for a people looking "more to utility than to the antiquated forms of a Portuguese University." He predicted that it would be necessary "to condense and modernize the course of instruction" if the drop in registration was to be arrested.

An anonymous document of about 1840, entitled "Memorandum Offered to the Most Illustrious and Excellent Counselor Lomonosoff, Minister Plenipotentiary of His Majesty, the Emperor of Russia, to the Imperial Court of Brazil," recommended transfer of the academy to Rio de Janeiro because, as current books were almost unavailable in São Paulo, professors and their lecture notes soon became antiquated. "There are professors of great merit who, placed elsewhere, would certainly achieve fame in the Republic of Letters." Literary circles were "contraband," while student discipline was minimal and in 1835 approached anarchy when a youth who had struck his professor in public continued his course with impunity and received his degree. The memorandum prescribed that the director be given "paternal jurisdiction, even though the people might call it despotism." (VAMPRÉ, 1924, I, pp. 338-40.)

That the academy acquitted itself somewhat woefully in these years can be amply corroborated. In contrast to their cultivated Byronism of the mid-century years, their impassioned abolitionist campaigning of *ca.* 1870, or their open defiance of the Vargas regime (1937-1945), the students' academic spirit in these years lacked consistency and purpose. A report by the director in 1837 censured both students and professors for absenteeism, and instanced one mentor who had missed thirty-four days of classes in addition to his two months of authorized leave. But little punctiliousness could be expected when salary payments were quite irregular and when the director himself, Nicolau Vergueiro, forsook his academic duties for long periods to follow agricultural and political interests.

A striking example of student unruliness was reported by the director pro tem in 1842. A student (who was also a priest) had been failed for a "scandalous" examination in arithmetic and geometry. When the director, in company with the professor of rhetoric, left the academy, the young man approached to demand satisfaction. On being advised to withdraw he set upon the director with a cane, shouting that he was "a numskull, rascal, and thief." Luckily three students came to the deliverance of the academic cranium by holding off the assailant. (AN, 1842a.)

The following year an army-trained disciplinarian, Colonel J. J. Luís de Sousa, was named provincial president to trample out lingering embers of São Paulo's liberal Revolution of 1842. He was a figure made to order for arousing the antipathy of the students, and the inevitable run-in occurred in June of that year. In relating the incident to the minister of state, the colonel prefaced his dispatch with an account of how students had been making a mockery of city traditions and authority:

"Appearing in the churches, that group of thoughtless youths take possession of the main entrance and, forming close and compact wings, oblige devout families to pass between them, exposed to vile and indecent actions and to tart remarks offensive to decency. When the ceremonies of religious worship are celebrated, the group, changing their position, take station at the grille of the high altar, and, turning their backs to the Blessed Sacrament, remain facing the ladies, who become the target for their maliciousness, the object of their madnesses, to the great scandal of family heads, who cannot watch such loose and immoral proceedings in cold blood. No one dares make them the slightest admonition, for he would expect in return a licentious answer." Averring that he had done his best to temper the students' insolence by "pacific means," the president went on to relate the occurrence that forced him to violence. On June 15, while attending a play in the Opera House, he found the uproar and indecent hoots of students in the audience so obnoxious that he was forced to ask for silence, out of respect for the proper families present. Calm was restored till the fourth act, when "as if by signal" certain students climbed on the benches, stamping and shouting furiously to let it be known that "they were ready to challenge everybody, starting with the soldiers, who had borne the greatest insolence with excessive resignation." When warnings of the president and the chief of police went unheeded in the tumult, the latter "ordered the departure and finally the arrest of one of the principal authors of the riot" (who was the son of Martim Francisco de Andrada). The students then had the effrontery to shout that their fellow be released or that all go to jail. (AN, 1843a.)

It is only fair to complement the above with the version of those thirty-two students eventually jailed, which was set forth in a direct appeal to the emperor. The president, they claimed, had held up the performance by his late arrival. Then, perhaps because of "an inexplicably ridiculous susceptibility in this man who had never found himself in so high a position," he had misinterpreted the spectators' impatience as a personal affront and made a speech condemning the demonstration as worthy only "of a barbarous people." As the fourth act of the melodrama (on the stage) unfolded, the plot called for gunshots. The smoke produced in the audience "an almost general cough; these symptoms of genuine discomfort gave rise to a few exaggerations, or caricatures." The president broke into a tirade of fierce epithets and rushed to the stage where, brandishing the sword seized from a soldier, he shouted "that as president he would have respect and that if any as a man were capable of challenging him, let him do it, and that he was no parlor and hallway president like his predecessors." (AN, 1843c.)

Besides making vivid the way in which students were for the rest of the century to leaven city mores, these documents have bearing on the years under consideration. The academy was not yet providing its protégés with either an absorbing course of study or fruitful extracurricular associations — just as the city itself afforded few channels for their restless energies. National politics, moreover, did not suffuse city life, but were only a patina — so that students made *ad hominem* rather than ideological attacks upon unpopular public figures. Andrada, the student ringleader, was intelligent and well read; he subsequently took his doctorate and held a chair in the academy. Had he been a student twenty-five years later, the milieu would have favored more articulate opposition to the president than loud coughing in a theater.

The academic library was one source from which foreign ideas might be expected to disseminate. By 1840 it contained 7,000 volumes, comprised mainly of the worm-eaten Franciscan collection and donations from Bishop Dom Mateus and from the academy's first director. Nearly half the items were, Kidder found, "unread and unreadable tomes on theology." Contemporary books, including works of jurisprudence, were in short supply; belles-lettres and the sciences were scarcely represented. The director, however, had complained vehemently to the minister of the empire. Some authors from the list of about two hundred and fifty titles whose purchase he requested (1835) indicate the secular, utilitarian bent that he hoped to give the curriculum: Jefferson, Blackstone, Franklin, Godwin, Malthus, James Mill, Ricardo, Gibbon, Humboldt.[1] For a few years new acquisitions stood little used on the shelves. Yet gradually their ideas were to seep into lecture rooms to form the minds of a new generation, and into the public press to give fresh turns of thought and rallying cries to the people at large.

The perplexity and flatulence that characterized much intellectual endeavor of the early part of the century were evinced by Friar Francisco Mont'Alverne (1784-1858). As a student he had used the Franciscan library before its absorption by the Law Academy, and for a time he taught theology, rhetoric, and philosophy in the city; in the 1830's a close disciple of his was instructing in the Curso Anexo. Mont'Alverne's thinking was confused and derivative, antischolastic yet tangled in the formulae of his Fran-

---

1. The director untiringly requested European periodicals as well. By 1838 the following were being received: *Revue des Deux Mondes, Revue Botanique, Journal des Connaissances Utiles, Journal de l'Institut Historique, Bulletin des Sciences Agricoles et Économiques, Revue Encyclopédique, The Quarterly Review,* and *The Edinburgh Review.* (AN, 1835-1839.)

ciscan training. Exposed to systems propagated in the empire during the Enlightenment, it floundered in a pastiche of Locke, Kant, Condillac, and Cousin that purported to reconcile the sensualist and idealist positions. Mont'Alverne's philosophic incertitude foreshadowed the antinomies of the entering age, while his eclectic outlook, then a rarity in Brazil, was in later years to be defined with increasing assurance by apologists for materialist, bourgeois society.

A more supple and self-consistent mind was that of Júlio Frank. In February, 1834, another of the academy director's communiqués to the minister of the empire (AN, 1834) informed that Frank, a young man born in Saxony, who had been teaching elementary classes in the interior, was the only applicant for the chair of history and geography in the Curso Anexo, and was willing to teach English as well until another candidate should appear. The writer, with the usual circumspection regarding foreigners, wished to know whether in view of the teacher shortage it was allowable to engage him. The minister replied affirmatively, with the proviso that the contract be for a stated period in case a qualified Brazilian should later apply.

Frank is a controversial figure. Because he was a Protestant, he was buried in the patio of the law school after his premature death in 1841, rather than in sacred ground; for the academic community his tomb is still invested with the mystery which veiled certain aspects of his life. Afonso SCHMIDT (1942) has novelized Frank's career, portraying him as intellectually gifted, dedicated to his students, and as founder of a benevolent mutual-aid society, the *Burschenschaft*, for the latter. Gustavo BARROSO (1937-1938, II, pp. 33-66) implausibly identifies him as Karl Sand — the unbalanced theological student who, in Metternichian Europe, assassinated the dramatist Kotzebue as a tsarist spy; he indicts the *Burschenschaft* as a subversive, Masonic counterpart of the German student societies which inspired it, and calls Frank a practitioner of black magic and of "Judaized *bacharelismo*." What needs to be said here is that Júlio Frank's German background, his well-informed eclecticism, and — to whatever extent he practised it — his occultism combined to make him a precursor of the mid-century romanticist phase of both the academy and the city.

A letter in which he describes translating Poelitz' *Compendium of Universal History*, a commission he received from the central government, gives a measure of Frank's intellectual influence. The *History* was in three parts. The first, "Ancient to Medieval," he translated virtually as written. The second, "Medieval to the Discovery of America," he totally revised, adhering to the "excellent *method*" of the German original but expanding the histories of France, Italy, Spain, and Portugal. The modern period was yet to be done; there "the difficulties multiply, for a compendium however good, if designed for the program of a given foreign literary establishment, does not serve indiscriminately for the academies of any other country." (AN, 1837.) In other words, Frank was introducing European procedures, the fruit of Europe's experience, but saw that conditions of Brazilian life exacted recognition and unique resolution.

Throughout Brazil the church had been losing its role of intellectual leadership in the years since independence, leaving it to be assumed by the law academies. Many of the church's most vigorous spokesmen were now of Masonic and regalist persuasions. Mont'Alverne and Father Diogo Feijó were both Masons, while Feijó opposed clerical celibacy and, as minister of justice, made sure that the patronage which had been accorded the imperial government by a papal bull in 1827 was fully exercised. The infiltration of Freemasonry into the Brazilian church created a schism which would be painful to heal in later years and which compromised its traditional authority. The union of church and state under the Constitution of 1824 and the acceptance of Gallican views by leading clerics further undermined this authority by subjecting the church to the government's constant intervention in its affairs.

The activities of such leaders as Father Feijó were in contrast to, and were indeed directed against, the demoralized state of most of the clergy. In 1832 an appeal to the bishop of São Paulo from the parishioners of Penha protested of a vicar whom they held in "aversion," whose manners were "quite harsh and uncivil," and who displayed not "the slightest measure of the affability and friendliness that befit the character of a curate." (AESP, 1832d.) By the next decade the bishop was giving evasive answers to such complaints and leaving the provincial government to deal with refractory priests, who were indeed its own civil servants. The situation was summed up by a president who blamed the low degree of public safety upon "lack of religion and civilization" and called for "improvement in the quality of our clergy, especially of that part which, living in direct contact with the people, is better situated to influence their social and moral relations." (DISCURSO, 1848.)

If we turn to the general panorama of the city's life and endeavor in the mid-1840's, we find it little changed since a quarter of a century previous, though one senses a different atmosphere by very reason of the fact that the promises of the 1820's were as yet unrealized. The remarks of a traveling Austrian gentlewoman who saw the city in 1846 — though not as keen or exhaustive as those of previous voyageurs — serve as a clue.

Ida PFEIFFER (1880) shared Saint-Hilaire's housing problem of nearly thirty years earlier. She and her companions were refused lodging first by a German innkeeper, next by a Frenchman who sent them to a Portuguese, and finally by this last. The letter of recommendation was still a *sine qua non*. When the visitors inquired of their eventual host, another German, as to "the curiosities of the town," he replied with a shrug of the shoulders "that he knew of none, unless we wished to consider as such the botanical garden." After some reconnoitering, the author concurred. Her remarks are tinged with restiveness and melancholy: "[We] found more pretty houses than, relative to its size, Rio de Janeiro possessed. But the constructions lacked equally taste and style. The streets are wide enough but excessively deserted, and the general silence which reigns in all the city is interrupted only by the incessant noise of the peasants' carts....The [wooden] axles...are never greased, which produces an infernal music....All the men, except slaves, wear two large cloaks which they throw back over the shoulder; I even saw many women enveloped in broad capes....We visited several churches which have nothing unusual, inside or outside. We ended at the botanical garden which, except for a plantation of tea, offers nothing of interest."[2]

Permanent immigrants continued to filter in from Europe. Judging by the limited demand for their facilities and by their immense circumspection, one cannot suppose Mme. Pfeiffer's innkeepers to have been economic or social pillars of society. Much less so was a German in charge of the Botanical Garden who was

---

2. KIDDER (1845, I, p. 231) had in 1839 singled out the Botanical Garden as "one of the pleasantest locations," though noting its "rather neglected" appearance. The garden, used for sporadic agronomic experiments, suffered from a slim budget.

discharged for having let the promenade lapse into pasturage for his horse and eight oxen, or the four Germans who were employed to assassinate Líbero Badaró.

Only a handful of the immigrants kept an identity as advance agents for European city culture. One of these was the Parisian coiffeur whose art was to prepare ladies for the more sociable life of salon and ballroom and gently to mesh the idle wheels of their existence to the spinning gears of fashion:

> Carlos Gorsse, coiffeur from Paris and pupil of the leading artificers of this profession, advises the respected public that, having arrived in this city to practise his art, he has established himself on Rua do Rosário, house no. 29, where he can be sought at any hour to comb and cut the hair of Ladies and Gentlemen. He will make periwigs of all styles, hair-fronts on tortoise-shell combs, square fronts of wire naturally distributed, perukes, chignons, and all that pertains to his profession with the greatest perfection and in the most modern style. He makes powders of many qualities to tint white hair any color desired. He has an assortment of perfumes and jewelry.   (*O Farol Paulistano*, Nov. 19, 1831.)

Another was the Englishman Henry Fox, whose claims to omnipotence heralded the era of facile advertisement and the sway of catchpenny science over a credulous bourgeoisie. Fox offered for sale a "water of pearls" that cured ringworm and all epidermal diseases, leaving the skin "smooth and clear"; "anodyne drops," the only medicine known to cure toothache without harming the tooth; a "divine mixture," one bottle of which was a "certain cure for gonorrhea"; and "lily blossom paste," a dentifrice "especially recommended for ladies, for it not only preserves the teeth, but gives them new brilliance and delicious fragrance." (*O Futuro*, Dec. 7, 1847.)

With a few exceptions, such as these two, middle-class foreigners of the period seemed either to meet an untimely end, as did Júlio Frank and Líbero Badaró, or to become culturally absorbed, as were the German gunsmiths previously described, the German gardener, and the innkeepers.

Lower-class immigrants likewise failed to unsettle the social mold. In 1828, 336 German colonists were sent by an official agency in Rio de Janeiro to Santo Amaro and Itapecerica, in the rural environs of São Paulo city. The provincial government gave them subsidies in money and food (for a year and a half), land, cattle (to be restored or paid for in four years), tax exemption (for eight to ten years), and a salaried doctor and vicar (for a year and a half). Townsmen showed toward these settlers their customary suspicion of foreign arrivals. A "Patriot" complained in *O Farol Paulistano* (July 12, 1828) that the provincial subsidy, the "blood of our fellow citizens," had been wasted in importing "foreign and *(si vera est fama)* facinorous people...to colonize a country that does not need it." Some of the immigrants took to trades after a while, locally or in other towns. But many farming families found themselves near penury when the subsidies ran out. Moreover, the milieu exacted compliance. Isolated from the world and forced to work land that was none too fertile, the German settlers soon adopted the language, religion, and lethargic behavior of — and they intermarried with — the rural squatters, or *caboclos*. Today a handful of distorted German names is the colony's only recognizable survival.

Figures for immigration of foreign workers into the province show how this influx of the 1820's, which was a forerunner of the large schemes for colonization that were drawn up in the last quarter of the century, was absorbed and denatured, not to be repeated for twenty years or more:

1827-1829 (3-year span).......955 immigrant workers
1830-1845 (16-year span).......384 immigrant workers.

When in 1840 Nicolau Vergueiro subsidized ninety Portuguese colonists for his plantation at Limeira in the interior beyond Campinas, the enterprise was so unsuccessful that it was almost immediately discontinued.

Other pledges of the 1820's were also hanging fire. The House of Correction promised by the first president was still under construction in 1845. The jail itself was in chronically deplorable condition. Prisoners lay in filth on thin floor mats, where their restless minds turned to thoughts of hacksaws — one of which once implemented the escape of sixteen (AESP, 1832a) — or of the firewater that was often smuggled to them. A pair of bibulous inmates on a cleaning detail once kicked over two pots, putting the jailer to the annoyance of sending for lavender to drown out the enormous stench. Lunatics were at times committed to prison, though when questioned about some prisoners who were alleged insane, one jailer said he did not know "when some of them had entered there nor by whose order, as there was no record at all in their respect." (AESP, 1848.)

Improved street lighting was, like prison reform, slow in coming. The twenty-four swaying fish-oil lamps in use in 1829 emitted, at distant intervals, a mortuary glimmer that cast mobile tongues of shadow on the walls. Fifty were available by 1839, but malefactors still found them spaced to give ample protective darkness. Moreover, not only did stone throwers keep many lamps out of commission, but in the interest of economy illumination was provided only between dusk and midnight from the third night after a full moon till the fourth night after a new one. Lamplighters took an hour to light and an hour to extinguish their lamps and spent the whole day in cleaning and repairing them.

The citizens' drainage project of 1827 proved to be only stopgap. Seasonal river floods continued. The Assembly asked bewilderedly in 1835 "if there is known to exist any plan or information regarding the possibility and advantages of canalizing or moving the River Tamanduateí...; likewise if there exist any instruments of mathematics or physics that could be laid hands on for any physical or topographic enterprise." (AALPSP, 1835-1836, p. 61.) Two years later the Câmara was still requesting of the legislature that it destine funds for draining Carmo meadow.

Though swamp water was abundant, water for use was still scarce. An engineer commissioned by the provincial government presented a fine scheme for piping in 1842, but showed cavalier neglect for its immediate purpose by failing to indicate additional water sources.

The Santa Casa, still the mainstay of the ailing poor, received new quarters in 1836, and there were signs — such as Toledo Rendon's donation of four years' salary as director of the Law Academy — that leading citizens were interesting themselves more in its mission. Although a private "Philanthropic Society" engaged in several phases of charity work did exist at the time, neither private nor government initiative challenged the supremacy of the church and its orders in this field. Certain of the Santa Casa's dependencies, however, were in a state of neglect. The lepers in the lazaretto, most of them slaves, were badly cared for. Of 109 foundlings left in the new turning box between 1825 and 1831, 60 perished —

largely through the negligence of the wet nurses to whom they were entrusted. The ineffectiveness with which the Santa Casa, whose incumbency it was, ministered to prisoners and maintained segregation of the insane has already been noted.

It was by now recognized that the lack of graveyards was a cause of disease. In 1829 the Câmara resolved to have Daniel Müller lay out a cemetery at a distance from any residences. Later a deputy asked the Assembly to end the "superstitious and offensive practice" of burial within churches by providing public cemeteries in every town, where bodies could be interred seven spans deep, one and a half spans apart. But the cognizant commission shortly reported that there was no feasible way of circumventing the custom, which was enshrined in a national law. (AALPSP, 1835-1836, pp. 58, 129.) And so the practice carried on. A corpse would be brought into its church. Floorboards were lifted. A grave was dug, and the newcomer, generally not coffined, was laid to mingle with the bones of his forebears and with the dank earth. When the ground had been pestled and the boards replaced, pious ladies resumed their lengthy devotions directly above, communing in age-old ritual and in the fetid air that they breathed with those who had gone before. (Demolition work in the modern city center still lays bare these old ossuaries on occasion.)

The system for educating the living showed scarcely any more change during the 1830's and 1840's than the system for burying the dead. In the educational as in other fields, an ambitious blueprint had been set forth, a *Memorandum on the Reform of Studies in the Captaincy of São Paulo* (reprinted in J. Q. RIBEIRO, 1945), written by one of the Andrada brothers, Martim Francisco, and largely inspired by the writings of Condorcet. The *Memorandum* advocated a utilitarian curriculum for the primary and secondary schools of São Paulo that would stress vocational training and the development of individual aptitudes. In the years after independence, however, this document and the type of thinking that it represented had no measurable effect. The câmaras of the province made no attempt to systematize their schools or to furnish prepared teachers. In 1834 the Additional Act merely shifted responsibility for all public education (except law and medicine faculties) from the shoulders of the câmaras to those of the impecunious provincial governments. Although in 1835 Father Feijó expounded the need for a normal school before the paulista Assembly, it was eleven years before that body took action. In 1836 São Paulo city and adjacent parishes had a population of 22,000, only 1,000 of them literate. Besides the two seminaries founded by the first president, accommodating 19 boys and 33 girls, there were nine elementary schools with an enrollment of 267 boys and 63 girls. Since about one-half the population was under twenty years of age, it is clear that only a fraction of the city's children was being taught.

Surveys sponsored by the Câmara in 1832 revealed that all the city schools were "in marked neglect, perhaps because the government had not supplied equipment necessary for classes or owing to the faint enthusiasm animating the respective teachers." Absenteeism was high while diligence and discipline were weak, the more so since students had discovered that the new Lancastrian method eliminated physical chastisement. (AESP, 1832c.) Presidents of the decade 1835-1845 ceaselessly lamented the lack of trained teachers, the ruinous state of schoolhouses, and the absence of centralized school inspection. One suspects that KIDDER (1845, I, p. 302) praised one of the city's schools as "the most flourishing" in the empire simply because the good missionary found its pupils learning to read from extracts from Scripture. "Very appropriate lessons had been selected, according to the capacity of the little readers," he wrote complacently, "and could not fail to exert a most happy influence over their heart as well as mind."

The two seminaries typified school conditions of the 1830's. The first director of the boys' seminary often left his post; in 1829 his proxy was a youth of thirteen. One of the early teachers was quite incompetent and relied (in a caricature of modern techniques) upon newspapers for class material. The building was in disrepair. Slaves tended to abscond, leaving the youths with unmended clothes and a diet of colewort and corn flour. The boys' daily awakening was suited to the gloominess of their situation; at the given hour a pupil would cry out, "Awake, oh brethren, from sleep, which is the shadow of dreary death! Let us worship the Lord!" The girls fared little better. The building that housed them became dilapidated and overcrowded, and the returns of a lottery assigned for its upkeep were never delivered. A report of 1830 found creditable moral guidance and sewing classes, but no slaves for essential chores, no reading of catechism or the national Constitution, and — as the directress did not comprehend the subject — virtually no arithmetic. Complaints were later lodged against the lack of a

chaplain and an infirmary, the insalubrious refectory, and the enrollment of feeble-minded students.

The period in question was not without its innovations, but
their fitful nature pointed up the resistance of society to change.
A relevant example is the provincial government's attempt in 1836
to improve husbandry by creating an agricultural school just north
of the city. There freeborn orphans were to study Christian doctrine, civics, geometry, mechanics, chemistry, botany, and agriculture. In December, 1837, the director complained that the land was
"covered with ants and underbrush and the house quite in ruins."
A few vegetables had been planted, but the ten slaves assigned him
found time only for illness and attempts at escape. He requested
more slaves, cattle, tools, plants, and seeds. In 1838 the farm was
abandoned. (J. J. RIBEIRO, 1899-1901, I, p. 20.)

Another innovation was the Topographic Bureau, founded in
1835 and designed as a school for civil engineers, deposit for
geodetic instruments, and library of regional maps and highway
projects. The bureau opened with fourteen students and soon had
twenty-three, but by mid-century it had twice been suspended,
which showed its breath of life to be weak.

A Permanent Municipal Guard, authorized in 1831 by the general council of the province, was the city's first police force. One of
its duties was to hunt runaway slaves, or to break up their autonomous communities. Earlier this task had fallen to a "bush captain"
(capitão do mato), appointed by the Câmara whenever the need
arose. In conformance with a trend of the times, a permanent
agency created by a supramunicipal power now undertook the service. If any assignment was too perilous, the new guards' wages had
to be doubled or tripled at the slaveowner's expense. The constab-
ulary was well disciplined, but by the 1840's it was underpaid,
promotions were slow, and equipment and quarters had deteriorated. Like the Law Academy it was housed in a former convent, as
though to signalize the disintegration of ecclesiastical authority.

One significant piece of legislation was the 1836 law for provincial and municipal expropriation. This empowered the president
or, subject to his approval, the câmaras to seize private property in
the interest of public health and safety or for essential public works.
Here, seemingly, was explicit recognition of the traditional commonweal. Yet the procedure stipulated was that once eminent
domain had been declared, attorneys for the government and the

expropriated party were to present estimates for just compensation. If these appraisals did not agree, the judge was to designate a third party to fix an intermediate sum. In practice, the compromise came to be an arithmetic average, even if initial estimates were as disparate as 10 against 1,000 contos. The law stayed on the books till well into the twentieth century, into the era of the large-scale land seizures that accompanied the mushroom growth of the metropolis. Factitiously alloying public with private welfare, it came to serve the greed of opportunists at the expense of anonymous taxpayers.

It is small wonder that the time-bound patterns of town life were not to be infused with fresh energies and reworked under rational auspices in a short decade or two after national independence. The very fact, however, that the drift of local affairs proved recalcitrant before the new vitalities of the nation and of the age placed in question those vitalities of the city's past. It is significant that by the 1830's public festivals were losing something of their rich social content. The fruit-shaped water bombs of Carnival were much abused, and festival masks were taken advantage of for the commission of acts of violence. In 1842 a law was passed authorizing a public archive, as if in declaration that the city had come into a new phase, that it had a "past" which was concluded and discrete from the present. It was difficult, however, to kindle enthusiasm for the project; ten years later the president chided the Assembly for having taken no action: "There — spread among many departments and archives, unclassified, unappreciated, lying in oblivion, left to dust and larvae — are important documents, invaluable for your history with its wealth of glorious and heroic deeds." (DISCURSO, 1852.)

The information so far given in this chapter about the little provincial capital of the 1830's and early 1840's suggests that the action of the "catalytic" forces introduced after independence was considerably dissipated during the two ensuing decades. Either these forces were ineffectual, as in the case of subsidized immigration and the plans for material improvement and school reform, or else they produced restlessness and disorientation, as was largely the case with the Law Academy and the repercussions of national politics. The old order was obsolescent but tenacious, the new one still powerless to be born. The events of the Revolution of 1842, to be described in the next chapter, illustrate the uncertainty with which many townsmen were responding to concerns of national scope. The visit of Dom Pedro II to São Paulo in 1846, also to be described, signalizes the reconciliation of city and nation, and the universalizing of the culture of the court.

Bibliographical Note

KIDDER (1845), PFEIFFER (1880), and S. J. C. COELHO (1860) contain descriptions of the city in the 1840's, while MÜLLER (1923) is a fund of provincial and municipal statistics. The experiment with municipal prefects in 1835-1838 is described in A. FLORENCE (1937). A. da SILVEIRA (1890) and N. D. SILVA (1930) document the career and martyrdom of Líbero Badaró. L. R. de CARVALHO (1946) is a study of the thought of Mont'Alverne and contains a bibliography. SANT'ANNA (1939) tells the story of the Botanical Garden. The history of the German colony established in Santo Amaro is reconstructed in ZENHA (1950).

Chapter 6

THE REVOLUTION OF 1842

*I*N APRIL, 1831, Emperor Pedro I, refusing to give in to a popular demand that he reappoint a ministry which he had just dismissed, suddenly abdicated and embarked for Portugal. As his son Pedro II, whom he left behind, was only five years old, the government passed to a triune regency, supplanted by a one-man regency in 1835. The regency had to cope with bitter separatism in the northern provinces and in the extreme south, but was able to rely upon relative tranquillity in São Paulo, Minas Gerais, and Rio de Janeiro. In 1841, however, liberal factions in São Paulo and Minas Gerais began to chafe under the conservative regime to which Pedro II turned shortly after attaining his "majority" at the age of fifteen. In particular, three laws affecting Brazil's administrative schema, passed toward the end of that year, caused annoyance. Liberals felt them conducive to autocracy and to elimination of liberal officeholders (though in retrospect the measures seem sanely devised in the interests of political stability).

One of the foci for liberal resistance in São Paulo was a branch of the "Society of the Invisible Patriarchs," founded in Rio de Janeiro in 1840 under a secret directorate and comprised of five- to ten-man cells. Paulista liberals were nettled not only by the conservative legislation but also by feelings that the government was prejudiced against São Paulo and that local political offices were being infiltrated by "foreign" appointees. The defiance born of colonial isolation had receded into a persecution complex that was to recur even after São Paulo had become economically the most potent state of the country.

The provincial presidency had until July, 1841, been filled by a paulista, Rafael Tobias de Aguiar. As was inevitable, he was replaced by a conservative, and, when the latter proved too conciliatory with the liberals, still another appointment was made, in January, 1842. The new incumbent was José da Costa Carvalho, former bernardista and editor of *O Farol Paulistano*, and now the baron of Montealegre. Though long a São Paulo resident, the baron was locally suspect for being of Bahian birth. The militant liberal journal *Tibiriçá* decried the northern carpetbaggers in versified Afro-Bahian dialect:

> *HYMN OF THE BAHIAN GANG*
> *The paulistas are captive,*
> *They're captives of Bahians*
> *Who can dispose of them*
> *Like a Ruler Sovereign!*
> *Bahia's a city,*
> *São Paulo's a grot,*
> *Long live Montealegre,*
> *Down with the Patri-ot!!*
> *Mister Baron is Bahian,*
> *Bahian too the Inspector,*
> *Bahian as well the Civil Judge,*
> *And even the Promoter!*
> (A. A. de FREITAS, 1914, p. 403.)

For a time Montealegre's prospects seemed formidable. Many of his conservative supporters withdrew to safer havens in Santos or Rio de Janeiro, leaving him to confront forces captained by such leaders of caliber as Father Feijó, Nicolau Vergueiro, and Tobias Aguiar. The liberals were organized, armed, and ready — most of them — to take extralegal action.

What pertains to this study is the role of the city itself in the movement. It is obvious that the issues were in no wise municipal, but involved the relation of the province to the nation and, even more broadly, abstract concepts as to a government's attributes and sources of authority. It is also clear that these larger issues, owing to events and agencies already discussed, had come closer to the articulate townsmen, displacing concerns that were near at hand and open to experience. The city, that is, would soon be taking a less fortuitous part in national affairs.

This new dimension of awareness in the city, combined with its pivotal importance as provincial capital, identified São Paulo both as the probable point of outbreak and as the stronghold of the movement. The question awaiting answer was whether the townsmen had retained a capacity for common action while their intellectual horizons were widening. Certainly the conservatives who fled to the seacoast had not shown much fiber. Would the liberals' discipline and stamina measure up to the revolutionary role thrust upon the city by its new pretensions and prestige?

There had been one portent in April, 1841, when the Câmara informed the emperor that São Paulo viewed "with sorrow the spreading rumor" that the dismissal of Provincial President Tobias Aguiar was imminent. (ACCSP, XXXIII, p. 126.) The gesture was reminiscent of the municipal renascence of 1821-1822. The outcome was not, for Tobias Aguiar was replaced three months later. The Câmara, hamstrung by the Constitution and impotent to contend with the issues at stake, could not aspire to its focal command of two decades earlier. Indeed, when violence broke out in 1842, some aldermen kept to their homes on plea of illness, while those who convened scrupulously followed a trivial agenda that omitted all reference to the revolution.

A further sign that the liberals could not expect to find disciplined support in the city came after a rumor was received, in February, 1842, that the government was bringing troops up from the south. That night a Club of 170 Extremists *(Exaltados)*, who were less chary than the Invisible Patriarchs, roved the streets breaking conservatives' windows, engaging in skirmishes, and pillaging balconies to obtain lead for bullets. The following night the Exaltados met in a country chácara, armed and prepared to fight. At 1:00 in the morning, Tobias Aguiar appeared before them. Diplomatically he let them know that they were prejudicing a movement which was now in any case inevitable, and persuaded them to disband and take orders from superiors.

The revolutionary leaders finally received their agreed-upon signal for action when on May 1 the emperor dissolved the Chamber of Deputies. The liberal plan, drawn up by representatives from São Paulo and Minas Gerais, was to acclaim new presidents in both provinces, with Tobias Aguiar designated for São Paulo. It was by now apparent, however, that São Paulo city had ceased to be a useful base of operations. The liberals' schemes had long since been laid bare by abortive bursts of violence on one hand and by excessive temporizing and negotiation on the other. The flame of public enthusiasm had guttered, while the president of the province, the baron of Montealegre, had been forewarned in detail and had strengthened his city garrison with forces from other towns. The miscarried attempt of an armed band to invade the city on May 11 and seize the barracks was a final seal on the impotence of the city's liberals. Vieira BUENO (1899, p. 14), newly a bacharel and one of the Invisible Patriarchs, found security measures so effective that his carbine "had the fate to be buried, still virgin, in the latrine" of his residence.

Disillusioned, Tobias Aguiar eluded arrest in São Paulo and started west for Itu on May 13. But the revolution he had come to despair of was bound to burn itself out. In Itu, sympathizers rallied to him as their leader, committing him to journey on to the rebel city of Sorocaba. Here the Câmara, citizens, and soldiery acclaimed him president, and a proclamation was issued calling paulistas to arms against the alleged tyranny of the ministry and pledging fealty to the emperor. On the 20th, Father Feijó arrived from Campinas, crippled, weary of body, but snorting fire, and proceeded to publish the rampant, aggressive journal *O Paulista*. Shortly a "Liberating Column" of over a thousand men was formed. Its mission was the capture of São Paulo city which, though no longer a resilient center of revolt, was strategically critical. The rebels' hopes for a long-range victory were already prejudiced, but, by underestimating the time it would take Rio de Janeiro to receive the news and retaliate, they caused any chances for short-term success to run out.

Meanwhile the baron (later duke) of Caxias, whose leadership in the Paraguayan War of 1864-1870 was to make him Brazil's most revered military hero, arrived in Santos on May 21 with a "Pacifying Army." The following day he embraced his good friend Montealegre, the provincial president, in São Paulo. He found no opposition, and the Carmelites placed their hospital at his disposal, "which in present circumstances may serve as lodging for the officers arriving from Rio de Janeiro." (AESP, 1842.)

Dispatches from Montealegre to the minister of war (AN, 1842b) show how the government forces were coiled into a tight spring in the capital, then released to overpower the adversary in all directions. On May 30 he reported the rebels to be holding out in six major municipalities and in two small towns near São Paulo. Caxias had withdrawn from the latter, since his forces "were still very small and wholly unsupplied, and could not, before the arrival of reinforcements from the Court, hold those points against the rebels, whose tactics lay in their swiftness of approaching the Capital with all the strength they had, to see if they might yet surprise it before arrival of said reinforcements."

By June 2 the rebels, trying to effect better concentration and defenses, had vanished from the environs of São Paulo. Several days later Tobias Aguiar, trying to mask his despondency, took the field personally, but it was too late to rally his troops. They had been caught off guard and demoralized near Campinas. Unimpeded, Caxias marched into Sorocaba on June 20. From a window old Feijó, tottering on his crutches, shouted after his fleeing confederates, "Run, you weaklings and poltroons! I stay here to defend you!"

On the 25th, Montealegre informed the minister that the revolutionaries were dispersed and Tobias Aguiar was in flight. He further announced that the marchioness of Santos, erstwhile mistress of Pedro I, had been found in Sorocaba and would be detained pending advices. The marchioness had just solemnized a *de facto* liaison with Tobias Aguiar in the latter's hour of distress.

The Revolution of 1842 offers illuminating comparison with the Bernarda of Francisco Inácio, which had broken out in the same month, twenty years earlier. Both were revolts against provincial authority. In the case of the Bernarda this authority had no backing; the coup came off successfully in the capital, and opposition retreated to the interior. When Rio de Janeiro tried to regularize the situation, the city refused to deal with its agents. Bypassing all intermediaries, the Câmara appealed to the prince himself and instigated his trip to São Paulo. By 1842 the emperor's representatives were strongly entrenched in the capital. The city in those active weeks showed no will of its own, as Sorocaba, through its Câmara, was still able to do. The capital was beholden to the crown-appointed provincial overlord and his militia. The coup that was ventured there collapsed; it was the rebels, rather than partisans of a displaced regime, who decamped for the interior.

The 1842 Revolution made clear that the political figures of stature in the capital were no longer the rural patriarchs who lived in proud detachment on their fazendas, but rather the law graduates, whether statesmen or politicos, who were converging from the interior and from Rio de Janeiro with new methods of leadership, taking residence in the city proper, appropriating its press and rostrums, interweaving its interests and destinies with those of the nation. The rebel leader, Tobias Aguiar, was of this new nineteenth-century stamp. Generous, deferential, rich from the Sorocaba cattle trade, he knew how to ingratiate ladies in a ballroom and, though upright in his profession of rational principles, was not averse to political negotiation and compromise. His alliance with the marchioness of Santos gave São Paulo one of its most gracious and urbane households.

In brief, then, two aspects of the 1842 Revolution may be noted. One identifies it with the uncertainties of the years after independence. The Revolution found the citizenry of the capital with neither a will to effective common action nor a clear perception of the issues then at stake. The other aspect relates the Revolution to later events. Caxias went on from São Paulo to the pacification of Minas Gerais and Rio Grande do Sul, securing internal peace for the whole country. This was the period in which Pedro II, coming into maturity, was learning to assert his steadying hand. Brazil's political structure had been tried and fixed upon. The nation was emerging from uneasy adolescence and could look to releasing its economic energies in tranquillity with the aid of Europe's new technology.

In 1844 all who had joined the Revolution were amnestied. Two years later, the emperor signalized an era of good feeling by a journey with his wife through the southern provinces. On February 26, 1846, they received a handsome ovation from São Paulo city, where they remained, except for trips to the interior, till April 12. Tobias Aguiar, nothing daunted by a term in prison, was on the reception committee and in attendance at all the fêtes. Another liberal pronounced an eloquent eulogy of welcome. Pedro dispensed honorific titles with largesse, dozens of them to ex-revolutionaries.

Everything attracted the attention of this bourgeois monarch: the process of torrefying tea, lectures and defenses of theses at the academy, student dramatics, religious rituals, and balls in his honor where he danced with aldermen's daughters. In his own person the emperor authenticated the manners and values that had hitherto been somewhat timidly penetrating São Paulo: imperial grandeur, Europeanization, gay and lavish parties, romance, sophistication, scientific curiosity, material well-being, cosmopolitan big-city culture, the parliamentary code of behavior, the gentleman's education.

Changes coming over this city of the late 1840's were of a chemical rather than physical nature. They had little effect upon its outward appearance or the activities of most townsmen — nor would they for years, even decades to come. But certain ideas that had been in the air for a quarter of a century began, in the decade of, roughly, 1845 to 1855, more cogently to assert themselves. The city in fact began to show signs, which will soon be examined, of accommodating to its regional traditions the demands and endowments of a world beyond. At that same moment, however, the vatic cry of the poet warned of change and of forces which the boldest mind could not have conceived.

Bibliographical Note

AUTOAÇÃO . . . (1843) and CAXIAS (1931) contain important documents of the 1842 Revolution. Secondary accounts of the movement are found in PINTO JUNIOR (1879), J. B. de MORAIS (1907), E. V. de MORAES (1934), Martins de ANDRADE (1942), and A. de ALMEIDA (1944; 1945). O. T. de SOUSA (1942) is a biography of Father Feijó. The visit of Pedro II to São Paulo is treated in A. de A. SODRÉ (1945).

Chapter 7

ALVARES DE AZEVEDO
AND THE ROMANTIC TEMPER

But disorder is today the fashion! The beautiful lies in confusion; the sublime in what is not understood; the ugly is all that we can comprehend: this is romantic: come be romantic, let's go on to my future.

— J. M. de MACEDO, *A moreninha* (1844).

A SOCIETY AND its era are often conveniently symbolized in the work and personality of an artist. Colonial São Paulo did not offer the wherewithal or the stimulus for a potential artist to realize himself, to rise free of the community's immediate and self-consistent claims. By mid-century, however, though the destiny of most citizens was still cast along clearly marked lines, there were a few who found themselves encompassing strange contrarieties. The one who, during the romanticist years, most deeply felt and fully articulated the tensions of old and new was the poet Manuel Antônio Alvares de Azevedo (1831-1852).

The son of a law student, Alvares de Azevedo was born in São Paulo in 1831 but was taken to Rio de Janeiro in 1833. At the age of four he was so afflicted by the death of a brother that his health was impaired for the rest of his short life. He was a brilliant pupil, and his headmaster, suggesting one of his romanticist ambivalences, found him to unite "the greatest innocence of habits with the vastest intellectual capacity that I have yet found in America in a boy of his age." In 1844-1845, the youth returned to São Paulo for schooling. Giving vignettes of the city, his letters home conveyed his wonder at seeing "only one or two families in the Cathedral on Ash Wednesday" and described an elegant ball given

85

by the Baron Sousa Queirós, where the air was fragrant "with a thousand scents" of flowers and perfumes. But the boy's birthplace did not yet enchant him. Writing of a dance attended by "what here are called pretty girls," he announced that "São Paulo, withal, will never be like Rio." Though prepared to enter the Law Academy in 1845, Alvares de Azevedo was below the minimum age limit and did not matriculate until 1848. Through the writings of the young law student one may project a physical and, more important, spiritual image of mid-century São Paulo.

Alvares de Azevedo's mixed feelings toward the city as a place of residence suggest the complexity which underlay his literary personality. His earlier impatience with its provincialism did not abate. By 1848 the city had "not yet ceased to be São Paulo," which meant "tedium and boredom." A year later there were no diversions but "to walk along the streets bumping into stones....Reduced to staying in the house, for lacking any place to go and seeing no pleasure in wandering around the streets, I find myself in the greatest insipidity possible, eager to leave this tedious life of badly paved São Paulo."

Yet this same locale — which was in no sense physically overpowering like the Amazon jungle, the northern drought land of Ceará, Rio de Janeiro's extravagant bay, the great southern plains of Rio Grande, or even the contorted hills and red soil of Minas Gerais — held a subtle, insistent fascination. One evening the poet and some friends were returning from a leave-taking at the Tree of Tears: "And there in the distance rose the black city; and its lamps, swayed by the wind, seemed like those ephemeral meteors that rise from the marshes and were deemed by the traditions of northern Europe to be spirits destined for distracting wayfarers ...or stars of fire, sparks of some furnace of hell sown over the black field....

"I stopped and wondered at that beautiful sight! those ashcolored and smoky clouds! that solitary sky of stars...and alone, in the silence of the night which was drawing on, an unknown bird was pouring out its hymn of farewell to the day that had died away in the shadows."

Just as São Paulo's traditions do not boast the wealth and panoply of colonial Bahia or an exotic African or Indian popular culture, so its physical setting is a somewhat neutral one. The soil is neither rich nor sterile, the land neither flat nor mountainous, the climate neither frigid nor tropical. At the same time the natural elements which do exist fail to blend in the "homeyness" of many settlements in a temperate clime. They are unresolved, one might say, or pitched in a minor key, in a way that is haunting to some, lackluster to others. One of the city's distinctive features, for example, is its celebrated *garôa*, a heavy fog verging on precipitation borne in from the southwest by Pacific air masses; romanticists saw in it the mystery and melancholy of Byron's London.[1]

To state the theme less allusively, the history of São Paulo since Brazilian independence discloses, in many realms, a groping for rhythms and certainties. In their confrontation with the modern world the city's thinkers, artists, and men of action have been more tempted than many other Latin Americans to deny their history — to neglect their elusive creole, hinterland heritage and to grasp at ready-made and, in the new context, precarious solutions and ideals from abroad.

This generalization assists the analysis of mid-century literature; for the paulista plateau did not conspicuously yield the tried and true themes of occidental romanticism, such as a northern poet, Gonçalves Dias (1823-1864), himself part Indian, found among surviving folkways of the "noble savage" in Maranhão. In São Paulo, the themes were more latent and diffuse; to elicit them required a kind of tonal sensitivity. Unlike Alvares de Azevedo, many of his fellow students assumed exclusive attitudes. A case in point was their Epicurean Society, whose members wrote, talked, and lived in the Byronic manner, so much so that they caricatured their prototype and fell into orgiastic degeneracy and a morbid worship of death and its sepulchral emblems. One night some

1. Twentieth-century painters find that the setting of the metropolis retains this elusive quality. The late Lasar Segall told the writer that the gray and brown and ocher "tonalities" of São Paulo's environment allow the artist eclecticism and freedom for subjective expression. Similarly, Anita Malfatti says that she can do sustained work only in São Paulo, not in Rio de Janeiro; the latter's natural setting is too exuberant and overwhelming. Although these are private sentiments, possibly rationalizations, they call to mind Henry James' remarks in his preface to *The Portrait of a Lady* about the compelling beauty and traditions of Venice which drew him constantly from "the fruitless fidget of composition." In Venice, he wrote, "one finds one's self working less congruously, after all, so far as the surrounding picture is concerned, than in the presence of the moderate and the neutral, to which we may lend something of the light of vision."

"Epicureans" were roving about in the new cemetery, beating on tombs and declaiming Byron. Suddenly they were possessed of the idea that there should be a "queen of the dead." After obtaining some fearsome robes and hoods at a Masonic lodge they visited the house of a slow-witted demimondaine. She was seized, wound in a sheet, placed in a coffin, and carried to the cemetery. En route one youth, who had studied at Heidelberg, recited Goethe in the original. At the cemetery another was elected as the queen's lover. He pushed off the coffin lid, clutched the girl, and found her dead of fright. "I have kissed a corpse!" he roared, half in horror, half in triumph.

That Alvares de Azevedo attended sessions of the Epicurean Society is evident from macabre accounts in his *Noite na taverna* (*Night in the Tavern*). But the poet's extensive literary production and high academic attainment prove him not to have been a debauchee. His verse shows that he found in Byron something more elevated than a bacchanal appeal; and he once affirmed that the "immoral can be beautiful" but that "from the immoral to the vile" is only a step and (showing perhaps excessive charity) that Byron's verse, though immoral, never trespasses over the "abyss."

The distinctive complexity of Alvares de Azevedo's outlook is further borne out if one compares him with a fellow law student, F. de P. Ferreira de REZENDE (1944, pp. 262, 272). In his memoir the latter recalled that while at the academy: "[I began] to experience the first attacks of my hypochondria; and since then I have almost never ceased being a mere bearer of life's burden." In 1853 he contributed a piece entitled "Ignorance and Happiness" to a student magazine, which held that only the ignorant are happy and that science and felicity are incompatible — a view he maintained throughout his life.

This strain of alienation runs through much of Alvares de Azevedo's poetry and correspondence. In a letter of 1850 he wrote: "There is but one thing that could today give me strength: that I should die." The poet's solitary existence, closed up alone in my room, most of the time *reading without reading*, writing without seeing what I write, contemplating without knowing what I am thinking," seems in retrospect to forebode the denial of the artist and his creative spirit in the materialistic era that was to follow.

Yet with his melancholia the poet embodied a strenuous will-to-do, an urge to smash discreet idols and to look to a far horizon. "Without a philosophy, without a national poetry, how do you expect a nation?" he addressed a student society in May, 1850. "Can a colorless reflection of what happens overseas be the blood of a nation? Can scientific parasitism be the living condition for the intelligence of a people?... [When] protection and improvement for public lycées are denied and there is no will to clear away the pecuniary obstacles that bar the door of the academies to the poor class...then, gentlemen, our purpose is greatly served by a decision to realize an ideal of philosophic love and luminous advance."

Two months later Alvares de Azevedo referred to this speech in a letter to his father. He stressed that he entertained "no idea of exaggerated liberalism, and much less of republicanism," that he wanted less liberal fanfare and more liberal institutions. The Constitution's guarantees for primary and higher education were not being honored. As long as the masses were denied "the dissemination of scientific light," they were but "statues of clay."

Alvares de Azevedo, like the city he lived in, was forced to select from among foreign cultures and re-fuse their elements. "Eclectic synthesis" is a watchword that runs through his speeches. "The philosophic History of a People," he once said, in a vein reminiscent of Vico or Hegel, "is the study of actions and reactions of races among themselves, tending toward the great unitary goal." He even anticipated the "cosmic race" of Mexico's José Vasconcelos by seventy-five years in asserting that the world's races and cultures would all cross in the New World "to produce a new, stronger race, a finer civilization, a richer literature." Yet his writings were tinged — sometimes anguished — by his sense that the eclectic outlook must never ultimately deny the unique temper of the receiving ethos.

For our purposes his play *Macário* is his most revealing work in that it roots his ambivalences directly in the city. Macário, a law student, is traveling toward São Paulo for the opening of classes and falls in with Satan:

MACÁRIO

I'm anxious to get there. Is it pretty?

SATAN (yawns)

Ah! It's amusing.

MACÁRIO

Are there by any chance women there?

SATAN

Women, padres, soldiers, and students. The women are women, the padres are soldiers, the soldiers are padres, and the students are students. To speak more clearly: the women are lascivious, the padres dissolute, the soldiers drunk, the students vagabonds. This with honorable exceptions — for example, after tomorrow: you.

MACÁRIO

This city must bear your name.

SATAN

It bears that of a saint: almost the same thing. It's not the clothes that make the monk. Besides, that place is large as a city, dull as a town, and poor as a village. If you're not reduced to giving yourself to debauchery, killing yourself from spleen, or being a flash in the pan, don't enter there. It's the monotony of tedium. . . .

MACÁRIO

But, as you were saying, the women. . . .

SATAN

Under the shining cloth of the mantilla, through the veil's lace, with their rose-colored cheeks, black eyes, and hair (and what eyes and what long hair!) they are pretty. Besides, they're pious as a great-grandmother; and they know the modern art of interposing an Ave Maria with a flirtation, and giving a wink while telling the rosary.

MACÁRIO

Oh! the satin-smooth mantilla! the glances of Andalusia! and the skin fresh as a rose! the black eyes, very black, between the eye-lashes' silken veil. To press them to the breast with their "ay's," their sighs, their words cut short by sobs! To kiss the palpitating breast and the crucifix that dances on her neck! To squeeze the waist and stifle a prayer on the lips! It must be delicious!

SATAN

Ta, ta, ta! What an inventory! You seem to be in love, my Don Quixote, before seeing the Dulcineas!...But the girls seldom have good teeth. The city on its hill, surrounded by grassy meadows, has steep alleys and rotten streets. The minute is rare when one doesn't stumble against a donkey or a padre. A doctor who lived and died there left it recorded in an unpublished work...that virginity was an illusion. But withal, nowhere else are there women who have more often been virgins than there.

The poet, who tells in his poems and letters of his own quest for an ideal love, is as closely identified with the yearning student as with the Devil. This duality of São Paulo, its halftoned echoes of Hispano-Moorish romance and the mordant realities of a small Brazilian city, was a mainspring of its romanticism. Because Alvares de Azevedo so precisely specified it, the critic Sílvio ROMERO (1943, III, p. 267) called him, above all others of the generation, "a local, indigenous product, son of an intellectual milieu, of a Brazilian academy." *Macário* is one of the literary works that most clearly exhibit what the historian Sérgio Buarque de HOLANDA (1948, p. 241) calls the "voracious, subterranean crisis" wrought in mid-century Brazilian writers by the "transition from life next to the elemental things of nature to the more regular and abstract existence of the cities." Their romanticism "was artificial and insincere only in certain formal aspects," writes Buarque de Holanda. "The best men, the most sensitive ones, set about frankly to detest life — the 'prison of life,' to use the phrase of the time."

Bibliographical Note

Quotations from the writings and correspondence of Alvares de Azevedo are from the eighth edition of his complete works (M. A. A. de AZEVEDO, 1942). V. de P. V. de AZEVEDO (1931) and J. P. da V. MIRANDA (1931a) are biographies of the poet. Discerning critical analyses of his work are found in Azevedo AMARAL (1931) and Mário de ANDRADE (1935, pp. 67-134). HADDAD (1945) gives the background for the romanticism of the law students.

Chapter 8

A CULTURAL QUICKENING

A SALIENT INDEX of the romanticist years is the increased matriculation in the Law Academy. This
was, of course, not straightway noticeable in the size of graduating
classes, which for the period 1846-1851 hovered at a yearly average
of 16. But in 1852-1856, the average jumped to 35, and in 1863 a
peak of 111 was reached. With a total enrollment of some 600
students, divided equally between the Curso Anexo and the law
courses, the academy's prosperity was no longer a matter for doubt.

A generation after its founding, the new dimensions of inquiry
that the academy stood for and the careers of a literary or forensic
nature that it brought into reach had become a part of Brazilian
city life. The newly acquired works of Jefferson, Godwin, and
Ricardo were not sharing the dust of their theological shelfmates.
By mid-century, students had perceived the new challenges – and
new freedoms. They exultantly hailed the school's founding in one
of their journals:

> 11th of August. – The great Academic day was suitably
> celebrated by our youths, who could not in any way
> forget the anniversary of our literary emancipation –
> an anniversary that for all recalls the era when we freed
> ourselves from old Coimbra, where among strangers we
> went to seek the fruits of science.
>
> (*A Legenda*, Aug. 21, 1860.)

By 1850 the number of new periodicals to appear in the city
each year was fast increasing. This signified greater literary activity
on the part of the students, who under the empire (that is, until

1889) edited about one-fourth of the city's publications and contributed to many more. The first students' journal in 1830 had been
devoted to belles-lettres. It was this field — along with social and
natural sciences — rather than factional politics which most attracted them through the romanticist period. Only after 1847, however, did there appear journals of substance, whose pages not only
drew nation-wide attention to a triumvirate of student poets in
which Alvares de Azevedo figured but gave a start to such writers
of future renown as the novelist José de Alencar. One bacharel in
later years recalled of the journal *O Acayaba* (1852) that: "The
vices inherent in the style of youth — that is, abuse of metaphors,
prolixity of sentences, declamation — are here replaced, with some
exceptions, by a simple, clear, and elegant language. The choice
of articles and of subjects for poems generally shows very good
taste." (J. L. de A. NOGUEIRA, 1907-1912, VII, p. 87.)

A perusal of the organ of the student society Ateneu Paulistano
(1852) reveals, in addition to verse and literary criticism, a variety
of mature and probing articles on history, law, and even psychology.
Dispassionate study was given to such contemporary Brazilian
themes as: "Would the Existence of the Hereditary, Representative
Monarchy be Possible without the Existence of the Senate Appointed for Life?" and "Does Ministerial Responsibility Extend to
the Functions of the Moderative Power?" The tenor of the students' writing in these years was in contrast to their lack of intellectual concern in the 1830's, their ardent political and social
propagandism of the late 1860's, and their flippant and studied urbanity of the 1880's. It was at mid-century that their literary
endeavor most nearly measured up to the responsibility, incom-
mensurate with their years, placed upon them by a city which was
centered in its law school and by a nation which could boast
only two.

The academy's mid-century renascence suggests two complementary hypotheses: that it was adapting itself to the needs of the
times and that São Paulo (with the other regions of Brazil that
supplied students) was beginning to demand a different and better-
educated type of citizen. As a consequence of both, the student
had new prestige in local society; he "belonged." The thawing out
of restrictive mores in this period was in part society's response to
his activities and needs. If the colonial church can be considered
as a drawstring that united the classes in common belief, ceremony,

and pageants, mid-century students might be thought of as undoing the seams of class distinction by which the earlier community had been knit.

Indicative of the students' new immunities is an episode that occurred in the same theater where in 1842 (ten or fifteen years earlier) they had been so victimized by a provincial president. This time a hubbub was set off by a priest whose appearance in the audience inspired the students to a chorus of jests at his expense and one of their number to an impromptu burlesque of the litany. The subdelegate of police ordered the show to close, but the management hesitated, and when the provincial president appeared in his box it was rumored that he had been summoned to countermand the subdelegate. Immediately student sympathy swung to the underdog. When the president began: "It was at behest of the academic body...," he was cut off with: "Never mind! Never mind! Suspend the show!" Alluding to the dignitary's liaison with a local strumpet, one youth cried out: "It was at behest of Cristina!" The performance was therewith canceled.

A contretemps that occurred in 1854 similarly attests the student body's less vulnerable status. One evening an army officer appeared in a box in the theater and failed to remove his hat. The students shouted at him to uncover and cried out military commands. Conflicts between students and soldiers ensued for several days, till finally the president ordered the battalion in question to Santos.

Other incidents show how student buffoonery was loosening the mesh of custom and superstition. At one street corner stood a large black cross held in reverence by the citizenry. It became known that a certain Lothario was using it as a ladder by which to enter a young lady's second-storey bedroom. One night a band of students made off with the cross and threw it in the river, and the chief conspirator spread the news via his credulous washerwoman that it had been borne through the city by an angel choir.

In the early 1850's, a student (later an important magistrate) approached the house of some proper maidens and entered into conversation with the youngest, when she noticed that he was clad only in a sheet. He dropped his toga to the ground, "and as if a shot had been fired into a flock of doves, all the girls ran off shrieking — wishing but not daring to look behind." (F. de P. F. de Rezende, 1944, p. 298.)

Not only did students organize dances, but those given in

private homes became more frequent and more animated. To be sure, Alvares de Azevedo ruefully compared a "narcotic" cotillion to Rio's "thousand-and-one-night dances in all their magic of lights and brilliance." Yet on other occasions he was less splenetic, particularly if a gorgeously dressed lady caught his fancy. A certain masquerade was enlivened by three students who found a way to temper a steep admission charge. One of them — dressed as an oversized dowager — appeared, paid the fee, and was received by the company with guffaws. "She looks nine months gone!" "It's due any time now!" Whereupon the matron entered travail and brought forth two students from beneath her voluminous skirts.

The following newspaper account indicates how dances were bringing the city cosmopolitan standards and the conspicuous extravagance which they entailed:

DANCE. — The Most Exc. Senator Sousa Queirós offered yesterday to paulista society a charming night with the splendid and sumptuous dance by which he signalized the degree of bachelor in law conferred on his eldest son, the Most Illustrious Dr. Francisco Antônio de Sousa Queirós. The dance took place in the residence of H. E., a vast building decorated with taste. The company was large and select, luxury and wealth being noted in all the *toilettes.* Dancing lasted till 4 o'clock in the morning, and during the whole night gracious and attentive service abounded.

The urbanity and fine manners with which H. E. and all members of his respected family treated their guests are worthy of special mention.

(*Correio Paulistano,* Nov. 21, 1857.)

Implicitly, the last sentence sets "urbanity and fine manners" in contrast to provincial suspicion and taciturnity.

A traveler of the period exaggeratedly attributed the whole of the city's new ferment to student life: "The academic youths give the town, during their residence in it, a sort of fictitious life which, as soon as it is interrupted [by vacations], causes the town to revert, so to speak, to its state of habitual somnolence.

"The old city of the Jesuits should be regarded, then, from two distinct points of view. The provincial capital and the law faculty, the townsman and the student, shadow and light, changelessness and action, the suspicion of some and the often libertine expansiveness of others, and, in fine, a certain monotony of routine personified in the permanent population and the audacious ventures toward progress embodied in the transitory and fluctuating population.... Remove the academy from São Paulo, and that great center will die exhausted." (ZALUAR, n.d., pp. 194, 205.)

Despite an assertion by this same traveler that many students lived in "comfortable rooms, with many objects of luxury and taste," most of them were on short allowances. A group, generally of three to six, would form a "republic," pooling funds to rent a house, buy necessities, and hire a cook; additional services were provided by slaves who accompanied their young masters from home.[1] The most famous republic was the *Chácara dos Ingleses* (Englishmen's Estate), so called for having once been the home of some British engineers. The Chácara had a varied career: as a trysting place for Dom Pedro and his paramour, as a home for the girls' seminary, and eventually as the republic of Alvares de Azevedo and his brother poets and locale of the Epicurean Society. By 1850 its traditions, dilapidation, and gloom, its unkept grounds, its nearness to the potter's field, and its association with Byron's homeland made it a capital stage prop for romanticism. In *Macário*, Satan points out the Chácara as his own dwelling:

SATAN

I have a house here at the entrance to the city: to the right in front of the cemetery.... Get up on my shoulders. Don't you see a light in that palace darting past each of the windows? They know of my arrival.

MACÁRIO

What ruins are these? Is it a forgotten church?... Does no one live there? I have an urge to enter that solitude.

Often a students' republic was on a street lined with hovels whose inhabitants were impoverished and even meretricious. Yet such students could at any moment step from their plebeian lodgings into the ballroom of, say, the marchioness of Santos, by now the lady of greatest prestige in local society, whose house was richly

1. The republic, frequently composed of "compatriots" from the same province, showed an *esprit de corps* that is lost in today's prosaic rooming house. One can, however, visit old-style republics in the charming and traditional town of Ouro Preto (Minas Gerais), where students at the School of Mines still maintain them.

furnished, whose coach rivaled the bishop's, and whose daughters enraptured every heart. The marchioness herself might even harbor a student who had been injured in a street brawl, or pay a visit to one confined in his republic by illness to render personal services. The students' attitude toward women corresponded to their ambivalent associations. With the same ease that they patronized lusty, lower-class dances — daintily termed *sifilíticos* — they could dedicate a journal, A *Violeta* (1848), to *"Dames et Fleurs,"* whose columns, murmured an editorial, overflowed with "perfumes, longing, and melancholy."

A general leavening was becoming apparent in the behavior of all townsmen of higher standing. Their needs were no longer suitably accommodated by the patriarchal family, plantation, and church. Specialized agencies of the city were pluralizing the citizen's institutional allegiance, partitioning his social involvement, and thus rendering certain of his attitudes unrelated, even contradictory, each to another. FREYRE (1951, I, pp. 300-301) documents this development for Brazil as a whole, calling it a transition from "absolute patriarchalism" to "semipatriarchalism." Just as bureaucracies, banks, schools, factories, offices, and stores came to restrict the purview of the *casa grande,* or "big house," of the planter, so the provincial president, judge, chief of police, lawyer, headmaster, hotelkeeper, and commercial agent encroached upon the authority of the patriarch himself. From the viewpoint of women, offspring, and other patriarchal dependents, Freyre suggests, it was as if the change were being made from absolute to constitutional monarchy.

A São Paulo newspaper's sharp criticism of the window blinds of the colonial sobrado typifies the incursions upon the traditional, self-contained institution: "...someone has said that it is not right to declare war on the poor rótulas, which are very comfortable. Comfortable in what sense? For concealing the family, first-storey windows covered by sunblinds, as utilized in Santos, Rio de Janeiro, etc., serve the same purpose. And to conceal it from what? Are we a people of ugly hags? Besides, there is the grave question of morality. It is well to reflect on the motives for which something is hidden.

"The little towns of our littoral, many villages and cities of the interior have forbidden their buildings blinds of straw or wood. Are we less advanced, and is our morality inferior to theirs?

"It is moreover beyond question that the appearance of the provincial capital will greatly improve with the projected measure, that the danger of bumping into windows will disappear. And who knows what effect it will have on our customs?" (*O Constitucional,* Oct. 21, 1854.) Patriarchal habits, however, and popular affection for the romantic Hispano-Moorish rótula were persistent. Not until 1874 did the first ones come down.

Church processions, though becoming increasingly profane, and the patriarchal dances, though increasingly public, were too ceremonial for the needs of daily recreation. Students organized country excursions on foot or horseback, boating and swimming parties along the rivers, and, on occasion, a three-day hunting expedition; at night they roamed the empty streets with flutes and guitars, serenading girls with languid roundelays. In 1839 the Câmara sanctioned the first billiard parlor (although five years later a merchant was denied license to conduct a public lotto game from noon till 2:00 p.m. daily). A maker and tuner of pianos set up shop for a month, advertising his instruments in *O Governista* (Jan. 3, 1846) as a hallmark of "civilization" and a mode of casual "recreation for the fair sex." Another pastime was the daguerreotype. Wrote Alvares de Azevedo in 1848: "The mania for being daguerreotyped has spread here. . . . There is not a student who has not had his picture taken, or at least who is not planning to do so. Moreover it is cheap — for 5$000 one gets a small-sized colored picture in a simple frame. And not only students are infected; the disease is catching and the doctor is making money." Merchants were quick to detect and stimulate the people's penchant for spectacle:

NOTICE
Aerial Voyage
of the
Giant Balloon.

Sunday, the 24th of this month, the GIANT BALLOON, 34 spans in height and 70 in circumference, will ascend from the BAZAAR, Rua do Rosário no. 37, and since it is going to France for a new assortment of cloth and toys, no fee will be asked for watching its departure, which for the greater convenience of the public will occur in the street, between 4 and 5 in the afternoon.
(*Aurora Paulistana,* April 23, 1853.)

A traveler in São Paulo would still have found no hotels in the early 1850's, and the belief persisted that people, particularly women, who sought such lodging were immoral. For convivial supper parties there existed in 1852 only the dark, narrow rooms of the city's two restaurants. But by 1855 the first hotels were appearing, and the traveler J. C. Fletcher registered at one just as he might have in "Boston, Liverpool, or Geneva." These establishments, though modest, brought soirées out of the patriarchal sobrado into "neutral" ground, offered facilities for gaming, served an allegedly continental cuisine, and afforded relief from the slumbrous calm of provincial evenings. The Hotel du Commerce was open till 11:00 p.m. and on theater nights for an hour after the performance; it boasted a "clever and skilled" European chef, a bakery at the service of the public, and a billiard room. In its dining hall or private rooms the Hotel de France served theatergoers such delicacies as "tarts of cream and sweets, shrimp and chicken pies, and puddings ... with a good and varied meal." (*Correio Paulistano,* 1859.)

Students dominated the mid-century theater — as actors (even as ingénues), playwrights, and audience — and carried it, if not to an extreme of polish, at least beyond the inelegant productions of 1820. In 1830 a students' theater had begun to function within the academy itself, and three years later they founded their Teatro Harmonia Paulistana, promising to offer "decent dramas, appropriate to the intellect of the century" and to waken patriotism and civic virtue in the citizen's breast. (AESP, 1832b.)

The students presented all the popular tragedies, farces, melodramas, and pantomimes of the era, with an enthusiasm that was not to be stayed by an imperial decree of 1830 which forbade productions during the school year. In 1843 the director of the academy testified to the seriousness with which the elite regarded student dramatics, in a complaint to the minister of the empire: "The students, wasting their time in rehearsals for the theater, shirk their duty toward their studies. The invitation [to performances] of certain families to the neglect of others causes grave inconveniences which should be avoided. And to all this must be added the danger of their bringing to the stage things which perhaps embarrass persons placed in higher stations of the social order." (AN, 1843b.)

The muse of drama was no longer the mere female of easy virtue that she had been in Saint-Hilaire's day, and *Revista Dramática*

(July 22, 1860) praised the actress Deolinda on her death as a fine gentlewoman. Signalizing this new respectability, the provincial president asked the Assembly in 1852 for a more spacious theater, construction of which was begun six years later.

The world horizons and impetuous criticism of students were a healthy stimulant to Brazil's rudimentary theater. Playwright Alvares de AZEVEDO (1942, II, pp. 388-91) urged that companies no longer pander to the pit's desire for farces and melodramas. He pleaded for taste and discrimination, for a theater that would inspire men to reflection and finer emotions, for dedication to the great European traditions. Sometimes the corrective to hinterland bathos took an earthier form. One night Deolinda delivered with too heavy a touch her soliloquy: "Now that I am alone and no one hears me, I dare to say: Yes! I love him!" From the pit cried a student's voice: "I overheard!" Pandemonium broke out, the actress fainted, and the play was suspended.

The theme thus far asserted for the mid-century years is the city's emergent awareness of new possibilities for personal and social life. The word "awareness" is important. For São Paulo — as an academic city, as provincial capital, as an economic and diocesan center — stood fair to achieve a more controlled and selective "out-turning" than that of the little mestizo villages of the Americas upon which big-city ways suddenly impinge. Paulistanos had means for recurrently appraising regional history and culture, for enriching and diversifying them with new customs and ideals; and the students, however dissolvent their impact upon society, showed sensitivity to the traditions of the city. The larger forces into which São Paulo's destiny was being meshed were not so unmasterable and subversive of the old order as they later became. This conclusion is to be reinforced in a consideration of material, particularly economic, affairs. Meanwhile, we shall turn to the church to see how an age-old institution, flagging in its social and cultural responsibilities, might suddenly gather itself to counter criticism and secular encroachments and to reassert its leadership.

None of the three journals that appeared in these years to reprehend the church in the conduct of its affairs reflected the shallow encyclopedism characteristic of later, self-consciously "scientific" critiques. *O Amigo da Religião (The Friend of Religion)* was in fact edited by a cleric and pledged in its opening editorial (April 8, 1855) to "go to the churches of the Capital to hear the sermons preached here and offer frankly its opinion. But it will bear in mind the well-known situation of the clergy of São Paulo; it knows their difficulties, knows their grievances, and knows that, facing a struggle with material conditions, they lack the means for work and instruction."

It is significant that the bishop who tried (1852-1861) to shore up the church's waning prestige was the first paulista-born, non-Portuguese incumbent: Antônio Joaquim de Melo. Whether or not his primary dedication was to the realm of the spirit has been lengthily debated. A contemporary and disaffected cleric described him as "atrabilious, designing, anachronous, hypocritical," money-grubbing, and unfeelingly highhanded toward the lesser clergy. He also accused the bishop, as did O Amigo da Religião (Jan. 26, 1856), of condoning slavery. (CARMELLO, 1873.) A modern apologist paints him as a self-denying reformer: stern, honest, and impartial. (P. F. da S. CAMARGO, 1941.) Partly because of an early military career he was an autocratic disciplinarian, which soon cost him the favor of his cathedral chapter.[2]

Immediately on taking office, Dom Antônio ordered his priests to be tidy always in personal appearance and to wear proper vestments; to abstain from dancing, gambling, and other improper amusements; to hold aloof from politics and from commercial transactions for profit; and to open and close mass (which was not to be shorter than eighteen minutes) with prayers. A visit to the city's two convents revealed violations of cloister and lighthearted music-making, a situation which the bishop soon corrected. He also warned chapelmasters not to interlard sacred music with contredanses.

Dom Antônio forbade the nocturnal burial ceremonies – as being a mere "pretext for committing within the churches every kind of irreverence" – at the same time that a few European Protestants and members of the Câmara were opposing interment in the churches in the interest of public hygiene. A "Cemetery for Germans" was opened near the city center in 1851, half of it reserved for Catholic and half for non-Catholic foreigners, and the large Consolação Cemetery for Brazilians was laid out in time to receive victims of

---

2. During Christmas Night mass in 1854 an altercation broke out before a horrified public between Dom Antônio and the capitulars, causing suspension of the services.

the fierce smallpox epidemic of 1858.[3] The scientific outlook and the resurgence of the faith were in this case of mutual service. The church's long-standing shortage of trained priests was another need to be met in the face of secular challenges. Twenty-five years before Dom Antônio's accession, certain townsmen had unsuccessfully petitioned the imperial government for a local diocesan seminary. (AN, 1827-1828.) Dom Antônio had more luck. With a subvention from the provincial government, a seminary for aspirants to the priesthood was inaugurated in November, 1856. The intentions of the new school's administration were straightway made clear in the inaugural addresses of the vice-rector (who declaimed against the era's taste for novelty, urge for pleasure, and scorn of authority) and of the rector. The latter, after decrying the fallacies of Spinoza, Rousseau, Kant, and Cousin and the irresponsible liberalism of Feijó and Pedro I, admonished his listeners grimly: "Behold, gentlemen, what is given us to hear every day in this enlightened city, where the chosen youths of the Empire come to be fitted for civil, social, and political life. Behold the inference that modern impiety can draw from the anomaly of a Holy Religion preached by worldly ministers." (P. F. da S. CAMARGO, 1941, pp. 168-70.)

Lacking competent paulista priests, Dom Antônio staffed the seminary with European Capuchins. This enraged some of his subordinates, who accused the newcomers of grossly reactionary bias, of hedonism, and of neglecting the welfare of resident students. Soon, issue was joined with the law students. Protesting the bishop's recommendation that the academy, as a "focus of immoralities," be transferred to Rio, the student journal A Legenda (Oct. 1, 1860) animadverted upon the seminary's "half dozen corrupt friars, adulatory hypocrites, and ambitious ignoramuses ... who dream of the fires of the Inquisition and of absolutism."

The bishop, in turn, was well aware of the obstacles to re-Catholicizing society. As he wrote to the emperor in 1858: "Brazil has no more faith; religion is almost extinct there. Of religion only the exterior remains: great feasts that usually end in lower-class

3. There had been two earlier burial grounds for restricted use: a potter's field and a plot for deceased nuns.
   The first cemetery regulations of 1858 stipulated that the newly dead should be laid in an "observation room" for twenty-four hours before burial. If any came to life he was, if financially able, to pay the gravediggers who had kept watch and the overseer 100$000. (REGULAMENTO ..., 1858.)

revelries, and physical idolatry of images. But *that* which is the *way, truth,* and *life* is unknown. ... For the state at which we are arriving, Sir, for this paganism in the education of youth, for the collapse of the social order owing to the subversive and anarchic principles that corrode enlightened persons, I find but one remedy [:] ... a frank and loyal alliance with the Holy See. Thus the bishops, returning to their natural station, recovering their old moral force, ... will diligently strive to reform customs and improve education, and will come to the support of the country." (J. J. RIBEIRO, 1899-1901, II [2], pp. 684-87.)

So far we have examined the city's culture during the romanticist years in its literary, sociological, and religious aspects. One may conclude that life was, at least for educated and upper-class citizens, more permissive, less monistically patterned than it had been in 1820. The roles of the church and sobrado were less inclusive. New currents of thought, and new media for transmitting them, made possible a spectrum of more individualized politico-intellectual attitudes — in the same way that hotels, dances, theaters, and billiard halls gave townsmen a more plentiful choice among daily activities.

One may further conclude that romanticist São Paulo had acquired, in comparison with the city of the 1830's, new vitalities, tension, and self-awareness. The academy had taken root and was prospering. Students were more purposive in their literary, journalistic, and dramatic pursuits and imparted their energies to the city. Their cultivated romanticism gave São Paulo a self-image, one that interpolated regional and traditional with cosmopolitan characteristics. The church, at the same time, through its seminary and zealous bishop, was seeking to restore an age-old Luso-Catholic moral and spiritual base to society. This involved acceptance of new challenges and competition. It meant, that is, bringing the church into relationship — albeit one of tension rather than, for the present at least, reconciliation — with new customs and ideas.

Because its institutional fabric was still so strongly patriarchal, increasing numbers felt their city to be hidebound and parochial. Traditionalists, on the other hand, found it becoming materialistic and wantonly liberal. But when we follow a more open view, such as that in Alvares de Azevedo's *Macário,* we discover a milieu of compelling and *sui generis* qualities. As J. C. Fletcher wrote of São Paulo to a friend in 1855: "I am in a cold room, — such cold as I have not before experienced in Brazil. The moon is shining coldly;

men creep about in cloaks, (I wish I had one,) and the only thing that possesses caloric is the candle which throws its dim light upon this paper. I ought, however, to except the stirring strain of a distant bugle, that really fills the night air with a warming melody. ... I felt a more profound respect for San Paulo than for any South American city that I have yet visited. ... My feelings of respect, however, arose not from the size of the city, nor from its picturesqueness, but because there is a more intellectual and a less commercial air about the people than you see elsewhere in Brazil. You do not hear the word *dinheiro* [money] ringing constantly in your ear, as at Rio de Janeiro." (KIDDER and FLETCHER, 1857, p. 363.)

The traveler ZALUAR (n.d., pp. 195-99) — while acknowledging São Paulo's political activity and institutions, library, hospitals, churches and convents, academy and seminary, theaters, stores, commerce, "hotels crowded with travelers," and Botanical Garden — sensed that the city "preserves even today [c. 1860] in its inhabitants, customs, and usages certain traditional traits: the stamp of mysterious concentration that the Jesuits could impress everywhere, not only on the people and buildings but, what is more, on the natural setting and very environment that surrounded them.

"Hence the first impression that São Paulo wakens in the spirit of him who observes and studies the character of its inhabitants is the dual physiognomy of its people, with an obverse and a reverse — like a sphinx. . . . The character of the paulistas, pleasing and open in intimacy, though suspicious at first meeting, gives them a certain stamp of singular originality, which precludes confusing them with the inhabitants of any other province of the Empire. The speech of this people also has a quiescence and an accent that are peculiar to it."

Bibliographical Note

A sampling of the life and customs of the mid-century years may be gleaned from the letters of M. A. A. de AZEVEDO (1942, II, pp. 435-532). See also J. C. Fletcher's expansion of Kidder's earlier observations (KIDDER and FLETCHER [1857]) and the memoirs of F. de P. F. de REZENDE (1944) and ARAXÁ (1883-1884). The city's burgeoning salon life of this period receives attention in PINHO (1942) and RANGEL (1928).

Chapter 9

MATERIAL FULFILLMENT

*7*HE MID-CENTURY LEAVENING so far described was accompanied by lines of economic thought and endeavor which reflected the new industrial spirit of the Western World.

In 1850 only fifty concerns in all of Brazil were classified as industrial establishments, and in 1852 the paulista president found only seven "worthy of mention" in the province, five of them in the interior. (DISCURSO, 1852, p. 33.) The relation between the capital's political centrality and its economic development is seen in the fact that its two factories, alone of the seven, had official patronage. One, a somewhat "decadent" foundry, had received a loan from the Assembly and was obliged to maintain eight apprentices from the boys' seminary. The other enjoyed a tariff exemption because it produced hydrogen gas for an improved system of street lights.

Private initiative is not to be discounted, however, as affecting the city's early industrialization. The foreigner Jacob Michels, for example, had "the honor to announce to the respected public" in *O Governista* (Aug. 2, 1845) that his factory on Rua Direita was offering "a grand choice of hats of all qualities and finest taste." He was a good craftsman, his prices were reasonable, and soon his capital enabled him to purchase more modern machinery and to contract skilled European labor. In the 1850's he set up a brewery as an adjunct to the hat factory, the product being comparable in price and quality to European beer. As evidence of a preference that the capital seemed to enjoy over other paulista cities, one can cite a second hat factory — founded in Campinas in 1853 but transferred to São Paulo the following year by its German proprietor, J. A. Schritzmeyer.

Public figures began to see that if the city and its tributary region were to import a larger share of the increasingly abundant goods of the Western World, two changes were necessary: rationalization of the domestic economy to furnish exportable surpluses, and local control of that economy so that gains from more intense and efficient production could not be claimed elsewhere. This realization accounts for the founding in 1853 of the Society for Encouraging Agriculture, Trade, and Crafts. Its fifty-nine charter members were not merely planters and industrialists, but leaders from all realms: churchmen, engineers, professors, politicians. In his inaugural speech, the society's president urged that farmers discontinue old, "exotic practices," that they cease to set themselves against "the evidence of the facts, the truths of new agrarian knowledge." Slave labor was to be replaced by methods more consonant with progress and prosperity. The export trade was to be nationally controlled, so that its profits would remain at home.

The society's aims were comparable to those of the Economic Society projected in 1822, but they must be examined in the light of its respective climate of change. The new society was (like the romanticist poets) better informed to mediate between foreign ideas and local conditions, and its projects conformed strikingly with the analyses of those twentieth-century planners who are aware of the pitfalls of mammoth industrialism. The society was alive to the benefits of home manufacture, but saw that in the case of an indigent rural economy the prime concern must be with rationalizing agricultural production.[1] Accordingly the directors set about to distribute information on farm machinery, sponsoring an exhibit in the capital; to encourage better grades of tea, wine, cattle, and wool; to discover other products that might take favorably to local soil and climate; and to acquire new seeds from abroad. In October, 1853, a letter from the society to one Nathaniel Sands, a United States citizen, made him an honorary member for his services in introducing farm machinery and inquired under what terms he

1. Cf. the provincial president's report of 1858, which affirmed that agriculture was the "perennial source of prosperity and wealth for all peoples" and that industry, as it merely transforms agricultural products, had to wait until labor, capital, and technical skill were available. (DISCURSO, 1858, p. 21.)

would become a "correspondent for acquiring farm apparatus and instruments which the society intends to order from the United States." (INDUSTRIAL..., 1854-1856.)

A corollary to the society's espousal of free labor was the founding in 1856 of an abolition society by the law students. Although the latter was soon disbanded, after it had helped to free only one slave, it was the forerunner of the intense abolitionist and republican agitation of the 1870's. Moreover, it gave an indication of how political and humanitarian crusades were to set the impress of the city upon the hinterland, and how the city was to become the agency for rationalizing the rural economy.

With reference to nineteenth-century Brazil, Buarque de Holanda (1948, p. 203) has pointed out that an impersonal, abstract order (symbolized in Sophoclean drama as Creon) challenged the community's "domestic, family order" (symbolized as Antigone); the rise of the city was "a clear triumph of the general over the particular, the intellectual over the material, the abstract over the corporeal." In some ways, as we have seen, one might construe this transformation as having been an enrichment rather than a denial of, or a triumph over, the "domestic, family order" of the São Paulo of the 1820's. It was, however, ominous that the Câmara had been superseded in the vital field of municipal administration by a government of province-wide legislators, headed by presidents the majority of whom were not even paulistas. The following are examples of how the impotent Câmara was appealing to the president on routine and clearly municipal matters:

"This Câmara, as it has often made clear to Y. E., finds itself at present faced with important works that absorb the limited resources at its disposal; and lacking the means to incur further expenses for public works, it judges its duty to be to bring these facts to the notice of Y. E., whose concern for public improvements and whose most valuable aid lent to this Municipality have overcome not a few difficulties."

"The Municipal Câmara of this Imperial City begs H. E. kindly to indicate the appropriate width for the Santos highway at the place called Cambuci, where João José Ferreira, of this Municipality, is erecting a building continuation of which was forbidden by this Câmara since it threatened to encroach upon the highway."

"As the rainy season is approaching and as certain highway bridges and most of the bridges ... in this Municipality are already in bad shape . . .; and in view of the embankment that caved away next to Arouche Reservoir . . .: the Municipal Câmara of this Imperial City begs Y. E. kindly to have those places repaired so that traffic will not be interrupted, which is to be feared if repairs are not soon in coming." One might cite many similar requests for assistance in bridge and highway repair, work on the cemetery, improvement of street drainage, and other civic needs. (AESP, 1855a.)

A large part of each presidential address to the Assembly was devoted to affairs of the capital city: street lighting and paving, the House of Correction, the market and abattoir, the water supply, the Botanical Garden, the theater, flooded rivers,[2] the need for better fire-fighting equipment. One finds in these documents more and more references to foreign (especially French) engineers — Bresser, Bastide, Martens d'Estadens, Milliet, Günther, Bourroul — who were resuscitating stillborn schemes of the 1830's.

In 1847 Afonso Milliet was contracted to furnish the city with 160 lamps, burning liquid hydrogen gas, that were to be kept lit all night, except in bright moonlight. A new abattoir, designed by Europeans, was opened in 1852; its drainage, like that of the old one, ran into the Anhangabaú, but it was subject to a stricter sanitary code, requiring hygienic installations and medical examination of each animal. By 1860 many of the city's bad roads had been paved, most notably the rutted and filthy Beco do Inferno (Alley of Hell). The Botanical Garden (officially the Public Garden after 1838) received increasing attention as a site for recreation and experimental horticulture; ordinances were adopted to promote public sobriety, and in 1862 the French traveler Houssay (1877, pp. 5, 80) was enraptured by the flowers, arching trees, marble statuettes, and cool chalet of his "dear Promenade."

In 1852 the long-promised House of Correction was finished and placed under the Auburn penitentiary system. Prisoners were regularly and adequately fed; workshops, an infirmary, and, later, elementary instruction were made available. In short, the prisoners' life was disciplined with a view toward rehabilitation. The year 1852 also saw the removal of the insane from prison to a house, albeit a cramped, ill-equipped one, administered as an asylum. A decade later they were transferred to larger, though scarcely commodious, quarters. And by 1855 a public archive was functioning.

2. On January 1, 1850, a six-hour rain caused the Anhangabaú to overflow and carry off a bridge and fifteen houses.

Epidemics, especially smallpox and cholera morbus, continued to ravage the populace. In the plague year 1858, the Cathedral was almost bereft of worshipers in Holy Week, and the Câmara gave up its meeting place for use as an infirmary. But disease control, like other public services, was coming under unified, rationally planned direction. During the cholera scourge of 1855, the city was divided into four medical zones, in which specified pharmacies and doctors were responsible for taking swift action to check the plague and for making daily reports to the president. A municipal Sanitary Commission, empowered to call upon the police for assistance and to provide free care for the poor, supervised all phases of the campaign. The president, however, still relied heavily upon the time-honored, unofficial agents of welfare: religious orders and beneficent public figures. The baron of Antonina, hearing of his efforts, wrote in the Catholic upper-class spirit of charity to offer "the paltry means at my disposal for alleviation of those disabled poor who may be attacked by this terrible disease." (AESP, 1855b.) [3]

School reform continued to be hobbled by the Additional Act of 1834 which, by centralizing higher and decentralizing primary education, left the system as a whole, in the words of Fernando de AZEVEDO (1944, p. 330), "disorganized, anarchic, congenitally atomized." São Paulo's schools were still insufficient in number, in physical equipment, in personnel. Teaching methods were still antiquated. Schoolbooks, when available, were prohibitively priced. Yet the horizons of the romanticist years were not wholly closed to education. A reform of 1846 obliged the provincial government to provide all populated places with schools and to set standards for curricula and for the qualifications, salary, and tenure of teachers. A two-year normal school, recurrently a hope for twenty-five years, was established in the capital. (When it closed down two decades later, however, the school had graduated only forty teachers.) School inspection, which lacked incentive and uniformity, was centralized under a provincial inspector general by a law of 1851 that shaved away another of the dwindling municipal functions. The regulations of the two government seminaries were rewritten in the

3. In 1849 Rio de Janeiro suffered Brazil's first important yellow fever epidemic. Ocean traffic spread it to São Paulo's coastal cities of Santos, Ubatuba, and Iguape, causing 231 deaths. Eleven were stricken in the capital, but all had been infected elsewhere. Its altitude gave São Paulo city an immunity which would later contribute to its metropolitan growth. (REGO, 1873.)

1840's, and in 1854 the boys' school, where students were reportedly "barefoot but healthy," was equipped to train tailors' and cobblers' apprentices.

Notwithstanding the innovations which have been mentioned, however, it should not be assumed that the rash of mid-century reforms affected all phases of city life with equal strength.

The provincial police force, increased to four hundred in 1850, was given to drink and insubordination. Water pipes and new public fountains were installed after 1851, but the small diameter of the pipes did little to relieve the shortage, and slaves continued using polluted river water. The religious order which took over the lepers' home in 1855 failed to improve its conditions; as before, invalids consigned to it preferred their independence, and the government felt that the expenditure for an adequate asylum would have outweighed its utility.

By 1855 travel over the coastal escarpment was much easier; the road to Santos had been macadamized, was less steeply graded, and could accommodate carriages if not too heavily laden. Yet the potential benefit of this highway was partly offset by a provincial law of 1851 which authorized duties on intermunicipal trade. The paucity of many simple articles of commerce is attested by Alvares de Azevedo's requests to his family in Rio de Janeiro for such items as gloves, books, cologne, and glass candle shields.

The mutations which did occur in the city's economic and administrative life, however, and the prospects for the future which in these years took shape are better understood if they are related to a shift in the economy of the larger region. That shift was the advent of coffee.

Bibliographical Note

INDUSTRIAL . . . (1854-1856) documents the economic stirrings of the 1850's. Mid-century statistics for the province and its capital are found in IHGB (1855a; 1855b).

Chapter 10

COFFEE ... AND PREMONITIONS

*I*NTRODUCED IN BRAZIL in 1727, coffee planting was taken up throughout the country in the eighteenth century. The crop's commercial value was slight at first, and consumption was restricted to the producing region, or even to the plantation (fazenda). By the early nineteenth century, however, markets for Brazil's traditional agricultural exports (sugar, cotton, tobacco) were for various reasons being curtailed. This occurred precisely at a time when a world and, particularly, American demand for Brazilian coffee began to assert itself. In 1779 the port of Rio de Janeiro exported only a little more than a ton of coffee; in 1806 it shipped over 1,400 tons.

The first zone to be favored for intensive coffee production was the Paraíba valley, extending southwest from the province of Rio de Janeiro into São Paulo. The rainfall and climate, the rich and unexploited soil, and a pattern of life not too heavily determined by a previous monoculture all contributed to this end, as did the region's inner cohesiveness and its natural maritime outlets. So swiftly did planting proceed that coffee made up 18 per cent of Brazil's exports in the 1820's and 44 per cent in the 1830's.

Before the railroad era, the whole Paraíba region remained economically tributary to Rio de Janeiro — both overland along the valley and via the coastwise shipping of its ports, which lay over the Serra do Mar. The paulista capital, in the 1830's and early 1840's, was negligibly affected by the coffee boom, except for the passage to Santos of shipments from scattered localities northwest of the city. Of the province's total coffee production in 1835-1836 of 9,600 tons, 84 per cent originated along the Paraíba, while the

111

value of coffee shipped out of Santos was less than one-fourth that of sugar.

São Paulo city, as earlier pointed out, occupies an infertile zone, which blocked the advance of coffee once it had reached the western end of the Paraíba valley. A report of 1856 observed that this region contained a few trees on hilltops or along rivers but that its most usual vegetation was a ground cover "commonly called 'goat's-beard' which, serving no purpose, kills other flora introduced there." (INDUSTRIAL ..., 1854-1856, II, p. 74.) Potters rather than farmers found the best use for the soil.[1] North and west of this region, however, came rich land once again. In 1820 João VI, little suspecting that here was coffee's future heartland, had praised its fertility, climate, excellent and varied pasture, and abundant water sources, and had asked that cattle ranches be set aside there as dowries for the princesses. (DIHCSP, XXXVI, p. 96.) Given the swift and steady increase in coffee plantings after independence, and given the rapid exhaustion of land along the Paraíba, it was inevitable that coffee should "make the leap" into the paulista northwest — especially since that area had certain advantages over the Paraíba valley. The new region was not mountainous. Its broad, gently undulating plains would hold the riches of the soil longer and facilitate rapid construction of a well-knit system of transportation. Moreover, the land had large streaks of *terra roxa* (red-purple soil), a product of decomposed basaltic rock of volcanic origin that was highly favorable for coffee planting.

For São Paulo city the importance of the "leap" was that it made a vast, wealth-producing agricultural hinterland tributary to the provincial capital and its port city, Santos. The coincidence of the "leap" with the capital's romanticist years is suggested by the following figures for the province's coffee production:

	1836		1854	
	Tons	*Per Cent*	*Tons*	*Per Cent*
Paraíba valley	8,300	86	44,500	77
Northwest	1,300	14	13,000	23
Total	9,600	100	57,500	100

1. Santo Amaro, scene of the early attempt at German colonization, was at the zone's southern limit. Here lumber was cut for building houses in the capital, and grain, manioc, and cotton were farmed for the markets of São Paulo and Santos.

Production during those years, in other words, increased fivefold along the Paraíba and tenfold in the northwest.

The mid-century presidents' reports were increasingly concerned with the new crop. (DISCURSO, 1848; 1852.) In 1848 new plantings were reaching "colossal proportions." In 1852: "Coffee planting is ever more prosperous and promises this province a great future.

"Our planters now show a tendency to shift from planting sugar to planting coffee and tea, and the change is gradually taking effect. This tendency stems, as you know, from the fact that not only is the latter culture easier and more advantageous than the former, but it is less subject to misfortunes inherent in the wretched state of our routes of communication and the impossibility of vehicular travel."

In 1855 it was stated that coffee was tending to displace all other cultures, that tea offered no profits, and that sugar, because of high processing and transport costs, was finding mainly local markets. (EGAS, 1926-1927, I, p. 238.) By then Campinas, an important city fifty miles northwest of the capital, had seen its sugar production, mainstay of its prosperity, dwindle to less than a third of the output of thirty years earlier. The shift to coffee was in full career.

We have said that the northwest coffee region was tributary to São Paulo city — a relationship soon to be reinforced by the railroads that were to focus upon the capital. In what ways, the question arises, did the city's new relation to a coffee region differ from the old one to a sugar region? HANDELMANN (1931, p. 361), writing in 1859, claimed that coffee was a "democratic plant," that it led toward subdivision of the land and the welfare of the many; whereas sugar, with its need for heavy capital investment in land, labor, and installations, was essentially "aristocratic." Cassiano RICARDO (1942, II, p. 237), writing eighty years later, asserts that coffee democratizes by its need for free labor and that the privileged group which emerges forms an open rather than a closed class.

That coffee inevitably democratizes is disproved by modern Costa Rica, where the status of many coffee workers is changing from peasantry to peonage. The nineteenth-century social structure of the whole Paraíba valley, in fact, strongly resembled that of the traditional sugar culture. Coffee fazendas tended toward self-sufficiency; they were worked by slave labor, and planters constituted a proud, hereditary "baronage" whose life activity was almost wholly contained within the rural domains. As a rule, the only land to be parceled into small farms was exhausted and marginal.

The pattern of economic expansion in the northwest, however, was quite different from that along the Paraíba. Here the new coffee barons were not guided by the vision of a self-contained, colonial-type slavocracy. Indeed, the abolition of the slave trade by the Brazilian government at the very time the northwest was settled made such a vision illusory. One senses, rather, a correlation between the structure of the new coffee empire and the emergence of the provincial capital into an era marked by eclectic planning, cosmopolitanism, and the practical-mindedness that could lift a problem out of any broad and traditional context.

The clearest instance of this correlation is the way in which the planters tried to meet their labor needs. Nicolau Vergueiro — who, for being a statesman and director of the Law Academy, was a man trained in the ways and ideas of the city — pioneered the field in 1840 with his Portuguese colony at Limeira. That experiment, as we saw, was short-lived, but in 1847, "Vergueiro and Co.," financed by a loan from the provincial government, contracted to import 1,000 European colonists for various fazendas. Within a decade, some two dozen colonies, containing over 4,000 farmers, were under way in many regions of the interior.

Previous colonization in São Paulo (for example, the German settlement in Santo Amaro) had been officially sponsored, as were attempts throughout the century in other provinces to the south. Mid-century paulista schemes, however, represented private initiative. The essential difference between the two was that officially sponsored colonists lived on the land as proprietors, while the others were contracted under an arrangement known as *parceria.* By terms of the parceria system, an immigrant family was advanced its travel expenses, to be repaid with interest. On the fazenda it was assigned a certain number of trees to tend and a plot of land for its own subsistence. It received as payment either a fixed wage or a percentage of the income from the harvest.

The extension of the parceria system was reflected in a spurt of immigration (agricultural) to the province. The yearly average of 46 for the period 1830-1851 jumped to 982 for 1852-1857. After the peak of 2,125 in 1855, however, a sharp decline set in, and that figure was not surpassed until 1875. A revolt of Vergueiro's colonists in 1856 in effect marked the end of the mid-century experiment. Though some colonists had been victimized by onerous financial arrangements and irresponsible administrators, this failure of the parceria was essentially attributable to the disparity between rural living conditions in São Paulo and glowing promises of the planters' agents in Europe — a disparity that was disillusioning especially for those immigrants who had given up urban, middle-class professions.

Although slave labor was for years longer the mainstay of the coffee fazenda, the parceria foretokened how the city was to cast its image across the face of the country. For the parceria and the later, more successful schemes for mass immigration that were modeled after it were not agrarian colonization in the full sense, but the importation of a "mobile, rural proletariat that continually changed patrons." (Davatz, 1941, p. 1.) This connection between the city and the pattern of northwestern expansion becomes clearer if we recall the urban associations of the new planters. Nicolau Vergueiro has already been discussed; many of the other pioneers, including Vergueiro's own son-in-law, were law graduates and held positions of forensic and political eminence in the city. Urban experience had led them to envision a cheap, efficient "labor supply."[2]

With the Industrial Revolution, the labor pool, impersonally conceived, had been factored out of the close-knit, multiassociational economic community. "Labor" became an isolated variable, a factor of production — like plant, capital, or raw material. The old sugar aristocracy was perhaps no less profit-minded than the new coffee barons. But the latter were less custombound, more free to plan their exploitation with capitalistic singleness of purpose. New promises, as well as their new outlook, made such freedom possible: the wide swath of rich virgin land to the west; the fast-expanding world coffee market; the farm machinery and the marketing and credit facilities of the new industrial world; the railway network that would soon obviate the planter's need to be self-sufficient.

The exploitative nature of coffee planting, encouraged by the biotic demands of the crop itself, was outlined by a paulista in the national Senate (1858): "The conversion of fazendas from sugar

2. It is significant that the political economy taught in the Law Academy in the 1840's was that of the French "bourgeois economist" Jean Baptiste Say, who distinguished himself from the earlier Physiocrats by adopting a manufacturer's rather than an agrarian outlook.

to coffee has contributed . . . in São Paulo to the rising cost of foodstuffs. . . . When the farmer plants cane he can also, and does, plant beans, and some even plant corn at a greater distance so as not to affect the cane. And it all aids splendidly to prepare the soil for cane. . . . That occurred in the municipality of Campinas, whose lands are very fertile, when its crop was cane — and in similar municipalities that supplied the capital and other places with food-stuffs.[3] Meanwhile, that whole municipality of Campinas, and others, are today covered with coffee, which does not permit the concurrent planting of foodstuffs except at the start, when new. But when [coffee is] mature, nothing else can be planted and the soil itself is unproductive for foodstuffs, perhaps forever, or until after a period of long years." (HOLANDA, 1948, p. 259.)

The coffee boom was in part a creature of the city. But the creature almost immediately threatened the stability of the creator. The presidents of the 1850's complained repeatedly of the scarcity and high price of foodstuffs. Bacon rose in 1853 from $080 or $100 a pound to $800 or 1$000, then leveled off at $400. Beans, even in the troublous year 1842, had cost only 1$000 an *alqueire* (1.2 bushels); in 1857 they reached 20$000. And whenever an epidemic took its toll among the coffee workers, more slaves were diverted to the coffee fields from subsistence planting.

São Paulo city of 1820 — small in size, modest in its economic needs — had been in symbiotic balance with its immediate region. By mid-century both the low carrying capacity of the close-lying land and new perspectives of capitalist-type exploitation to the west were associating the city with a far broader hinterland. This asso-ciation was still to be symbiotic. The city made its impress upon the structure of the coffee realm, and its fortunes were in turn subject to the vicissitudes of a monoculture. But the new relation-ship of city and country was not the direct and intimate one that a visitor to the town of 1820 might have perceived. The com-plexities and forces now suffusing it precluded its being, in the sense that it once had been, self-corrective. Buarque de HOLANDA (1948, p. 260) points out that the conversion to coffee "increased the need for recourse to the urban centers, which distributed food supplies that had formerly been grown locally. As a result, the

3. It will be remembered that, in the 1830's, subsistence farmers began to leave the infertile environs of the capital, causing that city to depend upon a wider region for its food supply.

agrarian domain gradually ceases to be a barony and approximates, in many regards, a center of industrial exploitation. It is only in that sense that one may speak of coffee as a 'democratic plant,' to use Handelmann's expression. The planter who emerges from contact with it becomes basically a citified rather than a rural type, for whom the agrarian holding constitutes principally a means of life and only occasionally a place of residence or recreation. The formulae for good crops are not inherited from tradition and the community through successive generations, along with the lands, but are learned periodically in schools and books."

A consideration of São Paulo's romanticist years makes clear that the nascent coffee empire and the quickening of the city's life are inseparable from each other. What remains to be seen is how the fruits of that empire — which were in appreciable measure responsible for the city's new cultural and material acquisitions — were in the long run to act upon the "domestic, family order." In the short run, certain aspects, at least, of that order were broadened and enriched; but the 1850's also evoked portents which should not here be overlooked.

One can point for example to the demise of the Society for Encouraging Agriculture, Trade, and Crafts. In 1856 its president recalled how three years earlier it had been installed in the capital "under the most favorable auspices" by citizens who foresaw "the retardation and falling-off through which the agriculture of the Province was to pass," spurred as it was by the profit incentive while lacking the guarantee of a reliable source of labor. Yet the society's voice awoke no echo. When the fervor of the first plans died away, "everything cooled off; and the promises of collaboration for the expressed aim of the society were lost in space." (INDUSTRIAL . . . , 1854-1856, II, p. 85.)

Was the commercial spirit to outrun the agencies for its control? Would the scientific outlook dignify or demean the life of man? Such questions are suggested, at their most prosaic level, by the following notices which by chance appeared in the same issue of *Correio Paulistano* (Nov. 21, 1857). One was an "Important Hygienic Notice" to school teachers, offering the salutary advice that: "The emission of urine is a very important function. To hold in urine for 24 hours is more dangerous than to fail to go to stool for a whole week." The other was a factitious, testimonial advertisement for an "anti-syphilitic water," in which nineteen residents of the city declared "for the good of humanity" that the water had cured them in quick order of gonorrhea, its application being "easy, painless, and of no inconvenience to the stomach."

Earlier, the writings of Alvares de Azevedo were adduced as exemplifying a fertile interfusion of new and old perspectives. Yet the poet was himself cut off at the threshold of a career. And, whatever flashes of faith he may have shown in science, education, and the new philosophies of Europe, he wrote in an elegy at the end of his life that "we are condemned to the night of bitterness; the north wind snuffs out our beacons. We shall all, poor castaways, be rolled upon the littoral of death."

The critic Allen TATE (1948, pp. 100-3) has pointed out that certain nineteenth-century romanticist poets met frustration because, "under the illusion that all order is scientific order," they forfeited the use of poetic imagination. Poetry tried to compete with science but lacked any "systematic method of asserting the will." The inflated style of such poets signifies a "rhetorical escape" that endowed their "will with the illusion of power." Defying "the cruel and naturalistic world" and lacking means to comprehend and cope with it, they were inevitably broken by it. Alvares de Azevedo and his fellow lyricists were victims of this "romantic irony." They stand, then, not only for what there was of mid-century fulfillment, but also for prescience of the "naturalistic world" to follow.

The most explicit misgivings about the currents of mid-century life that I have found are in a letter written at the close of the romanticist years, in 1856, by Ricardo Gumbleton Daunt. Daunt, born an Irishman but become a staunchly Catholic and conservative Brazilian, writes from the stolid, traditional little city of Itu, west of São Paulo, and inveighs in the manner of a Tocqueville or John Calhoun against the new tenor of life in the capital:

"There are many who wish to see São Paulo grow in wealth and make outstanding progress, but little are they concerned if it occurs with the loss of the traits of paulista character. ... They see the Province as a productive machine and a possible means for increasing the budgetary income. I, however, though I do not wish to yield to them in my love for the Province, do not hope for so rapid a transformation. ... I shudder at the progress rapidly being made in planing down the saliences and hallmarks of paulista character and customs which some applaud as a guarantee of the unity of the Empire! In my opinion uniformity of thought, custom, taste, and character presages the decadence of any great Empire, for being in itself a forced and unnatural thing, it can emanate only from the undue influence of the Court or some other center and is always an index of a lack of spirit, of virility, in people thus uniformalized, who are in this fashion prepared for Despotism.

"I am therefore very positively piqued with the foreign tendency of many men educated in our law faculties who unite to centralist ideas a senseless admiration for institutions of other countries and other races and wish to treat us as if São Paulo were a *tabula rasa* where everything is about to commence, as in any North American colony. ... As soon as paulista history is in any of its branches disesteemed, as soon as one wishes to assume that nothing essentially distinguishes São Paulo from semi-foreign Rio de Janeiro, as soon as one wishes to maintain that São Paulo never had an old. robust, and fertile civilization — neither will the government be able to rule us to our satisfaction, nor will the opposition be able to indicate the remedy." (IHGB, 1856.)

Bibliographical Note

Afonso d'E. TAUNAY (1927-1937) is a fifteen-volume history of the Brazilian coffee industry, also available in a one-volume abridgment (1945). SIMONSEN (1940) is a less comprehensive treatment by an economic historian. Concerned specifically with the paulista region are: MILLIET (1946a), an account of the westward expansion of the coffee frontier; MONBEIG (1952), an able and thorough history of this expansion from a geographer's viewpoint; and a more fragmentary study by PESTANA (1927). The characteristics and decline of coffee planting along the Paraíba valley in the nineteenth century are analyzed in QUEIROZ (1950) and, for particular regions, in HERRMANN (1948b) and STEIN (1957a). TSCHUDI (1953), J. P. C. de MORAIS (1870), and DAVATZ (1941) present data on the operation and eventual failure of the parceria system. FORJAZ (1924) is a biography of Vergueiro. Afonso d'E. TAUNAY (1937) studies the beneficial effect of the coffee boom upon municipal revenues in São Paulo province.

The life and opinions of Ricardo Gumbleton Daunt are recapitulated in BOURROUL (1900) and DAUNT NETO (1942).

Part 111—City Growth

Chapter 11

SELF-DEPRECATION AND NEW IDOLS

*D*URING THE FIRST three-quarters of the nineteenth century, São Paulo showed no untoward gains in population. Most sources, whatever the date they refer to in this period, give its inhabitants to be 20,000 to 25,000; but this apparent stagnancy means merely that in earlier reckonings certain centers were treated as subordinate parishes, rather than as independent municipalities. In the figures below, reductions are made to insure comparability:

Parishes	1836	1855	1872
Sé	5,568	7,484	9,213
Santa Ifigênia	3,064	3,646	4,459
Braz	659	974	2,308
Penha	1,206	1,337	1,883
Nossa Senhora do Ó	1,759	2,030	2,023
Consolação (detached from Santa Ifigênia, 1870)	......	......	3,357
São Paulo	12,256	15,471	23,243

The total rate of increase sharpens after 1855. Penha, an outlying nucleus, follows this pattern, though Nossa Senhora do Ó, also outlying, shows no increase at all. Sé, the central "triangle," grows steadily. But it is the regions immediately adjacent to the heart of the city (Braz and Santa Ifigênia-Consolação) whose increment is strongest — a trend reflected in the expropriation (1863) of chácara lands on the Morro do Chá, where five new streets were laid out.

The faster population increase of 1855-1872 failed to signify,

122

however, that the promised material efficiency and embellishment of the city were becoming realities. In fact, the decade or so which followed the stirrings of the city's mid-century years had something of the anticlimactic quality of the decade which followed the eventful 1820's.

A penitentiary provided with vocational workshops was completed in 1867, but treatment of persons committed to the insane asylum or the lazaretto was in no way improved during these years. The Public Garden was still the only recreation park. The Provincial Assembly was still housed, observed HADFIELD (1869, p. 72), "in a very pokey, close room attached to the palace, with a miserably low gallery at each end for the public." In 1863 the fuel for street lamps was changed to kerosene; complaints persisted, and the authorities had to start negotiations for coal gas. Though the first public market was opened in 1867, the congested little stalls *(casinhas)* that Saint-Hilaire had remarked half a century earlier continued interrupting traffic in a small street within the "triangle." So traditional and convenient where they that, despite efforts of the Câmara, they were not to be dispersed until 1890, when a second market was inaugurated. The water supply, however, was the Gordian knot. Presidents, goaded by bitter townspeople and newspapers, complained ceaselessly in their reports. But funds were not available for tapping the one supply — in the Cantareira hills, some miles north — that an English engineer advised in 1864 to be both pure and ample. Then, during the Paraguayan War (1864-1870), cast-iron piping was not to be had, and for several years two public fountains were supplied by bitumen-coated cardboard pipes.

The whole field of public works was the presidents' despair. Large sums were spent but, said one incumbent, "without method, system, knowledge, or even the possibility of control" (EGAS, 1926-1927, I, p. 396) — a situation aggravated by the scarcity of competent engineers. As late as 1870 a president lamented to the inspector of public works that, despite its greater prosperity, "the capital of the Province has no decent illumination, no water to satisfy its inhabitants, no fountains, handsome plazas, monuments, or public buildings." (J. J. RIBEIRO, 1899-1901, II [1], p. 558.)

Though the appearance of the city had not deteriorated, neither had it appreciably changed. And residents and visitors alike, worked upon by a new chemistry of hopes and ideas, expected change. Colonial vestiges – unquestioningly accepted in 1820 and cherished as romantic in 1850 – were, by the 1860's, unpalatably archaic.

Alfredo d'E. TAUNAY (1944, pp. 15-31), who passed through in 1865, found Campinas more attractive and cordial. São Paulo's public buildings, especially the "small and generally poor" churches, left him unimpressed. The sturdy, time-honored taipa construction and the classic rótulas were wanting in taste. Streets were clean, but "their paving leaves something to be desired." He was unpleasantly surprised at the city's lack of activity (except for a "great afflux" of foreigners working for the railway), the people's reserve, and the seclusion of the women, who, on their infrequent ventures into the street, concealed their faces behind mantillas. It was at this time, in fact, that law students began to burlesque the mantilla by wearing it themselves in church or for Carnival.[1]

Ferreira de REZENDE (1944, p. 445), a former law student, returned to the city in 1868 for his first visit in thirteen years. His autobiography, though it admits he may have been prejudiced by love of his own province (Minas Gerais) or by the dreariness of his student memories, states that he was ready to depart in a few days. "Although it was then beginning to be said that São Paulo was prospering greatly, I found the city just as I had left it, discovering nothing new there except the railroad that had recently been built."

Paulistanos themselves – knowing that their province was fast becoming wealthy from coffee and that wealth in their century should equal material betterment – were impatient with the slow march of events. A modern city, they had been taught, meant "order and progress" (the phrase soon to be proclaimed throughout Brazil by its positivists). By 1860 their complaints were being publicized by a livelier kind of journalism that was politically committed to practical issues and spiced with stinging caricatures. (It was only after mid-century that journalism began to win general acceptance in patriarchal Brazil as a bona fide occupation.) Through the press the people recognized certain rights as theirs; and through it

---

1. In 1857 roving bands of middle-class business people had begun to bring Carnival merrymaking out into the streets, lending a more unrestrained gaiety to that occasion. In 1872, according to *Diario de São Paulo* (Feb. 15), the celebrators included "a band of 'women' in mantillas, among whom were not absent those seeking to profane the clerical gown."

their spokesmen, or those who claimed so to be, formulated popular claims. "We love the people because we are sons of the people," vociferated A Razão in 1862.

"We love the people but do not deceive them.

"We love the people and are not like those who cry out today, and tomorrow servilely beg protection from their oppressors....

"What do we want? ... What we want is total and complete observance of monarchical, constitutional, representative government: the integrity of and respect for all the absolute rights of man." (A. A. de FREITAS, 1914, p. 487.)

Public opinion! Ever more insistently "the people" were appealed to as an ultimate arbiter, with rhetoric of cajolery, ridicule, or flaming indignation. The liberal A Razão was in this respect no different from the conservative O País (March 9, 1866): "On the 3rd of the current month Dr. João da Silva Carrão left the administration of this province.

"Our sincere congratulations to the paulistas.

"What good did His Exc. do during his unhappy and demoralized administration?

```
0  0  0  0  0  0  0  0  0  0  0  0  0  0  0
0  0  0  0  0  0  0  0  0  0  0  0  0  0  0
0  0  0  0  0  0  0  0  0  0  0  0  0  0  0
0  0  0  0  0  0  0  0  0  0  0  0  0  0  0
0  0  0  0  0  0  0  0  0  0  0  0  0  0  0
0  0  0  0  0  0  0  0  0  0  0  0  0  0  0
0  0  0  0  0  0  0  0  0  0  0  0  0  0  0
0  0  0  0  0  0  0  0  0  0  0  0  0  0  0
0  0  0  0  0  0  0  0  0  0  0  0  0  0  0
0  0  0  0  0  0  0  0  0  0  0  0  0  0  0
0  0  0  0  0  0  0  0  0  0  0  0  0  0  0
0  0  0  0  0  0  0  0  0  0  0  0  0  0  0"
```

Owing to the still vigorous patriarchal structure, however, the party system was far from effective; political groupings frequently served merely to camouflage long-standing family rivalries. O Liberal (Jan. 27, 1869) complained that: "Parties are the adhesion of many individuals to the same principles, the same ideas, the same interest, and the same opinions.... But, if this be true it is so on the condition of not prejudicing the vital system of parties with the dominance of a group or a family. That dominance means the dissolution of the community and the breaking of certain moral ties that constitute party discipline by subordinating the pretensions of each individual to the opinion of the majority." Yet, continued the article, the Sousa Queirós family had so preponderated in the liberal party as to receive the provincial vice-presidency twice and to appropriate "most of the seats in the provincial assembly" and the "best civil posts and industrial concerns." One judgeship in the capital "became infeudated to the family. High positions in the national guard, provincial and municipal companies for highways and other public works, everything, in fine, was distributed by blood relatives or kinsmen."

São Paulo was the capital of a flourishing and important province. Its officials had promised efficient administration and impressive public works, commensurate with its dignity. Books, journals, travelers, and engineers from northern countries testified as to what might be expected. Yet São Paulo drifted in colonial somnolence.

"One day last week," reported *O Futura* (Aug. 23, 1862) in disgust, "a mad dog ran through the most public streets of the city, threatening all who passed.

"An old Negro, carrying a barrel of water on the Rua da Boa Morte, barely escaped being a victim of this animal's fury.

"The district inspector slumbers in deep sleep. The Municipal Câmara retains such employees as long as they pledge their electoral services. . . . The man in the street merits a little attention only on those days of great intrigue when he deposits his vote of confidence in the urn. . . .

"Near the bridge in Braz the embankment is such that a tilbury risks being turned on its side if the driver shows a soupçon of negligence.

"The Municipality of São Paulo does not heed these things. If it were a question of a little graft the aldermen would long since have opened wide their eyes and pursed their lips. . . . Braz deserves attention only when it's a matter of giving land grants to the clubmen of the elections."

A decade later, in 1872, *Diario de São Paulo* found the streets overrun with dogs, chickens, and "more nanny goats than people" (July 17), and indignantly protested that certain sections of "this imperial city of São Paulo, capital of the province,. . . are genuine cattle farms — but at the expense of the backyards of the poor. Will there be no remedy for this, gentlemen of the Municipal Câmara?" (Jan. 19.)

São Paulo's sluggish response to modern trends was ascribed by *A Epoca* (June 14, 1863) to a carry-over of the "feudal" mentality: "The policy of the feudal lords has been limited to militarizing the national guard, restricting the press, snatching away the citizen's guarantees, denaturing the institution of the jury, joining the police with the magistracy, slandering reputations, corrupting talent, stifling agriculture, disdaining the sources of national wealth, persecuting trade with iniquitous laws, and laying upon the country an enormity of imposts, burdensome in the extreme, but necessary for fortune-seekers to enrich themselves, their hangers-on, and the greedy pack who have praised their honesty and severity."

The laxity of the police force evoked particular displeasure. *Cabrião* (I, 28 [1867]) printed a pair of cartoons on the subject. The first showed two guardians of the law who had spied a fracas down the street: "It looks like quite a scuffle down there." "Well, let's blow our whistles." The second showed three crickets in police uniforms, with the legend: "If all the patrols do is whistle, they might just as well be replaced by patrols of crickets." *O Futuro* (Sept. 27, 1867) complained that the hazards of a nocturnal stroll were as great as they ever had been: "It is pitiful to see the disgraceful state that the citizens' guarantees have reached in this unhappy city.

"The police sleep soundly and criminals wander without fear, creating every kind of disorder and giving rein to their malevolent and evil instincts. Taking refuge in the indolence of the authorities, they strut through the streets and make them the scene of their crimes and depredations.

"The Glória district is not passable at night; cloaked figures occupy the loneliest and darkest places to insult and at times to set upon the passerby, threatening him with cudgels and brandishing the dagger and knife.

"Drunken soldiers, posted at corners, torment the neighborhood with the imprecations they shout, and they carry their boldness so far as to throw themselves on pedestrians to rob them with the greatest insolence....

"The delegate of police is under obligation to end all these scandals and to bring to a close the reign of immorality and cynicism."

The frailties of the public officials, rather than any general increase of lawlessness, seem to have been the actual source of irritation for critics. The appearance of malefactors in the streets at night was hardly a new phenomenon; furthermore, there were signs that the public morality inherited from the agrarian past had not seriously deteriorated by the 1860's. In newspapers of the period, for example, one comes across notices inserted by persons who have found sums of money which they wish to restore to the owners. One night in 1865 when tables for an alfresco banquet had, at the Câmara's order, been set up in the Public Garden, the affair was unexpectedly canceled; next morning the preparations were still intact, with not a spoon missing.[2]

City officials were far more active now than a quarter of a century earlier; but the concept of "material progress" which had dominantly emerged from the new orientations of mid-century was, as they made use of it, unimaginative, and it denied the traditions of the city. This fact was elaborated by *O Doze de Maio* (June 8, 1863) in an article entitled "Material Improvements": "There was in Misericórdia Square a stone fountain of elegant and solid construction, which until only a few years ago tolerably supplied the city with potable water, water that all went there with jugs to obtain. Then came the material progress people to paint the stone as imitation wood, ruin the conduit, and leave us without water.

"There was in Acu a most handsome bridge ... of freestone, graceful, elegantly constructed, a true work of art. The flood of 1850 carried off that bridge, and *material progress* built in its place a brute mass — heavy, formless, irregular, brutal, stupid — that would bring shame to the most ordinary mason.

"We had a botanical garden that drew the foreigner's attention by its selection of plants, the luxuriance of its groves, the regularity and symmetry of its planning. Then came material progress to change that oasis into an Arabia Petraea.

"We had in Carmo Square a patio — irregular, it's true, but

---

2. *Correio Paulistano* (June 16, 1864) reported, however, that the *troca chapeus* (hat changer) had joined the "vast gallery of social parasites." On leaving a barbershop he would "by mistake" exchange an aged, brimless hat for another customer's new one.

clean and traversable. Then came *material progress* to implant in its center an immense mound, obstructing passage with rubble and forming there a Tarpeian rock where those attacked by spleen may throw themselves off.

"We had greengrocers in the Rua do Comércio selling their greens, fruits, etc. *Material progress* dispersed the greengrocers, scattering them afar in all directions, and began to build in the mire of Carmo meadow a filthy trash-bin given the name of marketplace which is to be finished at a future time.

"Street-paving was improved, thanks to a few presidents troubled with corns who were for that reason unable to stroll along the ancient and infernal pavements. But this material improvement went no further. Not a tree was planted in an agreeable spot; not a plaza was spruced up. Everything remains as it came out of nature's hands."

This loss of faith in the motives and capacity of Brazilian administrators was paralleled by heightened reverence for customs and wares introduced by a growing nucleus of middle-class foreigners. Between 1855 and 1872, the nonforeign population of the commercial center (Sé) increased 16 per cent, from 6,989 to 8,111, while the foreign population more than doubled, rising from 495 to 1,102.

Hotelkeeping, we have seen, was a foreigner's specialty. An almanac of 1857 listed six "cafés, billiard-halls, and hotels." After 1860 more imposing hotels were built, such as the Itália, the Europa, and the Glôbo. By 1863 the six establishments of 1857 had become twelve, and citizens were criticizing the old lodginghouses as a social and economic canker. French cuisine was *de rigueur*:

> Hotel of the Four Nations
> managed by
> Mr. and Mme. Guillemet
> Furnished Rooms
> Meals sent outside for a reasonable price
> RESTAURANT IN THE PARIS FASHION
> • • •
> The kitchen, run by a skillful French cook, leaves nothing to be desired as concerns the taste and selection of foods.
> (*Correio Paulistano*, April 7, 1864.)

Alfredo d'E. Taunay (1944, p. 15), so critical of things "native," was unreserved in his praise of the Hotel Europa, managed by M. Planel, a Frenchman, whose choice, abundant food was served by slaves under soldierly discipline. The rooms were immaculate, the servants diligent, and M. Planel was being enriched "by opulent planters from Campinas who spend money there with largesse."

Foreign barbers, hairdressers, physicians, dentists, horticulturists, jewelers, tailors, dressmakers, and retailers of all sorts prospered. Among the barbers were the Portuguese Vieira Braga and the Frenchmen Teyssier, Biard, Bossignon, and Pruvot. When Teyssier returned to France in 1871, his employee, Inácio Pinto, took over the establishment, adding "Teyssier" as his own last name. Fresnau and Bourgade, both French, were the fashionable tailors, while the modistes were Mmes. Martin, Pruvot, Rochat, and Pascau. J. Joly advertised receipt of regular shipments of fruit trees, bulbs, creepers, and "all the most beautiful and modern plants of Europe." The bookstore of the Frenchman Garraux, founded in 1860, was the city's third and the best it would have for years. Germans founded a printing press and several famous eating houses, one of which generously served a "Hungarian" wine that was suspected of never having crossed the ocean. The Prussian Teodoro Wille established a business concern in Santos and São Paulo, and was the first merchant to export a sack of paulista coffee direct to Europe. Another German, Dr. Carlos Rath — physician, naturalist, engineer, litterateur, and painter — left at his death in 1876 a scientific collectanea that formed the nucleus of the Paulista Museum.

The English-speaking world was also represented. In 1870 Mrs. George W. Chamberlain founded the American School, from which the Mackenzie School of Engineering, affiliated with New York University, subsequently developed. CODMAN (1870, p. 71) met an American dentist in the city (probably one Horace Fogg), noting that others like him "find employment in all Brazilian towns, and in the mouths of almost all Brazilian women who can afford to avail themselves of their services." Britishers were not uncommon in the 1860's and were soon to multiply with the advent of railway engineers. Though the French were the couturiers, it was the English who outfitted the traveler and sportsman, while their contribution to the city's board was Bass beer. Newspapers even carried occasional advertisements printed, like the two following, in English:

ENGLISH BOOKS

J. Youds, Rua da Imperatriz n. 26, has just received a lot of novels published by the best English authors and also works for Engineers. They will only be for sale a few days more.   (*Diario de São Paulo,* Aug. 8, 1872.)

Macintosh's woter [*sic*] proof.
Cloaks.
Ponchos.
Overcoats.
Leggings.
Riding boots.
Saddle bags.
Valises.
Swimming belts, etc.
For sale at Henry Fox's Rua do Rosario n. 3.
(*Correio Paulistano,* Jan. 9, 1864.)

In a later notice Fox described his wares as being "articles for horse-back riding, rail or sea travel, all received directly from Europe at reasonable prices." It was this same Henry Fox, an English watch-maker, who made and for half a century tended the cathedral-tower clock — the keeper of a conscience which he had transplanted from industrial Britain.

Italians, still few in number, were as a rule of lower station. A handful were organ-grinders. Others became peddlers; an example was Antônio Pontrimoly, who at last earned enough to open a store (1870) called, as the proprietor himself was known, "Two Hundred Réis" — that being the fixed price of every article. One enterprising Italian inaugurated a stand in 1865 for renting tilburies and four-wheeled carriages, which indicated smoother streets, a larger city, wealthier citizens, and a demand for swift, clean con-veyance and for a new pastime. By 1868 there were five carriage stands.

Because of the common heritage, Portuguese subjects were less conspicuous, but throughout Brazil they had ever since colonial days been the backbone of the urban, commercial class. Of 4,633 commercial concerns and manufactories in São Paulo province in 1864, 776 were run by Portuguese, and only 381 by all other foreigners.[3] The Portuguese showed strong solidarity. In 1864 they formed a music society which offered Sunday band concerts in the Public Garden to full audiences representing all classes. The first private organization which effectively supplemented the inadequate welfare work of the government and the church was the Portuguese Society of Beneficence, São Paulo's first mutual-aid society, founded by 1859 by an eighteen-year-old bookkeeper and two tobacconists. The society started with a roster of 168. Its aims were to find employment for contributors, provide sustenance for needy members, rehabilitate disabled ones, and bury those dying in want; soon it acquired an infirmary. T. de P. FERREIRA (1940, p. 49) calls the efforts of this society the sole exception to the stagnant condition of social work in the city during the first half of the empire. All other institutions suffered from: "Lack of proper buildings; the limited resources that medicine still offered us; absence of capable directors, especially of specialized educators; deficiency of financial resources, despite allocation of provincial lottery income to works of charity; bureaucracy causing delays in government decisions."

The Germans showed similar group consciousness. In 1863 they founded a Society of Beneficence, like the Portuguese one, and in 1868 another society, Germania, for recreation and for making available useful, particularly industrial, knowledge. They also held private church services:

Deutscher Gottesdienst.

Sonntag, den 10 d. M. um 10 Uhr Morgens, soll Gottesdienst in deutscher Sprache in dem Hause des Herrn Blackford, no 10, rua da Constituição, gehalten werden; und sind alle Deutsch Sprechende freundlichst emgeladen [sic] demselben beizuwohnen.

F. J. C. Shneider [sic]
Evang. Pfarrer.

N.B. Man bittet, wenn möglich, Gesangbücher mitzubringen.   (Correio Paulistano, April 8, 1864.)

Though Schneider, a Presbyterian missionary, later despaired of his

---

3. The Portuguese were far and away supreme in Rio de Janeiro, where 4,813 concerns were in their hands, with 1,038 run by other foreigners, and 1,373 by Brazilians. (S. F. SOARES, 1865, p. 23.)

countrymen's apathy and returned to Rio de Janeiro, the São Paulo community established a German evangelical church in 1871. Under cover of the tolerant liberalism of Pedro II's reign, Protestant spearheads from abroad penetrated Brazil deeply. In São Paulo the English-speaking group outdid the Germans. In the 1830's Daniel P. Kidder had preached Methodism in this region, and a generation later American Confederate "refugees" from the Civil War brought a minister of that denomination to Santa Bárbara, near Campinas, where their blond, blue-eyed, Portuguese-speaking progeny are still to be seen. But the Presbyterians were the first to strike roots in the capital. In 1863, fourteen "Anglo-Saxons" attended the city's first service in English, performed by the Rev. A. L. Blackford, an American who had just arrived from the new Presbyterian nucleus in Rio de Janeiro. Within a year and a half this pastor had founded a church, and in the interior of the province a Brazilian ex-priest whom he had converted was about to begin an energetic, itinerant career of proselyting.

The British formed their own group soon after, starting with small, informal services at Henry Fox's residence that were soon shifted to larger quarters in the railway station — the city's new temple of progress and civilization! "In San Paulo," observed HAD-FIELD (1877, p. 170), "there are many English employés and mechanics connected with the railway, settled with their families, who, through the kindness of Mr. Fox, are thus supplied with religious instruction..., the consequence being that order and good conduct is the rule, and the English name is respected. There are also religious unions of Germans and Americans in San Paulo, the latter being a very zealous body, doing a great deal of good."

The foreigner in São Paulo, whether minister or maître d'hôtel, was by now proceeding with assurance, almost militancy, along certain lines that Brazilian leaders, under European influences, had themselves charted. The foreigner, then, was not assimilated to the extent that he had been in the 1820's, for the city was yielding its self-determined identity to an impending one of which the foreigner, rather than the native Brazilian, was the advance agent. The foreigner, clad with new authority, had to be "reacted to."

This reaction took three principal forms, separable merely for schematic purposes. The first was an attitude long rooted in the Portuguese heritage: the irony — with its wistful, impish, and bitter components — of the small nation that for a moment in its history had enjoyed world importance. "It is certain," writes Jorge DIAS (1953, p. 64), "that the Portuguese is ashamed before a Swiss for the high living-standard that the latter was able to achieve; yet were he the Swiss, he would be in the same way ashamed for having attained welfare without glory." As Gilberto FREYRE (1948) has made clear, the counterpart to British commercial expansion in Brazil was a kind of "reverse penetration," by which the culture eroded the attitudes of Her Majesty's subjects and unobtrusively brought them to acquiesce, often with affection, in Brazilian customs and outlook. The Brazilian talent for keen, though modulated mockery of self-important outsiders has been a subtle binding force in face of the foreign afflux.

There were many instances of this "creole malice" after work began on the British São Paulo-Santos railway. The first and much-vaunted locomotive reached the capital in 1864. *Diabo-coxo* (Aug. 27, 1864) wryly reported the event: "As the mighty staffs of the *Diario de S. Paulo* and *Correio Paulistano* proclaimed, the cars were greeted by a crowd of esteemed persons, among whom the illustrious journalists were conspicuous; ineffable enthusiasm reigned among all.

"Do not believe, however, oh respected public, this April Fool story. Such words were pure formality, serving as a preamble to all the accounts.

"Those who attended gaped open-mouthed at the strange thing. A few, more curious (if not witless), went near it to see if it were of iron or rubber!...Others muttered with scorn: 'I thought it would be something more costly; we could produce better in the Ipanema factory.' A muleteer at my side cried in admiration: 'There must be some ten people inside the box to turn the wheels!' Even a public servant of high station refused to attend because he didn't wish to be a witness of ill-fortune."

When, during the inaugural trial run, with many dignitaries in attendance, the iron horse got out of hand and killed two persons, *Diario de São Paulo* blossomed with the following stanzas:

> *We're going to have a new pagoda*
> *In the Garden very soon,*
> *Steam-engines are going to leave —*

Whoever wants to go, it's free —
Except they'll have no chance with me. . . .

The carriage runs along so quickly —
Who says he's afraid to die?
Everyone falls from the mountain,
The only one to shriek's the engine —
People die without a sigh! . . .

Who says he's afraid to die
On a roadbed that's so solid?
The promenade is most delightful,
There's drinking water on the Serra —
It will serve to bless the graves.

Mr. Play-it-safe died old —
And it's friendly to give warning:
If you want to go out riding
They have carriages (no danger),
Nice and cheap right there in Sé.

What do you mean? Now who can fear
A carriage open to the sky?
If it tumbles on the Serra
All you do is give a jump —
And, being agile, you won't die!

(A. A. de FREITAS, 1921, p. 104.)

Cabrião (no. 3, 1866), with appropriate cartoons, posed the riddle: "What's the difference between a criminal mounting the scaffold and a traveler ascending the railway's inclined plane [that is, up the Serra]?" "The criminal prays for the rope to break, and the traveler prays for it not to."

Often, however, this attitude of mocking irreverence yielded to forms of more overt commitment, the two main varieties being xenophobia and self-deprecation. The best example of an enduring national animosity was the feud, starting at mid-century and lasting for decades, between law students and the *caixeiros* (clerks or accountants) of Portuguese origin. The rivalry took many forms, including periodic fracases. The Portuguese, barred from student dances, gave soirées of their own; but despite the affluence of many caixeiros, the cooperation of the city's fair sex could not be won. Flames were fed one year when the students forced a Portuguese impresario to double the salary of his Brazilian prima donna.

(AN, 1867.) Near the end of the century, student contempt for astute, profit-minded foreign middlemen and economic opportunists died away when it was found that they, rather than the literary and forensic bacharel, stood to gain under the new conditions of life. The liberal journal *O Sete de Abril* (June 3, 1865) denounced the police for tolerating "prostitute dances," whose sponsors were "miserable Jews who demoralize our youth," avaricious foreigners who "tread the soil of our country, find a populous center where there is a large number of rich young men, and try to reap a profit by all means within reach." Anti-Italianism of a similar vein occurred in the speech of a deputy before the Provincial Assembly (1872): "In certain localities they have called in foreigners as curates of the soul, those sons of the Basilicata, those Neapolitans, those *lazzaroni* (with honorable exceptions) who come to Brazil and after taking a curacy — not in an evangelical and religious spirit but in that of profit — dare ascend the pulpit and there direct sermons at the people with such incorrectness of language that it sometimes disconcerts their listeners. Y. Exc. knows that the Italian pronounces his *r*'s in a harsh and heavy manner, and thus whenever the letter *r* appears in a word, he provokes the laughter of his audience." (I. Silva, 1941.)

Cabrião (I, 28 [1867]), after praising the deceased Bishop Dom Antônio for personal qualities, criticized him for having left the seminary in the hands of Italian and French Capuchins, whose regime stood for "the coveting of lucre, egotism, envy of similar institutions, laxity, and fanaticism with their train of hypocrisy and dissimulation."

Certain paulistas, however, wholeheartedly praised the foreign example, as instanced by the Yankeephile sentiments of a young engineer, A. F. de Paula Sousa, who was temporarily employed in the United States: "We, wretched Brazilian *citizens*, have no idea, nor can we have, of the immense esteem in which the Yankee holds the school. . . . Education is for the North Americans like the bread and meat that they need every day. Hence this is the most educated, most active, freest, and most powerful people in the world.

"Could we but imitate them! Could we but forget the old and corrupt formulae to which we live subjugated, oblivious that we too inhabit the American continent!" (Letter written from Chillicothe, Mo., Sept. 20, 1869, published in *Correio Paulistano*, Dec. 2, 1869.)

The affairs of the church, especially in view of the Protestants' quiet, purposeful discipline, were a further cause for self-deprecation. A *Independencia* (May 28, 1868), noting the increase in Protestant conversions, lamented: "Three things infect our clergy like leprosy — ignorance, concubinage, and ultramontanism." Later (June 14, 1868) it referred to a sermon of a Capuchin from the seminary: "What a shame for our clergy that the foremost and only preacher in São Paulo is a foreign missionary!"

The successes of the Protestants at this particular time are not hard to understand. HADFIELD (1869, pp. 70-74), in describing a Roman Catholic procession of 1868, spoke of "worship to dumb idols," a frequent lack of decorum, the women's delight in displaying finery, and a priest's energetic but "squeaky" exhortation from which little could be gathered "beyond that his listeners were a very bad lot, and required all the intervention of the saints." He implied that such ceremonies were not "conducive to the maintenance of the Roman Catholic Religion," pointing out that elsewhere in Brazil they had fallen off; São Paulo had been more isolated, and "the foreign element" was of recent advent.

Yet even through Hadfield's patronizing account one glimpses vigor and meaning in the procession. Rich and poor made money offerings without stint. Not only did he see "young girls dressed up as angels, bands of music, soldiers with fixed bayonets, the President of the Province, and all the dignitaries," but also "the hardy, bronzed, country race, men who travel over the country with mules, leading the life of gypsies.... They almost live in the saddle, and are a very fine class of men — true Paulistos." The procession still served, that is, its integrative function, bringing together classes and races, officials and citizens, as well as citydwellers and the "bronzed, country race."

Even at this time, however, processions were obsolescent. In 1869 occurred the last one for the brotherhood of St. Francis of Assisi (comprising professors, students, and employees of the Law Academy). The last of the colorful Corpus Christi processions, which carried the wooden image of St. George, took place in 1872, soon followed by the last burial procession. One who signed himself "Devout" asked readers of *Diario de São Paulo* (May 11, 1872):

"Why is it that for years the feast of the Divine Holy Spirit has not been held in the parish of Senhor Bom Jesus do Braz?" In the very year of Hadfield's procession, *A Independencia* (June 28, 1868) carried an article on spiritism by Allan Kardec. It limned the bleak spiritual horizons awaiting those who too hastily forsook their heritage for foreign idols as yet untried: "Spiritism is a science of observation and a philosophic doctrine. As a practical science, it consists in the relations that can be established with the spirits; as philosophy it comprehends all the moral consequences emanating from those relations .... [Spiritism] is founded on observation and not on a preconceived system."

Bibliographical Note

MORSE (1951b) is a general history of the city for the years 1855-1870. Of the visitors' accounts of São Paulo in the 1860's, those by HADFIELD (1869; 1877) are the fullest. See also: Alfredo d'E. TAUNAY (1944), F. de P. F. de REZENDE (1944), ZALUAR (n.d.), W. SCULLY (1866), HOUSSAY (1877), and CODMAN (1870). BARBUY (1936) recalls the period in a "novel of paulista customs of 1860." N. W. SODRÉ (1950) describes the increasing importance of Brazil's public press after mid-century. E. C. NOGUEIRA (1953) examines French cultural influences in São Paulo, while A. LEITE (1944) more informally enumerates English ones; FREYRE (1948) studies the impact of English civilization upon all of Brazil. M. SCULLY (1955) is a sketch of the Mackenzie School. LÉONARD (1951-1952) in his study of Brazilian Protestantism and WEAVER (1952) in her survey of the evangelical activities of Confederate immigrants give many side lights on the cultural history of São Paulo.

Chapter 12

NEW RHETORIC AND THE RAILWAY

SEVERAL CIRCUMSTANCES explain why, in the 1860's, the paulista region and its capital responded in so lethargic a manner — save for enterprising foreigners — to mid-century orientations.

In the first place, São Paulo city still had neither rail connection with its port nor a rail network reaching its new hinterland. Coffee shipment was therefore slow, costly, and cumbersome since, as had been the case with sugar, haulage by animal was necessary; Hadfield commented in 1868 on the constant passage through the city of mules, horses, and old-fashioned oxcarts bound to and from the interior. It was axiomatic in the 1860's that to plant coffee more than seventy-five or a hundred miles inland from São Paulo was foolhardy, for shipment would have consumed all profits, however fine the yield.

The state of transport meant that planters (*fazendeiros*) and, more especially, female members of their families would not often journey by horseback or, in the case of the latter, by oxcart to spend profits in the cities. Dona Veridiana, wife of the prosperous planter Martinho da Silva Prado, resided permanently on their fazenda north of Campinas, though her husband had graduated from the Law Academy and his father was a prominent man of affairs in the capital. She did make the trip when each of her six children was to be born (between 1840 and 1860), though once she miscalculated, gave birth at a farmhouse en route, and returned to the fazenda since there was no further purpose in continuing.

Another adverse factor was the failure of the parceria. Word of

139

the colonies' mismanagement reached Europe, and the Germans went so far as to forbid emigration to Brazil (1859). The yearly influx of agricultural workers to the province dropped from 982 (1852-1857) to 213 (1858-1874). Coffee, with its drain on the tight labor supply, was dislocating the economy. A British railway engineer paternally warned paulistas (1862) that they would have to change their ways to deserve and make use of future São Paulo-Santos line. "You must not tie yourselves solely to coffee and sugar." You must abandon manioc, "which has no food at all for the human body; it contains only starch, and starch does not make blood.... Your soil and climate can produce nearly all the products of the world," and he specified wheat, cotton, silkworms, cattle, horses, and sheep. (AUBERTIN, 1862, p. 24.) It is true that cotton planting and export received a short-lived impetus when the American supply was cut off by the Civil War, but this merely reflected the same opportunism of the coffee boom.

The planned diversification of effort championed by the Society for Encouraging Agriculture, Trade, and Crafts was forsaken. Though the tariff agreement that so signally favored British manufactures had in 1844 been rescinded, Brazil levied the new imposts for revenue rather than for fostering practical basic industries. In 1866 there were only nine sizable textile factories in the country, and the vigorous efforts of the famous self-made businessman, Viscount Mauá, to industrialize the nation were consistently counteracted (ca. 1850-1875) by the single-crop fixation. São Paulo's anxiety to emulate the achievements of industrial Europe hardly squared with its medieval attitude toward the labor that would enable it so to do. The "working class" was commiseratingly defined by Correio Paulistano (Nov. 14, 1861) as "the persons and their families to whom fate has not conceded a single advantage that is not acquired by the sweat and fatigue of labor."

Another trend of these years was a peculiarly urban phenomenon, the overextension of the credit system. Earlier, coffee planters had financed their ventures independently, using city middlemen, or comissários, as mere selling agents. In the 1860's, however, as mounting agricultural income seduced fazendeiros into more lavish outlays for their homes and pleasure, the planter class fell into debt; comissários, often taking advantage of the vagaries of the world market, emerged as bankers.

The fazendeiros' recourse to credit was quite in keeping with the times. Despite a slight commercial crisis in 1857, banks proliferated in the larger cities throughout the 1850's; in 1856 São Paulo city received a branch of the Bank of Brazil and in 1859 a Bank of São Paulo. Financial circumspection gave way to a craving to speculate. A Commission of Inquiry, representing a conservative point of view, reported to the emperor in 1859 that after the abolition of slave traffic: "The country found itself master of resources that had hitherto been applied to payment for imported Negroes. Brazilian customs were for the most part simple in the extreme, a model of frugality. It was not possible that commercial greed, the corrupting monster, should vitiate by a coup de main the well-grounded habits of centuries. It thus followed that, in the absence of real or artificial needs for employing the surplus from our exports, metal came back into use. . . . The government was induced by bad counsel to coin [the nation's] metal and thus to facilitate its introduction like an active poison into the circulatory veins. Not content with that great evil being done the country, it revived the fatal memory of banks of emission."

Despite "morbid British philanthropy," continued the report, the Brazilian slave was far happier than starved lower-class whites in England. "Far better the good Negroes from Africa's coast tilling our fertile fields than all the gewgaws of the Rua do Ouvidor; than dresses at a conto and a half for our women; than oranges at eighty réis apiece in a country that produces them almost spontaneously; than corn, rice, and nearly everything needed to sustain human life being imported from abroad; than, finally, ill-advised undertakings, far beyond the country's legitimate forces, which, disturbing the relations of society so as to produce a dislocation of labor, have contributed most to the scarcity and high prices of all staples." (J. NABUCO, 1949, I, p. 258.)

The nineteenth-century expansion of western European banking reflected that continent's industrial growth. Brazilian banks were partly a mere repercussion of the European system and partly a response to commercial prosperity, rather than to organic industrial development. They were therefore an encouragement to sharp speculation and overextended credit. In 1864 the ratio maintained by the Bank of Brazil between circulated paper and reserves, fixed by law at 2 to 1, reached 6.4 to 1. In September of that year came Brazil's first commercial panic.

Another Commission of Inquiry singled out abuse of credit as the immediate cause of the crash, then listed contributing factors: trade stoppage owing to a poor harvest; economic decadence of the country, including all branches of its industry; bad management of the Bank of Brazil; speculation in stocks; rising costs of government; excessive imports in relation to demand; bad planning of business ventures. (RELATÓRIO..., 1865, p. 77.) The credit and banking system, like so many urban by-products, had extended the city's sway over the country and was now heavily to tax the powers of analysis and the good will of those who would subject it to control.

Though ultimately contributing to a sense of national unity, the Paraguayan War was a further deterrent to "material progress" in the 1860's. Declared by Francisco López, Paraguay's megalomaniacal dictator, in answer to Brazil's and Argentina's meddling in Uruguay, it dragged on for over five arduous years (1864-1870). Perhaps the martial spirit of a Bismarckian era was the fillip necessary to a "progressive" nation. In any case São Paulo's law students were reported by O Brado da Patria (Feb. 15, 1865) to be dedicating themselves with patriotic fervor to equitation, the manual of arms, and, since they anticipated crossing jungle rivers, the art of swimming. The city as a whole, however, accepted modern war as it did the locomotive, with a shrug of the shoulders. Cabrião repeatedly twitted paulistanos on their reluctance to enlist and on their confusing medals with true bravery, while Diabo-coxo (Aug. 27, 1864) offered the reward of "carte blanche as recruiting agent" to any one who could "discover a spontaneous method of apprehending volunteers for the patriotic service of war." When Alfredo d'E. TAUNAY (1944, pp. 18-21) passed through on his way to the campaigns, the only homage proffered was by the students: a large banquet with copious wine, beer, and orations. He praised the ardor of the paulista volunteers, many of them "from the best families of the Province," but found the regular troops "unprovided with the elements most necessary for operations. The provincial administration has done almost nothing to prepare our expedition. We found here the greatest coldness toward military affairs: genuine indifference." In the absence of such deep communal feelings as had roused the townspeople in 1822, militant patriotism was the perquisite of a Europeanized elite.

The recruiting methods of President José Tavares Bastos (1866-1867) scarcely served to bolster morale. He once enticed a crowd into the barracks to see a review of the troops, only to close the gates on them and impress all eligible males into the National Guard. So fearful were youths of his agents that they remained hidden in their homes — although a few, reluctant to miss church services, were known to slip through the streets disguised as women. At length the president was forced to flee to Santos for his personal safety.

On the news of Brazil's naval victory at Humaitá (1868), however, the city burst into celebration for three days and nights, with lavish illumination, rousing band music, and general tumult. In 1870, after final victory, returning veterans brought home a triumphant flag given them five years earlier by paulista ladies that was now blood-stained, shredded by bullets, and blackened by the smoke of combat. Mass was held for them at the seminary, a 500-place banquet was served by the businessmen, and a bedecked city went wild with joy.

For São Paulo as for Brazil, the war, though in immediate terms a total wastage, objectified a national destiny to be won by conscientious effort and by dedication to certain clear-cut ideals. Before the war's end the nature of that effort and those ideals was formulated by São Paulo's law students, who are once again to be considered.

After Alvares de Azevedo's era the vitality of the academy in no wise decreased. The yearly average of graduates rose from twenty-three (1846-1855) to sixty-nine (1856-1865). The class entering in 1859 contained two future presidents of the republic (Prudente de Morais and Campos Sales), while the one three years later included Silva Paranhos (the future statesman, Baron Rio Branco) and the poet Fagundes Varela — these being but four names out of dozens that were to be famous under the late empire and early republic. The students' literary and journalistic output was larger than ever. "It seems incredible," gasped *O Futuro* (Sept. 16, 1862), "the fervor with which the students devote themselves to letters!" But although the broad eclecticism of 1845-1855, and romanticism itself, continued to be cultivated, the latter was never again given so consummate an expression.

The theater was increasingly patronized — by women now as well as men, for *Diabo-coxo* (Aug. 27, 1864) offered to impart the secret of perpetual motion in a woman's tongue to any who would "tell why certain ladies, during shows in the theater, never cease chatting a single moment." But student playwrights — even the gifted Sizenando Nabuco, production of whose drama *The Tunic of Nessus* inaugurated the new São José Theater in 1864 — failed to meet the standards enounced by Alvares de Azevedo. Public taste ran to shallow, imported dramas, musical pastiches, circuses, juggling acts, and acrobatics. Of one troupe, *Cabrião* (July 14, 1867) observed with customary sting: "The effort that this dramatic company makes to provide new and varied shows is noteworthy.

"Daily, comedies are announced that the public has for 6 or 8 years seen only once a week.... [The actors] should continue, ...and let them count on the taste of a public which always deeply appreciates a steady diet since this averts any disturbances of the stomach.

"Let them keep on like this, announcing 'a show for everyone,' that is, let the public be told: such and such comedies will be given invariably during so many years and at all shows.

"Thus we shall be spared reading the announcements and the 'displeasure' of finding anything new on the programs."

Two romanticist poets who attended the academy in the early 1860's seem solitary and displaced. Paulo Eiró entered in 1859 after four years of schoolteaching. He read widely and deeply, and went through an ill-starred love affair that evoked many poems. In his second year a persecution mania set in. He withdrew, intending to prepare for holy orders, but ended his days in the asylum. Fagundes Varela entered the Curso Anexo also in 1859, took part in dramatics, wrote much poetry (including lachrymose stanzas to the most brazen, popular, and well-to-do of the city's *femmes publiques*), and engaged in the Byronic attitudinizing of his predecessors. Given to hypochondria and alcohol, he was unable to finish his course at São Paulo or at Recife, where he transferred in 1865. The modern poet Manuel BANDEIRA (1946, p. 81) calls him "a carry-over from the preceding generation," "maladjusted to the civilization of cities" and able to concentrate on "work of no sort except literature." The Byronic star had dropped from the ascendant, and the sign of the one to supplant it was the word "science," which appeared in the titles of no less than five student journals between 1859 and 1866.

The academy's most distinguished class was that which entered in 1866. Among its members were the future statesmen Joaquim Nabuco and Rui Barbosa, the third president of the republic Rodrigues Alves, and the poet Antônio de Castro Alves.[1] NABUCO (1947, pp. 15-17) tells of these years in his memoirs. "In the situation in which I went to São Paulo for the first year of the academy, I could not help but be a liberal student." His father, a distinguished cabinet minister who had been president of São Paulo in the 1850's, wrote to him to spend more time studying, but the son too highly valued his freedom and "spiritual emancipation" as a journalist. He read omnivorously, dazzled by new ideas. Above all, 1866 was for him "the year of the French Revolution"; Lamartine, Thiers, Louis Blanc, and the Girondists "all passed in turn through my spirit; the Convention was in permanent session there." The seductive liberalism of Professor José Bonifácio the younger "dominated the Academy." Nabuco was liberal "of a single piece; my democratic weight and density were maximum." After immersion in Bagehot, however, he aligned himself, unlike many colleagues, with the monarchy rather than with republicanism. As for religion: "When I entered the academy I carried my Catholic faith virginal. I shall always remember the fright, the scorn, the confusion with which for the first time I heard the Virgin Mary treated in a liberal tone. Soon, however, there remained with me only the golden dust of nostalgia." Renan provided "the most perfect intoxication of the spirit that could be given."[2] In short, as Nabuco recalled decades later, "escapades and Bohemian living were out of style, and elegance and intellectual prestige were highly respected." (C. NABUCO, 1950, p. 12.)

The issue which gave urgency and focus to this new intellec-

1. Nabuco transferred to Recife in his fourth year, while Rui and Castro Alves came from there to São Paulo in the third. Castro Alves stayed for only six months.
2. This is not to say that among the students there were not a number of fervent conservatives and proclericals. Nabuco himself tried in later years to "reconstruct the complicated journey" back to Catholicism.

tualism, and directly challenged the humanitarian liberalism of the academic city, was the campaign for abolition. For as Brazil's center of economic gravity swung south into the paulista coffee lands, thousands of slaves were transferred, at exorbitant prices, from Minas Gerais and from the north; the province's 80,000 slaves in 1866 had doubled by 1873.

The precursor of the abolitionist movement was Luís Gama. Though born in Bahia of a consensual, interracial union, he was by right a freeman. His father sold him into slavery in 1840 as a child of ten. A contrabandist brought him to Santos whence he traveled by foot, with over a hundred of his kind, to Campinas. There, because of his Bahian "nationality," none would buy him, and the dealer returned with Gama to his house in the capital. The slave was taught manual skills and learned to read and write from a law student who boarded there. Eventually Gama secretly received proof of his free birth, fled his master, spent six years in the militia, and in 1854 returned to the capital as an amanuensis. Though his career as an untiring polemicist was baptized in 1859 by a book of his satiric verses lampooning Brazilian nobility, women's fashions, money lust, and mulattoes passing as whites, at the heart of his crusade lay the desire to free his race. *Diabo-coxo* and *Cabrião*, appearing in the mid-1860's, made good use of his spirited collaboration.

In 1868 the ex-slave's grass-roots abolitionism merged with the more programmatic crusade of the students. An academic society of 1863, called "Fraternization," had already managed to free some slaves. But it was the emperor's official recognition of the slavery question in 1867 that evoked "a general surge of the urban soul against the immense sorrow of human life on fazendas and in sugar-mills." (SANTOS, 1930, p. 100.) On April 1, 1868, a student "juridical and literary" society was held spellbound by Castro Alves' first public recital of his impassioned poem "The Slaves." Soon theaters, debating clubs, Masonic lodges, and cafés were turned into rallying points for aroused liberalism. In *A Independencia* (1868), Rui Barbosa, Castro Alves, and their coeditors urged foreign immigration and, to attract it, freedom of worship, universal suffrage and education, and truly representative government with ministerial responsibility. After mid-July, 1868, with the resignation of the ministry that was to have effected abolition, the campaign reached new intensity. "America" Lodge, formed by Rui, Luís Gama, and others who chafed at cautious tactics, demanded emancipation of all children born to slaves, a measure shortly enacted by the Rio Branco law of 1871. In a speech forty years later, Rui recalled that the activities of "America" Lodge were quite bereft of the Germanic occultism and cabalistic ritual that had invested Freemasonry during early romanticism:

"None of us cherished the superstition of Masonry. None sympathized with its secretive aspect. None was charmed by the mystery of its formulae. Our whole plan was to react in the open; every object of our activity was public; all our instincts conduced toward the light. So unscrupulous were we with traditional procedure that, against the constitutional rules of the order, it was forgotten to confer on me the rank of master in elevating me as orator of the lodge. From that post I combatted the venerable, illustrious Dr. Antônio Carlos, then my professor of commercial law, in defense of a project of mine that would oblige all members of that house to free the wombs of their female slaves and would make that promise a prerequisite of admission for future initiates. My proposal carried, the learned professor losing the dignity that he had held for us....

"At the same time we inaugurated...public lectures, in assignment of which I received as a theme the abolition of the enslaved. It was the first time, if I am not mistaken, that so daring a subject was aired among us in the public forum. And in São Paulo at that time it could have been dealt with only by the petulance of a student playing the antics of liberal radicalism, with his case resting on excessively little judgment." (RECEPÇÃO..., 1909, p. 160.)

By April, 1870, a ladies' emancipation society sponsored by "America" Lodge was winning wide success, not only toward its stated goal but also, according to Correio Paulistano (April 10, 1870), in freeing "the lady-emancipators themselves from the narrow, subdued life such as had been imposed on them by the mold of colonial times."

As orator, editor, and general campaigner, the student Rui Barbosa waged his fight indefatigably. Its climax came on the three nights in 1870 when from a balcony he exhorted an enthralled crowd of citizens and newly returned veterans. As he remembered the episode in 1921: "A boiling wave of patriotic heat gushed from that balcony, engulfing in its vortex the soldiers, the people, the street, and was from moment to moment ignited by patriotic cheers. The crowd yelled. The ranks broke into acclamations. A kind of short circuit operated on the human mass, and no one could then restrain the explosion of inflamed souls. The orator was not very much. But his speech had the vigor, courage, and audacity of truth deeply felt; and among his words flashed those of freedom, the constitution, order: reflections on the conservative regime that then weighed upon the country. The city authorities wished to suspend the three days of official celebration. There was talk of bringing the dangerous student to disciplinary trial. They even threatened him with actual punishment. But public fervor, inflamed by the defiance of local officialdom, would not let him be thrust aside.... [For three nights] the voice of the young liberal received those cheers still warm from the heat of battles — a heat which, imbibed there in the delirium of the impassioned throng, boiled up in waves of civism and was exhaled in hymns to liberty." (F. NERY, 1932, p. 39.)

This passage grandly attests to the reverberations struck by student campaigning; to a popular sense of destiny served by the juncture of liberal propagandism and the defeat of Paraguay; and to an urban populace that could, if aptly appealed to, erect itself as a supreme tribunal.

Castro Alves, Rui Barbosa's coadjutor and last of the great romanticist poets, was as symptomatic of his era as Alvares de Azevedo had been of his. The earlier poet was reserved, introverted, chary of notoriety, diligent in his studies, and in love only with ideal women of his dreams. Castro Alves was impetuous, self-assertive, neglectful of classes and examinations, given to public declamation and to incessant amours. If, returning to the analysis of romanticism, Alvares de Azevedo is the Shelley who becomes spiritually impotent before a scientific world and "falls upon the thorns of life," then Castro Alves leans toward an alternative solution. With the "crude, physical imagination" of a Tennyson he "enjoys something like the efficient optimism of science; he asks us to believe that a rearrangement of the external relations of man will not alone make him a little more comfortable, but will remove the whole problem of evil, and usher in perfection." (TATE, 1948, p. 103.)

The following passages from a letter of Castro ALVES (1938, II, pp. 556-59), written in São Paulo in April, 1868, show how the city's romantic mystery had become the mere backdrop for a salvational crusade: "You find me in São Paulo, land of Azevedo, beautiful city of mists and mantillas, the soil that weds Heidelberg to Andalusia.

"We sons of the north...dream of São Paulo as the oasis of liberty and of poetry, planted squarely in the plains of Ipiranga. Well, our dream is and is not reality.... If poetry lies in smoking up the room with the classic cigar while outside the wind smokes up space...with a still more classic garôa; if poetry lies in black eyes peeping through the rótula of the balconies or through the lace of the mantilla...then São Paulo is the land of poetry.

"Yes! for here there is only cold, but a cold of Siberia; *cynicism*, but *cynicism* of Germany; houses, but houses of Thebes; streets, but streets of Carthage...[:] houses that seem built before the world, so black are they; streets that seem made after the world's end, so deserted are they.

"So much for poetry. As for liberty,...I tend to prefer São Paulo to Recife....

"I should tell you that my *Slaves* are nearly ready. Do you know how the poem ends? (I owe São Paulo this inspiration.) It ends at the peak of the Serra, as dawn breaks over America while the morning star (Christ's tear for the captives) dies gradually out in the west. It is a song of the future. The song of hope. And should we not wait?"[3]

One day in November, 1869, while Castro Alves was hunting near the city, an accidental discharge of his rifle caused a wound that within three years claimed his life. It seemed almost as if the little agrarian town had made, as it passed into history, a gesture of protest against this northern "condor," as he has been called, and his apocalyptic vision of social justice.

By the end of the 1860's, then, it appeared that the broad and rather loose eclecticism of which Alvares de Azevedo had been a spokesman was being translated into an endorsement of a limited number of clearly defined values. Prominent among them were a few simple political and socioeconomic formulae, the *savoir faire*

3. Fifteen years later this very region of the Serra became a refuge for escaped slaves.

of Parisian coiffeurs and hotelkeepers, and the industrial energy symbolized by the locomotives of the new English railway. The railway, indeed, did its part, along with the abolitionist movement and the Paraguayan War, to animate the city after 1867.

The stages of preliminary negotiation for a trans-Serra rail connection can be related to phases of the city's development. Provincial laws had, during the 1830's, authorized a contract for a São Paulo-Santos line fed by a hinterland network of rail and river-steamboat arteries; the project, being uncertainly conceived and lacking guaranties for the huge capital it would involve, bore no fruit. Later, in 1855, the provincial president assessed São Paulo's coffee boom and its economic future in practical terms and was empowered by the Assembly to open negotiations with any company which, with a maximum capital of £2,000,000, would build a railway "from Santos to this capital and the interior." The next year Viscount (then Baron) Mauá and his associates received a ninety-year concession, and they managed by 1860 to capitalize the S. Paulo Railway Company, Ltd., in London. In November, construction of a roadbed from the port to Jundiaí, via São Paulo, was begun.

The British head engineer AUBERTIN (1862, pp. 4-9) complained of the Serra — so long a factor of São Paulo's seclusion and self-sufficiency — as a "dreadful phantom" hovering over his task; "all our efforts and intentions are dominated and harassed by it, as is the unhappy nation that finds itself oppressed by the hand of a malevolent despot." Day and night his associates, Messrs. Fox and Bolland, groped about "through dense forests among the monkeys, later emerging white as mushrooms." At length British technics mastered the 2,400-foot Serra by a series of inclined planes, graded at one foot in ten, and stationary engines for lowering and hauling up the trains. In February, 1867, the 85-mile line from Santos to Jundiaí was opened to traffic.

For a brief moment the railway's success was imperiled by the lowered rates of competing muleteers. The latter were benefiting by a newly improved trans-Serra highway, built perhaps as a pork-barrel measure but ostensibly at least with the very aim of holding down railway freight rates. Two weeks after the railway had been in service, Aubertin urged a reduction of these rates, since many shippers were returning to mules after having given rail service a try. His subordinate in Santos saw a "great quantity of wagons and mule teams unloading and loading produce as if there were no railroad right nearby." It was found that to ship sixty tons from Campinas to Santos cost 2:800$ if sent the whole way by mule, and 4:100$ if sent by mule to Jundiaí and thence by train. (AESP, 1867.) Moreover, the mule team, like the modern truck and to a degree the airplane, gave "door-to-door" service, while the railroad involved transshipments and tended, because of its centralized facilities and fixed arteries, rather to mold than to serve man's economic behavior.

That shipment by rail soon won the day, however, is shown by the S. Paulo Railway Company's early statistics. The number of passengers carried rose from 29,000 (1867) to 51,000 (1868) to 74,000 (1871), while the increase in freight was, proportionately, even sharper. The railway was opportunely finished for the burst of cotton production occasioned in São Paulo by the American Civil War. Moreover, it proved a strong stimulus to coffee planting, for the export of coffee via Santos rose from a yearly average of 24,000 tons in the years just before 1867 to one of 67,000 in those just after.

Certain contemporaries were slow to see the activity and expansion that the capital could anticipate by virtue of its strategic location upon this axial rail line and as hub of numerous projected ones. CODMAN (1870, p. 70) felt that "when the road is opened, as it soon will be, into the rich district of Campinas, this place [São Paulo] will lose its commercial importance." And J. F. de GODOY (1869, pp. 4-15), commenting on the decadence of the Paraíba valley and on the need to tie it into the São Paulo-Santos line with a feeder, ascribed to Santos a future that actually fell to the capital: "Imagine the future importance of Santos when it receives all the agricultural wealth from the south, west, and north of São Paulo and the south of the province of Minas Gerais; when its market becomes the seat of the great exchanges, the thousand transactions born of the productive exuberance of those richest of regions. Then Santos will be the great commercial emporium of São Paulo, becoming the propulsive center whence life and sap shall leave, through a thousand channels, for the remotest extremities of the great arterial system that covers such vast areas."

In the late 1860's, however, there were a few signs of the capital's new animation. The main assembly plant of the railway was located there, and in 1868 the provincial president urged that it be expanded with a foundry, eight forges, and a repair plant that could simultaneously handle at least ten cars. In the account of his second visit to São Paulo in 1870, after a two-year absence, HADFIELD (1877, p. 169) gave a good yardstick for the quickening of the city's life:

"Looking about the city and neighbourhood I perceive many improvements since I was last here, the city itself, together with the streets, being remarkably clean. Roads in the outskirts, which were formerly quagmires, have been bottomed...and are now in very good order; in fact, there can be no doubt that San Paulo is destined to a go-a-head, as the capital of the province and the central pivot of railway communication. Gas works are now in course of erection, to replace the existing oil lamps, and the Provincial Assembly has given powers to the Government to contract for a supply of water; so all modern conveniences will soon be found here."

Completion of the Santos line goes far to explain this new life-tempo. Writing twenty years later, Paulo EGYDIO (1889, p. 52) identified the event as "a new and vivifying breath" for "the social life of the province" and as heralding the modern economic era. "In 1868, the province of São Paulo let out the first shout in favor of that great sociological and economic principle, that the State and the political power cannot and should not intervene in the industrial world, since accrual of wealth and material development belong to the sphere of individuals and free associations."

Bibliographical Note

The history of the paulista abolition movement given in SANTOS (1942) is a broad introduction to the political and intellectual climate of this period. The memoirs of J. NABUCO (1947, pp. 15-17) and accounts of Rui Barbosa's years in São Paulo — A. G. de CARVALHO (1946), RECEPÇÃO . . . (1909), H. COELHO (1925), and E. LEME (1949) — evoke this climate in the persons of two eminent law students. SCHMIDT (1940), CAVALHEIRO (1940), and CARNEIRO (1937) describe the lives, attitudes, and times of three student poets, Paulo Eiró, Fagundes Varela, and Castro Alves respectively. For Luís Gama and his abolitionist crusade, see MENDONÇA (1930) and MENNUCCI (1938).

The antecedents of the Santos-Jundiaí railway are set forth in A. A. PINTO (1903, pp. 21-35). Its construction and early operation are described in HADFIELD (1869, pp. 55-65) and CODMAN (1870, pp. 62-68). FARIA (1933) relates the career of Viscount Mauá, who was instrumental in organizing the railway and was the commanding figure of Brazil's economic awakening in the third quarter of the century. CANNABRAVA (1951) is a painstaking study of São Paulo's cotton boom of the 1860's.

Chapter 13

THE ERA OF POSITIVISM

*7*HE DEVELOPMENT of the Law Academy during the
sixty years or so after its founding in 1827 has
served as a point of reference for identifying successive phases of
São Paulo city's changing orientation to the outer world. The academy was in fact one of the important agents of that change. As soon,
however, as São Paulo acquired the traits of a fast-expanding, poly-
glot, commercial and even industrial metropolis, the academy lost
its energies and leadership within the very ethos that it had helped
to precipitate. A knowledge of how and why the academy became
an almost vestigial institution illuminates the whole period in
question.

In a masterpiece of preterition the academy director reported to
the minister of the empire in 1879: "If it were not for the terror of
passing in your opinion as an atrabilious and peevish old man,
perhaps I would tell Y. Exc. that the defense of [doctoral] theses
has become a mere formality and that some have been such as to
place in doubt the seriousness of the academic degree required for
that act. I say nothing, however, for I do not wish it judged that
my words are allusive." (AN, 1879.)

Silva JARDIM (1879, pp. 6-15) fixed 1878 as the year of the
"eclipse." "The collective soul of the youths seems to have been
fragmentized." Literary affairs had been abandoned; so too had
serious dedication to politics. The students' political journalism was
"light, without depth, without criterion." Reflective of the 1880's
were the titles of weeklies like *O Entr'acto* and *O Bohemio (The
Entr'acte* and *The Bohemian)* and such bohemian, beer-drinking

153

circles as that frequented by Olavo Bilac, whose sentimental Parnassian verses later made him Brazil's most popular poet. *Revista Academica* (Oct. 1, 1885) observed that after 1868 political factionalism disrupted the students' solidarity, study habits, and literary endeavor. Their new *Revista*, however, did not propose to revive serious creative efforts, for "literature and the arts" would enter its columns "as a simple accessory" for soothing the reader. In 1889 the academy was pictured as yawningly inactive, its eyes turned to the past. "The clubs have shut down. The arena of journalism is nearly deserted. The tumultuous meetings have disappeared. Almost nothing is published now, and nothing discussed." (VAMPRÉ, 1924, II, p. 525.) Even the physical plant was in abandon. Walls were dirty, patios overgrown, windows broken, equipment in disorder and disrepair.

The students, of whom four out of five were reported to wear pince-nez glasses, assumed the role of debonair sophistication and, with it, an occupational franchise for bohemian eccentricity. One critic thought the only remedy for *os novos* (the new ones), as they styled themselves, was "to take a slipper and spank them till the skin comes off." This same writer recalled (1890) the students' diligence, discipline, and *esprit de corps* of twenty years earlier, contrasting them with *os novos*, who roamed the streets aimlessly at night, singing, halting carriages, forcing their way into streetcars without paying fares. On one occasion they surrounded an Italian in public, "obliging him to commit upon himself what Jehovah anciently forbade the dwellers of Gomorrha to do one to another." (J. S. de REZENDE, 1890, pp. 14-21.)

The bacharel degree, now a mere entrée to a niche in a bureaucratic urban order, no longer entailed pioneer responsibilities for marking out horizons of national life. As one professor observed in 1888, most students hoped only for "legal admission into certain careers," some going so far as to surrender all faith in their own abilities and to place all hope in "nepotism and political protection." (VAMPRÉ, 1924, II, p. 517.)

The watchwords of political and economic liberalism were now hollow; initiative had passed from the forensic education which had generated them over to the realm of "science." The humanist view yielded to the belief that society could be propelled toward perfection by external manipulation. As the novelist Júlio Ribeiro wrote (1885) in the *Diario Mercantil* of São Paulo: "The first requisite of modern education, as a base for social reorganization, is universality of knowledge.

"The *scientifically prepared* man must know, at least elementally, mathematics, physico-chemistry, bio-physiology, moral-psychology. He must have good notions of arithmetic, algebra, geometry, mechanics, cosmology, sidereal and planetary astronomy, geodesy, physical geography, geology, mineralogy, paleontology, botany, zoology, ·anatomy, histology, pathology, psychology, morals, anthropology, ethnology, linguistics, history and historical geography, industry, art, literature, sociology, legislation, politics.

"Furthermore, he must have solid classical studies." (J. RIBEIRO, 1908, p. 23.)

It is true that four natural sciences were added to the academy's preparatory curriculum in 1885, but a reform of the faculty as a whole in 1891 left it as legalistic as ever. The academy library was not current with its foreign periodicals, and the local German-language paper *Germania* stayed on the doorsill since the librarians could not decipher it. One student looked in vain for a basic exposition of positivistic theories recommended by his professor, and complained in *A Lucta* (April 6, 1882) that the library had at great cost acquired the ponderous works, written in Latin, of the sixteenth-century French jurisconsult Cujacius. The city's facilities for higher education were to be expanded and modernized only during the republican period, and a university was not to be established until 1934. Meanwhile, certain less ambitious enterprises were launched.

In 1874 a Society for Propagating Public Instruction, supported by public subscription, began free classes for a hundred students. Shortly the course took a vocational orientation, and the school became the Lyceum of Arts and Trades, giving industrial, commercial, agricultural, manual, and artistic training. By 1887 it had an enrollment of 680, a 5,000-book library, and a yearly subvention from the province. Although the long-decadent boys' seminary became defunct in 1883, its place was taken by the Lyceum, the Dona Ana Rosa Institute, founded by private philanthropy in 1874, and the Lyceum of the Sacred Heart of Jesus, founded by the Salesians in 1885. In 1875 Rangel Pestana — a precursor of the Brazilian republic — and his wife opened a girls' school (short-lived, however, for want of a subsidy) with a curriculum that included sciences, domestic economy, and "women's rights in Brazilian society." The German colony sponsored classes, and in 1880 the American School became the first in Brazil to give a course in accounting and stenography. The diocesan seminary, which by the 1870's gave a better education than the academy's Curso Anexo, was in 1879 reorganized to answer long-standing criticism of the foreign Capuchins and their methods.

In the field of public primary education, a provincial law of 1874 carried forward the intent of the 1846 reform by making schooling compulsory for boys of seven to fourteen and girls of seven to eleven in all towns having schools. The printing presses had made cheap primers available. São Paulo's literacy rate for persons over six rose from 5 per cent (1836) to 30 per cent (1872) to 45 per cent (1887), a trend partly attributable to the arrival of literate immigrants. The disparity between city and country shows up when one considers that in 1887 the province as a whole was only 29 per cent literate and had one teacher for each 1,156 inhabitants, while the capital had one for 596.

More widespread literacy, however, did not signify improved pedagogy. The Normal School, which, with sixty-one students, reopened permanently only in 1880, was an inadequate source of new teachers. Public primaries held to their traditional lines. A favorite method for instilling knowledge was to cause a whole class to repeat the lesson up to thirty times in deafening, sing-song unison. A teacher named to a primary "chair" might find it nonexistent and have to rent a classroom at his own expense. Undisciplined pupils, even though their mothers might ask that they be whipped for their intransigence, had to be tolerated since a teacher's tenure hinged upon a minimum attendance.

In short, the keynote of the 1870's and 1880's is that they saw São Paulo pass from being a town, colonial in appearance but serving the empire as an intellectual springhead, toward being a full-fledged city, economically dynamic and impatient with earlier political and literary programs except as they might justify or embellish materially conceived living. The era of "material progress" found São Paulo with inept primary schools, a handful of vocational schools, and no competent higher institutions — and this in a city which during the final quarter of the century leaped from tenth to second largest in the nation and became the focus of its most productive economic region.

The capitalist outlook, if not full-blown capitalism, was steadily invading urban Brazil. Meanwhile, the only formal set of principles that was winning appreciable recognition from those who were concerned about future patterns of the economy and society was the positivism of the French thinker Auguste Comte (1798-1857), coiner of the term "sociology." This was the philosophic view which held that the Western World was entering a higher stage of development in which scientific generalizations about society were for the first time feasible and were to become the basis for systematically imparting "order and progress" to human affairs. The spiritual energies for this new regime were to derive from an ostensibly naturalistic "religion of humanity." Positivism, however, did not widely inform São Paulo's institutions and, as a comprehensive philosophy, roosted somewhat precariously in the minds of but a few.[1]

Even more than in the allegedly laissez-faire industrial societies of the Northern Hemisphere, economic development in São Paulo fell haphazardly to individual initiative: to foreigners, to the few Brazilians who had gleaned skills and experience at home, and to Brazilians educated abroad. In 1874, according to *Correio Paulistano* (Jan. 22), there were enough Brazilian students in Cornell to publish a journal in Portuguese; eight Brazilians were enrolled in Lehigh (three of them paulistas) and four (all paulistas) in the University of Pennsylvania. A representative career of public service was that of A. F. de Paula Sousa, who was born in 1843, studied engineering in Switzerland, then came home to organize São Paulo's Water and Sewage Division and participate in republican campaigning. Later he worked in the United States for the Rock Island and St. Louis Railroad, but returned to São Paulo to direct railroad engineering and public works. In the 1890's Paula Sousa was successively federal minister of public works and first director of São Paulo's Polytechnic School.[2]

1. The city was introduced to Comte's ideas in the 1870's by *A Provincia de São Paulo* and, in the same decade, to Darwinism by Dr. Miranda Azevedo and to the social evolutionism of Herbert Spencer by the articles of Dr. Paulo Egydio in *Correio Paulistano*.

2. On his return from America, Paula Sousa wrote an article entitled "Rapid Sketch of Some of our Industries Compared to Those of the United States." He berated Brazil for bad roads, transportation, and mails; inadequate financial facilities; inefficient agriculture; bungling, overcentralized government; and its need to import the staples of life. (ALMANACH, 1875, pp. 49-57.)

São Paulo had, under the empire, no organized facilities for training such men as these. Nor could positivism enfold them, once they had managed a training elsewhere, into an ethos of common enterprise. Before the poverty of positivism in this regard is examined, it should be explained why the more sanguine, humanistic ideals of the 1860's were withering.

Republicanism, as a commitment to cast off monarchic government, became programmatic with the Republican Manifesto of 1870, drawn up in Rio de Janeiro by two graduates of São Paulo's academy: Quintino Bocaiuva, who had spent two years in the republican environment of Buenos Aires, and Salvador de Mendonça. Early in 1872 a Republican Party was organized in São Paulo city, and plans were laid for a province-wide convention to be held in Itu in April, 1873. At this point a certain faint-heartedness in the movement was exposed. Campaign issues, and particularly the stand on abolition, were formulated equivocally, with an eye to coaxing support from the slavocracy, and the fiery Luís Gama refused to attend the Itu convention.

In foregoing decisive espousal of abolition, the Republicans were left with but a few vague declarations of intention, such as those which comprised the main planks of the party platform of the paulista republicans in 1881: *Decentralization.* — Although containing plausible recommendations for reinvigorating municipal government, the burden of this appeal was for provincial autonomy. In a nation where organizing and technical skills were at a premium, the shortsighted separatism of paulistas hoping to aggrandize their now prosperous province was scarcely edifying.[3] *Public Instruction.* — With positivistic rhetoric, this plank endorsed freedom of teaching and elimination of religious instruction. "Official teaching cannot be subjected to the influence of philosophic schools; it must be in-

---

3. The flavor of paulista separatism — which, as the province's economic advantage mounted, assumed overtones of megalomania and a persecution complex — suffuses the following article from *A Provincia de São Paulo* (*ca.* 1887): "Will it not be nice . . . when São Paulo can announce in the *Times* or the *New York Herald* and other papers of the old and new worlds the following: The Province of São Paulo, having liquidated its affairs with the old firm Brazil Brigantino, Corruption & Co., declares itself constituted as an independent nation with its own firm. It promises, in its relations with other nations, to keep good faith in its business, and rectitude, magnanimity, and dignity instead of the duplicity, knavery, and cowardice of the old firm." (T. de ALMEIDA, 1934, p. 20.)

tegral, concrete, and as complete as possible a recapitulation of the truths affirmed by science." *Agriculture.* — The need for additional labor was vaguely set forth, with the stress laid upon a mere procedural aspect — namely, that immigration be privately sponsored and that it be administered provincially rather than nationally. *Abolition.* — The emancipation ideal was gently endorsed and a feeble party resolution of eight years previous quoted. Each province was to "achieve the reform more or less slowly, in accord with its private interests and with its greater or less facility in substituting free for slave labor." (PARTIDO. . ., 1881.)

Two of the signers of this platform had in 1875 become editors of a new paper, *A Provincia de São Paulo* (today the substantial *O Estado de São Paulo*), that promised to be a powerful vehicle for republicanism. But it denied political affiliation and, like the Republican Party, soon developed inhibitions stemming from conservative backing. In 1884 two of its more spirited collaborators were forced out and founded a resolute, incisive, popular journal, the city's first evening paper: *Diario Popular.* Only in the late 1880's, shortly before the end of the empire, was *A Provincia* to resume a more forthright position.

Meanwhile, practical abolitionism carried on, unyoked from specific political affiliation. Luís Gama's apostolic dedication braced the campaign till his death in 1882, when he was succeeded by an audacious and virulent law graduate, Antônio Bento.

São Paulo city was an ideal focus for the crusade. Earlier, at mid-century, there had been several chácaras in its outskirts where masters sent refractory slaves for corporal punishment. But there were also havens for runaways. In 1857 a notice in *Correio Paulistano* (Nov. 21) requested the return of a slave "seen in this capital with his face tied up and wearing shoes;[4] he is suspected to have some hiding-place in the suburbs." In like manner, fazendeiros throughout the interior advertised continually for escaped chattel in newspapers of the capital, which, as the number of slaves owned by citydwellers fell off, became ever more a mecca for fugitives. (São Paulo city had 4,075 slaves in 1855; 3,424 in 1872; and only 493 by 1887.) In the 1870's the Puerto Rican liberal Hostos (1939, p. 395) praised the "democratic evolution" and free-and-easy atmosphere of the capital, where whites and blacks, free and slave

---

4. Slaves were customarily not allowed to wear shoes.

frequented the same cafés and streetcars and could, in the Public Garden, "sit on the same bench, contemplate the same beauties of nature, admire the same statue, applaud the same musical band, ...judge by a common right the same absurdities, and with this same acquired habit learn a common respect of one toward another."

The Rio Branco law of 1871 (the law of the "free womb," by which children thenceforth born to slaves were to be freed when they became twenty-one), regarded by most planters as a "cease-fire" agreement, merely whetted Gama for total emancipation. In that same year he was able, by seizing upon legal technicalities, to win freedom for over a hundred slaves belonging to the estate of a deceased millionaire. Thenceforward the courts became an important arena for his campaign.

Antônio Bento was even more venturesome. Through persuasion and violence he won liberty for hundreds of slaves belonging to his acquaintances. One night he and several dozen followers showed up at the soirée of a wealthy matriarch. The latecomers brought their own music and festivity, and under cover of the confusion spirited away all their hostess' slaves. The office of Bento's journal, *A Redempção (Redemption)*, became the center of a network of informants and operators who abducted slaves from fazendas to havens in São Paulo or Santos, or to sanctuary in the Serra. In the capital, clerks, merchants, typographers, and a lay brotherhood of Negro workers rendered services; carriage drivers allowed free use of their vehicles and were an unfailing source of information. When Bento organized a procession displaying church images and brutal instruments for slave torture, the police dared not interfere. Not only did Bento release slaves, but he arranged with understaffed planters to receive them as salaried labor. At the time of final emancipation (May, 1888), he boasted that a third of the fazendas were manned by these ex-slaves.

At length, abolitionist fever became more widely contagious. In the capital, where it spread most easily, the Câmara began recording in a Golden Book the names of freed slaves and their owners; by March, 1888, none remained in bondage. On his visit to the province in 1886, the emperor gave at least half a conto in each place where funds for purchasing slaves' freedom were being collected. Prompted by the foreign colony in the capital, as well as by the realization that abolition in the United States had left

Brazil the only important stronghold of slavery in the Western Hemisphere, the press and public opinion took up the cry. Republican leaders made their stand unequivocal by the late 1880's. And the fazendeiros themselves met the challenge, founding in the capital an Emancipation Society (November, 1887) pledged to freeing all slaves within three years. Within a year of March, 1887, voluntary manumission liberated 40,000 of the province's slaves, and thousands more were without hindrance fleeing en masse.

The ease with which planters were converted becomes more understandable when we consider that their efforts to import free European labor were bearing fruit. In 1871 they had formed an Association of Colonization and Immigration which, aided by government subsidies, set about to introduce agricultural workers. The yearly influx of such immigrants was at first modest, but at the very time that mass manumission was winning general acceptance it took on sharp increments:

1885 —	6,500
1886 —	9,536
1887 —	32,112
1888 —	92,086
1889 —	27,893
1890 —	38,291
1891 —	108,736

The success of subsidized immigration was in part owing to the efforts of Queirós Teles (later viscount of Parnaíba), who in 1878 visited eight countries of western Europe and returned to praise their — and particularly Italy's — potentiality as a labor source. As provincial president (1886-1887) he helped to establish a new Promotive Society for Immigration, and he signalized the role of the capital as a labor market by building in it an enormous "Lodge for Immigrants," where new arrivals could board for a week without cost while awaiting assignment to fazendas. He tirelessly visited planters, political enemies as well as friends, urging them to build neat, healthful workers' dwellings so that he might justifiably counteract bad rumors about the lot of colonists that were reaching European ears.

It is therefore evident why, when the princess regent signed the "golden" Emancipation Law of May 13, 1888, slavery had already ceased to be a matter for contention in São Paulo province and its capital. Nor were there in the air any other soul-stirring issues. The coffee boom was assured its labor and its railways. The city, as will be seen, was assured industry, commerce, public utilities, banking, ornamental parks and buildings, cultural diversions, and a fast-expanding populace. Little demand existed for the political and philosophic speculation of earlier decades — except perhaps for fragments of federalist theory that might be invoked to chide the central government for siphoning off paulista wealth.

A few days after the "golden law" a São Paulo journalist, Hipólito da Silva, spelled out this apathy and lashed at the "neutral" republican organs: "What do we do now? Lay down our arms? ...I will not accept that.... The social question is solved. The political one remains.... We must come to life again! We must agitate! The abolitionist campaign, in the grandeur of its purposes, in part stifled propaganda for the Republic.... The Republican campaign has lived till now in the terrain of doctrine.... This alone is not enough." (A. A. de FREITAS, 1927b, p. 487.) Yet Silva's new journal, O Grito do Povo (The Cry of the People), lasted only six months.

Indeed, when in November, 1889, the republican coup d'état took place in the nation's capital, it came in response neither to a popular mandate nor to the oratory of parliamentary liberalism. Rather, it was a businesslike change of administrators, carried out under the watchwords of positivism.[5] In his allegorical Esau and Jacob the novelist Machado de Assis sharply depicted the inconclusiveness and lack of fervor which attended the coup.

It was in about 1870 that a "new bourgeoisie" of soldiers, doctors, and engineers — persons "nearer the positive sciences owing to the nature of their professions" — rose to prominence in the nation's intellectual life. Some who swelled the positivist ranks were "men disillusioned with the spiritualist eclecticism taught among us and which was merged with a verbose and useless rhetoric." Others professed to resolve the cleavage between inbred religious beliefs and the tenets of Brazilian republicanism. The positivists of Rio

---

5. Positivism, of course, lent itself to authoritarian as well as republican uses (as the Mexican científicos of this period under Porfirio Díaz well knew), for its aura of "scientific" definitiveness showed up to bad advantage the frequently sterile polemics between Brazilian liberals and conservatives. This helps to explain the four years of military autocracy which followed the "republican" coup (1889-1894).

de Janeiro, who were the most influential, were spearheaded by a group from the Military School, many of them from petit-bourgeois families. They constituted a "new elite, of a spirit perhaps somewhat different from that represented by the bachelors in law from Coimbra, Recife, or São Paulo, where most of the sons of the rural patriarchal families received higher education." (J. C. Costa, 1956a, pp. 134-44.) Of this Rio group, Benjamin Constant was instrumental in the coup of 1889, while Miguel Lemos and Raimundo Teixeira Mendes became apostles of a Comtean "religion of Humanity."

In São Paulo, positivist currents were less channelized and tended to mingle their waters with social Darwinism. For one thing, a glorious economic future for the city and province seemed so assured that to set up a formal intellectual cult would have been an empty elaboration. Secondly, the city had no institutions comparable in influence to Rio's Military School which positivism might infiltrate and lay claim to. The newly re-established Normal School became the leading positivist center. The Law Academy, however, because of its decadence and because of the remnants of its humanistic tradition, was not a suitable proving ground. Miguel Lemos (1884, p. 49) sadly reported in 1882 that a law student had, by writing in a positivist vein on the topic "Religious Liberty," evoked "a veritable persecution from his examiners and the council of the school." The paper was "immediately declared null," and the student had appealed to the minister of the empire.

Positivism did, to be sure, find limited footholds in the academy. As early as 1880 a student published a book (Werneck, 1880) purporting to reconcile a monarchist position with positivism, Spencerian evolutionism, and Helmholtzian materialism. Certain students received their degrees "under the invocation of Humanity," and several distinguished graduates called themselves positivists. When Lemos came to proselyte in São Paulo, however, he addressed his series of nine lectures (1881) to the public at large. "The nature of the intellectual milieu which I proposed to influence," he recorded, "presented a heterogeneous mixture of vague, incoherent, purely verbal positivism and social aspirations peculiar to persons who by the nature of their studies are accustomed to consider the reaction of society upon man." He faced attentive audiences that included magistrates, ex-ministers, professors, students, and ladies; the papers carried extensive résumés of his talks. After founding a

Positivist Society (of six members), he left with high hopes for the future of the movement in the city. (M. Lemos, 1882, pp. 61-88.) This "heterogeneous" milieu, however, resisted regimentation. When the republican journal *A Lucta*, edited by foremost writers and political leaders, adopted positivist chronology, it warned: "This does not imply any fanaticism or infatuation for orthodox positivist doctrines." (Sept. 1, 1882; the Comtean date was 20 Gutenberg, 94.) Moreover, the city's leading positivist, Luís Pereira Barreto, was a maverick. Born in Rio de Janeiro (1840), he had studied medicine in Belgium and returned, with positivist ideas, to exercise his profession in Jacareí, east of São Paulo. His two tomes of philosophy and his spirited polemic (1880) with a Protestant evangelist, G. Nash Morton, revealed him not, certainly, as an original thinker but as opposing any sort of absolutism, whether of religious creeds or of formal positivism. (L. P. Barreto, 1874; 1876; 1880.) His philosophy reached beyond prevailing currents to Locke, Berkeley, Kant, and Eduard von Hartmann. In criticizing the intolerance, opportunism, and mediocre leadership of the times he inveighed not only against the church, but against the false wisdom and morality of the Law Academy. Despite his secularism, he sustained the vision to commend the moral stand of the bishops of Pará and Pernambuco whom the government imprisoned in 1874 for their Antimasonic edicts.

Because of his adaptive, uncommitted thinking Pereira Barreto fell under the ban of the Positivist Apostolate in Rio de Janeiro. Miguel Lemos (1900, pp. 149-54) scolded him for looking to German and American as well as French models, for separating Comte's philosophy from his politico-religious schema, and for falling into "scientific Gongorism." Managing as best he could with the intellectual attitudes then current in Brazil, Pereira Barreto emerged as a forthright critic and, during decades of public life in São Paulo city, as a practical educator, economist, and scientist. More nearly perhaps than any local contemporary, he measured up to Alvares de Azevedo's ideal of the discriminating, world-conscious philosopher, effectually dedicated to his countrymen's service. Yet Pereira Barreto had not as a young man been formed by the city's institutions, and his was a voice of criticism almost alone of its kind.

In short, the intellectual life of the city appeared to enter a phase of attenuation in about 1870. This phase coincided with the city's genesis as a metropolis, or what one historian has called its "second founding." It therefore remains to analyze that surge of physical and economic growth which put an end to at least the external vestiges of the colonial past.

Bibliographical Note

Travelers' accounts and reminiscences affording panoramas and vignettes of the young metropolis include: JUNIUS (1882), KOSERITZ (1943), RAFFARD (1892), ANDREWS (1887), HOUGH (1934), LECLERC (1942), A. J. de CARVALHO (1942), E. V. P. DE SOUSA (1946; 1948), DAUNT (1957), and SÃO PAULO HÁ QUARENTA ANOS (1928). COMMISSÃO CENTRAL . . . (1888) is a mine of statistics. A. da S. JARDIM (1879), SÁ (1880), J. T. de M. ALVES (1882), and J. S. de REZENDE (1890) are contemporary reports on the Law Academy; in his biography of the poet Olavo Bilac, PONTES (1944) recalls the students' bohemianism. J. F. de OLIVEIRA (1932) and J. L. RODRIGUES (1930) present the recollections of a teacher and a student, respectively, in the primary schools. SABOIA (1939, pp. 35-6) gives information about Rangel Pestana's school for girls.

VIDA E OBRA . . . (1945) summarizes the career of A. F. de Paula Sousa. DORNAS FILHO (1939), PALMER, JR. (1951), and E. C. NOGUEIRA (1954) are accounts of the republican movement in São Paulo, while paulista abolitionism is treated by SANTOS (1942), A. E. de MORAIS (1924), ANDRADA (1941), and L. AMARAL (1940). The founding of the journal *A Provincia de São Paulo* is related in ARANHA (1937). RICCIARDI (1938) sets forth the career of the viscount of Parnaíba; the immigrants' Lodge which he built is the subject of HOSPEDARIA . . . (1939).

TORRES (1943) describes the rise and influence of positivism in Brazil from a Roman Catholic viewpoint; COSTA (1956a; 1956b), writing in a secular vein, sets the movement in its socio-intellectual context. The yearly circulars of the Positivist Apostolate in Brazil, first published in 1882, contain regional reports, of which the most useful for this study are listed in the bibliography as M. LEMOS (1882; 1884; 1900). Two works by J. F. de OLIVEIRA (1898a; 1898b) are important documents of the positivist movement in São Paulo.

It is PAULA (1936) in which the 1870's are depicted as the era of São Paulo's "second founding."

Chapter 14

ECONOMIC EXPANSION AND IMMIGRANTS

*T*O UNDERSTAND the city's heightened activity after 1870, one must first turn to the booming and, with new transport facilities, fast-expanding coffee frontier to the northwest.

Communication between city and fazenda — and among fazendas — was smartly improved when some Confederate expatriates from the United States began manufacturing a light horse-drawn vehicle which, for passenger traffic, was vastly more expeditious than the lumbering oxcart. The *troly*, as it was locally known, had a flexible chassis and spoked wheels (the rear two being larger) and was advertised in *Diario de São Paulo* (March 13, 1872) as follows:

TROLYS OF THE MELO COMPANY
These carriages, after the 15th of the current month, will be used for transporting passengers and their respective baggage from this station [São Paulo] to Valinhos or Samambáia [near Campinas] and vice-versa.... Trolys may be hired for any point on the road from this city to Limeira and Rio Claro, as well as for any other point within this municipality.

The troly's effect on rural isolation was comparable to that of the Model T after the First World War and the jeep after the Second.

Of immensely greater importance, however, were the railroads. Within eight years of the completion of the Santos-Jundiaí line, the four major arteries to the hinterland were in operation. These were

166

(1) the "Mogiana": from Campinas north into Minas Gerais; (2) the "Paulista": an extension of the Santos-Jundiaí axis, north-northwest through Campinas; (3) the "Ituana": from Jundiaí west through Itu; (4) the "Sorocabana": from São Paulo west through Sorocaba.[1] The last important line of this network that centered on São Paulo passed, not through undeveloped lands, but east-northeast along the now decadent Paraíba; generally known as the "Central do Brasil," it linked São Paulo with the nation's capital. A close correspondence exists between these five lines and the historic routes for overland travel and haulage.

Figures for São Paulo's coffee production, a sequel to those given earlier, show the definitive shift of coffee planting to the province's northwest quadrant, whose economic reach the railways had so extended:

	1854		1886	
	Tons	*Per Cent*	*Tons*	*Per Cent*
Paraíba valley	44,500	77	33,500	20
Northwest	13,000	23	134,500	80
Total	57,500	100	168,000	100

The Paraíba production had begun its decline, while that of the northwest, which had increased tenfold during 1836-1854, was once again decupled.

It was not only by making coffee more marketable that the railways served to settle the hinterland. The "Paulista," a private Brazilian concern, was the most enterprising in this regard. It began giving free passage in the 1880's to immigrant labor destined for fazendas. It opened up a vast zone by providing steam navigation on the Mogi-guassu River. It encouraged cattle raising by helping to establish Brazil's first refrigerated packing plant; by opening riverboat service to bring cattle into São Paulo from other provinces; by slashing rates to encourage cattle shipment from winter ranges to the capital; by furnishing refrigerated cars for the meat export trade. The "Paulista" offered low-interest loans and low-cost rolling stock to tributary railways, and later it counteracted deforestation

---

1. In 1875 the traffic on three lines (Santos-Jundiaí, "Mogiana," and "Paulista") totaled 235,000 passengers and 210,000 tons of freight. By 1890 both figures were over a million, and yearly profits had risen from 3,000 to almost 10,000 contos.

with its experimental arboriculture and large-scale eucalyptus plantings.

This is not to say that the mechanized era was without its inefficiencies. Owing to poor roads haulage by animal from fazenda to railway was slow and costly, and at the stations further wastage occurred, since coffee sacks were loosely tied and received little surveillance. Five different gauges of track entailed toilsome transshipments, while the variations in shipping charges led to the use of circuitous routes to market. Moreover, freight movements were predominantly one-way, from farm to seaport.

Now that railroads had expanded the possibilities, the exploitative, urban-capitalist nature of coffee planting could more clearly be seen. The planter's *modus operandi* which impoverished the Paraíba region and was extended to the northwest has been described as follows: "The extractive culture of the soil, which the planter saw himself obliged to practice, cannot be called agriculture. It desolates the fields and makes of them deserts. It brings no well-being nor does it offer assurance of stability.... Brazil has exported its own patrimony, its capital, its wealth represented by the land's fertility, in behalf of a small number of intermediaries. This explains the poverty of our rural populace and the prosperity of the cities, which are the middlemen's abode and operating center." (P. P. de CARVALHO, 1943, pp. 34-38.)

Writing in about 1909, Pierre DENIS (1928, p. 110) described how this conversion to monoculture, with its mechanized marketing process and parasitic middlemen, had aggrandized São Paulo and Santos at the expense of cities of the interior. The latter "are not and have never been coffee markets. The only markets for coffee are São Paulo and Santos, and the businessmen of São Paulo and the comissários of Santos are in direct contact with the planters. The cities of the interior do not serve as points of concentration for the harvested crop, but they do control the distribution of imported merchandise in the agricultural districts.... Each city has stores for hardware, cloth, and groceries from which the depots of fazendas are provisioned. They live also from the money trade. Planters find credit at small local banks, which are maintained by more powerful banks situated in São Paulo."[2]

2. By 1889 a Free Bourse, five banks, and four branch banks functioned in the capital. At that time banks existed in only seven of Brazil's twenty provinces.

By the end of the empire any number of notices such as the following were appearing in São Paulo papers to announce the ascendancy of the urban middlemen in agricultural Brazil:

COMMERCIAL OFFICE
OF
Augusto M. de Freitas
59 Rua de São Bento [São Paulo]
Buys any quantity of coffee.
Arranges the sale of coffee by lots in this market or in Santos, where transactions are made with important commercial houses. Receives products on consignment from the interior or abroad. Will undertake as agent any business in the interest of third parties. Buys and sells buildings, lots, plantations, notes of public or private debt, letters of exchange, etc.

(*O Estado de São Paulo*, Jan. 15, 1890.)

It was in the mid-1880's, largely owing to a sharp dip in world coffee prices, that urban comissários began to press their stranglehold on the coffee lands. Thitherto they had freely extended credit to planters, generally at 12 per cent, and had nearly as freely been willing to renew such extensions. But by 1885 the money market had grown suddenly tight. LAÈRNE (1885, pp. 183-97) learned that coffee was yielding "very little or *no* profits" and was informed by a fazendeiro that only 20 per cent of the planters were "free." In the event of "liquidation" 30 per cent could scarcely have paid their debts; 50 per cent were so "desperate" they would not have survived.

This pinch (which applied more to fazendas tributary to Rio de Janeiro than to those of northwestern São Paulo) was shortly relieved by a firmer market and by the influx of foreign labor. Yet the middleman's dominion was established. By the turn of the century, coffee, delivered in Santos to a "half dozen exporters" who set their own price, was selling abroad for ten times what the planter received. "The facility of credit, which planters not only used but widely abused, was not a foundation propitious for a solid, enduring structure," wrote A. A. PINTO (1902, pp. 92-98). "Nor are the reputations for benevolence, to which the coffee comissários have acquired title, of a nature to justify for all time a commercial system that is today so costly for being retrograde, archaic, and wholly incompatible with the needs of the situation."

It must not be thought, however, that a strict dichotomy was arising between a rural gentry and a city bourgeoisie — such as in colonial times existed between sugar planters and Portuguese merchants in northern Brazil. For the railroads were making it possible for the coffee proprietors, who had customarily lived on their estates or in towns near them, to enjoy a more comfortable and stimulating life in the capital and still remain in touch with their fazendas. JUNIUS (1882, p. 56) observed in 1882 that during the previous decade the city had received "countless rich families, born and long resident in different localities of the interior." As citydwellers of wealth, social prestige, and higher education, many coffee barons entered into urban economic activities — as railroad directors, industrial pioneers, and bankers (though never brokers and comissários) — or into pursuits familiar from student days of a forensic, political, or journalistic nature. Foreigners, whatever their class, and most Brazilians could far more easily be identified with exclusively urban or rural interests.

One of the most striking examples of this dual allegiance was the famous Prado family. Antônio da Silva Prado (1840-1929) and Martinho Prado Júnior ("Martinico") (1843-1906) were sons of that fazendeiro whose wife, Dona Veridiana, had visited the capital only for obstetric reasons.

Antônio became a bacharel in São Paulo (1861), then after a trip to Europe for a "bath in civilization" he entered politics and journalism in São Paulo. By 1866 he was clearing a coffee and cattle fazenda far in the interior. But he was not long away from city interests. Between 1872 and 1890 he was at various times: national deputy, founder of São Paulo's Jockey Club, president of the Imperial Economic Bank, a director of the "Paulista" railway, president of São Paulo's Câmara, journalist for conservative papers, head of the Conservative Party, minister of public works, minister of foreign affairs, member of the Promotive Society for Immigration, and president of the Bank of Trade and Industry of São Paulo. In 1889 Antônio, Martinico, and their father began clearing land in Sertãozinho, far to the north, that became, with 3,000,000 coffee trees, São Paulo's largest fazenda. After 1895 he engaged in numerous industrial enterprises and was from 1899 to 1910 prefect of São Paulo city.[3] This vigorous career shows not only the coexistence of agra-

3. That Antônio Prado found the spare hours to become eight times a father stretches credibility!

rian and urban interests, but also a symptomatic shift through the years from politico-ideological to economic affiliations. His term as city prefect is remembered principally for the tumultuous material growth that it witnessed.

Martinico took his law degree in São Paulo in 1866 (having fought in the Paraguayan War), was for a time public prosecutor in the capital, then in 1869 devoted himself to a fazenda in Araras, beyond Campinas. In 1876, about when the railway was reaching that region, he took up residence in the capital. He became, unlike Antônio, a Republican, was elected to the Provincial Assembly, and in those years established a new, more distant fazenda. In 1887 the Promotive Society sent him abroad to supervise the first levies of immigrants. After helping his father and brother with the venture at Sertãozinho, he took additional European trips in 1892, 1895, 1899, and 1900.

The hypothesis therefore is that certain graduates produced by the Law Academy before the late 1870's, though their training tended to be legalistic and literary, had nonetheless a broad-mindedness, a sense of dedication, an ability to act within a framework of humane ideals. The generation of Antônio and Martinico Prado, of Rui Barbosa and Joaquim Nabuco, dominated public life till, approximately, the First World War. So assuring was their leadership that it was hard to realize that they had been formed in a bygone era of romanticism and crusading liberalism, and to recognize that Brazilian institutions were no longer preparing men to address, masterfully and inspiringly, the complexities of an urban age.

Natural attrition of these leaders and, after 1902, ruinous coffee crises were by 1920 to leave the rural-urban aristocracy with but the tatters of social prestige. Another cadre of leaders, often of foreign descent, would emerge — traditionless, opportunist, generated by the city. The industrialization of São Paulo, which began a decade or two before the end of the empire, made it a spawning ground for such an elite and propelled the city itself into a role of commanding economic and political importance within the nation.

In 1874 one writer urged the diversion of private capital and foreign labor to industry so that paulistas might round out the last stage of a cycle from slave to serf to citizen. Only with industry, he explained, citing Comte, were "human faculties utilized according to the degree of development of each person." A decade earlier, he went on, capital had not been available for industry, since

it was bringing 18 per cent, 24 per cent, or more in private transactions. But with the example of the Santos-Jundiaí railway, "the
spirit of association and private initiative were born in that province,
as if by magic, to engender a progress based on order and characterized by industry." (N. F. LEITE, 1874, pp. 3-15.)

A partial survey of the capital's industries made in 1901 gives
the year of founding for 94 concerns. Of these only four predated
1870, while 41 were established between the years 1870 and 1890.
(BANDEIRA JUNIOR, 1901.) A small sampling of newspaper notices
conveys some of this activity. In 1872, G. Sydow & Co. announced
a large workshop with modern steam-driven machines from Europe
that would reduce the cost of cabinetwork by 20 to 30 per cent. In
1877, Luz Foundry advertised the manufacture of saws, sugar mills,
pumps, presses, iron gates and railings, water tanks, and agricultural machinery. And in 1879:

> Ernesto Heinke
> Mechanic from Berlin
> 5 Rua Vinte e Cinco de Março
> Offers to make fine tools for watchmakers, sculptors,
> marble-cutters, etc., etc. Makes any and all repairs of
> SEWING MACHINES, GUNS, as well as any fine metal
> instrument. Guarantees perfection, promptness, and very
> reasonable prices.   (*Correio Paulistano*, July 19.)

The city's first factory-size cotton-spinning and -weaving mill
was founded by the baron of Piracicaba (who was reputedly the
first to have made extensive coffee plantings west of the capital)
and his European-educated son, Diogo Antônio de Barros. In 1870
the latter acquired machinery from John Platt & Sons of Lancashire,
and by 1872 the mill was in operation with thirty looms and sixty
workers. By 1887 this and a second mill of Diogo Antônio's in the
capital had a total of 350 looms. There were ten other mills in
the interior, all of them in or near the cotton zone, but those in the
capital were far and away the largest and indicated it as the point
of future concentration.

This trend toward centralization had been pointed out in 1881
by a Portuguese businessman who urged his government to appoint
a full consul in São Paulo, since it was the "capital of the province,
two and a half hours from the port of Santos, and the center of convergence for all the railways from the province and the Court [Rio].
Its location indicates that it is here that exists the greatest number

of interests to deal with and where all questions can easily be solved. The consul who comes to São Paulo has near him the higher provincial authorities, with whom he can deal directly, and from here he can oversee every locality, which would be impossible in Santos." (A. A. S. MARQUES, 1881, p. 27.)

By 1887 the capital and its environs could boast, in addition to Diogo Antônio's mills:

A ceramics plant, employing 300 workers, producing 2,000,000 bricks and 1,000,000 tiles per year. (Also scores of small kilns, profiting by abundant raw material and the city's construction boom.)

Five large foundries.

A factory for calicos with 70 workers, producing 320,000 meters per year.

Four plants for wood manufacture, the largest with a 40 h.p. engine, 26 machines, and 78 workers.

A furniture factory with 32 machines and 100 workers.

Brazil's largest plant for producing lard and other by-products from swine.

A match factory with 80 machines, 120 workers, and an output of 250,000 boxes per day.

Two hat factories, employing 245 workers and supplying São Paulo province and its larger tributary region.

Hundreds of small plants and artisans' shops.

The city's population figures reflect its industrial and commercial expansion:

Parishes	1872	1886	1890	1893
Sé	9,213	12,821	16,395	29,518
Sta. Ifigênia	4,459	11,909	14,025	42,715
Consolação	3,357	8,269	13,337	21,311
Braz	2,308	5,998	16,807	32,387
Penha	1,883	2,283	2,209	1,128
N. S. do Ó	2,023	2,750	2,161	2,350
São Paulo	23,243	44,030	64,934	129,409

The outlying nuclei, Penha and Ó, once lively way stations for mule teams, were now left in quiescence by trains that chugged without loitering into the city's expanding heart.

A comparison of the censuses of 1872 and 1890 reveals the rise of a "capitalist" class, a migration of planters to the city, the increase of women in liberal professions, and, in general, a decline in rural pursuits in favor of commercial, industrial, bureaucratic, and intellectual ones. Foreign immigrants were of course the wellspring that technical and commercial occupations drew upon. At a managerial level, the scientific training of a Diogo Antônio de Barros or the directorial talent of an Antônio Prado was rare among Brazilians. The roster of industrial entrepreneurs abounded in such names as Raffinette, Nardelli, Kleeberg, Christofani, Fowles, Weltmann, Sydow, Maggi, Falchi, Stupakoff, Zimmerman, Scorzato, and Witte — while of the proletariat probably 75 to 85 per cent were foreign.

Van de PUTTE (1890, p. 34) observed that foodstuffs were generally sold by Portuguese and Brazilians, dry goods by Brazilians, Germans, French, and Italians. Italians were the principal retailers of shoes, tinware, and hardware. The bakers, pastry cooks, and tanners were French or German. Metallurgic plants belonged mostly to the English and Americans, with Brazilians and Germans next in importance. Portuguese and Brazilians did rough carpentry, while the more skilled joiners were Brazilians, French, and Germans.

It is easy to see how wealthy or middle-class Europeans might come to the capital on their own account (as they had, in smaller numbers, during previous decades), drawn by its spreading fame as a boom town or by firsthand reports from acquaintances. But allowing that until the mid-1890's most lower-class immigration was subsidized and thus destined for fazendas, whence came those foreigners who in the 1870's and 1880's appeared as textile workers and bootblacks, peddlers and day laborers? How was it that between 1872 and 1886 foreigners rose from 8 per cent to 25 per cent of the city's population?

The answer is twofold. First, the colonizing system fixed upon by the planters was, as has been shown, the capitalistic, urban-type "labor pool," which assured the immigrant his transportation and life necessities but kept intact the large estates. Once the colonist had worked off his obligations, he was free to drift elsewhere since he owned no land outright. If he were dissatisfied with fazenda life or came from an urban area in Europe, he would be inclined to drift cityward. And as the disparity between rural and urban opportunities widened, this drift became more pronounced.

Secondly, many subsidized immigrants stuck to the city's fingers, as shown by these fragmentary figures:

Period	Subsidized Immigrants to the Province	Number Remaining in the Capital
1879	424	198
January-October, 1883	3,955	1,322
April-July, 1884	2,032	380

(AALPSP, 1880; 1884.)

In 1887 the director of the Promotive Society for Immigration resolved to discourage artisans and merchants from embarking at Genoa for São Paulo and to attract more farmers. The society later informed that although most of the first immigrants it had obtained (1886-1888) went into agriculture, a number did find employment in the capital and other populous centers, stimulating all branches of industry. By 1889-1891 the trend had reversed, and only two-fifths were going to agriculture.

If the lower-class European were enterprising, he discovered that paulista society now offered considerable economic and even social capillarity. A common avenue for self-advancement was the peddler's trade. Laden with cheap staples and gimcracks of the city (or, if more prosperous, leading a mule or two), the peddler made his rounds of the fazendas, selling and bartering. His constant dream was to acquire capital for a small general store on a trafficked road of the interior, and eventually to open a shop or even a factory in a city, ideally São Paulo. The German Victor Nothmann, for example, starting out as a peddler, was in 1879 "admitted to register" as a businessman in the capital, and as years passed Victor Nothmann & Co. became one of its largest textile wholesale houses. By the 1880's it was the Italians, especially Calabrians, who monopolized peddling, although they were soon to be displaced by the even cannier Syrians.

The influx of Italians, who were by 1897 to outnumber Brazilians two to one in the capital, was a decisive phenomenon of the period. Though many hundreds came in the 1870's, the steady stream began in 1882. In 1887 the Promotive Society — won by their industriousness and eagerness to emigrate and by the steamer fare saved by embarkation from Genoa — swelled the stream to flood size. The figures for immigration via the port of Santos read as follows for the decade 1882-1891:

Italian	202,503	Belgian	851
Portuguese	25,925	English	782
Spanish	14,954	Swedish	685
German	6,196	Swiss	219
Austrian	4,118	Irish	201
Russian	3,315	Other	483
French	1,922		
Danish	1,042	Total	263,196

It was, in 1890, too early to perceive the rise to high estate of the Italians of humbler origin. Residents of Sorocaba, however, were in the 1880's coming to know thirty-year-old Francisco Matarazzo, who, undaunted by having lost at sea the merchandise he had brought from Italy in 1881, was experimenting with new methods for putting up lard. He was branching out into other foodstuffs as well, preparing to shift his expanding business to the capital, where a few decades later he would be recognized as South America's richest industrialist and peer of the proudest paulista lineages.

Yet the city was not always so kind to those who tried their fortunes there. Ex-slaves coming in numbers from the fazendas often found themselves living in wretched hovels, working for minimal wages at jobs such as garbage collection to which whites scorned to stoop. Opponents of emancipation professed it to be mainly they who swelled the ranks of alcoholics, criminals, and vagabonds; and it could indeed be proved that the suicide rate among the city's Negroes and mulattoes far exceeded that of whites.

Paladins of liberalism, on the other hand, absolved ex-slaves and Brazilians in general of parasitism. "Rare, very rare are the Negro beggars that one finds in this city," asserted Diario Popular (April 30, 1892). "And when that happens there is no doubt that they are true unfortunates who expended their youth and energies in labor that was never paid and who are today without succor. ... [The beggars] are all foreigners, and foreigners who did not become disabled here, foreigners who came from their countries beckoned by the fame of our generosity and who arrived to add a black note to our active life with the sad picture of their deformities."

Of whatever color or language these wretches whom the fortunes of the city had bypassed, there was to their lot a bleakness and anonymity that sharply contrasted with the colorful posturing

ABOVE — Rua São
Francisco *ca*. 1860.
The Anhangabaú
valley seen from the
central "triangle."
LEFT — Rua 15 de
Novembro in the
late 1890's.

A 20th-century
neo-colonial mansion
on Avenida Paulista.

The old Prado
house, a sobrado
built *ca.* 1840.

Courtyard of a
modern cortico.

PHOTOGRAPHS COURTESY
OF THE DEPARTAMENTO
MUNICIPAL DE CULTURA,
SÃO PAULO.

LEFT — Chá Viaduct
over the
Anhangabaú valley.
Behind it, the
Matarazzo building.
BELOW — The
metropolis: *fore-
ground,* the
Anhangabaú valley
and the Opera
House; *upper right,*
Avenida São João.

The new cathedral,
begun in 1913.

The Anhangabaú
valley and modern
architecture.

of the "popular types" of years gone by. However commodious the asylums of the metropolis, however spacious its jails, there was little in the entering age to match the mocking but tender affection in which the small provincial town had once held its self-indulgent "Watersnake" and its preposterous "Vinegar Tears."

Bibliographical Note

M. F.-J. de S.-A. NERY (1889) contains monographs on Brazil as a whole which set a context for São Paulo's economic expansion. MORSE (1952a) examines socioeconomic aspects of the city in the period 1870-1890, and many of the travelers' accounts and reminiscences given on page 165 contain economic material. EGYDIO (1889) is a contemporary interpretation of the economic awakening, and COMMISSÃO CENTRAL . . . (1888) is a statistical source; J. F. de GODOY (1875) is both descriptive and statistical. The early decades of railway growth in São Paulo are treated in A. A. PINTO (1903), while LAÈRNE (1885) is an analysis of the coffee industry in the 1880's. The lives of Antônio and "Martinico" Prado, and data on the whole Prado clan, are given in N. PRADO (1929), PRIMEIRO . . . (1946), and IN MEMORIAM . . . (1944). E. C. NOGUEIRA (1954) emphasizes the mingled rural-urban allegiances of São Paulo's elite. The achievements of Diogo Antônio de Barros are reviewed in MAJOR DIOGO . . . (1945). RAFFARD (1892), a contemporary account, delves into many aspects of immigration to São Paulo; PICCAROLO (1908; 1911) and SYLOS (1936) deal with Italian immigration; HYGIN-FURCY (1888) is a guide for immigrants; the activities of the Promotive Society for Immigration are documented in DIRETORIA . . . (1887) and SOCIEDADE . . . (1892). DEFFONTAINES (1936) is a study of Brazil's immigrant peddlers. J. de A. MACHADO (1905) gives statistics to prove the excess of Negro over white suicides in the city for the period 1876-1904.

Chapter 15

PHYSICAL EXPANSION

*W*E HAVE THUS FAR CONSIDERED the soaring immigration to São Paulo province and the city's new sources of wealth and avenues of enterprise, as well as the climate of attitudes within which they developed. The combined action of these factors was registered in the appearance of the city — in its new construction, expanding perimeter, and public utilities and institutions. City growth during and long after the 1870's and 1880's objectified the tumultuous will-to-power of which reflections have already been noted and which so distinguished the metropolis from the modest provincial capital which it superseded.

In 1886 an Italian, one Dr. Lomonaco, observed São Paulo as follows: "Alongside handsome *palacetes* [new, palatial upper-class residences], worthy of any great city, one still sees small, humble hovels, the taipa houses built by the first Portuguese colonists. In contrast to certain well-paved streets, with many buildings, appear others scarcely marked out, possessing few structures, covered with creeping grasses or bare earth, impassable when it rains.

"These disparities in the mode and materials of construction are found as much in the old section as in the new. There is no district, one may say, of which to affirm that its appearance is definitive. Hence, only in ten or fifteen years will São Paulo have a conclusive cast and acquire the style of a great and handsome city." (Afonso d'E. TAUNAY, 1946, p. 62.) That São Paulo has not even yet achieved a "conclusive cast" is part of its later story; for the moment the description takes precedence over the prophecy.

The most telling impetus to "material progress" was imparted during the presidency of João Teodoro Xavier (1872-1875). A professor of law and devoted public servant, João Teodoro was

178

given to the gently ironic custom of summoning to his office a "jury" of homespun citizens, whose verdict on a given issue he would offer to political leaders as "public opinion." During his term an amount equal to nearly half the annual provincial budget was spent to embellish the capital — an instance of the "Versailles complex" at work which helps to explain why wealthy planters were starting to move to São Paulo.

Streets were of prime concern. Those forming the central "triangle" received the city's first "parallelepipeds," that is, small rectangular paving blocks. Expropriations were made and landmarks demolished so that old thoroughfares could be widened and new ones cut through. Some districts were linked across unimproved lands — notably Braz, a low-lying area of rural chácaras and soon to be a populous industrial belt, which was given access to the city center and to the Santos railway station. The crumbling embankment overlooking Carmo meadow was shored up. The meadow itself was drained, and a public park, delicately named the Isle of Loves, was laid out on a small island in the Tamanduateí. New regulations provided for smart upkeep of the Isle and the Public Garden, refreshment pavilions and weekly band concerts in each, a sixty-foot observation tower in the Garden, and tree planting along certain streets.

In 1872 the kerosene street lamps were replaced by far more satisfactory gas lighting; the original 606 lamps were more than doubled by 1887, in addition to which the company, a London firm, served 1,430 buildings. At the end of the following year electric street lights, installed by a Hungarian concern, were displayed to crowds in the city center. Telephones were in service by 1884. In 1877, local capitalists, acquiring the services of British engineers, organized the Cantareira Company to furnish São Paulo dependably with water and dispose of its sewage; from sources in the Cantareira hills to the north nine miles of pipes were laid to feed a city reservoir. By 1882, long-thirsty fountains were gushing, streets could be washed down daily, and 133 buildings had water connections; by 1888, over 5,000 buildings were served. When on a June night in 1882 church bells rang out as of old to give alarm of a fire in the Hotel Hespanha, the citizenry, as of old, rushed to the scene to lend aid. But the modern age had made them passive bystanders, mere thrill seekers; the blaze was extinguished by a new fire department employing newly installed hydrants.

São Paulo now boasted the best water and sewage systems in Brazil. But the wand of applied science, contrary to its advance notices, bade a Pandora's box to open. Efficient utilities, appearing in this underdeveloped agrarian environment, reinforced the city's inordinately swift growth by increasing the attractions of urban life. The hills that furnished water and the Tietê River that carried off sewage for 50,000 or 100,000 people were, a generation later, to become ineffectual for a population ten and twenty times as great.

One by one the city's long-standing deficiencies received attention. In 1877, prisoners still in the old jail were moved to a section of the Penitentiary, and the jail was remodeled to give more spacious housing to the Provincial Assembly. A new slaughterhouse was provided in 1887. In 1890, a second market place finally drove the colorful stalls off the Rua das Casinhas. The Santa Casa, whose patients tripled between 1870 and 1875, had its small staff of ten increased by a group of French nuns; it moved to a commodious site in 1884 and the next year opened an Asylum for Mendicants that was soon tending over 100 inmates. The Portuguese Society of Beneficence, whose facilities and membership continued to grow, became the model for an Italian (1878) and a French (1881) society, while Brazilian incentive in the field of charity was represented by two societies under the aegis of St. Vincent de Paul.

It was, however, simpler for wealth and science to provide new facilities than for old habits and suspicions to melt away. The city's Vaccinal Institute was not effective nor well supplied for nearly twenty years after its founding in 1874. The breakdown of causes for death by disease in the city (1887) shows public and private authorities to have been sluggish in the realms of preventive hygiene:

Diseases of the digestive tract....	397	Measles	54
Diseases of the respiratory tract_	215	Smallpox	34
Tuberculosis	209	Genito-urinary diseases	26
Cerebrospinal diseases	207	Diphtheria	22
Circulatory diseases	145	Puerperal diseases	10
Typhoid fever	103	Others, or not specified	314
	Total	1736	

Over half of those who died each year were children under eight years old, a phenomenon then attributed to bronchopulmonary diseases, caused by quick temperature changes and the "hygrometric state of the air," and to gastrointestinal diseases, caused by improper feeding, hired wet-nurses, premature weaning, and impure cow's milk. (TAPAJÓZ, 1894, pp. 14-16.)

Through no efficacy of its services for disease control, the capital was spared the yellow fever scourge. Having ravaged Santos for decades, the disease struck even more fiercely in 1889-1892, erupting as well in Campinas and other inland towns. It was noticed, however, that a businessman named Hawkins, who visited Santos continually during its worst epidemics, was not stricken until 1893, when for the first time he failed to return to São Paulo for the night. Until 1892, in fact, every victim of the disease in the capital had inevitably just arrived from one of the afflicted cities. *O Estado de São Paulo* (March 19, 1890) censured the apathy of officials toward these cases: "Neither is the disinfection of houses in which deaths occur carried out with proper vigor, nor is there an attempt to isolate the sick persons who arrive, or frequently have already arrived, from the neighboring city [Campinas]." After 1892, a few yellow fever cases did originate in the capital, but always they were persons who had received crates from Santos which, owing to the overworked port facilities, had been stored for months in filth and dampness; only then did the government start a more systematic campaign of decontamination and quarantining. Immunized by its high altitude, the capital was, as mistress of the rail network, simply transshipping unsuspected mosquitoes to the hinterland. The fever's ravages were in direct ratio to commercial activity. For Campinas, São Paulo's rival, this was a compounded irony.

The city's immunity to yellow fever was a factor, though not a cardinal one, of its precipitant growth, the analysis of which is still lacking in certain important details.

New animal-drawn streetcars were a sign of São Paulo's areal expansion. The first line (1872) joined the "triangle" to the Santos railway station. By 1887 there were seven lines carrying 1,500,000 passengers a year; in addition, a small steam railway joined outlying Santo Amaro with the city.

For rich and poor alike the scramble for living space had begun. Liberdade, on the road ascending southward, became a "respectable" section. *Diario de São Paulo* (Oct. 31, 1877) announced an auction of thirty-meter lots along the projected Liberdade streetcar line: "The progressive increase of population and hence the daily rise in value of lands next to the city being inevitable,[1]

1. Paulistas, like all Latin Americans, have historically preferred real estate to other forms of investment. The collapse of the banking house of Mauá in 1875 gave fresh impetus to speculation in city lands.

this is a golden occasion of immense advantage for proprietors and private parties to obtain, with little sacrifice, lands on which to build a shelter for the family." For land near the railway station only humble pretensions could be made:

ATTENTION   ATTENTION
LANDS FOR THE POOR
This is the first time that lots are being sold in São Paulo for 200$000.
Who would think that in this city, in the picturesque district of Luz, there could be sold lots so cheaply, within the reach of all. . . .
For that price only he who will not trouble himself to verify the truth will fail to become a property-owner.
(*Diario de São Paulo*, Sept. 20, 1877.)

Foreigners, as might be expected, had a strong hand in the land boom. The French engineer Jules Martin contracted in 1877 to build a viaduct across the valley of the Anhangabaú, which was 600 feet wide, and link the city's central hill with the Morro do Chá, whose chácara lands were being subdivided. Chá Viaduct, completed in 1892, became a safety valve for the congested "triangle." A German, Frederico Glete, acquired (1879) extensive chácara lands west of the center in Campos Elíseos, laid out a dozen or more streets, and sold off his lots for an 800 per cent profit. Another German, M. Burchard, also engaged in real estate in this area and opened up the boulevard that traverses the aristocratic Higienópolis district.

The upper-class residential section was spreading out south and west toward Santo Amaro, capitalizing on the view and drier air that the rising terrain afforded. Details of a chácara, put up for sale in 1877 and later subdivided, serve to describe the region: "There is for sale the large chácara of upper Pacaembu, located half a league from this Capital, with an excellent house of residence, a kiln, etc., etc. It likewise has excellent pasturage divided into several fields, good water, good and abundant clay for bricks and even tiles, and extensive woods where there is enough timber for construction. This estate, which is half a league in depth and 2,400 yards wide, is wholly enclosed by boundary ditches and situated on a pleasant and charming site enjoying a delightful view." (*Diario de São Paulo*, Nov. 22, 1877.)

Unlike some of the historic highroads that converged upon São Paulo, railways kept to the river-level plains, skirting the central rise along the basins of the Tietê and Tamanduateí. The São Paulo Railway, partly because of its generous provision of sidings, came to determine an industrial belt that contaminated a wide arc east and north of the center, much of which land was already undesirable for being low-lying and dank. Within this arc, notably in Braz and Moóca, most of the proletariat were to live.[2]

It must not be thought, however, that the city flowed out concentrically into neatly demarcated zones of land use. The swift, unplanned, exploitative nature of expansion caused industrial, commercial, and high- and low-class residential areas to jostle and interpenetrate unexpectedly. The following shows how a boarding-house or small industry might intrude among exclusive residences:

CHÁCARA

Announcing for sale or rent the picturesque chácara Helvétia, located in Campos Elíseos Paulistano, in direct reach of four well-used streets and facing on Rua de Santa Ifigênia with streetcars at the door; has a spacious residence for a large family, or can serve as a hotel, health home, or school, or for any industrial establishment; large yard planted with European and native trees, garden, and lawn. Piped water from Cantareira.

(*Correio Paulistano*, March 30, 1886.)

A report to the state government in 1891 described the city's turbulent growth with certain apprehension: "Although founded over 330 years ago, São Paulo is a new city, whose general appearance is now marked by constant renovation of old buildings, which vanish rapidly, and by the numerous structures that make up the new districts.

"Two-thirds of the present city, certainly, is of very recent date.

"Looked at as a whole, São Paulo is a modern city with all the defects and advantages inherent in cities that develop very swiftly. Discrepancies in buildings and street-planning, very appreciable differences in level, irregularity of constructions that are always

---

2. Much of the high-lying, upper-class area had reddish, clayey soil that drained poorly. According to the season its unpaved roads were either quagmires or dustbins. The sandier soil of the proletariat belt, however, offered no compensation because the high water table subjected it to flooding.

erected without preconceived plan, large inhabited areas lacking indispensable improvements needed for hygiene, wide spaces either unoccupied or very irregularly utilized, and along with all this a population that has tripled in ten years, much activity, much commerce, extraordinary rise in land and building values, and a naturally pleasant climate." (RELATÓRIO..., 1891, p. 1.)

With this pressure of growth the authorities were ill adapted to cope. Public utilities could not be expanded fast enough. Street cleaning and paving, garbage and sewage disposal, and drainage of the lowlands were all inadequate. Rivulets and vacant lots were becoming pestholes. Iron fences put up to protect trees were being damaged or stolen. And the Câmara was hobbled by not being able to keep up with its tax collections.

The city center — with narrow, irregular streets and huddled on a hill whose arteries of approach sloped as much as 21 per cent — was, even with its later viaducts, almost unsalvageable as a metropolitan nucleus. Worse still, the municipal codes of 1875 and 1886 were largely restatements of time-worn ordinances applying to a small, static town, so that new districts were laid out without guide or control. The 1886 code, for example, was quite explicit that flowerpots should not be kept on window sills, that horses should not gallop through the streets (except cavalry on urgent business), that public masquerades could be held only during Carnival, that taverns frequented by vagabonds must close at 10:00 in the summer and 9:00 in winter, and that precautions against casualty must be taken at bullfights. Yet the only provisions for opening new lands were that streets should be straight and sixteen meters wide and that plazas should be square. This "two-dimensional," gridiron planning produced a city that was disarticulated and unprepared for its increasing flow of traffic.

One of the presidents did in 1886 request "circular boulevards" to permit vehicles en route from one suburb to another to avoid traversing the city center. But these concentric *Ringstrassen*, simply a modified form of checkerboard planning, were not introduced for another fifty years. The city's new cankers could have been removed only by the vision and will of its administrators and by a renascence of communally felt responsibilities among its citizenry. In so rawboned and conglomerate a city this was much to hope for. Certainly the mere enshrinement of ideals in municipal codes was ineffectual. Some of the 1886 ordinances were quite opportune —

such as those requiring proper sewage disposal, cleanliness and ventilation of lower-class multiple dwellings, and isolation of insalubrious factories. Yet a survey of slum conditions in 1893 revealed that disregard for these measures was victimizing a large segment of the proletariat.

The sallies of the municipal and provincial governments into public works were numerous but fragmentary, and betrayed the lack of a bold, coherent vision of the city. Two of the new parks, for instance, though handsomely gardened, were a waste. A park laid out in the Municipal Square (1880) served to congest the traffic that converged upon two churches, a theater, the Câmara, and the Assembly, while the fragrant bowers of the Isle of Loves had to compete with the old shoes, bones, rusty cans, and putrescent bedclothes of an adjoining dump.

This history does not purport to describe city life of 1820 or 1850 as having been idyllic. By most material standards the population was, class for class, doubtless better provided in 1890. Yet in the earlier periods there was a certain correspondence between human behavior, experience, and expectancies on one hand and, on the other, the composition and tacit or avowed obligations of classes and institutions. By 1890 only a portion of the citizenry could — thanks to birth, luck, enterprise, or ingenuity — profess to see such a correspondence. Many others, pricked by the city into new awareness, were perceiving stubborn discontinuity between raw experience and prevailing ideals, whether the ideals of republicanism, Roman Catholicism, positivism, applied science, industrialism, or, loosely for most, "the modern age."

Bibliographical Note

In addition to the travelers' accounts and reminiscences given on page 165, see Afonso d'E. TAUNAY (1946) and RELATÓRIO . . . (1891) for general descriptions of the city and its geography in this period. (The latter, a manuscript in the Municipal Library of São Paulo, is quoted in part in NOVAES [1905].) COMMISSÃO CENTRAL . . . (1888) contains relevant statistics. President João Teodoro Xavier's report of 1873 is reproduced in PAULA (1954). The problems of the city's water supply are treated in R. H. de MELO (1935); BARATA (1875), ARRUDA (1888), and TAPAJÓZ (1894) are useful for demography and municipal sanitation, while GODINHO (1898) and STRAIN (1899) deal with the yellow fever question. CODIGO DE POSTURAS . . . (1875; 1886) contain the municipal ordinances for this period; the 1886 code is summarized in MILLIET (1946a, pp. 159-64). The concentric "circular boulevards" were advocated in RELATÓRIO . . . (1886).

Chapter 16

THE NEW BOUNDARIES OF LIFE

A GUIDING THEME of this history — namely, the emergence of a nucleated urban order within a dispersive agrarian one — has been near the surface throughout the preceding three chapters: in the discussion of positivism, in the description of credit facilities and public utilities, in the account of the geometric subdivision of private and municipal lands, and in the controlling assumption that the cogs of the city were at many levels meshing into those of the industrial world at large. An unequivocal hint is the fact that by the 1870's provincial statutes no longer defined the city as extending along main highways to certain chácaras, but circumscribed it with an artificial line, the "city limits." Fuller use of economic and demographic "statistics," increasingly available during this era, would have given even stronger emphasis to the "triumph of the abstract over the corporeal."

The present chapter will be an attempt to objectify certain "trends" and "processes," to suggest what citification meant by 1890 in terms of citizens' experience, behavior, and hopes. Upper-class architecture, which yielded important clues to the town of 1820, is once again of service.

Through much of the nineteenth century, there was in São Paulo little distinction between the professions of architect and engineer. As long as construction was of taipa, this circumstance did not preclude comeliness; for, as has been noted, the geometric solution imposed by taipa conduced to straightforward functionalism without demanding, indeed without accommodating, the esthetic ingenuities of an architect. By the 1870's, however, taipa was looked upon as drab and rustic; and the long-lingering, romantic rótula met extinction when *Diario de São Paulo* (Dec. 23, 1873) announced

186

that, by order of the Câmara, "the inextensible period for replacing rótulas, casements, lattices, doors, or windows that open outward ends the 31st of the current month." The methods of immigrant builders began to revolutionize the construction business in the 1870's, at the very time when the coffee planters were building more munificent city residences. The first changes were of a technical nature and were rung by artisans;[1] not until the 1880's did the city become worldly-wise enough to import architects. Artisans might change taipa for bricks; they might coat exteriors with stucco (which was more permeable than the bricks it supposedly shielded); they might affix extraneous cornices and friezes. But the structure itself and the social pattern which controlled it were not so quickly altered. JUNIUS (1882, p. 75) remarked that "the buildings in São Paulo, even new ones, do not depart from the style generally followed by all those of our country. Construction has not yet abandoned the heavy, monotonous, almost coarse architecture that the mother country taught us." The building standards of the 1886 municipal code revealed the persistence of an inflexible sobrado mentality: first, second, and third storeys were to be respectively 5, 4.8, and 4.5 meters high; doors were to be 3.2 by 1.3 meters, windows 2.2 by 1.1 meters, front walls 30 centimeters thick.

In 1917 the architect Ricardo SEVERO (1917, pp. 415-17), who himself popularized an uninspired neocolonial style, recalled the Italian stuccoers' abuse of "sculptured ornament applied to completely smooth façades without discretion, architectural composition, or minimal esthetic sense.... The thread of tradition was wholly lost in that eclectic labyrinth of foreign influences....Heed was no longer paid to the physical milieu, to the general topography, and to particular landscapes, or to the social scene with its uses and customs, its habits of family and collective life. The structural forms dictated by the materials of the country were not forthrightly adopted."

In the lást three sentences quoted, Severo refers to the more basic architectural changes in upper-class residences that occurred

1. Italian techniques came to prevail in São Paulo and were quite distinct from those of Portuguese masons, which set the mold in Rio de Janeiro, along the littoral, and elsewhere. The Italians, for example, preferred brick foundations to stone and used nails rather than screws in carpentry, which had the effect of changing the quality of certain woods.

shortly before the advent of the republic. Swiss chalets and luxurious palacetes appeared to attest the accrued coffee wealth and more frequent sojourns in Europe. In 1887 Lenita, the sensual heroine of Julio RIBEIRO's (1946, p. 69) novel *A carne (Flesh)*, imagines to herself buying "an elegant, graceful palacete with oriental filigree that would surpass and leave far behind those barracks of brick, those impossible scarecrows looming up: homely, extravagant, fazenda-type, cosmopolitan, without hygiene, without architecture, without taste. I would have it done under the direction of Ramos de Azevedo."

Francisco de Paula Ramos de Azevedo (1851-1928) became the grand vizier of this new architecture. Born in Campinas, he had worked as a young man with the "Paulista" and "Mogiana" railways, then studied engineering in Belgium (1875-1878). He returned to Campinas, worked on the reconstruction of its cathedral, and in 1868 established himself in São Paulo, engaged to build a new provincial treasury. More engineer than architect, more entrepreneur than engineer, Ramos de Azevedo, with his associates, set up a dictatorship over the city's taste that has only recently begun to crumble. His "style" was pinchbeck, derivative, and best described as promiscuous eclecticism with leanings toward the Renaissance. In scores of palacetes and public buildings, São Paulo still bears his stamp.

To understand more fully the way of life that the palacete stood for, let us pursue the wishful musings of Ribeiro's Lenita. Her home would be furnished with tables and writing desks bought in Paris by discriminating agents; Cordovan leather, Persian and Gobelin tapestry, Japanese *fukasas;* magnificent oriental chinaware ranged prodigally on shelves and consoles, in glass cases and cupboards of filigreed ironwood; porcelain from Sèvres, Berlin, and Vienna; Japanese bronzes, Venetian mirrors, Bohemian perfume bottles. Cabinets and *videpoches* would bulge with "ancient jewels, with chrysolites and diamonds set in silver, with old relics of gold from Oporto." Her cuisine "would shock tastes used to ground meat and loin of pork" with its smoked herring, caviar, partridge *faisandie,* roast lark, and every wine that was expensive and exotic.

With this heterogeneous and ostentatious ménage, the young lady's activities were to be quite in keeping. "I would have . . . a matchless Parisian *huit-ressorts* drawn by enormous, spirited, pureblooded steeds of dark color and the finest hair.

"I would be noted for the most elegant, daring, and even scandalous toilettes. "I would travel through all of Europe, pass a summer in St. Petersburg, a winter in Nice; I would ascend Jungfrau, gamble in Monte Carlo."[2] Though they must be taken as the daydreams of a self-centered nymphomaniac, these desires do not excessively misrepresent the prevailing temper of materialism and conspicuous consumption. The novel itself, finished in 1888, is in fact a sign of the times, being a Zolaesque, social-Darwinian jeremiad lacking art or compassion.

In 1887 the Portuguese critic Ramalho ORTIGÃO (1931) observed in a letter to Eduardo Prado that metropolitan Brazil was without taste and etiquette. The "enormous calamity" of "Brazilian civilization" was that Dom Pedro II's temperament was "absolutely unesthetic, fundamentally anti-artistic, rebellious to every notion of good taste.... The only serious work of his life consisted in making of himself a sage, and in that he failed....By his example he damaged as much as he could the art of conversing, of dressing, of receiving, of dining, of planning a menu, of leading a cotillion, of riding a horse, of furnishing a salon, of building a house, of writing a book." Society's reaction to the emperor's "dissolving action" was "singular": "The leading Brazilian men can compete with those from anywhere. The second-rate ones are perhaps at an excessive distance from the first. Or, ... there are no seconds. The first are immediately followed by the ninth- or tenth-rate. The mean is weak. The same happens with the ladies."[3]

Ortigão went on to praise the salon of his correspondent's mother (mother also of Antônio and Martinico Prado). Dona Veridiana had by now moved to São Paulo, where her house was a gathering place for such intellectuals as Luís Pereira Barreto, the ethnologist Teodoro Sampáio, the American geologist Orville Derby, the Swedish scientist Alberto Löfgren, as well as Eduardo Prado him-

2. A Provincia de São Paulo (June 5, 1875) advertised a Hotel Brasileiro in Paris catering especially to Brazilian travelers. On May 1, 1892, a round-the-world cruise for a hundred persons, which would take in the Chicago Exposition, was announced in O Estado de São Paulo.

3. Pedro's first visit to São Paulo had been in 1846. Three subsequent trips — 1876, 1878, and 1886 — helped further to bring the city into the social sphere of the court. Pedro was no less adroit socially and intellectually than most rulers of Victorian Europe; but he had traditions to create, while they had them, ready made, to draw upon.

self, an impassioned litterateur. Of Dona Veridiana, Ortigão remarked: "What expertness in the art of being pleasing!...What
a quantity of precise and just ideas casually dropped in the most
simple and unceremonious conversation! What...perfect good
taste in the choice of furniture and the choice of words!" Such
islands of refinement as Dona Veridiana's salon merely added to
the heterogeneity of high-bourgeois culture. So also did staunch
patriarchal survivals — for even in modern days some sons still kiss
their parents' hands and use with them the formal form of address.

The rail connection with Rio de Janeiro made it easier to
import foreign dramatic and operatic companies to entertain the
upper and middle classes.[4] This was as overpowering to student
theater as the big daily newspapers were to student journalism. The
old Opera House was torn down in 1870. But across the boards of
the São José Theater (reopened in 1876 after alterations) and the
"Provisional" Theater (built in 1873 during repairs to the São José)
paraded the most famed singers and actors of Italy, France, Spain,
and Portugal. The bombastic tragedian Ernesto Rossi was wildly
acclaimed (1879) by students and the Italian colony, and soon the
former, now become mere mimics, were soulfully declaiming:
"*Essere o non essere. Ecco il problema!*" Sarah Bernhardt made
two visits in the 1880's. Delirious students escorted her to her
hotel, spreading their topcoats for her to tread upon and shouting
"*Pisez sur nous, Madame!*" (it being maliciously rumored that the
French verb was heard with an unvoiced "s").

When Brazil produced a canvas painter of talent, he was spirited
off to a French atelier where he learned to paint in an academic,
preimpressionist style. Though the court was the most dependable
source of patronage, a few paulista artists — such as Benedito Calixto
de Jesus (1853-1927) and Oscar Pereira da Silva (1867-1939) —
remained in São Paulo painting canvases and decorating churches
and new public buildings. Calixto spent only a year abroad, where
he cautiously withdrew from an impressionist studio. He had some
of the ingenuousness but less of the vigor and originality of the
earlier Dutra and Father Jesuíno.

Largely because of its foreign colonies, the city had a musical
efflorescence. There were increasing numbers of voice and instrumental teachers. Chamber and symphony music was performed

4. One may sketchily estimate the city's class distribution in 1890 to have
been 5 per cent upper, 25 per cent middle, and 70 per cent lower.

by such groups as the Haydn, Mozart, and Mendelssohn clubs, the Paulista Quartet, and the 24th of May Musical Club — with Italian virtuosi predominating. Alexandre Levi (1864-1892), who was born and died in the city, was a composer of certain significance; despite his penchant for Schumann and Chopin, some of his works were genuinely Brazilian in theme and conception. Otherwise there was little creativity. Brazil's outstanding nineteenth-century composer, Antônio de Carlos Gomes (1839-1896), was born in Campinas and received encouragement from São Paulo's law students (for whom he wrote an Academic Hymn) to embark for Rio de Janeiro in 1860. A decade later he made his great triumph in Milan with his famous opera *Il Guarany,* and his years of fulfillment were not associated with São Paulo.

For the elite (though not perhaps for the middle- and lower-class Italian colony), to patronize musicales was an emblem of social distinction or, at best, a sentimental indulgence. This is confirmed by an account in *Revista Literaria* (May 5, 1887) of dilettantes of the Haydn Club attending a concert "with plenty of strong coffee in their stomachs to resist the temptations of Morpheus [*sic!*], God of classical music.

"I went to a concert in the said Club and noticed that there is not a single person there who is not deeply versed in *dissonant harmonies;* all of them perform a *duetto* with the players, for if the latter play some Hungarian hodgepodge in B, the former snore in falsetto voice in G."

Decades later, in a speech to graduates of São Paulo's Conservatory, the musicologist Mário de ANDRADE (1936) pointed out the artificiality of paulista salon music. For fourteen years he had asked his students the purpose of their studies; always they replied voice or instrumental training, never *music.* "If students come to the Conservatory with the sole purpose of studying piano or violin, if the ideal of those young people consists merely in the confusion and vanity that sacrifice the noble values of art to the hope of public applause, is it the fault of that fragile youth? It isn't. You are not the guilty ones, but your parents, your teachers, and the public authorities. Your error stems from a far more shameful and profound lack of culture, whose basis is the immoral confusion between music and virtuosity." The disadvantage, he continued, of São Paulo's orchestras and string quartets is that "in a deficient milieu like ours, where the lack of artists endowed with esthetic appreciation is desperate and where most of those who presume themselves cultured are mere pedants cashing in on the cult of self-worship,... such pedants demand immediate, limitless perfection, while the unlearned demand noise, rowdy music, no art, and a steady flow of sounds."

The growing middle class, whose appearance had made São Paulo atypical of the Latin American social pattern, of course found certain of these cultural pursuits open to them; and for less refined diversion they could attend races after 1876 in the new hippodrome or relax in the Stadt Bern, a beer garden with arbors, games, and an orchestra opened in 1877. There were circuses, bull-fights,[5] and an occasional public spectacle such as the inauguration of a new railway, the balloon ascent (1876) of a Mexican aeronaut, or the visit (1883) of Prince Henry of Prussia, brother of Wilhelm II. The first all-day picnic train trip occurred in about 1880, and shortly thereafter the French colony held its first kermess in the Public Garden. In 1877 the Normanton brothers from England opened a roller-skating rink which, along with a new form of exercise for the general public, offered "scenic skating" and variety acts. Their advertisement in *Diario de São Paulo* (July 5, 1877) appealed to consciousness of class and of the body beautiful:

> Skating is the most healthy, popular, and *fashionable* [word in English] exercise of the times; it guarantees one's necessary activity, invigorates the lungs, and gives the whole body a highly desirable grace and flexibility....
> "FIGARO" SAYS:
> Le patinage avec patins à roulettes, qui est le divertissement favori de la haute societé en Angleterre et en Amerique est à present un sport parisien.
> Let us make it
> NOW
> A PAULISTA SPORT.

5. *Diario de São Paulo* (Nov. 20, 1877) described one *corrida* as follows: "Only one real bull came out, which was the last. And as he was a bit more lively than the old nags that had appeared — and perhaps out of respect to the public — he did a little more, though even so the fight as it was handled was not worth the trouble.

"The horseman was a total fiasco, managing even to fall out of the saddle, which came undone from the fiery steed that he rode with such éclat." SAINT-HILAIRE (1851, I, p. 250) had long since observed the placidity of paulista bullfights.

An old-timer has recollected a year (1888) spent in a boarding-house as a law student. He not only gives a vignette of middle-class life, but shows how the student was passing from the independent "republic" to the anonymous rooming house. The place in question was on the second storey of a once elegant sobrado, whose ground floor belonged to a French hairdresser. (The "deterioration" of patriarchal sobrados in the city center was quite usual in that era.) "The boardinghouse gave the impression of Singapore, so diverse were its guests with their many languages. São Paulo's customs at that time were still very patriarchal: lunch from 9 to 10, dinner from 3 to 4. Afterward people went out replenished, toothpick in mouth — those well-off going to savor a delicious ice cream at 200 réis in Nagel's Sweetshop, the others as usual resigning themselves to decrying life's adversity, a topic of great and special predilection." The boarders were law- and normal-school students, lawyers, book-keepers, merchants, and public functionaries. "We ate at a 'round table,' always full and having two or three sittings." The guests, with their flow of chatter about everything that was or was soon to be in fashion, constituted a kind of "vocal newspaper." (PRIMEIRO . . . , 1946, p. 197.)

Those of the middle class whom São Paulo's economic opportunities did not favor might well, like these boarders, "decry life's adversity." According to *Diario Popular* (March 12, 1892) a small family could no longer live on 500$ a month, for it had to reckon with "the excessive price of primary foods, the dearness of clothing, the near-impossibility of paying for domestic service, the school, the doctor, the store, the fuel scarcity, and above all the immense complex of necessities that we create and can no longer go unsatisfied — all that combined with lack of foresight, absence of cooperative consumers' societies, disasters from the bourse's fluctuation in the dizzy period of expanding credit."[6]

The lower class, however, was more nakedly at grips with the problem of brute survival. For those of its members not housed by the traditional hovel of wattle-and-daub, the standard dwelling was the *cortiço* (literally, beehive), a multiple-family unit that settled the now valuable city land more densely. A typical cortiço, as revealed by the municipal survey of 1893, occupied the interior of a block, generally dank, low-lying land. It was formed by a series

6. The Câmara had long since relinquished control over the prices of staples which, at the time of independence, it was still effectively wielding.

of small apartments around a cramped patio, to which a long, narrow hallway gave access from the street. The average apartment housed four to six people, though its dimensions rarely exceeded ten by eighteen feet, with a height of about ten. Furniture, such as it was, took up a third of the space. Overcrowded sleeping cubicles lacked light and ventilation and were "hermetically sealed." Except in the rooms of northern Europeans, floors were so crusted with mud that the planking was not visible, and the dampness of the soil on which they rested caused the cheap, plain paper on the walls to peel. Interiors were blackened by flies and by the smoke of the stoves, which poorly constructed and maintained chimneys refused properly to vent. "The walls, bearing pictures in bad taste, have their plaster pierced by an infinity of nails and screws from which hang various objects of domestic use and working clothes. The furniture, unattractively arranged, is covered with piles of clothing to be washed." The main patio provided for its surrounding apartments a recalcitrant water tap, a laundry tub, and a crudely installed latrine. Paving and gutters were often lacking. Variations on the cortiço were: a single building (sometimes a converted sobrado) excessively subdivided; the dormitory-type *hotel-cortiço;* and improvised shacks at the rear of stables and warehouses. All were characterized by lack of air, light, space, cleanliness, drainage, and solid construction. (RELATÓRIO..., 1894.)

Cortiço dwellers would scarcely have been found sipping beer in the garden of the Stadt Bern. In 1883, however, octagonal kiosks, sporting streamers and garish posters, began to appear in parks and plazas and near the stations, selling coffee, sweets, and cheap alcoholic drinks. Just as the fountains had once attracted slaves, farm hands, and muleteers, the kiosks were a rendezvous for laborers, vagrants, soldiers, and lower-class women who effused a rich bouquet of firewater, body stench, and iodoform.

Such, then, in a few highlights, is the class spectrum of 1890. In terms of material well-being, its extremes were at a greater remove than in earlier years. Yet metropolitan complexity and anonymity had eroded many determinants of class status. Hence the disparity between palacete and cortiço took on an irony, and engendered a malaise[7] alien to the days of sobrados and wattle-and-daub huts.

7. National and racial tensions were one symptom of this malaise. In 1887 there were melees involving Italians and Negroes; next year occurred the most violent fracas of the feud between students and Portuguese tradesmen.

For a visitor to describe São Paulo fully and penetratingly was now more difficult than it had been for earlier travelers. The unperceived flow of its arteries of transport; the movements of currency and capital; the crosscurrents of ideas and attitudes — all conspired to make apprehension of the city a superficial and fragmentary, or abstract and statistical endeavor. Impressions of the roving observer, however, are not to be overlooked, particularly those made in comparison with an earlier period. "Junius," who left the academy in 1852, wrote a valuable record of his first return to São Paulo, thirty years later.

JUNIUS (1882) was struck by the quick, noisy tempo of life. Earlier, upper-class families had entered the streets only for occasional visits, always escorted by the paterfamilias; casual strolls for health or recreation were unknown. Cafés did not exist, and if a youth went to a restaurant for beer or even "water with sugar," he was held as extravagant and perhaps immoral. So few were the carriages that citizens hurried to their windows to identify the owner of any that passed. But now there were countless pedestrians, including unescorted ladies, attracted by fashion shops, sweetshops, cafés, restaurants, and concerts in the park. The once silent streets reverberated with the constant passage of streetcars and large, heavily laden wagons.

Junius was astounded by the profusion of artisans and shops and the luxury of their wares; the availability of toys and musical instruments, foreign wines and tobacco; the ease with which man or woman could acquire a Parisian wardrobe and grooming.[8] In Garraux' bookstore the widest line of luxuries and ornaments was on sale, along with a more up-to-date stock of foreign books and newspapers than could be found even in Rio de Janeiro.

To prepare a banquet in 1852, one started days ahead, arranging with a separate victualer for each of the several items (roasts, the tongues from Rio Grande, sweets, and other delicacies) and sending to Santos or Rio for wine or beer. Now, in 1882, there were restaurants and three big hotels where at 7:00 p.m. one could order a large banquet for the same night. The Grande Hotel — with its gas

8. Men's dress had become less formal. The frock coat — once worn by the academy's beadles and porters as well as by students and professors, and de rigueur even for horseback riding — was in 1882 not so much in evidence. For women the fashion of the 1880's was the bustle, which had superseded the long train of the 1870's and the hoopskirts of the previous period.

lamps, handsome candelabra, flowers, and large mirrors — found no equal in Brazil and was reminiscent of Europe's best.

Junius was impressed by the new suburbs, railways, public buildings, and the illumination and activity of streets after dark. Upper-class gardens, which once had grown only roses, scabiosa, pinks, dahlias, everlasting, and jasmin, now blossomed, thanks to European florists, with myosotis, azaleas, fuchsias, cacti, begonias, and many more. Most owners, however, could not name the new blooms; like other acquisitions, they had taken physical but not cultural root.

The foreign colony, once limited (except for the numerous Portuguese) to a handful of Englishmen, Frenchmen, and Germans known personally to everyone, had mushroomed and was numerically dominated by Italians. When asked which colony was best assimilated, Junius replied, "All of them, except the English." These subjects were dominated by Palmerston's notion "that the Englishman is the *civis Romanus* the world over.... In accord with this maxim is the belief of certain Englishmen who, I heard tell, understand that Companies formed by their compatriots constitute in any country *a State within a State.*

"If this be true, these persons could well be called *visionaries,* who assume that in every land they are in contact with Zulus."

Junius lamented, however, that this civilization of which Englishmen were self-styled apostles had been won at the cost of communal trust and security. "Formerly we could sleep in any house leaving the doors and windows open all night; nothing would be missing next day when we awoke." But now thieves were everywhere and, as policing was inadequate, often robbed in broad daylight; recently two unsolved murders had been committed.[9]

This hint of demoralization was confirmed a decade later in an article by a frequent visitor to the city who had always been amazed by its progress and fine homes but who went away this time in "deep sorrow." "São Paulo advances toward moral perdition. Anywhere that he turns the visitor finds vice increasing so unrestrainedly that the intervention of public authorities is essential to impede it.

9. *A Provincia de São Paulo* (Nov. 17, 1878) carried an appeal from "a victim of the thieves" urging exposure of the marauders and "pretty boys" whose thievery was becoming insupportable. "It would be well to recognize that many a youth who passes as honest in this city is part of the gang of robbers that now infests the whole province."

"In streets where formerly one saw only honest families and houses inhabited by persons with occupations today appear impossible faces that show — despite being covered with cold cream and *crème simon* and coated with powder — the ineffaceable furrows left by debauchery and sleepless nights spent in licentious immorality drinking goblets of simulated champagne among the cheap spangles of false love!" (*Diario Popular,* Oct. 27, 1893.)

The prostitutes of Saint-Hilaire's day had walked slowly in the shadows, never contumelious and never accosting (in fact, scarcely looking at) passers-by. They, and even tarts of the 1850's whom the law students sentimentally apostrophized, had a delimited function in society. They formed an "estate." The touchstone of commercial profiteering, however, subverted the bounds of that as of so many estates. *O Estado de São Paulo* (June 22, 1892) warned that "detestable exploiters of human misery" threatened to transform the "peaceful and moralized city" of ten years previous into a "vast brothel." São Paulo had become "full of those false hotels and rooming-houses maintained by more or less disguised pandering."

Once again we are confronted, not with the iniquity of the modern city, but with its lack of an indwelling system of norms to which behavior may be referred for reconciliation (even if immoral) or for censure. In many realms of city life we have traced the effects of this release from tradition. We have seen that cultural pursuits became more diverse, but that cultural expression became meager and unrelated to an as yet unapprehended life. We have seen that the city, by projecting its shadow across the hinterland, bade fair to derange the ecologic anatomy of a vast agricultural realm. We have seen how an imported rhetoric identified progress with material activity and accrual, and degeneracy with the traditions of an agrarian community. In short, we have witnessed a transition from a regional society having certain universal attunements to a cosmopolitan society having quite provincial ones.

A sense of loss did not altogether escape men of the time. Referring to a departure by railway from São Paulo, Lucio de MENDONÇA (1901, p. 309) wrote in 1877: "Soon the Locomotive, patron of progress and hence severe and inhuman for little egoistic tendernesses, would brusquely snatch us from there. With the railroads even these farewells had lost the old poetry. Formerly, the horseman who drew away from a beloved place went at a slow, contemplative pace, turning back his glance, and when he reached the rise whence the town could for the last time be discerned, he stopped and deeply suffused his soul with the sweet image that was to vanish at the first turn of the road. Today, emotion is fleeting and rapid, like all those of agitated and hasty modern living. The resting-place is there always, where much of our soul remains a prisoner to the old memories that do not die; it is the supreme moment; all will shrivel, as in a theatrical perspective, to a mere mechanical toy."

Luis MARTINS (1953) has written a book to suggest that the citified, university-trained generation which brought on the republican coup of 1889 was "parricidal." It subverted the rural patriarchy on a national and on a private, domestic scale; it dispensed with the long-standing symbol of paternal authority, Pedro II. In the later life and writings of this generation Martins detects a "complex of remorse" for its filial betrayal, a loss of faith in the drifting, authorityless society that was so largely of its making.

This remorse was a sequel to the prophetic misgivings of the romanticist poets. It appears generic to a modern urban society in which "logos" — or the quest for principles and for rational calculation of the isolated enterprise — transcends and denies the spirit, or tutelary "demon," of a traditional region. As the metropolis grew in size and complexity, its citizens were increasingly to feel the need to savor their lives more sharply — and in richer totality.

Bibliographical Note

Again, the firsthand accounts and reminiscences listed on page 165 serve as a background. DEBENEDETTI and SALMONI (1953) documents the Italian influence on São Paulo's architecture. J. F. B. da SILVEIRA (1941) gives an uncritical sketch of Ramos de Azevedo. PINHO (1942) describes the contemporary salon and cultural life of São Paulo and other Brazilian cities. The *fin-de-siècle* artistic milieu is treated by L. G. MACHADO (1948) as a prelude to his study of modern trends. CERQUERA (1954) is a history of opera in São Paulo. PIMENTA (1911) sketches the life of the composer Alexandre Levi, while C. P. de REZENDE (1948) describes Carlos Gomes' last year in São Paulo.

A graphic account of lower-class cortiço life is found in RELATÓRIO . . . (1894).

E. C. NOGUEIRA (1954) indicates the reservations with which the Freudian thesis of L. MARTINS (1953) about the "parricidal" generation of 1889 must be accepted.

Part IV—The Modern Age

Chapter 17

THE METROPOLITAN TEMPER

Life here is sad and tedious. You'll get bored, I assure you. . . .
Perhaps it would be better to go to Rio or São Paulo. For there
are the great commercial centers where you'd easily find a job.
The farm is a delusion; once you could earn a little money but now
business is no good.
             — J. P. da GRAÇA ARANHA, *Canaã* (1902).
Of the persons living on 17 farms visited . . . few have ever been
to São Paulo. One woman, 38 years old, has been there twice in
her lifetime. "São Paulo is too crowded," she says. "You get dizzy
from it all. Us folks from the country like it quieter."
             — DONALD PIERSON, *Cruz das Almas — A Brazilian*
             Village (1951).

*A*T THE THRESHOLD of the twentieth century we come
upon a city in flux, a city that is merely beginning to define itself, a city whose past is no longer sensed and
whose present and immediate future acquire special urgency —
a city that presses implacable questions. For great philosopher-
pessimists the city is the crucible of the age. In it the abstract and
symbolic become more immediate than what is seen and touched.
Architecture becomes geometry. Pattern becomes flux. Form becomes function. Sequence becomes simultaneity. Gods become
forces. Communion becomes communication. The estates of society become the masses. And one asks what powers of redemption, if any, the modern city contains.

Latin America has for two reasons posed the dilemma of urbanization with dramatic intensity. First, its recent city growth
has been of a compressed, haphazard nature, evoked by twentieth-
century international disorders and by the sudden mobilization of
untapped economic potentials. Second, in contrast to what has
occurred in certain European countries, there has been little op-

200

portunity to mediate the disparity between conditions of city life and those of the agrarian, quasi-feudal interior; so far no rural-urban equilibrium has been established.

It is these circumstances which are partly responsible for the speculation about antinomies between the isolated, closely knit "folk" society and secularized, individualized urban society which so frequently occurs in the writings of social scientists who have done field work in Latin America. If we compare the agrarian São Paulo of 1820 with the burgeoning metropolis of 1890, such antinomies seem largely confirmed. We detect linear progression toward what the sociologist loosely calls "disintegration." More-over, a glance at the twentieth-century city suggests that the trend has not reversed or abated, that the climate of life is permeated more than ever before by amoral secularism and opportunism; by transitory, partial, individualized relationships; by the neurotic urge for power, prestige, and possession. We find in abundance the hallmarks of that normless ethos described by the French sociologist Émile Durkheim as "anomy."

A closer look at the modern age, however, reveals clues that new modes of understanding, of planning, and of purposive asso-ciation are becoming available. Sometimes this is reflected in the act of vision achieved by poet, musician, or painter. Sometimes it is concretized on paper or in materials by an architect or city planner. Sometimes it is asserted more broadly and anonymously in the atti-tude or policy of a certain group, bureaucracy, or enterprise. The Spenglerian thesis that urban life is ineluctably decadent may have a cosmic verity. But its truth is transcendent and philosophical, not practical and sociological. Within any community, whether euphoric or "decadent" in the philosopher's sight, there exist potentialities for fellowship and, defining it broadly, for spiritual life. It may be that the metropolis is, by its temper, more conducive than the hamlet to thin, dispersive experience. Certainly it affords its inhabitants no fixed and unitary scheme of values. But it would be fatuous to deplore city life as inherently impoverished and to dwell on the truncation or ossification of all-providing preindustrial institutions without exploring what new means and symbols of human asso-ciation have come into reach. It is these latent or emerging possi-bilities which will be emphasized in the rest of this study.

With the passage of urban Brazil into the republican era the social historian Gilberto FREYRE (1944) associates a denial of

Portuguese-African heritage – of the customs, attitudes, culture, and humanitarian tradition of the colonial and imperial epochs. "The bad Portuguese habits of picking the teeth in public and of spitting noisily on the floor" were outlawed by a new Frenchified elite. Family heirlooms of silver and rosewood were auctioned off to foreigners and replaced by more modish acquisitions from Europe. Classics and humanities yielded to practical, technical disciplines. Children were baptized Newton, Jefferson, and Edison instead of Ulysses, Demosthenes, and Cicero. Harsh English words, such as "trust," "funding-loan," and "deficit," were injected into vocabulary. One spoke of the abstract complexities of coffee valorization, but no longer of the "valorization of the Brazilian man – of the man and of the people."

As Freyre intimates, the invasion of cultural influences often reflected merely an uncritical servility of *nouveaux riches* to foreign norms. When Georges CLEMENCEAU (1911, p. 268) visited São Paulo he found it "so curiously French in some of its aspects and customs" that for a week he "had not once the feeling of being abroad." Another Frenchman, GAFFRÉ (1912, p. 200), came to know one of the city's "*meilleures familles*" in 1911. They spoke French like Parisians and "day by day" followed the events, authors, magazines, and ideas of France; "one of the charming girls shows me the *Mode Illustrée*, which carries thither its practical advice and its kitchen recipes." In a deferential address to a Parisian audience a paulista of the period asserted that his compatriots were dependent for inspiration and guidance upon French museums and monuments, French libraries and theaters, French penal and police systems. "We go to knock at the door of your painters' and sculptors' ateliers, asking that they come to embellish our buildings and public squares, bringing us the magic colors of their palette, the seductive purity of the lines that take form under their chisel." (EGAS, 1910, pp. 8-12.)

It is hard to associate the dynamism of the times, however, with importations of so formal a nature. For in São Paulo, as in the whole Western World, the early years of this century were marked by childlike exuberance, by naive conceptions of "happiness" and cultural refinement, and by the naive belief that these commodities were inevitable rewards for pecuniary success in a world of increasingly numerous and remunerative opportunities. The most vital foreign influences were not those in which the city passively acquiesced but those which answered its new rhythms of life. Sports such as rowing, cycling, trapshooting, fencing, and the eminently popular "foot-ball" (that is, soccer, later to take its place alongside lottery-betting as the national sport) all came into their own at the turn of the century with their respective clubs or "leagues."[1] Another harbinger of the modern age was announced as early as 1896 in *O Estado de São Paulo*:

> Animated Photography
> Cinematography with the improvements of the great Edison, life with all its motion, the latest novelty which dazzles and enchants eyes amazed at such a discovery, is now showing on Rua da Boa Vista with a success that was easy to predict.
> He who sees it once does not fail to return....
>
> *Dixit.*

Movies objectified the quick flow of life, the surrender of established purpose and structure to the flux of immediate detail. As São Paulo's "futurists" were later to proclaim: "Pearl White is preferable to Sarah Bernhardt. Sarah is tragedy, sentimental and technical romanticism. Pearl is reason, instruction, sport, speed, joy, life. Sarah Barnhardt = 19th century. Pearl White = 20th century. The cinematograph is the most representative artistic creation of our era." (*Klaxon*, May 15, 1922.) The cinema was, however, more urgently a moral than an artistic catalyst. On a single day in 1917, for instance, newspapers advertised: *Chastity* (a film "posed in the nude"), *The Naked Virgin, Ruth the Innocent, The Audacious Woman, The Merchants of Love, The Sinful Woman.* Perhaps the most impudent notice had appeared a decade earlier, in 1906:

> Sant'Anna Theater
> . . . . . .
> Today the talking cinematograph will once again show the interesting scenes of the *Life, Passion, and Death of Christ*, along with new comic acts and popular songs.

Reminiscences of this period that have appeared in recent years

---

1. *O Estado de São Paulo* (May 31, 1902) used all the following English words in a single account of a soccer game: foot-ball, match, teams, referee, forwards, passes, goal, schoot [*sic*], goal-keeps, half-backs, yards, kick, full-backs, half-time, charge.

describe, despite their nostalgic sentimentalizing, a milieu of "folk-loric" vigor. Night life — in the cafés, cinemas, streets, and new cabarets — was more sharp and lively than in the luxurious movie palaces, chic bistros, and slovenly taxi dances of today. Immoralities were knife thrusts into the puffy body of decency and tradition, and had not yet subsided into the weary cynicism of amorality.

An almanac of 1913 listed thirty shops in the city that sold or repaired gramophones and forty-six cinemas and "diversions," among them such names as Bijou, High Life, Iris, The Skating Palace, and the Edison and Radium cinemas. Foremost of the channels for this new cultural invasion was the *café chantant,* a replica of the Parisian cabaret, with wrestlers, acrobats, Arab tumblers, and, most important, heavily rouged and painted cocottes from many lands. According to *Vida Paulista* (Sept. 12-13, 1903), the spicy, rollicking cabaret Politeama attracted upper crust and bohemians alike with its "singers of every sex, type, and manner" and "put an end to the ephemeral life of the national theater, condemning true Art to complete ostracism." It was the Politeama which presented São Paulo's first nude dancer. Sar Farah, an Egyptian girl, would appear on the stage, render a song, and suddenly, before the spectator's ecstatic gaze, open her elegant velvet cape like Phryne before the Areopagus.

Mlle Sar Farah's was something of an existentialist "gratuitous act." For she performed at about the time when a certain traffic inspector — in conformance with an ordinance which banned "immoral verses and sketches" on public walls — was declaring (1902) that "the prohibition of signs with figures representing the midwives' profession is a necessary measure, for it is patent that many of those signs offend public morality with the naked figures of newborn babies." (SANT'ANNA, 1937-1944, III, p. 264.) Misoneists and custodians of ancient morality, however, found their prohibitions powerless. A later journal, *A Garôa* (Sept. 30, 1921), taunted that the modern flirt was, like the automobile, a necessary import. "Customs barriers went down for automobiles; there was no protectionism possible. The 'flirt' didn't have to force a lowering of excessive imposts but entered like the silks of the famous couturières, disembarking on the beach...at night, without the inspector's catching on to the trick."

A commanding figure in this ambience of shattered mores and conspicuous prodigality was the "Colonel." The Colonel was a political boss from the interior who — in his golden age of 1890 to 1920 — manipulated local elections, controlled the sale of lands, exerted pressure to determine railway routes that would favor his bailiwick, and served loyal constituents as a father bountiful. One finds it hard to judge him severely. Just as the bandeirante once left civilization behind to explore and dominate the backlands, so the Colonel, representing rural interests, appears from the coffee fields to become the lavish, self-assured master of the metropolis. This personage was overawing to Mme Pommery, the little cocotte of Spanish-gypsy and Polish-Jew provenience in a novel by Hilario Tacito (1919, pp. 61-62, 83-85):

"'What did you say? The gentleman is a Colonel? But he didn't have the uniform....'

"'That doesn't matter.... Here when a customer isn't a doctor he's a colonel....'

"'Ah!...And the Colonel pays for everything?...What's his name?'

"'Colonel Pacheco Isidro; of course he pays for everything. He has five fazendas! Deputy. Political boss of Butucuara. Party director....'

"'But, tell me, are there many colonels here, many doctor-colonels?'

"'Oh, there are!...It's like this!!' And she brought her ten fingers together. 'A harvest!'

"'My God, caramba!...What a lovely land!'"

Mme Pommery shortly became informed as to the care and handling of colonels. "The 'financial capacity of the Colonel' was the cornerstone, axis, and soul of her whole system. One had to take his measure exactly and exploit him exhaustively later....The permissiveness and abnegation of the colonels was a point more than proven. It sufficed to lure them to proper surroundings — where temptations of the flesh and the bottle would be suitably combined with pageants of spectacular luxury — to see them divest themselves of everything, even their shirts....The use of champagne at thirty milréis a bottle must be considered compulsory. And professional services must be rendered to no one for less than a hundred milréis. The colonels should in short order be instructed and convinced that to pay less is ignoble, and not to drink champagne a turpitude....

"The city was becoming transformed in plain sight; it was

growing, becoming beautiful. The Municipal Theater would soon be inaugurated. Coffee, in the doldrums for so long, was feeling the first stimuli of valorization. From all points fazendeiros were crowding to the capital, all opulent and avid, all of them, to break the long abstinence of the bad days just past in a newborn life of pleasure and abundance.

"New customs and new institutions had, then, necessarily to appear in all spheres of society."

In the first decades of this century, it is clear, city life took on a pungent style, which was to hypnotize the *avant-garde* writers and artists of "Modern Art Week" in 1922. Beneath the garish boom-town exterior, however, problems and threats were beginning slowly to be discerned. The state's Department of Labor, which two years later was forced into urgent measures to meet São Paulo's first industrial crisis, warned in 1912: "São Paulo should remember that no social problem is wholly foreign to it and that the apparent simplicity of its life does not absolve it from meditating questions which disturb peoples further advanced." São Paulo was "a focus, in short, ready to discharge, soon perhaps, an electric current in all spheres of activity." (*Boletim do Departamento Estadual do Trabalho*, Nos. 1-2, p. 9.) It can be seen, then, that the mores of prodigality exemplified by the "Colonel" were serving to consume "electric currents" of the metropolis which had not been guided into functionally relevant patterns.

Under the empire, Caio PRADO JUNIOR (1945, p. 220) has observed, the businessman exclusively dedicated to the calculus of pecuniary gain was only a "figure of secondary importance, ill esteemed and carrying little weight." In 1890 the republic swept him "into a central and commanding position." Immediately abusing his greater freedom and powers, the businessman precipitated a financial crisis that ominously reflected the propulsive forces of the times.

In São Paulo, financial activity became inordinately intense. VEIGA FILHO (1896, pp. 122-25) was amazed that business corporations had "in this market alone a nominal capital totaling about a million contos." The crash came in 1892, and with it an "acute state of crisis." The price of land in one city district fell from 4$000 to $500 per square meter. Shares of the "Paulista" railway dropped from 850$ to 260$. Two hundred cars were withdrawn from daily service on the São Paulo Railway. The Bourse and many factories were closed. Sixteen banks and forty-seven companies were liquidated. Most threatening of all perhaps, as a harbinger of sociopolitical malaise, the "popular class had to...make withdrawals from its accumulated capital."

Speculatory fever was responsible also for the coffee crisis of the early twentieth century. Between 1890 and 1900, forty-one new municipalities were created in the state, most of them on the coffee frontier, while the number of coffee trees rose from 220 to 520 million. It was, however, the urban intermediary, not the planter, who largely profited. He bought at low prices during the four-month harvest season and sold during less competitive months; as exporter, it was he who absorbed the windfall accruing during the 1890's from the depreciation of Brazilian currency. By the end of the decade, however, the world coffee market was saturated, and the price tumbled to its 1880 level. In 1905, eleven million sacks, or 70 per cent of yearly world consumption, existed as surplus, since the five-year maturation period for new plantings had prevented swift curtailment of production. Intermediaries, though not wholly unscathed, continued to benefit from currency inflation; but planters — staggered by the price fall and plunged into debt by the maintenance of overexpanded enterprises, salaried labor, and their more lavish style of life — lost all security.

The correctives devised to answer the crisis were "valorization" (strategic purchase and sale of coffee by the government to steady the market) and official restriction of new plantings. Subsequently coffee enjoyed booms during World War I and the mid-1920's. Not until the vast oversupply and collapse of 1929, when coffee was used as fuel for locomotives, did valorization stand clearly forth as characteristic of a central illusion of the urban mind. It is the illusion, long since exposed by Karl Marx, that statistical indices are a more important basis for economic reform than the analysis of modes of production and institutional structure.

The crisis which first jarred the man in the street into a sense of being congenitally victimized by urban institutions was that which followed the outbreak of World War I. This event touched off a violent price rise in São Paulo. The rise was artificial and speculatory since, despite ample stocks of commodities on hand, domestic as well as imported items were affected; moreover, the initial panic was not followed by steady, proportional price increases. Many factories met the crisis by curtailing production to two or three days a week, and thousands of workers, whose functions had been marginal and precarious, were thrown out of employment.

In a series of searching analyses (see *Boletim do Departamento Estadual do Trabalho,* Nos. 12-19), the Department of Labor pointed out the urgent need to "guarantee the industrial wage against those fluctuations, too violent to be natural, which depopulate the fields and bring plethora to the cities — in the incredible incongruity of a barely incipient rural industry alongside an urban industry which already threatens to graft the problem of pauperism into the normal life of the State." The Department indicted "pernicious urbanism" for hypnotizing growing thousands of foreign immigrants and native farm workers with an illusory promise of employment and prosperity. Urban factories were regulated by no adequate social legislation and offered no assurances of job tenure; they were subject to the "deceptions and disasters" of the coffee monoculture and of industrial organization that ineffectively met competition. In good times a worker found ready employment, but he could never "make himself necessary." "He is almost always superfluous, parasitic, tolerated." Without warning "tens of thousands of unemployed may appear where a few days before there seemed to exist only well-being and tranquillity."[2] This indeed is what happened in 1914. To meet the emergency the Department established soup kitchens and, to eliminate top-heavy middlemen's charges, produce markets that reduced the prices of staples by as much as 50 per cent. Three streetcars were commandeered to give free passage to farmers bringing comestibles from the suburbs.

But the root of the problem was the rural situation — and the paradox of undermanned plantations crying out for more laborers. In three months (August to October, 1914) the state government moved 12,000 workers from the capital to the interior; by June, 1916, the number had reached 30,000. From this experience it was clear to the Department that "valorization of the countryside," making small farms and the necessary benefits available to the independent farmer, was a prime condition for "de-urbanization of the capital." Such counsel, however, did not prevail throughout

2. Ironically, the Department itself had declared only two years earlier, in 1912, that the city's textile plants, which then employed nearly 12,000 workers, were in a position to expand facilities for employing 6,000 more.

the bureaucracy. A prefect's report of 1914 naively boasted that: "São Paulo is equipping itself to be a great industrial center, something like Chicago and Manchester combined." The new phenomenon which the uneasy drift and confluence of human beings was forcing to the attention of city administrators was that of the crowd — *la foule.* In 1909 Pierre Denis (1928, p. 112) remarked: "*Saint-Paul est avec Rio le seul point du Brésil où l'on puisse voir une foule.*" One factor contributing to the rootlessness of the lower classes and to the expendability of their services was the passivity of the proletariat. A report on São Paulo's industries in 1901 observed that workers lived under miserable conditions; yet when they protested the wage cuts that were generic to the vagaries of home industry, they were always "obliged by reflection and by circumstances to return to work, resigned to the conditions which pecuniary difficulties forced the industrialist to impose." (Bandeira Junior, 1901, p. xiv.)

The most effective workers' leadership in the first two decades of the century came from the anarchists. They helped to organize strategic strikes, and their *ad hoc* "leagues" for combatting food scarcity, avaricious landlords, high prices, and press censorship occasionally bore fruit. But little progress was made toward the goal which they professed to be primary, namely, imbuing the sense of workers' solidarity. The puritanism of paulista anarchists led them to take a long view of the inevitable "new society"; to value workers' theaters and cooperative vacation communities above agitation for short hours and high wages; and to withhold recognition from compulsory institutions (the state) by eschewing political participation and electioneering. Partly as a result of this policy, syndical groups were by the 1920's still structured weakly along mutualistic lines — organized variously by trades or groups of trades, by city districts, or by single factories — and exercised little power in public life. The anarchist ideal of spontaneous association, reminiscent of São Paulo's earlier years, was not adequately translated to accord with realities of the modern metropolis.

The socialists were more conventional in their tactics and, when they met in São Paulo for the Second Brazilian Socialist Congress (1902), urged foreign workers to become naturalized so that they might vote. The congress pledged itself to work for a long list of material benefits and assurances for labor and, more broadly, to create solidary associations of class-conscious workers and bourgeois intellectuals. The socialist movement, however, retained an improvised, artificial character. Its intellectual and largely European leadership failed to answer local situations or to arouse sustained popular enthusiasm. "What is most resorted to among us is what might be called the *socialist liturgy*," wrote A. E. de MORAIS (1905, p. 8); "everything is confined to brilliant externals and buoyant declamation, for the most part sincere but bereft of practical significance."

Despite their loose organization, however, it appeared for a moment in May, 1906, that the workers might be starting effectively to resist their employers. A strike was called against the "Paulista" railway to protest highhanded action against a worker and to exact an eight-hour day and other concessions. The strike spread to the "Mogiana" and to industries in Campinas and São Paulo. In the capital, violence flared up, and certain law students showed active sympathy with the strikers. But the latter were too feebly organized and equipped to oppose vested powers that were wholly indisposed to recognize proletariat interests. A report of the "Paulista" scornfully branded the strike as having "genuine anarchist character" and boasted that, with "the ever prompt and solicitous aid of the government," the company was soon running its trains again, "conceding nothing to the strikers and dismissing from service those employees who as leaders of the movement became responsible for the damages incurred." (RELATÓRIO..., 1906, p. 11.)

The general strike of 1917 far more effectively registered new social alignments. That strike, touched off in June with a demand by workers in a large cotton-textile factory for a 20 per cent wage increase, spread throughout the city and by mid-July immobilized over 20,000 workers who had been suffering from sharp inflation. In reporting the event *O Estado de São Paulo* (July 12, 1917) was forced to sympathize with the workers: "The truth is that at present the situation of the worker in São Paulo is in general the very worst." As in 1906, there were persons who raised the bugbear of anarchism and terrorism. But the press, the government, and even a few industrialists now recognized the legitimacy of the workers' demands and their right to organize. The secretary of justice and a Committee of the Press, representing the newspapers, became mediators, and the workers' basic requests were filled.

One could, of course, easily exaggerate the workers' new status. Under state President Altino Arantes (1916-1920), foreigners with socialist beliefs were at times deported, habeas corpus was violated, and force was employed for strikebreaking. The leftist journal *O Parafuso* (Nov. 3, 1917) pointed out a specific irony in the administration of justice. The state Tribunal had just convicted a dedicated anarchist leader (whose reputation has subsequently approached saintliness) on a trumped-up charge of robbery and, in the same session, acquitted an official of the powerful Matarazzo concern who on damning evidence had been charged with counterfeiting "Italian" olive oil. Two months later *O Parafuso* moved to Rio de Janeiro to escape censorship.

Despite occasionally successful strikes, the workers of Brazil's large cities have not displayed discipline, group consciousness, and ability to generate leadership. They have achieved prominence less as a force assertive of its own demands than as a passive, mutualistic body to which more militant powers have been making increasingly direct appeals. Here in fact is an essential condition of the society. For in western Europe — as Georges Sorel, Roberto Michels, and others have demonstrated — the urban lower classes were largely responsible for creating their own spheres of power. In São Paulo — as in other areas where industrialization and urbanization have been of recent and diluvial rather than slow, organic development — agrarian attitudes persist. In the early 1930's DEURSEN (1934, p. 306) found that São Paulo's worker, compared to his European counterpart, was "content with his lot, materially speaking," and that, "life being after all less difficult and the struggles of industry less acute than in the old industrial countries, conflicts over wages and work have scarcely any *raison d'être*, and class war practically does not exist."

The Communists, whose party appeared in Brazil in 1922, were perhaps the first group systematically to manipulate the lower classes for private purposes. Many of the early ones were anarchists discontent with the slow progress of their own movement and loyal to genuine socialist aims. But leadership soon fell to opportunists who exploited the common man's misery, tried to hypnotize him with mass meetings, and urged him to violence. Marxist literature was circulated by publishers as a commercial venture, for Communists did not trouble themselves with formal indoctrination. Their policy, made necessary by an ever-shifting platform, was to mystify rather than educate. In Luís Carlos Prestes, whose "Prestes Column" eluded the government in a stirring odyssey through the backlands (1924-1927), they found a glamorous vanguard symbol of resistance to oppression that transcended political formulations. Though many intellectuals became disillusioned with Communism during the 1930's, its appeal has been strong for workers of São Paulo and for Santos stevedores. In recent years, despite the illegality of the Communist Party, political administration of Santo André, an industrial subcenter of São Paulo, virtually passed into Communist hands. It is perhaps as much Communist influence as it is the taxes and congestion of the capital which makes decentralization attractive to industralists and has effected a hegira of factories to small, outlying towns. This alarmist attitude exaggerates the Communist threat beyond its inherent importance.

Since the 1930's more powerful interests have entered into competition for the worker's allegiance. The first administration of the late Getúlio Vargas (1930-1945) made a strong play for the support of the growing proletariat with its program of social legislation. Though many measures, such as the founding of *IAPI* (Institute of Old Age and Industrial Pensions), were constructive, the latter phase of the regime, known as the "New State" (1937-1945), syndicalized labor in paternalistic, virtually authoritarian fashion, interfering with the workers' freedom of expression and association and with their right to strike. Given labor's relative docility, this paternalism abated after 1945 only in its more coercive aspects.

The church, too, is trying to instate itself with the people. A prevalent attitude it seeks to counteract is that of two Italo-paulistas in one of Mário de Andrade's short stories: "They never went to mass. Religion was only taking off your hat when you passed in front of churches. Why they took it off they didn't know. They'd seen their father do it, and lots of others. They did it too. Custom." Catholic pageantry is obsolescent in the world of sports and movies, and working people have slowly withdrawn from religious processions, leaving them to girls, widows, and spinsters. Urban change and uncertainty, moreover, have made magic (a first cousin of scientific manipulation) more appealing for many than immemorial church devotions. This is attested by the city's large number of spiritist circles, which occur both in a "lower" form, tinged with African fetishism, and in a "higher" one, the bourgeois, European variety.

One would be misled, however, if one were to judge the church's response to secular encroachments solely by the windiness of its continuing pronouncements on the evils of gambling and the dignity of the family. Writing at the turn of the century, Father Julio MARIA (1900-1910, p. 123) identified the republican era as a period of "combat" for the church, after its "decadence" under the empire and its colonial "splendor." Since the separation of church and state in 1890, and the detachment of the ecclesiastical from the civil hierarchy, the church has been freer, and in fact more obliged, to appeal directly to the people with a modern program of "social action." It sponsors workers' associations, gives domestic aid and counsel, and, through its Catholic Electoral League, advises voters. A spearhead organization is the Social Action of the Jesuits of São Paulo. As described by one of its leaders several years ago, Social Action has the functions, first, of "consultation," or furnishing data toward the solution of social and economic problems of groups and organizations and, second, of "direct action," such as sponsoring medical clinics and courses of training for workers, engineers, and managers. The immediate goal of Social Action is not so much redemption of the masses as providing a Catholic education for young men who are to assume key positions in the industrial metropolis. In 1946 the church's educational facilities were greatly enhanced by the establishment of the Catholic University of São Paulo, with faculties of law, science, letters, and engineering and a school of journalism.

The "exploiting" industrialist has, paradoxically, certain advantages in the face of this competition. Unlike the Communists he can, if so minded, offer the worker both doctrinal consistency and long-term material benefits. Unlike the government he has the incentive to personalize labor relations and eliminate bureaucratic red tape. Unlike the church he has no reason to make social assistance contingent upon profession of the faith. *SESI* (Industrial Social Service) and *SESC* (Commercial Social Service) were both created in 1946 under sponsorship of employers' groups. They are devoted to resolving workers' domestic and legal problems, broadening their social horizons, giving job training, raising living standards, defending real wages — and, like the church, to subsidizing the education of promising youths to key technical and managerial positions. In its first year *SESI* set up thirty-seven supply posts in São Paulo city which undersold retailers by 30 to 50 per cent and forced general price cuts in staple foods.

A domestic problem handled by *SESI* in 1948 which came to

the writer's attention illustrates the nature of its activities as well as some characteristics of the depressed portion of the working class. The family in question had six members (recently reduced from seven with the eldest daughter's elopement) who lived in a small brick hut on the city's outskirts. The father was a welldigger earning about twenty-five dollars a month, half of which went for rent. The mother, in bad health for ten years, could not supplement this income since she had never learned how to sew or make sweets, and she lived too far from the city to become a domestic. The home had no electricity and only a little impure water from a shallow well which the husband, unable to pay an assistant, could not deepen. The whole family was illiterate; they ate only rice and beans, except for occasional greens given by a friend, and slept, six of them, in three beds. The eldest boy, a ten-year-old, had obtained some seeds from a gardener but planted only herbs. The first act of the SESI worker had been to make the mother get a certificate attesting her marriage. With this, the husband was able to obtain a worker's passbook that entitled him to medical assistance for his wife, schooling for his children, and, for himself, night courses that might lead to a better-paying job in industry. It was also the social worker's hope to persuade the mother that she take in laundry and to induce the eldest boy to plant something more nourishing than herbs.

If this family — originally from a fazenda and living despairfully in a city whose ways were only partly understood — is typical of a sizable portion of the lower class, it is evident why the underprivileged have not displayed more discipline and militancy. As for the underdog who manages to better his status, he does so under the patronage of a vested interest or else, through luck or ingenuity, capitalizes on unexpected opportunities of an expanding economy and relatively permissive society; in either case he receives little incentive toward "class solidarity."

Its perennial general strikes might suggest that the workers of France are oppressed by economic inequalities. Yet when a French social worker (LEBRET, 1951) conducted a housing survey in São Paulo in 1947 he discovered that the bulk of the French people were by comparison well housed and had the skill of turning a few modest rooms into comfortably furnished quarters. In São Paulo comfort was a function of mere space rather than of adroit homemaking. Its housing, far more than France's, was polarized into extremes. Thirty-seven per cent of the cases surveyed were unimprovable hovels or near-hovels, sometimes accommodating eighteen persons in two rooms; 24 per cent were substandard but improvable; 20 per cent were comfortable or luxurious and included many mansions of twenty rooms or more. Only 19 per cent were average, or "satisfactory," dwellings. Similarly for eating habits — the diet of São Paulo's poorer classes centers in rice, beans, bread, and coffee, while that of the wealthy abounds in imported delicacies. The art of devising a varied, healthful menu within the limits of a modest budget is one which is rarely practised by any of the classes of the city.

That the various discontinuities in the society have not been more subversive may be ascribed to the city's paternalistic traditions (some of them now being re-created in new guises) and to the social fluidity and permissiveness of the current years of change. In speaking of class structure and tensions one cannot properly apply economic or political class criteria that obtain in western Europe or America. One must seek out *local determinants* of status together with the *expectancies* of the various status groups. If there are no expectancies, as with the welldigger described above, there is little threat to the social order. If expectancies are realized, as with a gradually promoted public functionary of humble origin, there is likewise little threat. Unrest occurs only when expectancies are denied — as when an informed semiskilled worker is repeatedly denied privileges, or when a well-born professional man is crushed by inflation, or when a powerful industrialist is blocked from political influence.

It is relevant here to mention the status of women, whose "emancipation" so often introduces anxieties into society via the family. In 1886 a woman was for the first time appointed to work in a city post office, while the Law Faculty matriculated its first woman in 1898 — by which time thousands of them had entered stenography and industry. A rise in the female suicide rate for the city seemed to reflect a growing conflict among women's social involvements:

No. of Suicides and Attempted Suicides

Period	Male	Female	Per Cent Female
1876-1895	191	37	16
1896-1904	326	127	28

It has in the twentieth century become ever less common for women to marry before the age of twenty. The following figures show how wide the disparity between city and country in this regard had grown by 1937:

Age of Woman at Marriage (1937)	São Paulo State	
	Capital	Interior
Under 20	25%	46%
20-24	46	39
Over 24	29	15

As with workers, however, so with women — the immediacy with which the industrial crowds in upon the patriarchal age has produced a reorganization of their economic activities far greater than that of their emotional loyalties. Although women are no longer subject to the more humiliating patriarchal taboos, and although increasing numbers embark on successful professional careers, the majority, even the many who hold jobs, acquiesce in the tradition which assigns priority to their domestic interests. As for the unmarried girl, however much the metropolis may have liberalized chaperonage and the family-controlled courtship, her role continues to be defined by a "virginity complex" which, among upper- and middle-class circles, generally dooms a deflowered girl to spinsterhood or concubinage. The male whom this androcentric society so favors is still free to indulge in the patronizing attitude which one of his sex expressed years ago in the feminine journal A Mensageira (Oct. 15, 1897): "Till now we have esteemed the woman merely as a creature of feeling; we must now see her also as an intellectual creature — for it is necessary that she think in order that she may feel more nobly."

In spite of the growing allegiance which the ideal of romantic love is winning in Brazilian cities, the divergencies between the realms of male and female culture preclude the "intimate association between spouses which is usually expected in the United States." Were this cultural and social distance between them to be bridged, however, speculates Emílio WILLEMS (1953, p. 342), it "would probably lead to an increase of friction and conflict within the family." Along with its cohesiveness the metropolitan family preserves, from patriarchal times, a wide radius of extension. A recent survey indicates that one may expect a resident of São Paulo to identify from thirty to five hundred relatives, many of them also living in the city. Partly because of the continuing vitality of the extended family, so typically modern an institution as the stock market has failed to develop in urban Brazil; "the most important joint-stock companies are owned by kin groups which handle transfer of stock as a purely domestic matter. In fact, despite heavy industrialization, a stock market, comparable to that of other industrialized countries, does not exist at all." (WILLEMS, 1953, p. 343.)

The continuing interaction of the patriarchal and industrial orders imparts an intricate, unresolved character to the pattern of social determinants and expectancies in São Paulo. The following class schema for urban Brazil, devised by Ralph BEALS (1953, p. 334), is a useful introduction to the picture:

	(Elite tends to define self racially but ideologically opposed to discrimination in economic and political matters.)
	Landholders turning to industry, banking, commerce.
UPPER:	High government officials.
	Heads of church and army.
	Many professional men.
	Declining number of intellectuals.

(mild breaching of barriers)

	Managerial.
	Middle bureaucracy.
	Storekeepers.
MIDDLE:	Some professionals and intellectuals.
	Teachers.
	Some service personnel and technicians.
	White-collar workers.

(increasing breaching of barriers)

	(Little racial discrimination; few barriers to marriage. Large groups of extremely impoverished.)
	Petty civil servants.
LOWER:	Small shopkeepers.
	Artisans.
	Working-class groups.

Of special importance is the increasing class mobility, the gradual obliteration of lineage as a criterion of status. Though commonly hailed as an omen of "democracy," this may well portend something else if mobility is down rather than up — if, for instance, the aristocrat becomes déclassé or the white-collar worker is proletarianized. Further, the erosion of traditional status determinants opens new expectancies throughout society. This in turn increases the potential for disequilibrium, for there is a successively wider scale of points at which political malfeasance, economic instability, or social intolerance can upset expectancies and induce tension. Much depends, therefore, upon the foresight and *noblesse oblige* of those in controlling status. Despite occasional philanthropies and their organized ventures in social welfare, however, members of the elite display a minimum of these qualities in their way of life. When some years ago the Frenchman MOURALIS (1934, p. 8) visited São Paulo's luxurious Hotel Esplanada he found that: "The refinements of manner borrowed from old European societies and displayed with ostentation give the effect of unwitting caricature and in no way conceal sentiments of primitive crudity. One swiftly has the impression that all is false in this room — save the jewels."

Many *grā-finos*, as the wealthy are called, are parvenus without cultural roots enjoying bloated, lightly taxed profits. Their faster pace of life has caused an American complex of martinis, night clubs, Cadillacs, and sportive week ends to displace Gallic affectations of the recent past. In 1945 the marriage of Matarazzo's granddaughter was preceded by eight receptions, twenty-six dinners, and twenty-three suppers; the ceremonies proper lasted three days and cost $300,000. *Time* (Jan. 21, 1952) vicariously gloated that a young industrialist was building his fiancée "a million-dollar house in suburban Santo Amaro with two Turkish baths, a shooting gallery, a bowling alley, and an outdoor swimming pool. It will also have a 130-ft. indoor swimming pool with a cascade of water 30 ft. wide and 21 ft. high at one end. By swimming through his waterfall, [the owner] will find himself in a grotto equipped with bar, bath, and bed."

How to translate *noblesse oblige* into the terms of a nontraditional society is a dilemma of São Paulo and of the modern world at large.

Bibliographical Note

The case studies of Latin American communities, which supply the data for polemics over the "folk"-urban dichotomy, are too numerous to be cited here. The pioneer study was by REDFIELD (1930) of Tepoztlán, Mexico; his subsequent analysis of four communities of Yucatán (1941) allowed him to elaborate more fully his conception of the "folk-urban continuum." In a restudy of Tepoztlán, Lewis (1951) sets forth important qualifications of Redfield's theory. A collection of articles on the whole subject, which includes bibliographies, appears in *Ciencias Sociales*, IV, 23 (Oct., 1953), published by the Pan American Union. Pierson (1951) is the study of a rural community only sixty miles from São Paulo and discusses the influences of the city upon it. B. Ferreira (1954) is a popular treatment and Petrone (1955) a more scholarly one of São Paulo since 1900. Hummel (1901) and A. M. Pinto (1900) are accounts of the city at the turn of the century, the latter providing comparisons with an era forty years previous. Casabona (1908) records the notes of a French visitor. More pungent evocations occur in the reminiscences of C. Marques (1942; 1944) and the novel of Tacito (1919). Economic aspects are emphasized in the account of P. Denis (1928). Mouralis (1934) and Matthews (1956) afford vignettes of city life in more recent years, while J. Silveira (1946) gives a journalist's caricature of São Paulo's upper crust, the grã-finos. The anthropologist Corrêa (1935) impressionistically contrasts the inhabitants of São Paulo with those of Rio de Janeiro.

C. M. D. de Carvalho (1910) provides an economic background for the early twentieth century, while Mission . . . (1909) gives indices of economic expansion for the period 1887-1907. Schompré (1911) deals with São Paulo's Bourse. Lalière (1909) describes aspects of the coffee industry, the financial history of which is summarized in Monbeig (1952, pp. 94-106). The country-to-city migrations are treated in F. M. de Carvalho (1942b), Zanotti (1946), V. U. de Almeida and Mendes Sobrinho (1951), and J. F. de Camargo (1957). The *Boletim do Departamento Estadual do Trabalho* and Departamento Estadual do Trabalho (1915) are useful for the labor market and conditions of work during the 1910's and 1920's.

Leuenroth (n.d.) and Piccarolo (n.d.) treat the anarchist and socialist movements respectively, while Mello (1949) is an account of Communism in São Paulo by an embittered renegade; Pisani (1937, p. 416) lists Italian fascist organizations in the city during the Mussolini era. Loewenstein (1942) uncritically analyzes the first Vargas regime; Duarte (1946b) is an indictment of it by a São Paulo journalist; Nobre (1950, chap. VIII) describes censorship of São Paulo's press under Vargas; Vieira and Silva (1955, pp. 299-342) details administrative changes in the city under the New State. Episcopado . . . (1942) is an example of the local clergy's continuing concern with conventional morality, while the magazine *Serviço Social*, published by São Paulo's Jesuits, evinces a growing awareness of the opportunities for social work in the commercial-industrial world. E. de A. Whitaker (1940) describes some of the city's spiritist centers. The functions of *SESI* in São Paulo are set forth in Simonsen (1947).

The studies of the middle class in Latin America edited by Crevenna (1950-1951), though they contain no data for São Paulo city, provide suggestive comparative material. F. de Azevedo (1948) in his study of the sugar industry and political life in Brazil indicates the composition of the new urban elite. Drawing upon the censuses of 1920 and 1934, Herrmann (1943) points out the changing "demographic-professional structure" of São Paulo city and state. Davis (1935), Secretaria da Agricultura . . . (1940b), and Araujo (1941b; 1947) are surveys of lower-class living standards in the city; the housing question is studied in Teles (1940-1), Pierson (1942a), Idort

(1942), ARAUJO (1945), and LEBRET (1951), and the dietary question in ARAUJO (1940b), IDORT (1941), F. P. do AMARAL (1943), and PIERSON (1944). LOWRIE (1936) surveys the city's agencies for "philanthropic assistance," and J. E. FRANCO (1944) details the state's welfare facilities for minors; O. de GODOY (1940) studies the "factors of criminality" in the capital. A. ALMEIDA JUNIOR (1940) gives figures to show the later age at which marriages are taking place in São Paulo. An early study of suicide in the city is J. de A. MACHADO (1905).

BANCO DO BRASIL (1954), is a geo-economic statistical synopsis of São Paulo state and its capital. For special needs one should consult the many publications of the Departamento Estadual de Estatística.

Chapter 18

INDUSTRIALISM

In the school maintained by the Dante Alighieri Society they
taught the following sequence:
"Where was Christopher Columbus born?"
"In Genoa."
"Who takes care of the coffee in the State of São Paulo?"
"The Italian."
"Who invented the Ford car?"
"Count Matarazzo."
— PLÍNIO SALGADO, *O estrangeiro* (1926).

*M*OST OF THE PROMINENT Latin American cities
developed as bureaucratic, commercial, and
cultural centers. Their customs, society, city plan, and rhythm of
life were not shaped by the demands of industry. It is chiefly in
western Europe and the United States that one finds the cities
which came to importance with the Industrial Revolution and which
best exemplify industrial conditions of life. São Paulo is the most
notable exception to the Latin American norm. It began attracting
industry shortly before 1890, at the very time of metropolitan expansion, and today exhibits Latin America's largest industrial concentration. In São Paulo, however, the casual observer is not
oppressed by the grime and soot or by the labyrinths of brick and
steel and the relentless convergence of humanity that characterize
the industrialism of certain northern countries. The city expanded
radially in a burst of undisciplined energy. Industries and homes
are scattered with a prodigal use of space that leaves unexpected
open and unimproved areas. One has at least a visual sense that
São Paulo is built on land, that it occupies a geographic setting,
that it is not an "asphalt jungle."

Within this general cast, however, standard problems of the

221

factory community may readily be discerned. Little else could be expected when the mere accouterments of industry were accepted as in themselves a blessing and sign of progress. *Diario Popular* (March 2, 1892) buoyantly described "the loud, merry song of the Italian at work" and "the noise of the forges" in a city district which had become "a lovely workshop, a gigantic factory for future paulistas, the new generation destined by its Old World industrial heritage completely to transform, for the better, the physical and commercial aspect of our land." The absence of zoning regulations to sequester these "lovely workshops" has through the years victimized householders. Typical is an early group which complained to *O Estado de São Paulo* (Aug. 14, 1896) that a new sawmill was burning wood shavings "whose soot is carried by the winds in all directions, penetrating houses and blackening everything."

Transportation lines have not been planned with an eye to the routes between home and job that are used by the bulk of the workers. Schemes devised at the turn of the century for neat, symmetrical subway lines, luckily never put into effect, seemed largely concerned with bringing well-to-do playgoers to the Municipal Theater. Not until 1948 did subway engineers pry into workers' travel habits with an "origin-and-destination" survey.

Another lingering problem is workers' housing. The municipal commission which investigated cortiços in 1893 recommended demolition of substandard residences and construction of inexpensive, spacious, hygienic workers' communities, where truck farming might round out a family's income and activities, and bring the city's socioeconomic life into better balance. "A city like this, surrounded by the amplest terrains, by broad lands suited for any construction, should not harbor in its bosom those dens called cortiços where the strongest health withers and the imprudent worker, in quest of an illusory and fatal saving, almost always encounters the germs that dispatch him." (RELATÓRIO..., 1894, pp. 49-54.) Municipal laws of 1897, 1900, and 1908 were an effort to induce public and private agencies to create cheap, salubrious housing centers in uncrowded areas. But to this as to any swiftly expanding economy, long-range plans and the sense of interclass community were alien. A project of the industrialist Jorge Street, which distributed profits annually to workers and made their children's education compulsory, was perhaps the sole exception to the following observation of the Department of Labor (1912): "Few are the industrialists who concern themselves with the problem of workers' homes. Of these none does so in a humanitarian or altruistic spirit." (*Boletim do Departamento Estadual do Trabalho,* Nos. 1-2, pp. 35 ff.) A report by the state president in 1925 declared the "lack of hygienic housing" to be "progressively more serious." "The law authorizes the government to remove tenants from improper dwellings and distribute them proportionately in tolerable ones. But the housing shortage and the protests that such measures evoke under the circumstances obstruct the action of the Sanitary Service." (MENSAGEM..., 1925, p. 37.)

In 1940, 40 to 60 per cent of the citydwellers suffered from substandard conditions. A survey of 261 cortiços in that year (TELES, 1940-1941) revealed that only 43 per cent of their inhabitants were in sound health. Part of the cortiço problem could be explained by the city's lack of decent low-cost dwellings and by the workers' need to congregate near their place of employment because of the inadequacy and high cost of transportation. Remedies for these deficiencies have been increasingly sought in the 1940's and 1950's. Though projects of private industrialists tend to favor better-paid workers, the government's Institute of Old Age and Industrial Pensions has been constructing large communities of low-cost, unpretentious homes and apartments with all the appurtenances of social, educational, and commercial life. Rents are figured to approximate one-third of the tenant's income and to yield the Institute 3 or 4 per cent on its capital, both ratios being low for Brazil.

The analysis of the city's physical shortcomings in the 1940 survey was, however, less significant than the habit of mind, partly responsible for and partly bred by the cortiço, which it depicted. Poverty, overcrowding, and the women's need to be absent from the home as wage-earners, of course, contribute to the cortiço's lack of order and hygiene. But of comparable weight is the "absence of domestic education," for it was sometimes found that cortiço proprietors, despite their high incomes, live under the same insalubrious conditions as their tenants. The cortiço, in other words, is not to be expunged by mere physical rearrangements; it embodies a mental attitude, a traditional unconcern with comfort and hygiene, and, often, a compulsion to live, at whatever disadvantage, near the excitement, commotion, and bright lights of the urban center and its thoroughfares.

In searching for ways to enrich the communal life of unprivileged workers, planners must examine and learn from the social organization of the cortiço itself. The housing problem will not be solved by mere expenditures of money and resettlements of persons. To a greater degree than slums and tenements of other cities, São Paulo's cortiço, with its one-storey grouping of rooms around a central court and common facilities, allows for social cohesion. In spite of their squabbles and intrigues, persons born and raised in a cortiço of, say, two hundred dwellers develop sociability and the habits of mutual aid and shared experience. Those who plan the decentralized, self-sufficient workers' towns must see the cortiço not simply as an unhealthy canker, but also as an institution which, within narrow limits, meets human needs and embodies social attitudes. The cortiço retains, in however degenerate a form, aspects of the preindustrial "neighborhood" and its face-to-face relationships. This mutualistic spirit, like that of the early labor syndicates and anarchist leagues, should be in some manner preserved and utilized by the industrial metropolis.

Just as the city's proletariat has distinctive traits which must affect any future dispositions, so have the anatomy and functioning of its industrial park.

The leading characteristic of São Paulo's industry is that it developed recently in an agrarian, "underdeveloped" nation, largely in response to external, international factors. To nations such as Brazil it became evident in the second half of the nineteenth century that western Europe was evolving economically (and thus "progressing" culturally, so it was held) at a rate of change that was geometric rather than arithmetic. The market for industrial products was in that era far more elastic than that for agricultural ones. Brazil, like many other countries, discovered that to continue trading off farm exports for manufactured imports in a free international market would soon ruin its economy. Its protectionist tariffs of the early republican period were imposed in answer to this threat.

Though stimulated by international wars and depressions, Brazilian industrialism is primarily a function of this long-range situation. Novel industrial patterns therefore appear, for Brazil must import techniques — such as machine technology, or systems of banking, credit, and marketing — from lands which evolved habits of mind and social organization along with them. Attitudes and social changes cannot, however, be incorporated like machines or railways; one cannot legislate into being the capitalist ethic, namely, the habit of impersonalizing and standardizing socioeconomic relationships and of basing upon them a "rational" calculus of profit and loss.

The fact that Brazilian industry is largely a political necessity means that it survives under paternalistic auspices. Although paternalist measures can animate specific ventures, paternalism as a social philosophy is incompatible with the capitalist ethic. Caio PRADO JUNIOR (1945, p. 273) has described as follows the placid, "parasitic" prospect awaiting Brazilian industries in about 1920: "They will not undergo the struggle for conquest and expansion of markets which constitutes the great stimulus for capitalistic enterprises and is primarily responsible for the dizzy progress of modern industry. It can be said that markets will come to them in an appeal for home production of articles which the country's financial situation has prevented from being purchased abroad. . . . Brazilian industrialists will live as a family, a peaceful family within which opportunities are fraternally distributed." It is always within this context that the apparent dynamism and antitraditionalism of São Paulo's industry must be viewed.

Given the inevitability of Brazil's industrialization, the emergence of São Paulo as a focal point was hardly surprising. The city's nineteenth-century climate of change has already been discussed. It was defined by liberal, cosmopolitan ideas and institutions taking root in a town whose modest colonial traditions were, ostensibly at least, displaced with ease. It was in addition defined by the coffee boom, that is, by an exploitation which freed rural entrepreneurs, workers, and capital accumulations to migrate from country to city — and then in time of agricultural crisis actually impelled them to do so.

If, now, we examine a rough semicircle with a fifty-mile radius extending from São Paulo west to Sorocaba, north to Campinas, and east to Mogi das Cruzes, we find that it unites six more tangible ingredients for an industrial park.

(1) A rail and highway network with connections, via São Paulo, to the port of Santos.

(2) An accessible, populous market enjoying a higher living

standard than most of Brazil. The region referred to now contains 5 per cent of the area of São Paulo state and 40 per cent of its 9,500,000 population; it has easy commerce with the rest of the state and with neighbors to the north, west, and south.[1]

(3) Raw materials. Staples for such basic industries as textiles, ceramics, cement, furniture, and food-processing all exist locally, and São Paulo is favorably placed to receive iron, coal, and petroleum of Brazilian or overseas origin. In 1951 Brazil's first inter-city oil pipeline was opened between Santos and São Paulo, tripling the petroleum delivery that the overburdened railway had made from the port. An oil refinery, located between São Paulo and its port and capable of meeting about one-third of the country's needs for finished petroleum products, began operations in 1955. The government's big Volta Redonda steel mill is in the Paraíba valley; very recently an even larger mill, which is eventually to produce a million tons a year, was opened in São Paulo itself.

(4) Capital. Initially a by-product of the coffee boom, it was supplemented by the limited funds and high business acumen of enterprising immigrants, notably Italians and Near-Easterners.

(5) Labor. Europeans originally subsidized for work on fazendas were the early nucleus of the labor force. They were joined by waves of "spontaneous," or self-financed, immigrants attracted by São Paulo's temperate climate, economic opportunities, and freely negotiable short-term labor contracts. Between 1908 and 1920, Santos received 190,000 subsidized immigrants, nearly all of whom went, at least initially, to fazendas, and 340,000 "spontaneous" ones, of whom 80 per cent took jobs with industry, trade, or railways in the capital and other cities. Many such foreigners supplied technical skills, metallurgic and mechanical for example, which São Paulo's schools did not yet teach.[2]

1. The major entities of southern Brazil that fall within São Paulo city's economic reach (São Paulo, Rio de Janeiro, Espírito Santo, Minas Gerais, Paraná, Santa Catarina, Rio Grande, and the Federal District) contain only 18 per cent of the nation's area but 50 per cent of its population, 71 per cent of its highways, 74 per cent of its railways, and 89 per cent of its electric power.

2. During the quarter-century after 1908, a million foreigners entered via Santos and slightly over half a million departed. Japanese showed an overwhelming tendency to strike roots; Portuguese, eastern Europeans (except Russians), and Near-Easterners were moderately stable; Italians and Germans emigrated in almost the numbers that they arrived. Urban immigrants were much less apt to remain than agricultural, which intensified the permutations of São Paulo city.

After World War I, non-Mediterraneans figured prominently in the levies. Between 1925 and 1929 eastern Europeans, many from dissident minorities created by Versailles, were nearly a quarter of the total, and Japanese, settled by an agency that their government had founded in 1917, over a tenth. In 1930-1934 the Japanese rose to 28 per cent, while the once-dominant Italians, by now under fascist aegis, dwindled to 3 per cent. In 1934 the restrictive immigration quotas of the Vargas regime cut the influx to a trickle. São Paulo's need for factory and farm labor, however, continued to be served by internal migrations. These had been accentuated in 1927, when tens of thousands, drawn by São Paulo's coffee prosperity and traveling under grueling conditions, fled a severe northeastern drought.[3] In 1935-1939, 96 per cent of the state's 285,000 immigrants were Brazilian nationals. Since World War II, arrivals from overseas have increased only moderately, owing to the government's insistence that foreigners be skilled farmers who will revitalize home agriculture and not compete in urban jobs. In 1950-1952, for example, 560,000 nationals entered, as against 100,000 foreigners; of the latter, Portuguese, Italians, and Spaniards comprised over three-quarters.

Though the five factors so far given must be taken as an interrelated complex, the final one may perhaps be isolated as a precipitant, without which the heavy industrial development in the years and aftermaths of two World Wars would have been far milder.

(6) Hydroelectric power. In the early 1890's a fifty-kilowatt steam engine supplied the city's electric lights. By 1900 the S. Paulo Tramway, Light and Power Co., Ltd., organized in Toronto, had absorbed the earlier company along with the two city transit systems. Shortly a dam and a power plant were completed west of the capital on the Tietê. When it was perceived, however, that waters of this river would, in their gradual descent inland, never meet the city's fast-growing needs for power, the "Light" constructed a series of dams in the swampy valleys of the Tietê's affluents, close to the rainy crest of the Serra. Waters which had reached the Atlantic via the River Plate after an inland course of 2,500 miles were then pumped from vast reservoirs to plunge directly down the littoral escarpment. At the end of 1953 the "Light" had an installed capacity of 1,000,000 kilowatts and, as the city's power

3. A drought in 1952 brought over 1,100 persons per day into São Paulo state from the northeast.

needs have been critically in advance of this amount, the capacity has been at least doubled since then. The city's electric-power consumption per residential consumer is now higher than that of Chicago, and the "Light," with assets of $700 million, is Canada's largest foreign investment.[4] In a country whose fuels are scarce and of low grade, it is clear, a power supply such as this can be expected sharply to concentrate industry. By 1940 São Paulo state accounted for roughly half the value of Brazil's manufactures and the city alone for one-quarter.

Having characterized the trend of Brazilian industrialization and having suggested reasons for São Paulo's eminent role, we are now to examine the structure and special attributes of the city's industrial park. Its fortuitous and heterogeneous mode of growth is a common denominator of the aspects to be discussed.

Corporate structure. Industry here suddenly invaded an agrarian society where surplus funds were by preference invested in securities bearing strong guarantees of a fixed return, such as mortgages, state bonds, and bank securities, or in ventures which promised swiftly to double or triple their capital. Real estate frequently combined the assurances of one with the exorbitant premiums of the other. With few funds available for run-of-the-mill risk ventures, industrial capital was usually furnished not by numbers of "anonymous" shareholders but by the entrepreneur, his family, and a few friends having faith in his personal qualities.[5]

Francisco Matarazzo's "United Industries" is the most striking example of such an enterprise. Matarazzo, a modest immigrant, as we have seen, who had lost his initial capital at sea, transferred his affairs from Sorocaba to São Paulo at the end of the last century, and was soon dealing in grain and flour. In 1900, assisted by British capital and technicians, he built his first flour mill. Next he began to make sacks for his products and in 1904 put up a large textile plant. This led to cottonseed-oil mills and thence to soap and toiletries. Packing cases were then necessary and, to produce them, sawmills. So it went. By the outbreak of World War I his textile plants were engaged in spinning, mercerizing, and dyeing. The war itself stimulated expansion and profits. *O Parafuso* (July 7, 1917) even accused Matarazzo, who had been created a count by the

4. In 1956 the company became, for legal purposes, a Brazilian concern.

5. When industrial ventures are financed by loans the customary interest rate is 12 per cent. Industrial profits run at an average of 18 per cent.

Italian king for his services, of secretly yearning to subscribe to the war loans of both sides so as to prolong the conflict and his heightened income.

By 1925, ownership of the United Industries with their many home and foreign branches was represented by 150,000 shares; over 70,000 were held by Matarazzo and most of the rest by his family. Matarazzo was the agent for the Bank of Naples and for the Fiat company. He controlled ships, railway cars, trucks, and an insurance business. His industries had ramified into artificial silk, chemicals, distilling, perfume, candles, varnish, ceramics, oils, tanning, meat packing, metallurgy, salt and sugar refining, carpentry, and plaster. He died in 1937, bequeathing Latin America's foremost industrial empire, and the world's largest personally operated one, to his son. Francisco, Jr., has more than doubled, perhaps tripled, the size of the enterprise, which in 1949 had a listed capital of $33 million, reserves of $54 million, and gross sales of $137 million, and which has been said to make 90 per cent annually on its paid-up capital. By 1952 the firm employed over 30,000 workers in 367 plants. The bleak and impeccably dressed Francisco, Jr., controls his empire from a pigskin-paneled office that is fitted with a buzzer system to summon top executives, who, on leaving, must bow their way backward from his presence.

Other Italians, like Crespi, Siciliano, Scarpa, and Gamba, and Near-Easterners, like Jafet and Maluf, paralleled Matarazzo's achievements, though less spectacularly. Common to all was a shrewd perception of the character and potentials of paulista economic life. Their modest origins left them without preconceptions derived from formal acquaintance with the theories and institutions of European capitalism. They worked their multiform empires up from nuclear basic industries and always in directions where consumers' wants, available resources, and their own ingenuity were effective. Skilled at improvising unconventional industrial and financial arrangements, they were careful not to rely heavily upon agents, either in Brazil or abroad, for basic capital or for essential steps in the industrial process.[6]

The day after Matarazzo's death, *Diario de São Paulo* (Feb. 11,

6. The pattern of industrial control by family *grupos* is showing some signs of change. For example, an American investment company called Daltec has, since 1946, bought millions of contos of stock in small, successful paulista concerns, passing it on to investors at a modest profit. Stocks are said to have become as easily purchasable as lottery tickets.

1937) suggestively compared two great industrialists: Viscount Mauá of the nineteenth century and Matarazzo of the twentieth. A full analogy would have set the former's hampering commitment to imported ideas, procedures, and institutions against the latter's flexible and pragmatic improvisations. The sequence of these two men symbolizes a phase of what the sociologist Roberto Michels called (though without adopting the rigid dialectics of classical Marxism) the "metabolism" of society. A change had occurred in the system of economic production, and the incumbent leading class, proved unadaptable, was joined and partly displaced by persons of lower status who were uncommitted to prescribed habits and rhetoric.

The vast majority of industrial concerns, of course, do not expand like the giants referred to. Throughout the city large, well-equipped plants coexist with small shops, even domestic ateliers, using long-outmoded techniques. At the turn of the century, BAN-DEIRA JUNIOR (1901, p. xi) remarked that hundreds of manufactories were hidden "in places that the Public does not see." These ateliers successfully competed with large-scale production because their overhead was negligible, because their proprietors took profits out only for subsistence, and because consumers were concerned with prices of articles and not habituated to examining their quality.

These particulars continued to hold true. Of 8,400 establishments in the city classified as factories in 1941, 6,000 employed twelve workers or less and 7,800 employed a hundred or less; only 170 employed over five hundred. Continuance of small-scale, often exploitative hand labor is attributable to the flaccidity of the syndical movement and to the excessive profits that big firms are forced to yield. Moreover, large-scale production does not run at standard efficiency, which is the next aspect to be taken up.

Factory efficiency. Despite the recency, by world reckoning, of São Paulo's industrial boom, much of its plant equipment is overage. Lack of a strongly competitive market, lack of local heavy industries, and lack of foreign exchange with which to import capital goods have conspired to keep in use machines that date from the early expansion of forty or fifty years ago. During the economic crisis of the 1930's, in fact, when the problem of underconsumption was diagnosed as one of overproduction, the federal government prohibited the importation of textile machinery. São Paulo, it is true, has been able to produce a few capital goods. During World War I local firms were forced to turn out machines for processing farm products. Since the 1930's equipment, such as band saws, boilers, hydraulic presses, machines for the paper and chemical industries, and machines for processing cotton and vegetable oils, has also been produced. The Institute of Technological Research, founded in 1934 as an adjunct of the Polytechnic School, has assisted considerably in this realm.

Even allowing, however, for these developments and for changes wrought by World War II, it remains true that many plants are antiquated and badly run. In the 1940's LANARI JUNIOR (1945) showed the rolling mills to be "deficient and uneconomical" and copied from aged models; rolling, he claimed, took twenty man-hours per ton, a figure which should cover the whole metallurgic process from the mine to final lamination. O. Pupo NOGUEIRA (1945) found vast sums lost yearly to the textile industry by faulty use of power and improper lubrication. "As our industries grew under a regime of empiricism, we cling to empirical methods of work, with the general result of scanty, defective, and expensive products."[7] A committee of the UNITED NATIONS (1951, pp. 17-49) reported that, although São Paulo state's textile machinery was modern for Brazil, only 35 per cent of the spindles and 12.5 per cent of the looms were new.

The United Nations report, however, points out a group of factors more important than overage machines as a cause of plant inefficiency. These include, first, inadequately specialized production; second, improper conditions of manufacture: uncleanliness, sloppy maintenance of machines, lack of humidity control, and yarns of unreliable quality; and third, the use of superfluous labor. This last is in turn related to: perpetuation of old-fashioned work patterns; an excessive increment of unskilled labor in relation to jobs created by new investment; the combination of low wages and high prices; weak commercial competition and the existence, partly owing to deficient transportation, of monopolistic trading areas. The report concludes that most of these disadvantages can be remedied ex-

7. The dearth of engineers is of course relevant; Brazil has only one-quarter as many, proportionately, as the United States. In the 1940's the deficit of industrial engineers was estimated at 30-40 per cent; one year a single factory in São Paulo proposed to hire the entire graduating class of the Polytechnic School.

peditiously and at moderate cost by rationalizing techniques and reorganizing personnel.

It is of course theoretically true that persons of any land could, as biological organisms, be regimented in a fashion to attain comparable levels of output. What the United Nations report fails properly to consider, however, are the cultural implications of industrial efficiency. To change this single factor in an economy is to change the whole intricate scheme of human values and incentives, as exhibited by consumer, producer, and worker. If broad, humanistic controls are not employed in rationalizing industry, it becomes likely that men will be manipulated as statistical entities. That production figures absolutely and universally define maximum "efficiency" and social well-being is a myth. Efficiency in its full sense is not quantitative. Nor can it directly and swiftly be achieved by manipulation of men and machines. It is rather a by-product of rich, self-consistent relationships within a community of men, and is specified in terms of their given culture. We are led, then, to consider São Paulo's workers.

Labor. In a little more than twenty years the state's industrial workers have swelled from 150,000 to 900,000 and those of the city itself from 100,000 to over 500,000. This rapid growth of the labor force and its scanty professional training combine with disorders of the freewheeling economy to produce marked occupational instability. Fluctuation within professions, mobility among professions, and rural-urban migrations are all exhibited. (Though the attraction of urban life and wages causes migrations to be primarily country-to-city, the war crisis of 1914 and the industrial one of 1931 induced contrary movements.)

Writing in 1934, DEURSEN (1934, p. 302) found the professional *esprit* of Europe largely absent: "Here the common man changes his métier with surprising ease. Today a cabdriver, tomorrow he will decide to be a butcher..., only to open later on a café or little general store which, dissatisfied once again, he will give up to take work as a laborer, or simple 'operative,' in a factory, a construction project, or public works." O. Pupo NOGUEIRA (1935, p. 40) comments in a similar vein: "Our worker, then, is a nomad of labor, rarely coming to have that attachment to calling which forms working dynasties in lands of older and more advanced industry than ours."

Though such workers hamper productivity, they nonetheless have compensating endowments, and it is from the full and integrated range of the workers' qualities that the industrial park should take its complexion. The fact that many are by origin rural and the fact that much land in and near the city is cultivable suggest a class of suburban factory-farm workers. The dual occupation would, in a sociocultural sense, offer a fuller life to a working family. It would cushion them against fluctuations of São Paulo's somewhat disequilibrated industrial system. And it would help solve the problem of feeding the capital of a state in which between 1935 and 1950 (making no correction for inflation) the value of manufactures increased twenty-four-fold and that of farm products less than seven-fold.

This last problem was foreseen over sixty years ago by *Diario Popular* (April 25, 1893): "São Paulo grows swiftly and fearfully and will shortly be a vast city and great center of population and consumption. It is necessary, even urgent, that it start now to plan its future food supply, or else it will soon find itself (if such is not already the case) at grips with scarcity, high prices, and hunger." The article went on to denounce the effects of coffee monoculture and to suggest ways of stimulating food shipment to the capital and developing its agricultural environs.

In 1935, however, a poll of 204 workers' families revealed that only fifteen had gardens and only nine kept more than ten chickens. It was claimed that, with the aid of cooperatives, manioc, sweet potatoes, corn, pigs, and chickens could have been raised in almost half of the workers' districts, appreciably trimming their inflated living costs. (Davis, 1935, p. 151.) A model was furnished by the Melhoramentos paper plant outside the city. By 1940, 80 per cent of its 1,500 workers were using company lands for grazing and agriculture; the company in turn bought their produce at market prices and through its depots inexpensively sold them supplies.

São Paulo's worker possesses extensive if not intensive occupational experience. As high rates of absenteeism attest, he does not accept diligence and assiduity as self-sufficient ends. He is not yet regimented by large, impersonal syndicates and factories to the point of his acquiescing in a permanent routine for the sole assurances of tenure and long-term wage increases; security and income are but a sector of a larger range of incentives.

Private and public plans that will stabilize the industrial economy must therefore treat the worker and his family as human beings, not as creatures to be predictably shuffled about in physical and pecuniary arrangements. The divers interrelated functions of Industrial Social Service are a recognition of this need. *SENAI* (National Service of Industrial Apprenticeship) is another pivotal agency. Its tasks are to vest youthful workers with professional skills and *esprit* and, a more imaginative one, to mediate between the foreign, codified procedure and the unique conditions of Brazilian life.

Persistent Catholic-agrarian attitudes that distinctively imbue São Paulo's economy are often at variance with imported modes of industrial organization. *Jôgo de bicho,* a popular game of chance attached parasitically to official lotteries, compensates for this hiatus between the common man's inclinations and urban ways that exact his compliance. MOURALIS (1934, p. 7) spoke of its "redoubtable spirit that allows blind hope to destroy the love of work and stresses the instability of all things." The strict morality attending the game's highly informal conduct should suggest to industrial planners that social "efficiency" awaits any institution answering deep-seated needs.

São Paulo retains qualities of the face-to-face community, however sparsely articulated, which have elsewhere vanished and whose recovery is dearly sought. The success and efficiency of the industrial park rest less with production indices than with the measure in which it comes to enshrine regional, sociocultural traditions. Foreign technics and solutions must be received with high discrimination, that they may serve rather than dictate the design of industrial growth. In short, the shrewd pragmatism of a Matarazzo issuing freshly and recurrently from present, angular realities should — in other ways and for other ends — inform the legislator, industrialist, technician, foreman, and labor leader.

São Paulo's industry apparently exhibits no decisive movement toward monolithic amalgamation. And the scarcity of industrial capital, whatever its disadvantages, has at least spared the economy the evils of overcapitalization and top-heavy corporate combinations. Lucila HERRMANN (1947, p. 91) proved that in the early 1940's the expansion of the industrial park "was attributable to the numerical increase of small plants employing few workers." Another of her conclusions (1948a, p. 6) stressed the significance of this trend for the milieu we are considering: "In small factories — where contact between owner and worker and among the workers is primary, that is, direct, face-to-face, more intimate, and of a nature more affective than formal — a stronger solidarity is engendered; this is more favorable to job stability than large factories, where contacts between owners and the mass are indirect and formal."

Factors of demand and production. The city's industrial park reflects the needs of consumers having limited buying power. Although the per capita income of São Paulo state is three times that of Brazil, it is only one-third that of the United States. Light basic industries demanding a minimum of skilled labor and capital have always predominated. In 1952 the major categories, and workers employed therein, were: textiles (97,000), mechanical and electrical appliances (95,000), building and furniture (53,000), foodstuffs (36,000), clothing (32,000), chemical and pharmaceutical (29,000), glass and ceramics (18,000), and others (77,000).

Certain anomalies, however, are to be considered. The industrial market is still in process of growth and definition; large sectors have never been competitively exploited. Neither the knowledge nor, more important, the incentive exists for determining its precise lineaments and for adjusting production accordingly. When Sears, Roebuck was preparing to open a branch in São Paulo, a representative asked a Brazilian manufacturer how the unit price for 10,000 dozen clothespins would compare with that for 1,000. "Higher, he answered, because expanded production would involve him in more work, and anyway, if the item was going to be so hot, why not charge the public for it? Many an industrialist has told Sears he is making out all right with present volume and a 50 per cent markup, so why expand and get liver trouble (the Paulista variant on U.S. ulcers)?" (SEARS, ROEBUCK IN RIO, 1950, p. 151.) The store opened in 1949 with 500 employees, 95 per cent of them Brazilian and all participating in a profit-sharing plan. During the first day, the nylon-stocking counters, which undersold local competitors by 40 per cent, were deluged with customers, the stock of 1,000 refrigerators sold out, and the pyrex and enamelware cooking utensils were gone in a few hours.

Although most of São Paulo's consumers live on slim resources, the highly unequal distribution of wealth causes a small but articulate group to demand and pay excessive prices for luxuries and semi-luxuries that require the most advanced industrial techniques and divert productive forces from the basic items. Radio receivers serve as an example. In the United States there is one set per five inhabitants, in Brazil only one per thirty. São Paulo accounts for 90 per cent of Brazil's output of radio equipment, for which it employs 10,000 workers.

The spasmodic production movement characteristic of new industry is exaggerated by the influence of foreign concerns. Many are directly represented in São Paulo by large factories, assembly plants, or stores, the leading American firms being — in addition to Sears, Roebuck — General Motors, Ford, Anderson Clayton, International Harvester, Firestone, and Otis Elevator. Though such plants serve as organizational models, they also provoke erratic shifts in the supply-and-demand schedule by introducing new products, designs, and techniques that have been elaborated only gradually in their home countries.

Extraneous pressures and an indifference to the shape of the total market therefore restrain São Paulo's industrial plant from properly answering basic needs of the entire consuming public. Lucila HERRMANN (1947, p. 98) confirmed this statistically and reported, "on the one hand, a greater concern of industrialists with products serving urban life, at the expense of those serving rural; on the other, heightened interest in products less essential to life but subject to large profits, and slackened interest in manufacture of articles more essential to life and health."

In concluding this section it should be emphasized that the judgments explicit and implicit in the foregoing pages add up to no program. The only certainties advanced are that living traditions are not to be denied; that concentration, quantity, and short-term profits do not adequately gauge industrial strength; that a region industrializing in the twentieth century can be easily misled by the design and solutions of one that industrialized in the nineteenth. These principles serve public and private interests indistinguishably and, unless São Paulo's industrial economy is to lapse into permanent disequilibrium, must be acknowledged.

São Paulo should learn from rather than imitate its predecessors. Western Europe and, especially, the United States have incurred onerous "social costs" with their industry. Many of these costs do not yet severely weigh upon São Paulo. They include such items as: regimented and routinized lives; loss of warm and living modes of primary association among men; commercialized human relations and ascendancy of the profit motive; polluted cities dissociated from the natural attractions and freedom of the country; squandered resources and ruinous cyclical recessions; the wastes and degenerative cultural effects of competitive advertising. Such costs, some of them long since painfully incurred by its agricultural exploitation, are already accruing to São Paulo's industry. Ways might yet be found, however, to avert the full toll — and to redefine industrial efficiency.

Bibliographical Note

A principal source for São Paulo's industrial expansion is the monthly magazine *Revista Industrial de São Paulo*, founded in 1945; of particular value are its historical surveys of individual industries. BANDEIRA JUNIOR (1901) is a partial census of the city's industrial establishments at the turn of the century; BANCO DO BRASIL (1954) and the publications of the Departamento Estadual de Estatística contain present-day statistics. DEURSEN (1934), though somewhat outdated, is the best general analysis of the structure and dynamics of São Paulo's industrial park; N. W. SODRÉ (1947-1948) is a disorganized account of its growth; HERRMANN (1947; 1948c) presents statistical and interpretive studies of its functioning. B. da C. CALDEIRA (1935) is an analytical history of São Paulo's textile industry. STEIN (1957b) is a thoroughly documented analysis of the development of the cotton textile industry in Brazil. Among the many journalistic accounts of the contemporary "boom town" are BIG TIME . . . (1950), No. 1 BOOM CITY . . . (1951), CITY OF ENTERPRISE (1952), MARTIN (1955), and BRAZIL'S CITY . . . (1957).

For studies of immigration see p. 292; C. S. ANDRADE (1952) analyzes Brazil's internal currents of labor migration to São Paulo. RAMOS (1904) describes the advent of electric power, while PENTEADO (1942) discusses the possible effect of the new reservoirs upon the city's garôa. LUCROS . . . (1948) gives indices for the profit structure of São Paulo's industry. H. F. LIMA (1954) surveys the principal industrial concerns in twentieth-century São Paulo, giving sketches of many industrial pioneers. The founding and growth of Matarazzo's empire are recorded in ATRI (1926, pp. 115 ff.), IN MEMORIAM . . . (1937), and WYTHE (1949, pp. 163-64); EVEN BILLION (1952) reviews the achievements of his son and successor. The industrial empires of Gamba and Scarpa are discussed in ATRI (1926, pp. 154-61) and of Siciliano in PICCAROLO and FINOCCHI (1918, pp. 127-38). PRODUÇÃO . . . (1947) analyzes the production of capital goods in São Paulo; INSTITUTO DE PESQUISAS . . . (1939) summarizes the origin and growth of the Institute of Technological Research. IDORT (n.d. [b], pp. 87-123) and UNITED NATIONS (1951, pp. 17-26) examine aspects of industrial efficiency. WILLEMS (n.d.) and HERRMANN (1948a) discuss problems raised by the "mobility" and "fluctuation" of the labor supply. The growth and difficulties of technical and vocational education in São Paulo are set forth in H. A. SILVEIRA (1935), SECRETARIA DA EDUCAÇÃO . . . (1937), and REIS (1945); MANGE (1944) explains the functions of *SENAI*. The story of Sears, Roebuck in São Paulo is told in GOOD-NEIGHBOR SEARS (1949) and SEARS, ROEBUCK IN RIO (1950).

Chapter 19

THE METROPOLIS AS POLIS

"You're sending us to the trenches, but will you come along too?"
—PAULO DUARTE, *Palmares pelo avêsso* (1933,
published 1947).

HROUGHOUT THE WESTERN WORLD during the decades
preceding World War I, there was a minimum of
pressure upon political leaders and institutions to formulate techniques and plans corresponding to the new configurations of industrial life. Except for the clashes in outlying colonial regions,
an era of peace seemed to have descended. Faith in technology
and industrial initiative was a sufficient catechism. It served to
justify delivery of human communities, by constitutional democra-
cies and "benevolent" tyrannies alike, into the hands of a relatively
few economic entrepreneurs. Social critics were not yet sufficiently
informed, articulate, and influential nor were aggrieved parties
sufficiently organized and militant to impede the process.

In a world climate such as this it was not surprising to find in
dynamic São Paulo city, whose population was increasing after 1895
at a rate of 25 per cent every five years, a municipal administration
bearing little relation to the multifarious dimensions of metropolitan
life. It is true that in 1898 executive power was centered in a "single
alderman" called the "municipal prefect." The nation's republican
Constitution of 1891, however, had only vaguely defined the purview of municipal rule. "The States," it provided, "shall be organized so as to assure autonomy to the municipalities in all that affects
their particular interest." It was left to state legislators to specify
this "particular interest," with the result that vested political factions
reduced the municipality to a mere administrative entity and deprived it of statutory protection against interference from the state

(such as the state enjoyed vis-à-vis the federal government). A state law of 1906 made clear the bureaucratic artificiality of the municipality when it defined municipal revenues as consisting in part of proceeds from the sale of lands adjacent to "settlements of over a thousand souls in a radius of six kilometers from the central plaza."

The colonial tradition of municipal commonweal had been in eclipse too long for it suddenly to reappear in an era of political factionalism and bureaucratic routinization, of which the "central plaza" mentality was a by-product. City governments in fact failed to utilize even such powers as the republican Constitution accorded them. Though one paulista president avowedly abhorred (1905) "curtailment of the freedom of the municipalities," he nonetheless found that most of them "have not been able usefully to employ the taxes they collect and always postpone the execution of urgent measures, expecting everything to come from the State Treasury." (EGAS, 1926-1927, II, p. 177.)

State administration, however, was itself scarcely exemplar. In the 1890's Eduardo PRADO (1904-1906, II, p. 265) likened the divisions of Public Works and Sanitation to "two wagons carting the Treasury's money." There were "terrible contests and rivalries. Which could cart off more money?" On one occasion Public Works needed Sanitation's excess cement, but Sanitation, instead of making a direct transaction, sold to an intermediary, who resold to the rival division at a profit of 8$000 a barrel. Another time both agencies were engaged in works along the Tamanduateí. Sanitation built a culvert for drainage. Public Works dug a canal which not only served the same purpose but bisected the culvert, rendering half of it useless. The Treasury took a loss of over 1,000 contos. Subsequent years provide a harvest of analogous instances.

São Paulo and a few other Brazilian capitals which underwent rapid change at this time expanded therefore without benefit of long-range planning by political authorities. Their model, to the extent that any existed, was the vigorous uncontrolled growth of the young American cities. The prefecture of Antônio Prado (1899-1910) left little more than a few isolated monuments, such as a new market and the imitative and pretentious Municipal Theater. As a city engineer of the period admitted, the government did not guide but could only timidly and unimaginatively embellish São Paulo's growth, "leveling and extending the city streets and planting them with trees, opening parks and improving the trajectory of a few streets in the old section — resolving merely problems of the moment since resources went no further." (V. da S. FREIRE, 1911, p. 92.)

São Paulo city, as a political entity, was failing to serve its inhabitants. But, in direct proportion to this failure, it was coming to serve political machinations of state and national scope — a fact made explicit by the revolt of 1924.

The background of this revolt is to be found in the unchallenged supremacy of the Republican Party and its moral disintegration. Writing in *O Estado de São Paulo* (Sept. 2, 1919), Mário Pinto Serva said that the Republican forerunners of 1870 had "wanted to seize the power of the imperial dynasty and deliver it to the people." But twentieth-century Republicans, a "bastard generation," had made a mockery of elections and cheated the people of their power, maintaining it "in their own hands as a monopoly." Party platforms were issued personally by candidates or incumbents in the form of empty generalities. The nation at large had, in fact, no unified, doctrinal party. The Republican Party was inconstant and multiform. It received definition only from local political situations within the states. It was a function of space, time, personalities, and "the ceaseless contest for ministries, municipal prefectures, and state and federal sinecures." Its "sole objective was power." (CARMO, 1948, p. 22.)

The Law Faculty was by the 1920's an antechamber to the party. Students had long since abandoned their concern with current intellectual problems and their claims to political and literary leadership. They no longer took stands on public issues and held rallies only to adulate influential figures. The foremost student organization, the 11th of August Center, was a proving ground for the world of political intrigue. Academic diligence was slack, and law was studied so that it might, in future careers, be adroitly evaded. A. de Alcântara MACHADO (1940, p. 333) wrote that the "bacharel graduates without knowing how to draw up a power of attorney. But when it comes to hyperbolizing (manifestations to the government, excursions in special trains at the government's expense, messages applauding the eminently patriotic action of the government) and oratory (anniversary speeches, nationalistic speeches, commemorative speeches, speeches of welcome and valediction) the bacharel is a doctor." If São Paulo's colder climate originally determined the site of the academy, continued the critic (p. 111), "the temperature finally hardened brains and energies. Today's youth is refrigerated. Even more so than Armour products."

Without means to assert its claims, the general populace of the nation "oscillated between rage and sarcasm, hoping for any cataclysm that would clean out all this villainy." (SANTOS, 1930, p. 437.) It was the army that had the discipline and organization for overt action. The republican regime had done little to insure its loyalty, and the military showed themselves increasingly restive after 1910. Finally in July, 1922, an army revolt in Rio de Janeiro protested the election of President Artur Bernardes. A few junior officers had been detailed to instigate the defection of São Paulo's "Public Force" (state militia), but they lacked the prestige for the task. São Paulo remained calm, and the revolt in Rio de Janeiro was suppressed. Certain of the seditious officers, however, managed to escape imprisonment and to shift their conspiracy to São Paulo, some of them assuming false names and occupations. Here, abetted by persons still anxious to remove Bernardes, they set about to win allegiance from elements of the local army garrison and the militia.

From their headquarters in São Paulo city the conspirators established contact with garrisons in other states and kept in touch with their chief, General Isidoro Dias Lopes, in Rio de Janeiro. Elaborate plans were laid for seizing control of the city; after the coup, troops were to move eastward and, reinforced by contingents from Minas Gerais, march upon the national capital. On July 3, 1924, Isidoro Lopes left Rio de Janeiro for São Paulo, and in the early morning of the 5th the revolt broke out. The commander of the local Military Region, who had taken no precautions to forestall the action, was surprised and imprisoned in the first hours. About one-half of the men in uniform in the city, including soldiers, police, and firemen, went over to the rebels, swelling their strength to 3,000 or 3,500 men. On July 8, the "legalists," outnumbered and demoralized by this insurgent force of Isidoro Lopes, fled to Mogi das Cruzes, twenty-five miles east of the capital. Here they were joined by troops of the government and of other states, till they eventually reached a strength of 14,000 to 15,000.

With regard to São Paulo city, the critical aspect of the revolt was that it bore no relation to the life of its people. The rebels seized the city purely by reason of its prestige, industrial power, and strategic location. They had hoped that the proletariat might be induced actively to support their cause, and to that end some of them gave workers free access to commercial stocks of merchandise and food. Although Isidoro Lopes himself tried to ingratiate his regime by denying responsibility for any lawlessness and by doing all possible to maintain public order and municipal services, fine wines and foreign delicacies appeared on many a poor man's table.

The rebels, however, could evoke support neither from São Paulo's citizenry nor from elsewhere in the nation. The fact was that Isidoro stood for nothing. The program he publicized dealt in perfunctory fashion with political mechanisms to be enacted by a future constituent assembly. For persons who chafed under the oppressive Bernardes regime and longed for a taste of democratic leadership, the disillusion could not have been sharper. "Not a single idea, not a principle was taken up and comprehended, firmly and solemnly. There were only vague phrases, designed for simple rhetorical effects, showing not the slightest trace of proper knowledge of the affairs of state and of the moral and economic needs of the country." (SANTOS, 1930, p. 456.)

Nowhere, in fact, could the common man look for leadership. State President Carlos de Campos had hastily retreated to Mogi das Cruzes and his forces were bombarding São Paulo as an open city, at times firing merely for the psychological effect. The "legalists" knew their cause to be so lacking in appeal that they variously described the revolt to their own soldiers as a mutiny of the state militia for higher wages, an uprising of Italians, and a general strike. Under such circumstances, and in view of the fact that military targets and personnel in the city went virtually unscathed while civilians suffered sizable casualties, it was an excessive irony for Carlos de Campos to announce: "I am certain that São Paulo prefers to see its beautiful capital destroyed rather than legality in Brazil."

As for industrialists and, in general, those known as the city's "conservative classes," they made it repeatedly clear that political programs were of little consequence and that they were willing to come to terms with any regime as long as violence and damage to the industrial park could be avoided. The most vivid statement of this attitude was made by the president of the big-businessmen's Commercial Association: "We are not moved by tears shed by the people, who mourn the death of hundreds of unarmed citizens. We are not moved by the sobs of our wives and children who are resignedly and loyally suffering the severities of a situation neither created nor deserved by us.

"Our appeal is made ... so that the economic and financial annihilation of São Paulo state, the most prosperous member of the Federation, may be obviated."

In another utterance he disclosed his suspicion of the working class and, by implication, his lack of sympathy with the common people: "There exist in the city highly dangerous anarchist elements, Italians, Spaniards, Russians, and those of other nationalities, who await only the opportune moment to subvert the public and social order." (J. C. de M. SOARES, 1925, pp. 79, 95.)

The "danger" of anarchy, however, stemmed less from the alleged presence of foreign agitators than from the fact that the citizens found no public authority which represented their interests. The people had only distant curiosity about the conflict; in referring to the combatants they never said "we" and "they" but, like spectators or victims, designated both sides as "they." When the bombarding began the people had no cause to remain. To expedite civilian evacuation the rebels ordered heavy cuts in train fares. By July 17, 200,000 persons had left the city. Ten days later the rebels, having failed to attract any popular support, were also withdrawing. In an unpublished proclamation on this occasion General Isidoro revealed how the city had been gratuitously exploited for purposes ill-defined and foreign to it. São Paulo had been "merely a first step, a means of impressing the nation." "Our main objective was and is a revolution in Brazil which will raise the hearts, shake the nerves, and stimulate the blood of an enfeebled, exploited, derided, and enslaved race." (DUARTE, 1927, pp. 243-44.)

In the aftermath of disillusion following the 1924 revolt, idealistic members of the younger generation, together with certain older, experienced politicians, founded the Democratic Party in São Paulo (1926). For a reform movement to achieve momentum, however, in the most prosperous and politically powerful state of the union was not easy. Coffee rode on the crest of a boom, and the nation's president, Wáshington Luís (1926-1930), was a paulista who had restored civil liberties and was pursuing economic policies eminently favorable to his home state.

The collapse of the coffee market in 1929 threw the coffee empire into crisis and bewilderment. In 1930 President Wáshington Luís designated a fellow paulista, Júlio Prestes, as his successor, giving the state another favorite son as chief executive in its hour of need. Yet Prestes' election — insured by government control of election machinery — by no means promised the decisive measures and inspiration that the depression called for.

Meanwhile a new coalition, the Liberal Alliance, supporting the candidacy of the popular, demagogic southern *gaúcho* Getúlio Vargas, was winning acclaim throughout Brazil. The alliance was bolstered by the adhesion of influential Minas Gerais, the state which had been alternating the presidency with São Paulo and was disgruntled at Wáshington Luís' violation of the agreement. In São Paulo many members of the new Democratic Party saw in the alliance a challenge to the entrenchment and stagnancy of the Republicans. But since the alliance represented interests alien to São Paulo's political hegemony, paulistas found no grounds for enthusiastic commitment to either side. Numbers of them, looking in confusion for a hero who transcended political formulations, urged the return of General Isidoro.

In October, 1930, Vargas and the Liberal Alliance, backed by the army, asserted control of Brazil and forced the resignation of President Wáshington Luís. A diary kept in São Paulo city during that month by the Frenchman MOURALIS (1934, pp. 192-230) clearly portrays an indecisive citizenry confronted with the nebulous rhetoric of power politics: *Oct. 8.* The southern states of Santa Catarina and Paraná held by the revolutionaries. "Nervous anxiety" throughout the city; shopkeepers pull down their blinds, anticipating fighting. *Oct. 9.* Pernambuco to the north in revolutionary hands. Many have left São Paulo for fazendas or small towns. *Oct. 11.* São Paulo state encircled by the alliance; a general movement against its economic supremacy is threatened. The city displays "the greatest calm"; the townsmen "seem not to attach much importance to all that is happening." *Oct. 13.* Fighting in Minas Gerais. "Here the same indifference still reigns. Newspapers are concerned with the new street lighting." Young men await news of the rebels' success and pay no attention to the order for mobilization. *Oct. 16.* The national government can rely only on São Paulo, Bahia, and Rio de Janeiro. Mobilization partially effective among São Paulo's lower classes but not at all among the elite. Business circles worried over the deposition of Wáshington Luís.

Oct. 18. "This evening the aspect of the 'triangle' has completely changed." Nearly all stores have closed their blinds; the police are well armed. Everywhere "a vague disquiet." People wonder about the effects of occupation by the revolutionaries. "São Paulo sees itself conquered and is afraid." *Oct. 24.* News comes of the army revolt in Rio de Janeiro. An uprising also breaks out in São Paulo. Pro-government newspapers are sacked. All stores and cafés closed. Machine-gun fire. A few shouts of "Viva Getúlio Vargas!" People in the streets seem more curious than worried; they look on with "a discreetly ironic air and doubtless reflect that this means a lot of time lost."[1] *Oct. 28.* Life and traffic are again normal in the city. The first gaúcho troops are received by a large, curious, partly enthusiastic crowd. Many prominent people "who had showed themselves fiercely legalist on the evening of the 23rd became, after the 25th, convinced revolutionaries." Even certain Republican politicians have now gone over to the new regime. *Oct. 30.* Vargas arrives in the city amid mild acclamation. The gaúchos seem like troops of occupation. *Oct. 31.* Paulistas evince "malaise"; many who supported the revolution are apprehensive of its consequences.

Townspeople, the lower and middle classes, remained passive during the movements of 1924 and 1930. But it was not the passivity displayed nearly a century earlier, during the Revolution of 1842. For the people now were being reached by the press, radio, cinema, politicians, ideologies. Communists were publicizing, in however cryptic a fashion, the great Russian promise. Italian fascists, in an appeal to the *italianità* of their compatriots, were glorifying Mussolini's welfare state in the Italian-language press and through their local organization (the "Fascio Filippo Corridoni di San Paolo," founded in 1923) and its several youth movements;[2]

1. LIMA SOBRINHO (1933, p. 242), describing this same day, recorded greater excitement but the same absence of orientation: "The impression is that of a great whirlwind. Everyone runs pellmell without knowing where he is going or even what he is fleeing. . . . That city in terrified flight from a danger that no one sees is something hallucinating." A striking insight into the people's relation to politics was afforded by the fact that manifestants set fire to lottery shops, "as if to avenge their lack of prizes from the two games of chance, politics and the lottery."

2. When the Ethiopian war broke out in 1935, Count Matarazzo pledged supplies to Italy and promised to hold open the jobs of any of his employees enlisting under the Duce. Though fascism was too remote a phenomenon for its creed to make critical inroads among working-class Italo-paulistas, many influential ones had to shift ground quickly when Brazil declared war on the Axis in 1942. After the war, however, the city's amorphous ideological climate allowed easy assimilation of fascist émigrés from Italy's upper professional class.

in a counterappeal, exiled Italian socialists had founded a group named for Giacomo Matteoti. With greater propagandistic effect, movies were popularizing the American ideal of cheery, comfortable homes and conspicuous, sportive leisure for all classes.

Words, slogans, large ideas, distant cities and countries — all these, the citizen now realized, had relevance to his immediate life. But from the controlling political level came so many conflicting and fluctuating directives, with such an admixture of personal opportunism, that it was difficult to commit himself to a cause. In other words, a citizen was incorporated into a world extending far beyond the city in ways he had not been a century previous; but neither he nor his leaders clearly perceived the modalities of incorporation, nor how to achieve their regulation.

On assuming power Vargas appointed "interventors," usually young army officers, to replace the state presidents as part of his program of political centralization. The interventors sent to São Paulo, which Vargas especially wished to bring to heel, effected social reforms but displayed only a limited sense of human realities, refused to work with liberal groups like the Democratic Party, and were sharply resented as non-paulistas. One, an arrogant young lieutenant (who became Brazil's Coordinator of Economic Mobilization during World War II), was forced to resign for his ill-considered bolshevizing. Another, a doctrinaire positivist, believed beggars to have equal rights with all men and released those lodged by the government, lending a grievous aspect to the central streets of the capital.

For fifty years paulistas had harbored the suspicion that the federal government was plotting against their state's progress and hegemony; they were wont to refer to São Paulo as a locomotive pulling the other states like twenty empty freight cars. By 1932 this suspicion was fanned into flame. The words "constitution," "autonomy," and "legality" sprang to life. The Democratic and Republican parties, hitherto irreconcilable, became a Single Front in February, 1932. When on May 22, Minister of Justice Oswaldo Aranha, subsequently famous for his international diplomacy, arrived to mediate "the paulista case," he encountered a rally of tens of thousands in São Paulo city: workers and aristocrats, Communists and industrialists, doctors and lawyers, gentleman planters and white-collar workers, students and professors. Persons of every political belief made speeches. All had suddenly found agreement in the paulista cause. After being pelted with eggs and tomatoes, Aranha returned in failure to Rio de Janeiro.

On July 9 the solidarity prefigured by the rally was concreted by São Paulo's declaration of hostilities against the central government. The people's fervor was more reminiscent of 1822 and 1868 than of 1924 and 1930. "In every window and in every street," wrote an eyewitness, "we see streamers and flags fluttering with the colors of all the states.... The populace, brimming with unexcelled patriotism, fills the streets and with delirious hurrahs and vivas runs to the barracks, vibrant with patriotic songs and shouting: 'We want arms to defend São Paulo, to save Brazil!' " (ALVES SOBRINHO, 1932, p. 75.) Men, women, and children, doctors, technicians, and professional men flooded the improvised headquarters, demanding to be sent to the front. Shortly the Law Faculty was taken over as a center where volunteer units were formed to fight alongside the state militia and insurgent detachments of the army. Fifty thousand men were eventually put into the field.

Money contributions poured in. A Campaign for Gold received donations of gold articles to a value of over 3,000 contos in the interior and over 6,000 in the capital. A public subscription to assist soldiers' families amassed 1,000 contos in three days. Girls who organized a Campaign for Eggs gathered thousands of dozen eggs for trenches and hospitals; some Syrian girls started another campaign to collect raincoats. Industrial, commercial, and retail associations all embraced the cause, as did the various foreign colonies. Though the task of policing the city had to be assumed by civilians, violent crimes diminished and no license was taken for property depredation.

Frustrated in its hopes for the adhesion of Minas Gerais and Rio Grande do Sul and unable to receive military supplies from abroad, São Paulo was thrown upon its own industrial park for war matériel. Federal propaganda among the workers caused no defections, and they cooperated fully with employers and technicians. An appeal went out for scrap metal, and within a few days the amount turned in exceeded available storage space. Guns, flame throwers, gas masks, helmets, and bombs went into production. After some mismanaged experimental tests which caused loss of life, grenades and mortars were also manufactured. Armored trains and, for nearby rivers, armored launches were devised. Two 150 mm. guns were taken from emplacements and, with the aid of

World War I illustrations in the *American Locomotive Cyclopedia,* mounted on cars of the São Paulo Railway. By the end of September, 240,000 new and recalibrated rounds of ammunition were produced daily. Though paulista projectiles and bombs were not uniformly effective, the opponents came to respect them, and at one point São Paulo was delighted to intercept an enemy radio message reading: "Order Navy tighten blockade São Paulo receiving foreign munitions."

The Institute of Engineering and the Polytechnic School furnished hundreds of engineers and technicians to handle the severe problems posed by military operations, logistics, and administration of civilian life. In some cases Polytechnic students were called upon to perform ballistics calculations for badly trained army officers. When the fighting was over, paulista engineers had thousands of miles of roads, trails, and telephone lines to their credit.

The movement of 1932 dramatically revealed that the metropolis, no less than the agrarian town, holds a potential for orchestrating individual, professional, class, or factional interests within the larger perspective of community. What was also disclosed, however, was that conviction and hope can in the modern age be sustained only by levelheaded planning of a highly complex order. Enthusiasm, uninformed by head-on discernment of reality, contributes to its own defeat. Public passion is today more tenuously related to effective social action than once was the case.

The paulista war effort, which collapsed at the end of three months, was doomed by prematurity and miscalculations. The initial advantage of surprise was not followed up in a determined advance upon Rio de Janeiro. Then, when it turned out that proper measures to insure the alliance or neutrality of neighbor states had not been taken, military commanders and strategy were unprepared for sustained combat on many fronts. Further, there had not been time properly to convert the industrial park. Troops received ample sweets, wine, and toothpaste but, despite valiant efforts, insufficient fighting equipment.

In a more important sense, there was no psychological adjustment to the dimensions and implications of the task undertaken. There was no continuity between plans and action on one hand and emotional warmth on the other. An opponent justifiably asserted passive expectancy to have been the fatal weakness of São Paulo's campaign. "It waits for Rio Grande — and General Waldomiro

Lima breaks through Itararé to Buri. It waits for Minas Gerais – and troops of the 4th Infantry Division take Guaxupé, Casa Branca, São José do Rio Pardo and, presto, knock at the gates of Campinas. It waits for another pacifist revulsion in the capital of the Republic. It waits for Sr. Artur Bernardes. It waits for Sr. Borges de Medeiros. It waits for ships which are to bring arms from Europe. It waits for planes which are to come from Argentina and Chile. . . . It waits for the Antichrist.

"Never in Brazil was there so much waiting!" (Afonso de CAR-VALHO, 1933, pp. 70-72.)

Military operations were disorganized largely because no sense of mission was communicated to the troops. "The climate of political exaltation was restricted to the denser urban centers, and the consistency of the values that should have inspired the 'revolutionary action' was small in relation to the movement's sizable proportions." (FERNANDES, 1949a, p. 32.) Many professional officers were bereft of idealistic fervor. And, though volunteers often showed exemplary devotion, certain cultured youths were reported to have retreated from one bombardment shouting "Sauve qui peut!" – leaving common troops in the breach who were unversed in French.

The exaggerated optimism of his newspapers had not prepared the paulista soldier for the opponents' superior numbers and equipment. He was sharply disillusioned to find that the flags, tumult, and factitious appeals to bandeirante traditions of his capital city bore no relation to grim realities of trench warfare. It was the disillusion, not of the man of faint courage, but of the man incompletely informed, the man betrayed by outworn, inadequate, or opportunist political formulations. Referring to 1932 and earlier, Sérgio Milliet (CAVALHEIRO, 1944, p. 241) wrote that "the youths who followed old and, many of them, professional politicians were soon disillusioned and gradually abandoned the fight. Before understanding that the problem was purely one of education, they entered the Revolution of '32 with enthusiasm. It was this which at length opened everyone's eyes to our terrible dearth of men."

In political as in economic life, what had occurred was that, in São Paulo and in Brazil, nineteenth-century institutions were no longer molding capable leaders. By the 1920's, initiative was passing to persons without formal training and culture. Such persons came naturally into mastery of the premises and rhetoric of modern urban

life, and, though they had inherited no humanistic traditions or commitments to public service, some were shrewdly alive to the anxieties
of the people. Just as the new industrialists sometimes manufacture cheap, sturdy basic goods and sometimes shoddy, overpriced
luxuries, so the new politicos, according to the direction of their
immediate interest, sometimes astutely serve the public good and
at others ruthlessly exploit their constituents. The new leaders, that
is, disingenuously pursue private ends and in so doing may fortuitously serve the community. They are twentieth-century pioneers,
with techniques that tell much of their society. What remains is
to redefine public interest with an eye to the logic and implications
of these techniques, to create norms of leadership and to invest
public conscience with the discernment, incentive, and means to
assure fulfillment of such norms.

A formal instrument for articulating and rendering effective
public conscience is the primary and superior school system. In
1933 various firms and business and civic leaders financed the
inauguration of the Free School of Sociology and Politics of São
Paulo, the first advanced course of study in the social sciences in
South America. Oriented to American rather then locally regnant
European canons of sociology, the school in its first year conducted
ground-breaking surveys of immigration and of farm and city living
standards. In subsequent years it has commendably served its principal aim of training specialists for private and public administrative careers.

In 1934 the state founded a Faculty of Philosophy, Sciences, and
Letters to meet the crying need for a center of disciplined humanistic studies and, more specifically, to train secondary-school teachers
of higher caliber. Its standards elaborated in large part by selected
professors from Europe and the United States, the faculty has come
to assume the Law Academy's abandoned role as the city's —
perhaps the nation's — liveliest intellectual center. The faculty forms
part of the University of São Paulo, founded the same year and
incorporating such pre-existing bodies as the Law Faculty (1827),
the Polytechnic School(1894), the School of Pharmacy and Odon-
tology (1899), the Luiz de Queiroz Agricultural School of Piracicaba
(1901), the Faculty of Medicine (1914), and others. In 1946 a
Faculty of Economic and Administrative Sciences was added. For
the future it is planned to bring together the scattered components
of the university in an American-style "university city." The campus

lies to the south of São Paulo and abuts on the grounds of Butantã, the famous research institute for snake antitoxins. This pressure for a cohesive university with its independent life illuminates the decadence of the Law Academy. A century ago the latter was a pre-eminent institution in the city. The student body enjoyed a clear identity, while its ideas and doings were of public significance. Then, as the interests and energies of city life enlarged and ramified, the metropolis engulfed the academy. Students were dispersed anonymously in boardinghouses with tradesfolk and office workers. The city, insensitive to their intellectual concerns, deigned only to snicker at their pranks.

The metropolis is now too large and complex a community to reincorporate the student in a commanding role. The plea for a university city is therefore a plea for an autonomous subcommunity providing proper facilities for work, leisure, and healthful living, engaging the whole scale of a student's interest and activity, restoring him to participation and responsibility. The law students' lively defiance of the repressive Vargas government (1937-1945) showed their spirit to have been latent, not extinct. An ideal university city — even granted its artificial aspects — would provide, in William James' phrase, a "moral equivalent" for eliciting such spirit.

In the matter of public citizenship a critical function of São Paulo's institutions of higher learning is to staff and, directly or indirectly, to plan the primary school system. Statistically the primaries have been efficacious, for the city's literacy rate for persons over six has risen from 45 per cent (1887) to 75 per cent (1920) to 85 per cent (1946). Creating a literate populace, however, is less to solve a problem than to open a new range of educative responsibilities. Unfortunately the state-wide Code of Education (1933), designed to vitalize the primary curriculum, was largely vitiated by cramped facilities which since 1928 had forced many schools to "process" three and even four shifts of pupils each day.

After conducting an extensive poll of informed opinion on São Paulo's schooling problems, the educator and sociologist Fernando de AZEVEDO (1937, p. 170) concluded that the primary was not yet commonly regarded as "a focus of moral life, or, more clearly, a 'home of education.'" For the school to become this, "pupils cannot be isolated from teachers under pretext of an aggressive discipline.... Familial cordiality between students and their masters, who become the guides and counselors of youth, should be one of the basic traits of the new school whose social influence is exerted simultaneously through lessons and through an environment of moral elevation, mutual trust, and reciprocity of affections."

The question of political education is thus inseparable from that of general education, and "political" must in essence mean, as it did for Aristotle, "social." The attempt artificially to inculcate the rational outlook and to induce awareness of ideological abstractions is a fruitless one. Formal disciplines of the classroom must continually interact with experience. A *political* life is one which is *social*, or *lived*. Transcendent political issues of the modern nation become meaningful to the citizen only as he approaches them through participant association with fellows.

The *metropolis* of São Paulo cannot directly revert to the ancient *polis* of 10,000 householders — or even, less ambitiously, to the São Paulo of a century ago. In spite of danger signals which have appeared, however, it need not be regarded as irrevocably over-extended and fated for the decadence of the Spenglerian megalopolis. Planners in divers realms may find a viable concept in that suggested by the city-within-a-city projected for the university — namely, the multiform polis, having many interwoven communities of residence, profession, cultural and intellectual interest, sport and recreation. In this light the stereotyped class in civism, the local headquarters of a national political party, the political tract on a library shelf, or the speech broadcast from Rio de Janeiro has a far lower potential for political education than does the urban or industrial planner, the architect of a workers' town, the local labor syndicate, the parish church, the neighborhood playground, the sport club, or the Department of Culture (São Paulo's municipal bureau for cultural advancement).[3]

The best evidence of its citizens' potential for purposive, co-operative life is São Paulo's relatively peaceful assimilation of immigrants, for today only one of every four or five paulistas has two Brazilian-born parents.

The nineteenth century, as we have seen, witnessed certain

---

3. A *sine qua non* for the "multiform polis" — for its complex interbalance, its internal play, its ceaseless, many-phased self-analysis and -correction — is civil liberty and municipal autonomy. After the collapse of the first Vargas regime these were restored by the Constitution of 1946. Though the late Sr. Vargas, a prototype of the new-style politico, was re-elected in 1950, he shrewdly disinclined to resuscitate his "New State."

contretemps involving foreign groups. That an increasingly competitive metropolis should exhibit a degree of suspicion toward the immigrant was, particularly during the decades of large-scale and not immediately assimilable levies, only to be expected. Suspicions appeared not, however, to signify smoldering, endemic violence. It took clear incidents to set off fracases. A minor disturbance ensued, for instance, when in the early years of the Italian influx a witless Italian impresario gallantly dedicated a dramatic performance "to the Brazilian colony." More serious was the "Question of the Protocols," which arose over Italian indemnity claims and over alleged outrages against Italian crews in Brazilian ports.[4] Four years of recriminations were climaxed in 1896 when Italy's *opéra-bouffe* consul in São Paulo marched through the city streets at the head of two hundred compatriots and a brass band shouting "Viva Italy" and "Down with Brazil." This led to shooting and casualties, to assaults upon the paving and signs of the streets called "Italians" and "Prince of Naples," and to temporary police suspension of all newspapers and amusement places.

The city's foreign quarters all preserve a measure of identity. Sometimes this permits of freakish assimilation, as in the case of a Turkish immigrant who lived for thirty years in the Spanish quarter and adopted Spanish rather than Brazilian customs and language. The poet Guilherme de ALMEIDA (1929) once recorded his impressions of the various districts: Hungarian women in calico dresses. "Shawl over the shoulder. Kerchief on the head. Necklaces and necklaces. A trace of long-ago gipsydom." A spotless Japanese restaurant whose little waitress, "serious, distant, honest, among curtains of gay cretonne with figures almost as Japanese as she, informs crisply: 'No meals for whites!'" The German quarter of bars and pianos. "In each bar is a piano. At each piano is a German. For each German a stein. . . . People of peaceful discipline and poetic professions — florists, musicians, photographers, orthopedists, tapestry-makers, masseurs." The Jewish quarter with its synagogue and stores of ready-made clothes, furniture, and furs, "always and always." Tall Baltic women "with black astrakhan manteaux and milky legs above white tennis shoes (the best maids in São Paulo)." In the Spanish quarter the odor of "canvas and onions. Sacks of

4. Sailors are perennial troublemakers. On December 18, 1945, three tipsy jack-tars "on liberty" from the U.S.S. "Little Rock" (a prophetic name, it turns out) caused a scuffle in São Paulo by their indiscreet ogling.

grain open their mouths and yawn, obese and swag-bellied in storeroom doorways; strings of onions drip from the roofs, twisting
against dirty walls, sharply fragrant like moist braids.... Little
shops. At each one a woman in mourning on the balcony. On each
woman in mourning a fortune-teller's face. White-powdered without rouge." The Near-Eastern quarter, kingdom of gewgaws.
"Showy hardware. Cheap trinkets. Showcases: soaps, bead necklaces, cloth, playing cards, shawls, fountain pens, tins of shoe polish,
gramophone needles, neckties, rugs, watch charms, sandals, suit-
cases, pins, chromos, mirrors, bobbins, dolls, narghiles, tools....
People walking or standing. Only men. Not a single woman.
... Blond Syrians, from Beirut, Damascus, Jerusalem, buttoned up
in rubber coats, undulant and majestic like the waters of the
Euphrates, perfumed with mulberry and tobacco.... Dark Arabs
crying their language of dry, parched, sandy consonants... Armen-
ians with penetrating, oily eyes... Serious Persians... Subtle, hard-
working Egyptians... Proud Kurds with their suspicious tribal air
and the scorch of a distant sun on their rough skin... Turks... But
for São Paulo they are all Turks!"

These quarters are in no sense ghettos. National concentration
is largely for occupational and economic reasons. Syrians cluster
because their peddlers and stores have monopolized a large segment
of the dry-goods trade. Jews have maintained traditional commercial specialties. Portuguese and Japanese form suburban nuclei
as truck farmers. Britishers and Americans have means that allow
them to gather in the garden-suburbs near the sport clubs and good
schools.

None of the quarters contains a majority of the citydwellers of its
respective nationality. Multiplying opportunities for economic pur-
suit and social capillarity disperse even the more differentiated,
cohesive non-Latin groups. Syrians as well as Italians have married
into aristocratic "400-year" families and acquired mansions on elite
Avenida Paulista. In 1941 a study of the city's Jews (Assimi-
LAÇÃO..., 1941) revealed that only a few of those who had arrived
twenty-five years earlier were still to be assimilated; that while
Jewish immigrants rarely married Brazilians, one-half of their
children did; and that incompatibility among Jewish groups is
greater than that between Jews and Brazilians.

Florestan FERNANDES (n.d.) shows through an examination of
telephone directories that in the decade 1934-1943 persons of for-

eign birth and descent entered the status-conferring professions of law, engineering, and medicine in larger relative increments than native Brazilians. Law and the careers that it makes available are traditionally the purview of long-rooted families. But Italians are rapidly entering this field, showing themselves to be the group "that is most seriously competing with the natives, in an effort perhaps to establish political status corresponding to its new social and economic situation." (The falling-off of foreign immigration in the past quarter of a century has of course rendered the assimilation problem less critical.)

Negroes are a somewhat special case. From slavery they inherit the stigma of low socioeconomic status which, it may generally be said, ceases to attach to a Negro once he achieves economic or professional success. As a small (less than 10 per cent), readily identifiable minority group, however, colored persons are logical scapegoats in a fluid, increasingly competitive society which does not furnish, to the extent of the preceding patriarchal regime, ceremonial outlets for tension. In 1941 over 200 persons in the city were interviewed who had specified white domestics in "help wanted" notices. The range of explanations led the investigators to conclude that Brazil's traditional discrimination against Negroes for their low status and against markedly Negroid features has here been slightly infiltrated by discrimination against Negro blood. (Oracy NOGUEIRA, 1942.) In São Paulo, unlike northern Brazil, African survivals have been absorbed into the prevailing occidental culture, while the ritual fetish cults have disappeared. Yet the twentieth century has brought the city an outcropping of Negro journals, recreation clubs, and organizations for welfare and advancement. Since the Negro is now culturally assimilated, such associations have the object not of preserving Afro-Brazilian ways but of assailing attitudes that give him racial identity.

By and large, however, the city's color line, in keeping with Ibero-Moorish heritage, is loosely defined. Although many private clubs do not admit Negroes, there is no real segregation in São Paulo. A federal law of 1951 ended the occasional refusal of rooms to Negroes by the luxury hotels. A belt containing a high proportion of Negro and mulatto homes near the center of the city is largely explained by the frequent poverty of colored persons and by the tendency of many white immigrants to remain separate from native Brazilians — white and Negro alike. That the visible degree rather than presence or absence of a Negro strain is a status determinant is suggested in Flávio de CAMPOS' *Planalto* (1939, p. 173), a novel about São Paulo life, by a character who contemplates a mulatto girl: "And after all, *she isn't so very dark*. And if she were ... what importance has color? Stupid bourgeois prejudices, an excuse for the slavocracy" (my italics). A. de Alcântara MACHADO (1940, p. 64) points up the mildness and flexibility of racial attitudes in the following incident: "One of São Paulo's football [soccer] leagues organized two games between a Negro and a white team. One of the players was a mulatto. And so the solution to the problem was for him to play the first game with the Negroes and the second with the whites. Thus no one had cause for complaint.[5]

Whatever human tensions it harbors, São Paulo, certainly in the world of today, is a challenging example of the coexistence of diverse peoples. Its absence of decisive national and racial antagonisms — and, as was earlier demonstrated, of deep and long-standing hostility among the classes — is a rare and prized ingredient for the political community which Aristotle long ago envisaged.

5. The very malleability of racial attitudes — and with it the knowledge that discrimination is often suspended — places many persons, notably São Paulo's educated mulatto, under excessive tension. BASTIDE (1943, p. 32) observes in this connection: "In the United States the caste line is so clear that resentment is expressed in clear conscience, even more so in the case of mulattoes or educated persons. In Brazil, on the contrary, it insinuates itself silently, like a gnawing vermin."

Bibliographical Note

The relation of the municipality to state and federal administration in republican Brazil is treated in JAGUARIBE (1897) and NUNES (1920); J. J. RIBEIRO (1907) is a guide to the municipal organization of São Paulo state, as determined by the law of 1906. O. e SILVA (1940) is a collection of documents pertaining to municipal reorganization under Vargas; M. de CARVALHO (1942) defends the termination of municipal autonomy under the "New State." O. M. CARVALHO (1937; 1946), MEDEIROS (1946), A. SEVERO (1946), and MOREIRA (1947) are antiauthoritarian treatments of the modern problems of the Brazilian municipality. The dispositions relevant to the administration of São Paulo city itself are gathered in PREFEITURA ... (1936; 1947).

MESQUITA FILHO (1925), a São Paulo journalist, examines the sociopolitical climate of the 1920's; DUARTE (1927, pp. 284 ff.) and A. de A. MACHADO (1940, pp. 105-11, 332-33) comment on the politicizing of the law students. AMERICANO (1924) is a fairly balanced interpretation of the 1924 revolt; J. C. de M. SOARES (1925) and DUARTE (1927) are apologies for the "conservative classes"; POLICIA ... (1925) is an official indictment of the "subversive movement"; NORONHA (1924; 1925) is an account by the commanding general who was captured by the insurgents; COSTA and GÓES (1924) is an eyewitness report by two intellectuals.

The historical treatment of paulista "nationalism" given in PALMER, JR., (1950) is a useful background for the 1932 movement; so too are BRAGA (1921) and LOBO (1924), which put forward paulista claims to hegemony and special attention. COARACY (1931), LIMA SOBRINHO (1933), R. JARDIM (1932), and A. MIRANDA (1934) are narratives of local events related to Vargas' assumption of power. Accounts of the 1932 movement itself are plentiful, among them: H. de C. e SILVA (1932), the version of the commandant of São Paulo's state militia; KLINGER (1933), the depositions of five military leaders who served São Paulo; ALVES SOBRINHO (1932), H. de ANDRADE (1932), and CASTRO (1934), accounts by paulista patriots; PACHECO (1954), the diary of a law student who volunteered for the paulista cause and was soon disillusioned; Afonso de CARVALHO (1933) and GONÇALVES (1933), statements by partisans of the federal government. DUARTE (1947) is a foot-soldier's view of the fighting, a book from which FERNANDES (1949a) generalizes about "the sociological study of war." Logistic and technical phases of the paulista offensive are covered in N. de REZENDE (1933) and MORGAN (1934), while RELATÓRIO . . . (1940) documents the Campaign for Gold.

In a poll of twenty educators, F. de AZEVEDO (1937) spells out the problems of São Paulo's whole education system. MOACYR (1942) surveys education in São Paulo during the 1890's, and VALE (1924) does so for the early 1920's. The structure and history of the University of São Paulo and the plans for the university city are given in AMERICANO (1947) and E. de S. CAMPOS (1954); INFORMAÇÕES . . . (1935) sets forth the methods and purposes of the School of Sociology and Politics. HUTCHINSON (1957) is a study of university education and social status in São Paulo. IDORT (n.d.[a]) and R. de MORAES (1947) discuss the problem of training persons for municipal administration in São Paulo.

The Italian "Protocols" affair is treated at length in SCHMIDT (1947) and in the newspapers of the period; shorter accounts appear in VAMPRÉ (1924, II, pp. 622-23) and EGAS (1926-1927, II, pp. 102-104). For studies of immigration to São Paulo see page 292. DEPARTAMENTO DE CULTURA (1936), LOWRIE (1938a), and ARAUJO (1940a; 1941a) analyze the distribution of immigrants within the city, while A. ALMEIDA JUNIOR (1945) proves that their descendants are gaining admission to the Law Faculty in increasing numbers. MARTUS-CELLI (1950) investigates attitudes toward national, racial, and regional minorities in the city. Studies of specific national groups include PISANI (1937) and CASTALDI (1957) on the Italians, KNOWLTON (1955) on the Syrio-Lebanese, BIALOSKORSKI (1933a) on the Poles, CALLAGE (1934) on the Hungarians, and CRISSIUMA (1935) and WILLEMS (1948) on the Japanese. BASTIDE (1943) sets a background for the analysis of the Negro question in Brazil. BASTIDE and FERNANDES (1955) is a near-definitive study of the history and present status of relations between white and Negro in São Paulo; MORSE (1953) is a far less ambitious conspectus of the same subject. The many studies of present-day racial attitudes in the city include LOWRIE (1938b; 1939b), Oracy NOGUEIRA (1942), BICUDO (1945; 1947), and GINSBERG (1954); BASTIDE (n.d.[a]) correlates race and suicide in São Paulo and, in (n.d.[b]), surveys the Negro press of São Paulo state. The study by PIERSON (1942c) of the Negro in Bahia gives some consideration to São Paulo and is useful for comparison.

Chapter 20

MODERNISM

São Paulo! commotion of my life. . . .
—MÁRIO de ANDRADE, *Paulicéia desvairada* (1920).

*A*T THE END OF THE LAST CENTURY the processes of change and expansion in the city were so intense, and apparently so self-propulsive, that intellectuals tended to retreat to an ivory tower, or else to assume apologetic functions. Pierre DENIS (1928, p. 112) remarked in 1909 that: "The society of São Paulo is less given to literature, diction, and eloquence than that of Rio; though one feels it to be more active, São Paulo is not the capital of Brazilian letters. It is impassioned over economic questions." Here is a striking contrast with Fletcher's letter of 1855, quoted earlier, which ascribed a "more intellectual and a less commercial air" to São Paulo, where the word "money" was not "constantly ringing in your ear, as at Rio de Janeiro."

"Material progress" outran the formulations of its own spokesmen, for by 1900 intramural squabbles had split apart São Paulo's clique of positivists. Indeed, the most capable minds appeared to be fumbling. A learned newspaper polemic in 1901 over science and religion, between Luis Pereira BARRETO (1901) and Eduardo PRADO (1904-1906, IV, pp. 165-273), revolved largely around the marginal issue of anticlericalism. The central question as to the ways in which technological change relates to human culture and freedom was assumed to answer itself. Prado, a fervent Roman Catholic who had bitterly attacked the culture and "imperialism" of the United States in his *A ilusão americana* (*The American Illusion*, 1893), asserted religion and material achievement to be compatible, alluding to the United States and Canada as religious

258

countries and to Thomas Edison as a "very believing" Christian. Only the generation born after 1890, which had from childhood experienced São Paulo as a metropolis, was congenially to articulate the modern age. A student circle like that of Ricardo Mendes Gonçalves, who graduated from the academy in 1906, was still in the bohemian, Parnassian tradition of twenty years previous. Gonçalves, the future writer and publicist Monteiro Lobato, the future anthropologist Artur Ramos, and other young literati lived in a yellow chalet called "The Minaret." Though the group later made substantial, sometimes brilliant, contributions to Brazilian letters (except for Gonçalves, who killed himself while young), none in his student days showed traces of the "modernism" which is soon to be discussed. Known as the "hound pack," with Gonçalves "the hound that bays at the moon," they took long country walks during which they assumed roles from Daudet's *Tartarin de Tarascon*. Students of a decade later continued to resist new modes of expression; their journal *O Onze de Agosto* (July-Aug., 1916) commended the "beauty and polished form" of Parnassianism and called contemporary art trends "nebulous and pedantically hypocritical."

Popular magazines at the turn of the century had no political or artistic commitment. Their contents were disconnected, superficial, and designed to soothe and divert rather than to stimulate the reader. Caricatures had lost their sting. The first issue of *Vida Paulista* (Sept. 12-13, 1903) was announced as "more sketch than journal": "We will not preach any new idea; we will not overthrow the government with articles, nor arouse agriculture with pictures, nor spur industry with prose, nor with the same weapons develop commerce."

Modernism, by which Brazilians mean their awakening to the themes and idiom of the twentieth century and of their own country, is not to be taken, however, as a spontaneous product of São Paulo's "Modern Art Week" of February, 1922.[1] The movement grew from fragmentary responses which had for some twenty-five years been filtering into the conventional attitudes and rhetoric. The journal *Zé Povo* (Oct. 12, 1911), for instance, in spite of its shallow and derivative poems, had a quick, kaleidoscopic flavor:

1. Brazilian "modernism" is to be distinguished from the "modernism" of Spanish America, where the term designates the cultural renascence and Parnassian, symbolist movement of 1880-1915.

"Zé Povo is complete. Nothing escapes; it knows all, sees all, watches all, tells all; it's more than the Pathé Journal. It rambles hither and yon. It goes to football, theaters, movies, regattas, teas, dances; frequents the political and literary circles; visits the 'triangle,' Café Guarani, Castelões Teashop." O Eco (July, 1916) recognized the diversity of the metropolis and its demand for direct, practical counsel without "partisan color or religious overtones." It contained "theoretic-practical advices about agriculture, ranching, aviculture, electrical devices for small industries"; it addressed the philatelist and puzzle-solver, maintaining special sections for housewives, young ladies, and children with useful suggestions about fashions, healthful sports, and matters of general interest.

A more substantial literary endeavor was Revista do Brasil, founded in 1916 and revived in the 1920's by Paulo Prado and José Bento Monteiro Lobato. The Revista's wide range of lengthy, serious articles recalled the high quality of the mid-nineteenth-century reviews. And, though its tone was conservative, it finally printed a few younger writers: articles by Mário de Andrade, reports from Paris by Sérgio Milliet, and commentary from the United States by Gilberto Freyre, then a graduate student at Columbia University, who enthusiastically wrote of having discovered Mencken, O'Neill, Amy Lowell, Charles Beard, Dreiser, and Sinclair Lewis.

Editor Monteiro Lobato was a vigorous innovator and social critic. He first caught the public eye during World War I with a letter on page one of O Estado de São Paulo which decried the effects of slash-and-burn agriculture. In 1918 and 1919 he published three widely read books goading the urban conscience for its neglect of the hinterland, which he symbolized in the figure of a lethargic countryman, Jeca Tatu. In 1920 he founded a publishing house, Monteiro Lobato & Co., and set about to develop a reading public and to disseminate books by Brazilians. Although the house failed financially in 1925, it gave São Paulo's publishing industry an impetus which was to bring it into rivalry with that of Rio. Monteiro Lobato's patronage of young, experimental writers, his pungent and ironic literary style, and the sting with which Jeca Tatu caricatured the hitherto neglected or romanticized caboclo appeared to mark him as an apostle of the modern spirit. His forte, however, was the casual insight and polemical rapier-thrust; his larger judgments tended to be sentimental and his nationalism too sociological.

"Paranoia or cynicism," his scornful critique of the expressionist canvases of the young artist Anita Malfatti, exhibited in 1916-1917, showed up the limits and flaws of his vision. To explore freely the contours and symbols of twentieth-century themes was left for younger minds.

It was, according to Mário de ANDRADE (1942, p. 16), about six years before Modern Art Week that "the conviction of a new art" came to "a little group of paulista intellectuals." Perhaps the single most provocative influence was the paintings of Anita Malfatti, who had just returned from Europe and from studies in the United States.[2] In New York, she later wrote, she had once seen "a very brilliant red spot right in front of the sun. A voice asks: What is the secret of happiness? I stopped. The voice goes on: You seem to be the spirit of happiness, and the spot grew small and vanished. I then realized that it had been an automobile." (RASM, p. 17.) It was not long before another painter, Emiliano Di Cavalcanti, the poet Guilherme de Almeida, and the novelist Oswald de Andrade, who has been called the *enfant terrible* of the movement, were holding daily meetings in the bookstore O Livro. Soon others joined them. Authors read new poems and books; more exhibitions were held; musicians played new works. And the idea of the public sessions that were organized in February, 1922, as Modern Art Week gradually took shape.

The "Week" represented the efforts of a group of men and women about thirty years in age who, with diverse outlooks and media, had found a common enterprise in trying to penetrate and render into form the flux of modern life. Although certain of them eventually defined the artist's social mission with uncompromising rigidity, one of the modernists' primary services was to reincorporate art and society. During the previous half-century, art had come to mean virtuosity; the virtuoso was isolated from his milieu by a routinized vision of it and from fellow artists by the competitiveness of their interchangeable talents. The modernists were once again, like the romanticists of 1850, artists-in-community.

2. An earlier exhibition, by the young Russian-born, German-trained artist Lasar Segall in February, 1913, had been received sympathetically and without commotion. Young modernists were not yet ready for him, while Philistines found him no threat to the prevailing order, so far was his expressionism removed from the accepted academic style. Nine years later, during Modern Art Week, Segall's works evoked the same derision accorded to other modernists.

They held periodic gatherings in Mário de Andrade's house, in the elegant mansion of Paulo Prado, in the bookstore O Livro, in the office of the review *Papel e Tinta*. They took headlong flights into the night in the green Cadillac of Oswald de Andrade. They corresponded with fellow artists in Rio de Janeiro and abroad. "During those half dozen years we were really pure and free, disinterested," Mário de ANDRADE (1942, pp. 30, 33) later wrote. "No one thought of sacrifice, no one treasured the unintelligible, no one imagined himself precursor or martyr."

Modern Art Week was celebrated in the Municipal Theater, an imitation of the Parisian *Opéra* which stood for the very cultural attitudes that modernism sought to explode. The inaugural speaker was Graça Aranha, a patron from the older generation widely known for *Canaã*, a thesis novel about rural Brazil; his speech on "The Esthetic Emotion in Modern Art," "illustrated" by poetry and music, was kindly received but threw little light on the aims of his protégés. The piano playing of Guiomar de Novais was applauded, though she too fell short of being a full-fledged modernist; in an open letter in *O Estado de São Paulo* (Feb. 15, 1922) she protested the "exclusive and intolerant character" of the proceedings and described herself as "saddened by the publicity given to satiric references to the music of Chopin." The composer Heitor Vila Lôbos, who had hitherto done most of his music-making as an accompanist for moving-picture houses, caused a commotion by appearing with a slipper on one foot (because of a corn). In spite of this "futurist" eccentricity, his music received favorable notices.

It was not musicians but painters and writers who elicited furor. Scandalous gossip about them was invented and circulated. Canvases by Anita Malfatti and Segall were attacked with canes.[3] Readings by poets and novelists were rendered inaudible by hoots and catcalls. One newspaper suggested that the modernists had planted claques to aggravate the uproar. Certainly, the poet Menotti

3. New York's "Armory Show" of 1913 (the year of Segall's first São Paulo exhibition) evoked an identical reaction, and for identical reasons: "Unlike the French public, which had seen modernism evolve step by step, the American public had no preparation to help them understand the wild-looking pictures with which they were suddenly faced. Newspapers printed headlines usually reserved for murder trials, and citizens stormed through the doors to rock with vituperation or laughter. Thus began the hysterical furor about 'modern art' which still shouts down rational discussion of contemporary painting." (FLEXNER, 1950, p. 90.)

del Picchia went out of his way to provoke tumult in a speech that began: "The automobiles of the planets careen dizzily along the highway of the Milky Way. . . . The constellations play in a jazz band of light, syncopating the harmonic dance of the spheres. The sky seems a huge electric billboard that God set up on high to advertise for eternity His omnipotence and glory. . . . What an error! Nothing could be more orderly and peaceful than this vanguard group, freed of traditional totemism, alive to the policed, American life of today." (BROCA, 1942.)

What was striking about the young modernists was not, however, their insolence and iconoclasm but their self-consciousness and missionary dedication. In an open letter to Menotti del Picchia following the "Week," Mário de Andrade wrote: "We finally achieved what we wanted. Really, friend, there was no other means to acquire celebrity. . . . We had only one resource, to fabricate the Modern Art Carnival and let the parrots talk. They tumbled like parrots." (BROCA, 1942.) And the first modernist review, *Klaxon* (May 15, 1922), spoke of the "Week" as medically necessary: "Damp, chilled, rheumatic with a tradition of artistic tears, we made up our minds. Surgical operation. Excision of the lachrymal glands."[4]

That the 1922 group had not been doctrinally or stylistically unified was evident after 1924, when manifestoes and magazines of such cliques as "Brazilwood," "Green-and-yellowism" (the national colors), and "Anthropophagy" (a reference to the aborigines) began to counteract European currents with nativist and nationalist appeals. As 1930 drew near and political restlessness increased, artistic programs were infiltrated by political credos.[5] Novels by such

4. This clinical attitude toward the complacent bourgeoisie was carried to its ultimate a decade later when the gifted artist and engineer, Flavio de CARVALHO (1931), kept his hat on during a Corpus Christi procession to test whether respect for individual rights was stronger than religious formalism. His flirtatious manifestations, he claimed, left female worshipers, particularly the homely ones, quite oblivious of their devotions — till finally he was pursued by the crowd and came under temporary police custody.

A quarter of a century after this "experiment," the artist tried another. He strode through the city streets dressed in his "suit of the future": a colorful blouse, yellow sandals, and a short skirt. Again a crowd gathered, but this time they were more jocular, and some even promised to adopt the style. The bourgeois capacity for indignation appeared to have weakened by 1956.

5. A plebeian forerunner of socially committed art had been the anarchists' Social Theater Group, founded in São Paulo in 1922, the year of Modern Art Week; its first play was called *Proletarian Flag*.

writers as the self-styled "mural" novelist Oswald de Andrade and fascist-oriented Plínio Salgado challenged the supremacy of poetry, since they were better vehicles for social concern.

After 1930 it is hard to speak of "modernism" as a single phenomenon. Even among the nonpolitical, ramification of interest and emphasis became extreme. There were nativists, Europeanizers, Americanizers. Some continued to shock the bourgeois; others courted the underprivileged; others created worlds of private symbolism. There was increasing exchange with other cultural regions of Brazil. There was interplay between the arts and research disciplines. For many, modernism became social anthropology; recovery of neglected folklore; study of Brazil's social, economic, and political institutions; ethnology and philology; or literary criticism. The philosophically inclined were attracted to the less schematic, less deterministic systems (notably the Germanic thought diffused by Ortega y Gasset) and to an eclectic, historically oriented quest for a Brazilian "ontology." "Modernist" also was the plea of Paulo DUARTE (1938) for rehabilitating and preserving documents, art works, and architecture of the past, a task in large part assumed and ably carried out by the local branch of the Service of the National Historic and Artistic Patrimony.

Those who kept to artistic creativity displayed similar diversity. In the catalogue of one salon of painters in the 1930's, the critic Sérgio Milliet wrote that they represented "a state of spirit" rather than "a school." "And that state of spirit," he pointed out, "is that of our contradictory century, pained and joyful, troubled and mystical, disillusioned but nonethless constructive." Likewise the literary reviews assumed an attitude of serious, pluralistic inquiry. *Revista Nova* (March 15, 1931) opened its pages to "combativeness, ferment of ideas, conflicting currents, search, and discussion." *Clima* (May, 1941) announced its title to signify a " 'climate' of curiosity, interest, and intellectual ventilation." The editors had multifarious interests but looked beyond the encyclopedism of positivists and evolutionists; they hoped to mediate among the realms of the modern mind and to avoid facile systematizing. This exploratory, self-critical phase of modernism was in some measure a response to an atmosphere of world crisis and to the disillusion engendered by the inadequate leadership and ideals of the paulista revolt of 1932.

The modernist movement, becoming ever more labyrinthine, may be said to have lasted some twenty-five years, or a generation.

Its terminus was marked perhaps by the death of Mário de Andrade in 1945, or perhaps by the appearance of a group of young poets whose skilled, hermetic verse was advertised as "neo-modernist." One cannot say, however, that modernism has been "superseded." Like romanticism, it was "a state of spirit," not a body of dogma, and therefore an open, not a closed system. And, it may be surmised, the roots of modernism are more deeply struck than were those of romanticism; its ramifications have been more diverse and conscientiously explored, and they continue fruitfully to interact. It appears to be a threshold to cultural maturity, and to an era of organic, less spasmodic cultural change.

Although São Paulo was not exclusively the cradle of Brazilian modernism, the city and its Modern Art Week imparted a spirit and impetus to the movement. The critic Alceu Amoroso Lima explains this, first, by pointing out that modernism — with its "esthetics of noise, color, light, movement, raucous impression, protest, scandal, rupture with the obsolete and established" — reintegrates art into modern life. He then identifies São Paulo as the Brazilian city in which artists were most fully dominated by components of this life: "motor, asphalt, radio, tumult, rumor, open-air life, great masses, big effects, the cinema carried into the other realms of art and stamping them with its esthetics of splintered reality, imagistic illusion, superposition and distortion of forms, primacy of technique over nature and of rational or irrational effect over nostalgic and lyrical inclination." (B. de FREITAS, 1947, p. 321.)

Rio de Janeiro was a less likely point of outbreak for a cultural "revolution" because of the leisurely, ceremonious internationalism of its elite and because of its folkloristic popular culture. Not only, however, did the international affinities of São Paulo reflect the vitalities of its trade and industry, but the city was oriented by tradition and the economy to a broad hinterland, rather than to a colorful, circumscribed region. The paulista mind, as earlier suggested, is less preconditioned, more free to select and to synthesize. It is a paradox, though not a puzzling one, that São Paulo, perhaps the country's least "picturesque" city, should sponsor the most urgent inquiries into Brazilian culture and into its world significance.

Social factors are also to be considered. Commercial, materialist, fast-moving São Paulo had produced the cautious, literal-minded subject of Mário de Andrade's "Ode to the Bourgeois":

I insult the bourgeois! the nickel-plated bourgeois,
The Bourgeois-Bourgeois!
The well-made digestion of São Paulo!
The man-ham! the man-buttocks!

This creature, living with no margin of culture, confidence, or humor, cannot risk being a loser and becomes the ideal, the inevitable target of the revolutionary. "Now in malicious Rio," wrote Mário de ANDRADE (1942, p. 28), "an exhibition like that of Anita Malfatti might have caused a public stir but no one would have been carried away. In ingenuous São Paulo, it created a religion."

Along with the bourgeoisie and parvenus, moreover, São Paulo could boast a small aristocracy having the cultural self-assurance to patronize modernism. Sunday gatherings of intellectuals at the home of Paulo Prado, himself an author and famous for his sardonic *Retrato do Brasil (Portrait of Brazil)*, recalled the earlier salon of his grandmother, Dona Veridiana; and in 1924 he subsidized the magazine *Knock-out*, successor of *Klaxon*. Another aristocrat, Dona Olívia Guedes Penteado, also maintained a modernist salon, and a member of her family was the first to buy a painting from Di Cavalcanti.[6]

As long as the movement was supported solely by the indulgent rich, however, and until it found ways to enter the lives of the people at large, modernism could be little more than a cultural incrustation. Official subsidies, to be sure, were forthcoming soon after Modern Art Week. Anita Malfatti and the sculptor Victor Brecheret received pensions to study abroad, and one of the latter's statues was purchased for a public park. Performances of Vila Lôbos' music were sponsored in other countries. In fact the Municipal Theater had been made available for the "Week" itself at no cost. These, however, were isolated subventions. The prefecture was in no way prepared to sustain an integrated, many-phased cultural program. Its contract in 1926 with an Italo-Brazilian theater company made clear that bureaucrats still judged culture in terms of quantity, spectacle, and European affiliation. By the terms of the

6. Recently the *nouveaux riches* have found that to patronize modern art is not only safe but socially advantageous. Their discovery has endowed the city with elegant museums and theaters, but lack of criterion makes their patronage occasionally capricious and uninspired.

contract, the company was to produce, between May and September, "a repertory of operas, a repertory of popular musicals, an Italian or French dramatic repertory, at least two symphony concerts directed by a world-famous conductor; optionally, any other dramatic spectacle, operettas, dances, recitals of virtuosi, and so forth, at the discretion of the Prefecture." (Municipal Law 2955, April 6, 1926.) Mário de ANDRADE (1934, pp. 247-67) remonstrated that the troupe performed only worn-out *Toscas* and *Traviatas*, that it engaged incompetent artists, and that in any case the high admission charge turned away students and the general public: "Let us cease that absurd pretension, the display of luxury of the mere few and not of the city, simply because in its present economic, intellectual, and moral situation the city has no reason or wherewithal for showing off."

Mário de Andrade himself finally received the chance in 1934 to direct a new municipal Department of Culture, assisted by a staff of able colleagues. Among the many functions that it undertook were to hold contests in the fields of history, theater, folklore, and music; form a symphony orchestra; develop educational cinema; install a public record library; organize popular orchestras and traditional fiestas; restore and publish historical documents; conduct surveys of the municipality that would help to improve its economy and encourage tourism. Later a modern, skyscraper library was built, administered as a dependency of the department. Mário de Andrade's central purpose was to enrich the daily life of the common people and, through playgrounds and kindergarten libraries, that of their children. In spite of accomplishments that won international fame, his larger design was curtailed by political pressures, and he finally left the department with a bitter disillusion that hastened his early death. Yet three years had sufficed for him to prove that modernism was not a pose and was at home with the people, and imaginatively to develop new areas of municipal service in their behalf.

In his life and writings Mário de Andrade was the incarnation of modernism, as Alvares de Azevedo had been of romanticism. He embodied its introspection and its social consciousness; its narcissism and its iconoclasm; its intellectual preciosity and its sidewalk slang and familiarity; its lyricism and its raucous barbarity; its nostalgia and its antitraditionalism. He poked fun at the pianist

Guiomar de Novais for her attachment to Chopin and Schumann, and also wrote a sensitive study of the rural samba of São Paulo. Prose fiction, poetry, musicology, research into folkloric or scholarly themes, sociology, criticism of all the arts were each within his province. Mário de Andrade was responsive to the cultures of Europe, the Americas, the regions of Brazil, and to their interplay. His was pre-eminently a city mind, attuned to imperatives of the outer world and free to range across and to interpret the things of Brazil. This city mind, moreover, gave a fixed center to his imagination: São Paulo. Sérgio MILLIET (1946) calls him: "Above all an urban poet, without a single rural landscape, without bucolic images, but immersed in city coal-smoke, pointing out factories and skyscrapers among the mists of his Piratininga." His poetry from the early *Paulicéia desvairada* (*São Paulo Hallucinated*, 1920) to the posthumous *Lira paulistana*, Milliet continues, expresses a love grounded in psychological ambivalences and poignantly sublimated in the city which is still "adolescent, assuming form, hesitant between the feminine tenderness of certain cities like Paris and the masculine strength of others like Chicago."

The modernist, like the romanticist of a century ago, finds São Paulo to lack the salient traits of a Rio de Janeiro or Salvador. What overtly characterizes São Paulo — movement, speed, lights, traffic, skyscrapers, factories, money — is universal, with no explicit voice or design. To encounter the city's *genius loci* demands a particular sensitivity. Sometimes it is discovered, as MOURALIS (1934, p. 148) found it, in a small restaurant where students and *"petits fonctionnaires"* chatter over a fragrant *feijoada* and coffee; or perhaps, as for the poet Guilherme de Almeida, in the foreign quarters, where laughter and rhythms of other lands, not yet wholly absorbed, lend the city an accent of mystery; perhaps in secular fragments of ancient beliefs, heterogeneously pooled in the common man's corpus of magical acts and phrases; perhaps in the ageless ditties (*trocinhas*) of children at play; perhaps in the impromptu samba, beaten out by bootblacks on their shoe boxes, bottles, and tins; or perhaps in the anonymous ballad (modinha), slangy, unromantic, factual, journalistic, rudely versifying the sensational crime or disaster — so different from the deftly satirical, politically conscious balladry of Rio de Janeiro.

Writers and artists find that São Paulo offers an idiom congenial to the elusive and many-dimensioned, partly bitter and partly yearning quality of the modern world itself. One finds this idiom in the images of Mário de Andrade's verse: in the city's winds and garôa, its April afternoons, its "millions of roses," its little seamstresses, its bulky streetcars, its "horrible cathedral made of pretty stones." One finds it also in the intense yet delicate "tonalities" of Segall's canvases which, according to the novelist Jorge Amado (*Diretrizes*, April 24, 1941), reflect a mystery hidden in the city's bars, in the twilight of its Plaza of the Republic, in its quiet family suburbs with tree-lined streets. One finds it in the quick, allusive, catalectic Italo-Brazilian dialogue of A. de Alcântara Machado's city tales and sketches; in the wistful but vibrant lyricism, the shifting rhythms, the subtle polyphony of the music of Camargo Guarnieri — which contrast with the more telluric, symphonic mode of Rio de Janeiro's Vila Lôbos.

The folklorist Amadeu AMARAL (1949, p. 127) once made a distinction between the popular music of paulista countrymen and that of urban balladeers. The former "lives in tradition and of tradition. It is simple, monotonous, plaintive." Its rhythm falls naturally in with the "ageless measure of seven- (or less commonly five-) syllable verses, arranged most of the time in regular strophes." The music of the city balladeer, however, is of the moment. It draws unpredictably on a host of traditions, and exhibits the diversity, freshness, and early obsolescence of a world of flux and fashion. It is "complex, capricious, melodic, with a great variety of rhythms, comprising verses of every measure and strophes of every type."

Persons of an older generation had been unable to discern the vigor and relevance of the city's daily vernacular. Predisposed to a classical concept of "culture," the scholar A. A. de FREITAS (1921, p. 48) once accused the city's common man of "intentional, calculated, and selfish disdain" for failing to commemorate the exploits of the colonial bandeiras in popular Homeric epics. The work of the modernists has been to reveal that, when man lives with a curtain between himself and the world of immediate experience, symbols and idiom for expression, and for coherent thought itself, will elude his grasp.

Bibliographical Note

J. P. da SILVA (1922, pp. 167-82) surveyed the literary scene in São Paulo on the eve of Modern Art Week, finding much activity but as yet no "school." The career and writings of Monteiro Lobato are carefully examined in CAVAL-

HEIRO (1955); CRUZ (1948) is a perceptive critical study. PRODUÇÃO E CONSUMO . . . (1947) and CAVALHEIRO (1948) trace the history of the city's publishing industry.

The best guide to Modern Art Week and to the subsequent movement is S. COELHO (1954), a collection of descriptive and interpretive articles with a bibliography for the period 1922-1937. M. da S. BRITO (1954-1955) is a well-documented study of the "Week" itself and its antecedents. For journalistic accounts of the "Week" see contemporary São Paulo newspapers and BROCA (1942). The keenest analysis of modernism is by its most versatile spokesman Mário de ANDRADE (1942); see also RASM (1939), G. de Almeida's chapter "São Paulo e o espirito moderno" in SÃO PAULO E A SUA EVOLUÇÃO . . . (1927), MORSE (1948; 1950b), and, for painting and plastic arts, ANDRADE FILHO (1947) and L. G. MACHADO (1948). FUSCO (1940) deals with the second phase of modernism, the decade of the 1930's. The contrasting attitudes of first- and second-generation modernists, many of them paulistas, are set forth in the symposia edited by CAVALHEIRO (1944) and NEME (1945) respectively. For the verse of the "neo-modernists" see Revista Brasileira de Poesia, founded in São Paulo in 1947.

A memorial issue of the Revista do Arquivo Municipal (CVI, Jan.-Feb., 1946) devoted to Mário de Andrade contains articles on his life, personality, mind, and writings. The functions of the Department of Culture are outlined in F. PRADO (1936a, pp. 39-75; 1936b, pp. 97-107); Mário de Andrade's frustrations as its director are brought out in DUARTE (1946a) and in his letters to Duarte, published in O Estado de São Paulo (Feb. 25-27, 1947).

The city's library facilities are discussed in GROPP (1940) and M. L. M. da CUNHA (1947); see also the magazine Boletim Bibliográfico, founded in 1943 by the Municipal Library of São Paulo. The articles by ALVARENGA (1942; 1943) describe São Paulo's library of recorded music and document the musical taste of those who frequent it. J. da V. OLIVEIRA (1950; 1952) lists the city's musical institutions, indicating the people's listening habits, while CERQUERA (1954) gives the history of opera in the city to 1951. The collection and activities of São Paulo's new Museum of Art are described in F. B. e SILVA (1954).

A number of studies of the city's popular culture exist. See A. de A. MACHADO (1940, pp. 35-37, 190-5) for the street ballads; FERNANDES (1944) for magical aspects of the city's folklore; FERNANDES (1947) for the children's ditties (trocinhas); FERNANDES (1952) for popular riddles (adivinhas); T. de LEMOS (1941) for the sambas of the bootblacks; E. de A. WHITAKER (1940) for spiritism. Amadeu AMARAL (1948) deals with many aspects of urban and rural folklore in São Paulo.

Chapter 21

ANATOMY OF THE METROPOLIS

Dona Bianca went to bed without turning off the light. . . . And she closed her eyes to imagine herself in the most expensive palacete of Avenida Paulista.
—A. de ALCÂNTARA MACHADO, *Brás, Bexiga e Barra-Funda* (1927).

*I*N THE COURSE OF THIS HISTORY, the term "city" has been used more and more to point to the scale of expectancies and "mind-set" of the urban population, rather than to designate a physical entity. In this final chapter it is fitting to return to the more basic concept developed near the outset of the study — namely, the city as a nucleus of buildings, activities, and services, having a particular geographic situation.

In 1890, as we have seen, São Paulo had already begun to expand in all directions from its central hill. To the east, low-lying Braz with its railway station (Rio-São Paulo line) and its Lodge for Immigrants was fast becoming a district of small commerce and workers' quarters. Luz Station (Santos-São Paulo line) to the north was another center of activity, with land here also being settled by poorer classes. The south and southwest had not the stimulation of a railway line and terminal, and were only beginning to feel the pressure for residential space. But, to the northwest, the new residences on subdivided chácara lands by now plainly advertised the urban culture and interests of the ascendant elite, as did the newly beautified Plaza of the Republic, formerly the bull ring.

It is not easy briefly to characterize this concentric growth,

271

which has occurred at immense speed[1] through the agency of private transactions and profit-minded real estate companies, without auspices of zoning regulations or a controlling plan, and frequently in defiance of the logic suggested by topography. "Vertical" change — that is, functional changes within already settled areas — is as unpredictable as the "horizontal." It is true that a study done in 1935 by Lucila HERRMANN (1944) of a vital radial, Avenida São João, corroborated the general schema of urban evolution formulated by the American sociologist E. W. Burgess. She found that the avenue, originating in the city's economic and bureaucratic center, proceeded through a zone of small commerce in economic and moral deterioration, then, successively, through zones of modest residences, of upper-class residences, and finally suburban zones of industry and small commerce. The city's other main radials, however, do not conform to this schema, and even Avenida São João has, in the years since the study was made, appreciably departed from its predicted stages of development.

Speaking in broad terms, however, one may say that the pattern of the city's growth has been determined by the basins of the Tietê and Tamanduateí to the north and east and by the high ridge to the west and south. This pattern is complicated by many streams that gully the elevated land, most importantly the Anhangabaú with its affluents which cut off the hill upon which the city center stands. Today, moreover, new topographical determinants are introduced as the city encroaches into the Pinheiros valley to the west and the Cantareira hills to the north.

One of the most dramatic developments has been the progressive occupation of the high land by the *haute bourgeoisie:* an advance after 1890 through Higienópolis up to Avenida Paulista on the crest, then down the southwest slopes into the "Gardens." This movement correlates with the rise of the traditionless, industrial-commercial elite. It is reflected architecturally in a shift from the modified fazenda-type dwellings of the coffee barons to the ostentatious hodgepodge of styles — including classical, Florentine, English, Near-Eastern, and neocolonial — of Avenida Paulista. It is also reflected in the abandonment of the ideals of a sophisticated

1. Between 1934 and 1940, for example, the population increase within a 2-mile radius of the city center was less than 10 per cent. Between the 2- and 4.5-mile circumferences it was 50 per cent; beyond 4.5 miles it was 85 per cent.

and Frenchified leisure class (which were implicit in the name "Campos Elíseos," or "Champs Élysées," given to an early upper-class district) in favor of the ideals of an energetic, Anglo-Saxonized plutocracy dedicated to "home," sports, and comfort, an image popularized by the work of English urbanists. On April 1, 1893, *Diario Popular* asserted that São Paulo was striving to achieve the "grandiose proportions of Anglo-American cities" and identified Higienópolis, with its atmosphere of English "cottage squares," as one of the city's prettiest spots and "the favorite locale of the English and Americans, yankees."

The Tietê-Tamanduateí arc today girdles the ridge with rail-ways, proletarian quarters, and zones of commerce and industry, while the apartments, rooming houses, and modest dwellings of the expanding commercial and bureaucratic middle classes occupy interstices in both upper- and lower-class areas. Formerly aristo-cratic quarters near the center are a favorite point for middle-class infiltration, although centrally located luxury apartments allow ex-ceptions to the flight of the elite to spacious, gardened sites on the outskirts. The area just described, the rising land with its girdle, exhibits unexpected open spots, especially along the rivers and steep gullies, where squatters' huts, stray animals, improvised gar-dens, and football fields appear. But mounting land values, urban-izing programs, and gradual canalization of the Tietê are inducing progressively fuller land use. This area might in fact be called the core of the modern city, as the little "triangle" was in the last century.

Outside this modern core are a large number of heterogeneous suburban nuclei, half assimilated into the city and ranging from an urban, industrial subcenter such as Santo André to rural villages lacking electricity and piped water. These perimetric satellites are usually traditional, formerly independent settlements. Though each has a variety of relations with the encroaching metropolis, they fall roughly into three functional categories:

(1) *Residential-recreational.* Some of the suburbs to the east, along the "Central do Brasil," and to the north and northwest are predominantly middle- and lower-class residential. Santo Amaro to the south — long ago the site of the modest German farm colony — has become, owing to lakes created by the hydroelectric dams, a middle-class excursion center, while the wealthy have week-end chácaras and even permanent homes there. The cool hills and

forested park to the north offer similar attractions (and are a site for hospitals and sanitariums). In fact the "week end" in a suburban chalet, like the vacation at the seashore or a mountain spa, has become a fixed institution for those able to afford it. Originally a fad popularized by Hollywood, the "week end" is becoming an ever more necessary escape from the pace and tensions of the city. The tendency to scorn rustic life and quiet, evident after about 1880, has reversed itself. So far, however, São Paulo lags behind the large cities of Europe and the United States in providing facilities for the mass exodus of its lower classes on holidays.

(2) *Agricultural.* The city environs have, in spite of the unfavorable soil, always supported agriculture. Some is of a sporadic or subsistence nature, while some is commercial and helps — though, as has been shown, to only a limited extent — to feed the city. In recent decades Japanese immigrants, most of whom first worked on fazendas, have intensified suburban truck farming (sometimes with excessively exploitative methods) and modified the urban diet with their greens and potatoes. The two most important zones are to the northeast along the "Central do Brasil" (vegetables, fruit, vineyards, flowers) and to the southwest (corn, potatoes, beans, rice, manioc, fruit), where in 1927 the Japanese organized the Agricultural Cooperative of Cotia;[2] chácaras in the northern hills have also come into importance since 1920. Clay kilns and preparation of charcoal are prominent extractive industries of the suburbs. Wood for charcoal is gathered under primitive conditions and, as scrub growth has locally become sparse, it must now be supplemented from sources as far as 250 miles away.

The Japanese have much more effectively stimulated suburban farming than have government projects. A proposal by the bishop in 1887 for a Trappist agricultural school near the city awoke no official response at all. When in 1905 Prefect Antônio Prado finally created a Municipal School of Pomology and Horticulture to promote cultivation of unused suburban lands, the school came to specialize in grafting ornamental trees and plants, introduced the study of French, and was eventually suppressed owing to the incompetence of its directors.

One official venture was longer lived: three suburban agricul-

2. By 1957 this cooperative had nearly 5,000 members. Their farms, mostly small fruit, vegetable, and poultry farms, covered 300,000 acres and were tilled by 1,500 tractors.

tural colonies, made up largely of Italians and Tirolese, created in 1877-1878 by the provincial government. Hardships and maladministration were weathered, so that by 1887 the colonies supported 1,300 persons growing vegetables, fruit, tubers, sorghum, and osiers for sale in the city. A house and plot could be bought at moderate terms for cash or on credit, with the "assurance of the quality of the lands and above all their good location with respect to transportation routes." (IHGB, 1891.) By 1907 the São Bernardo nucleus alone had 2,100 members from fourteen countries, living together in harmony. In relation to the needs of the growing city, however, such colonizing experiments have been on far too limited a scale, and plans are still afoot to encircle the city with truck farms.

(3) *Industrial.* São Caetano and Santo André to the southeast comprise the most important industrial subcenter. Industries were attracted here after 1890 by cheap land and the facilities of the trans-Serra railway, and today they include some of the city's largest plants, such as Kowarick for woolens, Rhodiaceta for artificial silk, Firestone, General Motors, Lidgerwood for machinery, and Pirelli for copper wire and cable; beyond Santo André a second perimeter of industrial satellites has already begun to appear. Westward along the "Sorocabana" lie industrial Lapa and industrial-residential Alto da Lapa, site of the Armour packing plant. Farther out is the subcenter Osasco, which developed in the late nineteenth century from the fazenda of an Italian and now has textile, ceramic, match, and meat-packing plants. Northwest, on the São Paulo Railway, is the diversified and rather badly planned industrial nucleus of Pirituba. In some cases a single plant has formed an isolated industrial community: Portland Cement and the Melhoramentos paper company to the northwest and, to the east, a big nitrochemical plant in São Miguel.

The metropolis, however, must today be considered within a larger context than that of its close environs. For, whereas in 1890 it contained only 5 per cent of the state's population, it now has 30 per cent, with its life much more intimately bound to that of the interior. For the health of both city and country, stable, efficient, and diversified agriculture must replace cyclical, monocultural exploitation. And a prosperous rural population enjoying local equivalents for the primary facilities and opportunities of the metropolis must be developed as a check against fluctuating mass migrations and chronic congestion of the capital.

The "central plaza" mentality, so restrictive in city planning, is even more disastrous when it operates on a regional scale. Just as the central plaza has profited at the expense of the suburbs, so the city itself is favored over the countryside. The traditional unit of political administration is the urban nucleus. Although on maps the municipality is an urban-rural complex comparable to the American county, in practice a "municipal" improvement — such as provision of electricity, telephones, water, or sewage disposal — predominantly benefits the municipal *center*. Tax rates, credit and banking facilities, health and sanitation agencies, syndical and professional organizations, and the distribution of schools, teachers, and technicians are all designed to favor the citydweller, especially if he inhabits the capital.[3] In 1946 there was one physican for every 550 people in the capital and only one per 3,100 in the interior. A rural priest sometimes must singlehandedly administer a parish that has the same area — though far worse transportation facilities — as that of a whole diocese in Europe. Young lawyers rarely start their careers in small towns: "Sustained by jobs that are often low-paying and even humble, they will not leave the capital, and they cherish the illusive hope of becoming successful lawyers there." (R. de A. SODRÉ, 1944, p. 138.)

The price and distribution system of the metropolis has, especially since World War II, been critically prejudicial to the small farmer living fifty or a hundred miles away. Though the retail price of onions, beans, corn, or potatoes may be as high as six times the farmer's production costs, middlemen's commissions sometimes make it more lucrative for him to sell produce locally, or to restrict planting, than to market in the capital. Cattle ranchers in the northwest of the state and impoverished fishermen along its coast have for decades been similarly victimized by urban profiteers and "trusts." The marginal economy of the countryman and the undernourished workers and inflated food prices of the city constitute an irony yet to be resolved.

Railroads have in the twentieth century continued their pene-

3. A municipal law of the capital (no. 2965 of April 15, 1926) concerned with telephone service clearly discriminates against the isolated farmer: "In the rural districts . . . the Concessionary undertakes to establish local services, always within a radius not exceeding three kilometers of a suitable point, which will be the central station, chosen in agreement with the Prefecture when there have been at least sixty requests for telephones."

tration of the interior, connecting the capital and its port with far-flung pioneer regions and economic possibilities. By 1952 the state had 4,800 miles of track (21 per cent of the total for Brazil), compared with 2,100 fifty years earlier. But in fanning out westward along crests of ridges — with detours to accommodate powerful private interests — railroads have accentuated the rural-urban contrast by leaving large, unserved interstices. The excess of railway exports over imports reflects the inaccessibility and poverty of the rural populace; in 1939, for example, the "Sorocabana" station in the capital received 890,000 tons from the interior but dispatched to it only 210,000 tons. The advent of the resistant, durable, and easily repaired Ford car, followed by the truck, bus, and jeep, did much to decentralize transportation facilities and to encourage subdivision of fazendas by making diversified truck farms economically feasible. Yet, even so, the state highway system, originating in a comprehensive plan of 1920, has tended to parallel the railway net and to focus upon the capital as a center of irradiation — as evidenced in the competitive squabbles of railway and trucking interests. Although the state's system has increased from 65 miles (1921) to 4,900 (1952) — and is supplemented by over 50,000 miles of federal and municipal roads — the connecting roads are insufficient and poorly maintained, subject in the northwest to sand drifts and impassable in the clayey terra roxa after heavy rains.

In spite of the attendant difficulties, however, decadent coffee lands, especially along the Paraíba valley, have shown signs of recuperation in the recent past. Landholding has been sharply decentralized since the collapse of the coffee market in 1929, when owners of large fazendas began to parcel out lots to their tenant farmers. One manner of doing this was to allow the tenant to plant half his plot to coffee and half to whatever crops he chose; after delivering a portion of his coffee to the fazendeiro for a stipulated period, perhaps 60 per cent for twelve years, the tenant would become outright owner of the plot. Subdivision was assisted by the "Paulista" railway, which bought up fazendas, parceling and reselling them to maintain production and traffic along its lines. Since the Depression, diversification of crops to feed the cities and production of raw materials for manufacture, such as cotton, have been widely taken up. At the same time industry, attracted by lower land prices and freedom from congestion, is invading the interior along newly electrified railroads, east into the Paraíba valley, north to Jundiaí and Campinas, west to Sorocaba.[4]

Possibly air transportation will in the near future appreciably advance the task of knitting the cities and hinterland of São Paulo, allowing the region to dispense with a fully articulated rail and highway system. As compensation for their special problems, "underdeveloped" areas enjoy this privilege of bypassing hitherto normal stages in realms of technological and other development. The state's five airports in 1945 were fifty-six by 1951; the number of passengers annually handled by São Paulo city's Congonhas airport has passed the million mark and increases rapidly, giving it the reputation of being the world's third busiest airport (after New York and Chicago). Small two- and four-passenger planes, maintained by individual fazendas, supplement the commercial air network.

At least certain features, then, of a traditional city-country symbiosis seem recoverable under auspices of the technology and complex forces and institutions of the modern age. It is well, however, to enter the caution of the anthropologist Emílio WILLEMS (1944) regarding the extension of urban influence into isolated rural areas. "There exists no basis of understanding which can jointly serve urban civilization and the multiplicity of backland cultures." When the two impinge, urban man must searchingly ask: "What qualities are desirable for the countryman to acquire in contact with civilization?" Much of rural "lethargy" and "backwardness" has an integrative, protective function. "Let it not be forgotten that the caboclo's self-sufficiency is his sole defense and keeps him at a distance from the growing instability of the capitalist economy." Given the inevitability with which urban culture encroaches upon the hinterland, the question as to the relative "happiness" of the caboclo and the citydweller seems academic. Yet urban man should constantly pose it — for the understanding and awareness of human values which such contemplation affords.

To place the metropolis in its larger setting is to reveal that the

4. It must not be forgotten that the economic health of the whole tableland hinges upon the efficiency of the port of Santos, its major outlet to the world and the port which handles nearly one-half of the nation's foreign trade. Santos has since 1925 been chronically congested; ships have at times been delayed for months, thus causing foreign exporters to charge higher rates for cargos destined there. At present, plans for dredging and for enlarging the docks are in progress.

notion of "city limits" is a formal one, that city and country inter-penetrate within a broad geographic continuum. One must return, however, to the urban nucleus to find the city's expanding energies most clearly objectified.

In the twentieth century São Paulo's population has doubled every fifteen years. It reached 240,000 in 1900, 500,000 in 1917, 1,000,000 in 1933, and has now passed 3,000,000, which places São Paulo ahead of Rio de Janeiro as Brazil's largest city and South America's second largest. To keep pace with this growth the building boom has been phenomenal and has eased off only in time of depression or war. In 1920 there were 1,900 new constructions, 4,000 in 1930, 12,500 in 1940, 21,600 in 1950, and 29,000 in 1952. In some years the figure is three times as great as for Rio de Janeiro. Recently the number of buildings over ten or fifteen storeys has mounted sharply, most of them office or apartment skyscrapers spawned by exorbitant land values of the congested city center.

The unrelenting demand for living space and the chronic in-flation of the twentieth century[5] have made real estate and the construction business a bonanza for speculators. The following table shows the soaring cost of land per square meter within the various perimeters of the city:

Year	"Triangle"	Central Perimeter	Urban Perimeter	Suburban Perimeter	Rural Zone
1916	1.000$	165$	23$	3$	$10
1936	4.500$	600$	100$	36$	7$50
1943	8.000$	1.000$	150$	60$	12$00

(The perimetric categories are somewhat artificial, since they give no idea of the disparities that exist within all zones.) Today a square foot of ground-floor space in the "triangle" costs up to ten dollars, or as much as it would along Manhattan's Wall Street.

Before 1913, private concerns bought up lands at minimal prices or simply appropriated them with no payment at all to the city. They would then lay out whole districts in a chessboard style that bore no relation to topography and sell off their lots. The goal was to cram as many lots as possible, all of identical size, into a given area. Frequently a speculator left vacant property or a half-built house to stand for years as an eyesore while he awaited its appreciation. (Vacant lots often appreciate more rapidly than lots

5. The index for paper money in circulation passed from a base of 100 (1930) to 162 (1940) to 732 (1948) and shows no signs of leveling off.

with houses.) When sold, many plots were virtually unimproved and lacked arterial connection with the rest of the city. At times even the logic of aristocratic privilege was challenged – as when attractive hilltop sites were sold to poor people who had no means to embellish them, while the rich moved into the well-planned "Gardens" to jostle a workers' district on the swampy west slope of the city's central ridge.

A municipal law of 1913 was an attempt to protect the public interest by setting norms for large-scale real estate ventures, but its spirit did not transcend the geometrism of the 1886 ordinances. Another law ten years later provided more wisely for public convenience and hygiene, but it was regularly circumvented by ingenious schemes for clandestine districting of new lands.

Municipal legislation pertaining to districting and construction was brought together in 1929 in the *"Arthur Saboya" Building Code,* which, with revisions and accretions, is still in effect. Like the old "Laws of the Indies" of the Spanish colonial empire, the code is an amalgam of unimaginative minutiae and vague advice that bears the proviso "whenever possible." It has been criticized for its lack of a coherent zoning plan; inadequate provisions for the approval of building plans and supervision of construction; faulty handling of the problems of public health and safety; deficient regulation of the real estate business; and absence of any esthetic criterion. The code in fact bans certain modern building solutions which in hygiene and comfort are superior to its own norms.

An exception to the exploitative regime of private districting has been the "City" Company. In 1911, glowing prophecies of São Paulo's future by the French architect J. Bouvard inspired E. Fontaine de Laveleye, a Belgian, to buy up some 3,000 acres of city lands. His tracts he in turn sold in 1912 to the City of San Paulo Improvements and Freehold Land Co., Ltd., organized in London with a fourteen-man board of directors that included himself and Bouvard. Engaging the services of the English urbanist Barry Parker – known for his planning of the garden city of Letchworth, the garden village of Earswich, and the civic center of Oporto – the "City" began to carry out long-range plans for residential districts. Though it has developed middle-class and workers' as well as luxury communities, the "City" is best known for its creation of aristocratic Jardim América, which set a model for contiguous "Jardins," or "Gardens," later planned under other auspices. In return for providing contoured streets, shade trees, utilities, strict zoning regulations, clear land titles, and a few model homes, the "City" required that the purchaser comply with its stipulations for the size of residences and upkeep of grounds. As a result Jardim América is an attractive and peaceful district, if one excepts its architectural heterogeneity and the graceless style, for which the cinema is in part responsible, of English bungalows and California-Miami dwellings.

The "City," however, did not eliminate speculation by those who bought its lots and could at best provide only occasional planned and stable islands in the urban maelstrom. Within the broad pattern set by the river basins and central ridge, the rule has been planless intermingling of commercial, industrial, and upper- and lower-class residential zones, which induces rapid, wasteful "contamination" and sudden, speculatory appreciations. Land set aside for parks and playgrounds is insufficient, often perfunctorily and inconveniently situated, and, with some exceptions, designed more for ornament than for use. VIOLICH (1944, p. 103) found São Paulo "to possess more jumbled land uses in a small area than any other city" visited by him in Latin America.[6]

Before referring further to the city's functional maladjustments it is well to recognize that large expenditures by public and private agencies in the twentieth century cause its services to compare favorably with those of most of the world's metropolises. Public utilities, transportation arteries, recreation areas (including a large stadium), facilities for hygiene and sanitation, hospital and social welfare services have been developed, in spite of persistent material and administrative deficiencies, to a degree exceptional for a Latin American milieu. It must also be kept in mind that many of the city's dislocations are attributable simply to the rapidity of its population growth, which no amount of foresight or resources could have been expected fully to cope with. The following observations are therefore limited to aspects of urban maladjustment which seem primarily to stem from defective human vision before the complexities of modern city planning.

---

6. Zoning problems, some of them now irremediable, were addressed by a Department of Urbanism which the prefecture created in 1947. It is to be hoped that future urbanizing will not wholly absorb the city's sectional diversity and unexpected rural vistas into the dull homogeneity of the standard metropolis.

Water supply, for example, has been a chronic problem. The Cantareira reservoir, made available in 1882, has been repeatedly supplemented by other sources, including filtered water from the Tietê River. But water distribution, which is made difficult by the city's ridges and valleys, has never kept pace with population. Crowded new districts have often been left wholly dry. In 1945 the city was estimated to need 135,000,000 gallons per day but received an average of only 100,000,000; in dry spells this average flow is sharply cut — during the 1925 drought, for instance, by 55 per cent. If we review the early years of the expansion of the water system, the factor of sloppy planning clearly stands out. In two years alone (1892-1894) the daily flow was raised from 1,600,-000 to 7,100,000 gallons. During the subsequent decade, however, it was found that no account had been taken of the city's differences in level, since the diameters of the pipes were improperly scaled and the system as a whole was not subdivided; further, mains were laid so close to defective sewage conduits that water was discolored and contaminated with typhoid germs.

As for street paving, the granite stones introduced in 1873 are still standard, although asphalt, first used on the rich man's Avenida Paulista, is more and more common. The former are available in nearby quarries and are serviceable for heavy traffic, but they have not generally been laid to meet proper specifications. Often of irregular sizes and set in loosely packed sand, the paving stones are easily dislodged, wear out tires, and accumulate dust in their interstices.

A pointed but affectionate caricature of São Paulo's streets, reminiscent of *Cabrião* and *Diabo-coxo* in the 1860's, was drawn by Mário de Andrade in his folk novel *Macunaíma* (1928): "The said arteries are all embroidered with flitting scraps of paper, little sailboats of fruit rind and, especially, with extremely fine and very playful dust in which a thousand and one specimens of voracious microbes are dispersed daily to decimate the populace.... And not content with this dust being raised by the movement of pedestrians and by braying engines called 'automobiles' or 'trolley-cars,' ...the diligent ediles contracted for some anthropoids — monstrous, slate-colored, unisonous centaurs — to whom is assigned the title Public Sanitation; *per amica silencia lunae*, when traffic has ceased and the dust rests innocuously, they emerge from their mansions, drawn by mules and with tails whirling in the manner of cylindrical brooms, to raise the dust from the asphalt, rousing insects from sleep and inciting them to action with huge gestures and horrendous cries. These nocturnal duties are discreetly conducted by miniscule lights placed at such distant intervals that darkness is almost total and the activities of evil-doers and thieves are not disturbed."

Public transportation over these streets has been another problem. Since the city is circular with radiating transit lines, traffic is unevenly distributed, being light at the extremities and excessive at the heart; interconnection among outlying districts is almost non-existent. In 1939, 93 per cent of all passengers leaving the city center took their conveyance from terminal points. One-hour waits in long queues are not uncommon, a double nuisance since paulistas share with Parisians the familial custom, now obsolescent in Rio de Janeiro, of returning home each day for lunch.

When in 1927 the prefecture rejected the Light and Power Company's plan for a thorough overhaul of the transit system, the company, though its contract was to run for another fourteen years, refused further to renovate or expand its streetcar lines; a 44 per cent increase in passengers for the period 1934-1940 was therefore handled by a constant number of vehicles. Streetcars were supplemented after 1926 with buses, but these were owned by dozens of concerns, most of them lacking the organization and services proper for maintenance. Since World War II all transit lines have been merged in the Municipal Collective Transport Company, which is acquiring large modern buses, trolley buses, and "trailer-tractor" buses. Better organization and equipment, however, are only a palliative. The crux of the problem is how to get hundreds of thousands of people, converging daily from all directions, in and out of (or for many, through or around) a city center whose circulation has not wholly been solved by viaducts, in which the bulk of the city's offices, banks, department stores, and modern theaters are concentrated, and in which new and taller skyscrapers continue to soar.[7] Transportation is thus subordinate to city planning.

7. In May, 1957, it was announced that the Municipal Transport Company had authorized a contract with a West German corporation for construction of a sixty-mile monorailway network at an estimated cost of nearly $300,000,000. The scheme was strongly opposed by the Brazilian Institute of Engineers as being extravagant and insufficiently planned, and as entailing excessive expropriation and demolition in densely built-up areas. At that moment the city already faced a possible deficit of $11,500,000 and the transport company one of $17,600,000. (The New York Times, Jan. 7 and May 6, 1957.)

São Paulo's city plan has been badly bungled. Not true planners but old-fashioned engineers elaborated it. The guiding criteria have been geometrism rather than functionalism and an esthetics of pretentious façades rather than of inviting, many-dimensioned forms consonant with region and era. This outlook was evident in an early project of 1910, submitted by Ramos de Azevedo and others, which proposed three wide avenues for the city center, not in answer to experienced needs but as a showpiece for the independence centennial; the chief function of the trajectories was to intersect at the site of a massive monument. "The magnificent perspective to be enjoyed from the center of this plaza . . . will be comparable only to that viewed in Paris from atop the arch in the Place d'Étoile." (ALBUQUERQUE, 1910.)

A year or two later a more practical plan went into effect. This was to enlarge the "triangle," widen some of its streets, reroute its streetcar lines, beautify nearby river basins, and improve its connections across the Anhangabaú. A progress report in 1924 showed many though not all of the goals to have been achieved. Meantime, however, the program had become obsolete, which was not surprising, since its sponsors had accepted the undersized "triangle" as a permanent nucleus and neglected to plan the teeming new suburbs.

The 1924 report was itself based on two quite restrictive principles. One of them, answering more to an inferiority complex than to the needs of the people, called for a showcase capital "which we paulistas may take pride in and boastingly exhibit to foreigners who visit us. At present São Paulo has very little worthy to be seen by the foreigner and offers in fact many deplorable and distressing aspects." The second principle was illustrated by a diagram of two concentric perimeters intersected by radials. São Paulo was to have six such radials; five were already in use or being constructed, while a "perimeter of radiation" lying well outside the "triangle" had for some time been under study. (In recent years a second, outer perimeter has been projected.) It was to so simplistic a formula, then, that city planning was converted: ". . . in sum and essence we reduce the whole problem of *remodeling the city's system of circulation to the study of six large radial avenues and a perimeter of radiation.*" (MAIA and CINTRA, 1924-1926; authors' italics.)

A subsequent *Project for a Plan of Avenues for São Paulo City* by the engineer and later prefect F. Prestes MAIA (1930) embellished the formula with a profusion of citations in foreign languages and photographs of São Paulo and leading world cities. It also contained rose-tinted sketches of the future metropolis: a lurid pastiche of Caesar's Rome, the Paris of Louis XIV, and modern New York. They depicted viaducts groaning under the weight of massive skyscrapers; gloomy, authoritarian palaces commanding vast esplanades; and a mélange of artless, ornate architecture that included even a pagoda style. The plan, known to São Paulo's architects as "The Divine Comedy," was followed fifteen years later by a more restrained progress report, *The Improvements of São Paulo,* known as "Purgatory." (F. P. MAIA, 1945.)

The radials-perimeter system, elsewhere called the loop-and-spoke plan, is not inevitably mischievous; São Paulo's recent viaducts, river-bed expressways, and traffic tunnel are in fact absolute necessities. Execution of the total plan, however, was delayed until expropriation costs had become astronomically high, so that individual projects were timid and obsolete on completion. If the city now has difficulty circulating and parking its 165,000 registered motor vehicles, what may be expected when in the near future that number is doubled?

The enterprise, moreover, exhibits certain specious aspects, such as the expressways that make frequent grade crossings or the viaduct that receives a second level for a future subway with no promise that it lies along a suitable subway artery. More important, the loop-and-spoke system, unsupported by broader planning, can become positively deleterious, as C. McKim NORTON (1953, p. 86) has pointed out:

"The policy of building express highways into and around the center of cities is valid as far as it goes. It will bring a limited number of persons to central city areas in private automobiles and will provide expressways for mass transport by bus. It will divide metropolitan areas into large sectors within which developments of almost any form and type can take place. But without land-use planning and control in the central areas and within each of the outlying sectors bounded by segments of the 'loop-and-spoke' system, the expressways will add to, rather than relieve, congestion.

"Experience indicates that new circumferential highway facilities are soon overloaded unless land-use controls keep new developments in scale with the highway which stimulates them."

Persistence of the "central plaza" and "broad avenues" mentality is an obvious key to São Paulo's problems. Metropolitan growth has been so recent and swift as to seem almost a fantasy. Paulistas want the overt and time-honored testimony of a grandiose "city center." Much twentieth-century "planning" has consisted merely in efforts to move parts of this center, notably smart shops and theaters, out of the "triangle" and across the Anhangabaú. This is not decentralization, but enlargement and enhancement of the monolithic nucleus. The late advent of automobiles, moreover, which appeared in appreciable numbers only in the mid-1920's, helped to postpone a vision of the expansive, subnucleated, swift-moving modern city, its arteries and cell tissues biologically rather than geometrically elaborated.[8]

A few functioning subcenters do exist, industrial-commercial Braz most conspicuously, along with certain peripheral nuclei. A few radial streets offer stores and cinemas at a distance from the center. A few big department stores are invading the suburbs. Planned, outlying communities for factory and white-collar workers are appearing. But the decentralizing, or pluralistic, habit of mind — which, as already suggested, is relevant as well to the arts, political leadership, and industrial and rural planning — does not yet orient the field of urbanism in broad, decisive fashion. More important, the people themselves are under hypnosis by the thrills, dazzle, and grandiosity of the metropolitan heart. To center their primary activities and emotions in the neighborhood community seems to many a dreary, provincial prospect. No urbanist, however inspired, can impose a city plan upon people indisposed to accept it. The magnetism of the city center has weakened the townsmen's "habit of community," and it is at this point that the *political* (or, *social*) problem, discussed earlier, converges with that of the urbanist.

One reason for the failures of urbanism in São Paulo has been the exclusion of architects from planners' councils. For the architect is far more intimately concerned than the engineer with the

8. On Feb. 16, 1922, *O Estado de São Paulo* noted with dismay the increase in automobiles and traffic snarls: "And if in the next ten years the city should continue developing as it has been, which everything points to, then our streets will be inadequate for automobiles; the center, with streets of such modest width and with all its alleys and angles, will be acutely constrictive for public thoroughfare."

In modern São Paulo I have seen a street on which cars drive up on the *left*-hand sidewalk to pass oncoming trolleys.

traditions, habits, and tastes of specific groups of men, both their living communities and their associations for work or recreation. And since his works are for the eyes of the public, the architect is trained to render function esthetically.

Modern architecture and good architects were late to appear in São Paulo. For decades the field was free for builders, predominantly Italian, who conceived of structure as façade and silhouette, and whose jumbled, derivative, ostentatious styles were branded by *O Commercio de São Paulo* (Jan. 29, 1896) as the "ridiculous amalgam" observable in "recent urban constructions, whether private or public." In public buildings, such as the palatial Paulista Museum, built at the site where Pedro I declared Brazil's independence in 1822, a neo-Renaissance design was for a long time favored, though there were outlandish exceptions. At the time of World War I, Vítor Dubugras, who taught in the Polytechnic School, promoted the modish and ornamental *art nouveau* and, through his architect friend Ricardo Severo, an artificial neo-colonial style that Monteiro Lobato's writings helped to popularize. The disordered eclecticism of the new Law Faculty, the neo-Gothic Faculty of Medicine (influenced by American universities), and the forbidding, fascist-inspired Matarazzo building are more recent examples of the façade-maker's tradition.

At Modern Art Week in 1922, architecture was ineffectually represented, and when the young architect Rino Levi returned from study in Italy four years later, he found modern trends still unrecognized except in some articles by Mário de Andrade and in Gregori Warchavchik's "Manifesto of Functional Architecture" (1925). The prevailing outlook was defined by the architect of the "Sorocabana" railway station in the magazine *Arquitetura e Construções* (Aug., 1929), who affirmed local tradition to be "Latin." "We cannot accept here the architecture of Germans, Slavs, and others, whose ethnic origin was niggardly in its bestowal of that great talent." This assertion was somewhat anachronous, since reinforced concrete, then being used to great effect in São Paulo, was a technique introduced by eastern Europeans. According to its editors, moreover, the magazine took as its model "chiefly the American reviews," while the writer himself praised non-"Latin" builders of Yankee skyscrapers, who had exerted "enormous efforts in applying old architectural styles to those buildings, not contemplating a new style because they realize, 'There is no art without style, and no style when one searches for it.'" With reference to modernism and to Le Corbusier (apparently not a "Latin"), whose inspiration Brazil was, soon after, rewardingly to assimilate: "The snobbery of the current generation of modernists offers us, in lieu of the age-old, magisterial art, a series of reckless creations that reveal only elegant ignorance.... The houses of Le Corbusier might suit Tartars, Kurds, and Hebrews who, having no architecture of their own, were using that of others and suppressing the elements of beauty, namely, the ornaments."

Soon, however, modern architecture began to come into its own. One of the early experimenters was Flávio de Carvalho, whose work, though erratic and at times awkward, broke completely from imported models that bore no relation to the Brazilian scene. Following the example of such men as Rino Levi and Bernardo Rudofsky, an Austrian who arrived in 1938, architects began to discriminate among techniques and solutions from abroad with an eye to the particular needs of São Paulo. Hospitals, motion-picture theaters, and workers' communities were boldly designed for the comfort and movement of large concentrations of people. Attention was paid to the seasonal cold which distinguishes the climate from that of Rio de Janeiro, and buildings were faced to catch the afternoon rather than the morning sun. Office and apartment skyscrapers were stripped of stuccoed embellishment, and the structures made possible by the lightness and flexibility of reinforced concrete were increasingly explored. Walls came to be thought of not as unwieldy supports of brick but as ductile partitions, or as an epidermis mediating between living space and outer environment.

Certain private residences are as striking as the public buildings. The home of Rino Levi and Rudofsky's Arnstein and Frontini houses have a quality that might be called lyrical, with their well-knit patterns of rooms and patios; their sliding partitions that allow house and garden to interpenetrate; their modulations of contour, volume, and light; their accentuation of regional building materials; and their plain walls set off by shifting outlines of semitropical foliage. It might almost be said that the handsome suburban chácara of a century ago has been recreated in the techniques and idiom of the modern age.

For architects, however, who are aware of the city's potential for beauty and functional service, it is sharply frustrating to be confined to individual constructions, often private homes that merely enhance existing comforts of the wealthy or else skyscrapers that intensify the city's congestion. It is small wonder that many architects would welcome a politico-economic arrangement whereby their fuller vision of human life would replace that of the engineer to serve, not the isolated, over-privileged individual, but the community, the manifold communities, of the modern metropolis.

Bibliographical Note

For the geography, ecology, and growth patterns of the city, see MONBEIG (1953; 1954), PRADO JUNIOR (1935b; 1941), and DEFFONTAINES (1935a). BANCO DO BRASIL (1954) presents useful statistical tabulations. JAMES (1933) is a comparative study of São Paulo and Rio. AZEVEDO FILHO (1954) contains information about a local urbanist and philanthropist who was prominent at the turn of the century. Studies which stress the city's construction boom include: R. de ALMEIDA (1929), MENNUCCI (1929), ARAUJO (1935), and N. M. CALDEIRA (1939; 1940a; 1940b; 1940c). HERRMANN (1944) is a sociological analysis of an urban cross section, taken along an important radial avenue. The disposition and function of São Paulo's suburbs are analyzed in A. E. de AZEVEDO (1943; 1944; 1945), while HELLER (1943; 1944) depicts the formation, growth, structure, and vicissitudes of a typical suburban nucleus. The settlements of Japanese in the environs are treated in A. R. de MELO (1935, pp. 45-48); SAITO (1954-1955) deals with their Agricultural Cooperative of Cotia in a thorough monographic study of "cultural transplantation." A. R. de AZEVEDO (1945) describes the suburban charcoal industry. R. de A. e SILVA (1941) is a study of the industrial subcenter of Santo André.

The chronic disparity between urban and rural living standards, and the urban methods of exploitation of the hinterland, are pointed up to particular effect in MENNUCCI (1941); see also J. P. da V. MIRANDA (1931b), P. P. de CARVALHO (1943), PEREIRA (1938), JAMES (1946), and IDORT (1947). HAMBURGER (1954) assesses the impact of the metropolis upon rural family structure. *Revista do Instituto de Café* carried many articles in the 1930's describing the effects of the coffee crisis upon the rural economy of São Paulo; BIALOSKORSKI (1933b), PRADO JUNIOR (1935a), and MILLIET (1946a, pp. 73-120) are studies of rural working conditions and of the development of small holdings. SECRETARIA DA AGRICULTURA . . . (1940a) indicates the lines along which the Paraíba valley is recuperating economically. The problems of distributing food cheaply and adequately to citydwellers, and of properly compensating rural producers, are set forth in PIERSON (1951, pp. 71-75); the meat industry is considered in GOUVEIA (1938) and ZALECKI (1938b), bread in ZALECKI (1938a), fish in BOJANO (1940), and beef and milk in DUNCAN (1955). A useful background for economic questions is the cost-of-living indices for 1913-1934 in M. CARDIM (1936).

C. P. da SILVA (1913) is a report on the condition and needs of São Paulo state's rail, river, and highway system at the threshold of the automotive era. J. J. da S. FREIRE (1914) and A. A. PINTO (1916) are studies of railway operations in the state and of their impact on its economy; MATOS (1940), MONBEIG (1940, pp. 135-46), and N. W. SODRÉ (1948) are more recent analyses, while RICARDO JUNIOR (1933) and PASCOALICK (1941) are concerned with individual railways. The state's highway network is the subject of Assis (1933), Mendes (1940), and Simões (1940a; 1940b). Macmillen (1925) depicts the overcrowded docking facilities of Santos in the 1920's; Villas-Bôas (1947) and Aspectos . . . (1947) outline the subsequent developments. Functional maladjustments of the city itself are broadly surveyed in V. de Barros (1945) and International . . . (1950). An essay by L. P. da Silva in Annaes do 1º Congresso . . . (1931, pp. 87-137) describes methods of clandestine districting of new lands. The "Arthur Saboya" Building Code, with its revisions, is given in Netto (1947); criticisms of the code are found in Eiras (1934), IDORT (1942, pp. 125-32), and a paper of A. Albuquerque in Annaes do 1º Congresso . . . (1931, pp. 301-10). P. Barreto (1933) gives data on the founding and early achievements of the "City" Company, while the zoning problem is studied in F. P. Maia (1936) and Lefevre (n.d.).

C. Ferreira (1898) and E. da S. Prado (1904-1906, III, pp. 73-75) document the inadequacies of water distribution in the city during the 1890's; subsequent studies of the water system include F. S. R. de Brito (1911), R. H. de Melo (1935), and P. P. Whitaker (1946). Amadei (1928) is concerned with the city's street paving. The growth and chronic problems of the transportation system are treated in Prefeitura . . . (1928), Le Voci (1936), IDORT (1940), Rudolfer and Le Voci (1943), Leão (1945), Abraão Ribeiro (1946), and Modernizing . . . (1948). Chemin de Fer . . . (1904), Novaes (1905), and Requerimentos . . . (1911) contain early, unimplemented schemes for subway construction and indicate the formalistic nature of such projects.

The successive phases of city planning in the twentieth century may be traced in the following projects and progress reports: Prefeitura . . . (1911), Maia and Cintra (1924-1926), and F. P. Maia (1930; 1942; 1945). The industrialist Vilares (1946; 1948) has also contributed studies on urbanism in São Paulo.

R. Severo (1917) is a critical study of early twentieth-century architecture in São Paulo and in Brazil. P. R. Magalhães (1935) describes the building of São Paulo's Municipal Theater. Goodwin (1943), Kidder-Smith (1944), Sitwell (1944), and Mindlin (1956) are surveys of modern Brazilian architecture which make references to São Paulo. Debenedetti and Salmoni (1953) is a study of the Italian influence upon São Paulo's architecture. For photographs and plans of specific recent projects see: Nurses' School . . . (1950), Instituto Central . . . (1950), Teatro Cultura . . . (1950), and Office Building . . . (1952). See also the magazine Habitat, founded in São Paulo in 1951.

General Bibliographical Note

7HE SCHOLARLY PUBLICATIONS AND RESOURCES of São Paulo
city's Departamento de Cultura are summarized in MILLIET
(1938) and SHAW (1938). Those of the Arquivo do Estado de São Paulo are
discussed in INSTITUTO DE ADMINISTRAÇÃO (1948, no. 30, July). The regulations and history of the Arquivo do Estado are given in PEQUENO HISTORICO . . .
(1953). M.W.V. da CUNHA and SOUZA (1947) analyzes the publications policy
of São Paulo state.

A. LEITE (1954, pp. 403-558) presents a wide-ranging and indispensable
though rather slipshod bibliography of some 10,000 items pertaining to the
history of São Paulo city and its region. The bibliographies of MINISTERIO . . .
(1922-1929, I, pp. 476-80), LOWRIE (1939a), and FERNANDES (n.d.[a]) are
limited to the subject of population and immigration. CANNABRAVA (1947)
is a critical analysis of studies in the field of Brazilian municipal administration.
MONBEIG (1941) and MORSE (1949, pp. 40-43) discuss some problems of
urban historiography in Brazil.

Newspapers are identified in the text whenever cited. TOLEDO (1898) lists
the periodicals of São Paulo province and state for 1827-1896, devoting pages
385-492 to the capital city. A fuller, more generously annotated listing for the
capital, covering 1823-1914, is given in A. A. de FREITAS (1914; 1927b).
NOBRE (1950) is a more recent compilation, with entries through 1945. A. E.
MARTINS (1912) and A. A. de FREITAS (1927a) offer informal commentary
on the local press and its traditions.

Toward a history of São Paulo, its outpouring of guides and almanacs
during the past century or so contributes a wide variety of information; publications of this nature which have been particularly useful for this study are
listed in the bibliography under ALMANACH, ALMANAK, and MEMORIAL. . . .
(For a fuller listing see A. LEITE [1954, pp. 405-6].) Of importance as reference works are four generous repositories of incident, legend, custom, and
personalities pertaining to the city's history: M. E. de A. MARQUES (1874), J.
J. RIBEIRO (1899-1901), A. E. MARTINS (1911), and SANT'ANNA (1937-1944).
On a smaller scale the reminiscences of A. A. de FREITAS (1921) are useful,
as are his fragmentary "dictionaries" of the city (1924; 1930). P. C. de MOURA
(1943) is a cicerone of the city's streets and plazas and their traditions. SÃO
PAULO E A SUA EVOLUÇÃO . . . (1927) is a miscellany of lectures on São Paulo's

history and culture. Commemorative editions of the city's newspapers, published on the quadricentennial date, January 25, 1954, offer a variety of retrospective articles by authorities in many fields; the supplement of *O Estado de São Paulo,* in particular, amounts to a historical encyclopedia.

The most noteworthy general history of the city since its founding is the highly readable, well-documented, lavishly illustrated three-volume work by BRUNO (1954); it is expository rather than interpretive, emphasizes customs and social history, and devotes only an "appendix" to the years 1918-1954. Afonso TAUNAY (1954a) is a shorter general history which gives selected details of the growth and transformations of the city to 1922. SAMPAIO (1900-1901), MORSE (1950a; 1952b), and MATOS (1955) are limited to the city's development in the nineteenth century.

Several scholars have placed São Paulo city in its geographical and ecological setting: MONBEIG (1953) in a broad, historically oriented study, PRADO JUNIOR (1935b; 1941) and DEFFONTAINES (1935a) in more intensive, specifically geographic ones. The Tietê River, an important natural determinant of the city's history, is treated by Melo NÓBREGA (1948). Maps of the city for various years in the nineteenth century are collected in COMISSÃO . . . (1954). MATTOS (1925) and FERRAZ (1940) are introductions to the climate of the region; São Paulo's distinctive heavy fog, known locally as garôa, is discussed in FERRAZ (1939).

As a background for the city's economic development, PRADO JUNIOR (1945b) is an able though strongly Marxist study of Brazilian economic history; SIMONSEN (1939) surveys the growth of Brazilian industry, BASTOS (1944) the emergence of capitalism in Brazil, and VIEIRA (1947) the evolution of Brazil's monetary system. PESTANA (1923) and MORSE (1951a; 1954a) are economic studies centering on São Paulo itself. AGUIRRA (1934), a historical examination of the budget of São Paulo city, is a corollary to the story of the economic expansion of the paulista region. Two informative surveys of immigration and colonization in São Paulo state are DEPARTAMENTO ESTADUAL DO TRABALHO (1916) and S. de A. AZEVEDO (1941); see also F. M. de CARVALHO (1942a), P. de M. CARVALHO (1940), A. R. de MELO (1935), and VASCONCELOS (1941). Drawing upon the censuses of 1872, 1890, 1920, and 1934, HERRMANN (n.d.) shows how shifts in São Paulo's occupational distribution reflect socioeconomic trends.

SANTOS (1930), a penetrating introduction to Brazil's political traditions, directly and by implication illuminates the city's political role within the nation. The presidents, governors, and interventors of São Paulo province and state for 1822-1939 are listed in HOEHNE (1941). M. W. V. da CUNHA (1947) is an introduction to municipal administration in São Paulo state, a field in which EGAS (1925) and DEPARTAMENTO ESTADUAL DE ESTATÍSTICA (1945a; 1945b) serve as reference works. Among the administrative institutions which have been given independent treatment are the Força Pública, or state militia, by P. D. de CAMPOS (1909) and E. ANDRADE and CAMARA (1931); the police force, by VIEIRA and SILVA (1955); and the fire department, by P. D. de CAMPOS (1908). T. de P. FERREIRA (1940) is a thorough historical survey of São Paulo's public and private agencies for social welfare. Since city administration has often fallen to provincial and state presidents, the annual *relatórios* of the latter, summarized in EGAS (1926-1927), illuminate many aspects of the city's life and growth. A few particularly useful relatórios are listed independently in their unabridged form: L. A. M. de BARROS (1946), DISCURSO . . . (1848; 1852; 1858; 1859), PAULA (1954), RELATÓRIO . . . (1886), and MEN-

SAGEM . . . (1925). J. C. de A. MARQUES (1874) is a compilation of provincial legislation, much of it relevant to the capital.

To the intellectual climate of Brazilian history, J. C. COSTA (1956a) is a valuable introduction, while MORSE (1954b) reviews the cultural and intellectual development of the city itself. Julio MARIA (1900-1910) and J. C. RODRIGUES (1900-1910) provide a background for religious concerns with their histories of Brazil's Catholic and non-Catholic institutions, respectively. P. F. da S. CAMARGO (1952-1953) is a study of the church in São Paulo to 1861. MOACYR (1939-1940, II, pp. 311-437; 1942) summarizes nineteenth-century educational policies in São Paulo, while MENNUCCI (1932) analyzes them as a militant reformer. INSTITUTO BRASILEIRO . . . (1946) discusses the problem of illiteracy and BUSCH (1935) the development of normal schools in São Paulo. J. L. de A. NOGUEIRA (1907-1912) and VAMPRÉ (1924) not only trace the history of São Paulo's Law Academy but, with their vignettes of professors and students, provide a wealth of information for the city's social history. PAIXÃO (1936), EGAS (1935), and MESQUITA (1951) are sources for the development of theater in São Paulo; CERQUERA (1954) gives the history of opera in the city. Y. de A. PRADO (1929), BRUNO (1944), and FRONTINI (1957) are brief surveys of the city's architectural styles, and ARROYO (1953) a study of its churches.

Although much of his concern is with northern Brazil, FREYRE's studies of the colonial fazenda (1946), of nineteenth-century urban culture (1951), and of the social effects of the transition to the republican era (1944) provide an indispensable context for the present history. Elsewhere (1943, pp. 76-133; 1954) Freyre has considered characteristics peculiar to the São Paulo milieu.

Selected Bibliography

$\mathcal{D}$OCUMENTARY COLLECTIONS AND ARCHIVES appear under the abbreviations by which they are referred to in the text. Their full titles or names are given in parentheses next to the listing. In addition, the following abbreviations have been used to identify the names of three journals which recur throughout the bibliography:

RAM   :   *Revista do Arquivo Municipal*
RIHGSP   :   *Revista do Instituto Histórico e Geográfico de São Paulo*
RISP   :   *Revista Industrial de São Paulo*

The variations in spelling and accentuation to be found in this bibliography are attributable to the fact that Portuguese orthography was standardized only recently in Brazil. The items have been alphabetized in accordance with the system that prevails in the Biblioteca Municipal of São Paulo and other Brazilian libraries.

AALPSP   (Annaes da Assembléa Legislativa Provincial de S. Paulo).
ACCSP   (Actas da Camara da Cidade de São Paulo).
AESP   (Arquivo do Estado de São Paulo).

1825.   Four members of the Câmara Municipal of São Paulo to the provincial president, May 14. Sala 10, maço 41, Capital.

1830.   Report to the provincial vice-president of São Paulo, Dec. 1. Sala 10, maço 42, Capital.

1832a.   Antonio Cardozo Nogueira to the provincial president of São Paulo, March 22. Sala 10, maço 41, Capital.

1832b.   Sociedade Harmonia Paulistana to the provincial president of São Paulo, Sept. 25. Sala 10, maço 42, Capital.

1832c.   Six members of the Câmara Municipal of São Paulo to the provincial president, Feb. 14; José Xavier de Azevedo Marques to the Câmara Municipal of São Paulo, Dec. 17. Sala 10, Capital, 1832.

1832d.   Thirty-two inhabitants of Penha da França to Dom Manoel Joaquim Gonçalves de Andrade, bishop of São Paulo (undated). Sala 10, Capital, 1832.

1842.   Six clerics to the provincial president of São Paulo, May 20. Sala 10, maço 51, Capital.

1848. Report by José Xavier de Azevedo Marques to the Câmara Municipal of São Paulo, Aug. 31, transmitted to the provincial president, Sept. 3. Sala 10, maço 51, Capital.

1855a. Câmara Municipal of São Paulo to the provincial president, May 9, Dec. 5 and 14. Sala 10, maço 62, Capital.

1855b. Baron of Antonina to the provincial president of São Paulo, Oct. 7. Sala 10, maço 62, Capital.

1867. J. J. Aubertin to the provincial president of São Paulo, March 1. Sala 10, maço 85, Capital.

AGUIRRA, JOÃO B. C.
1934. A vida orçamentaria de São Paulo durante um século. *RAM*, II (July), 27-34.

ALBUQUERQUE, ALEXANDRE DE.
1910. As novas avenidas de S. Paulo. São Paulo: Vanorden.

ALINCOURT, LUIS D'.
1830. Memória sobre a viagem do porto de Santos á cidade de Cuyabá. Rio de Janeiro: Tipografia Imperial e Nacional.

ALMANACH LITTERARIO PAULISTA
1875. — para o anno de 1876. São Paulo: Provincia de São Paulo.
1876. — para o anno de 1877. São Paulo: Provincia de São Paulo.
1879. — para o anno de 1880. São Paulo: Provincia de São Paulo.
1880. — para o anno de 1881. São Paulo: Provincia de São Paulo.

ALMANAK DA PROVINCIA DE SÃO PAULO PARA 1873.
1873. São Paulo: Americana.

ALMANAK PAULISTANO.
1857. São Paulo.

ALMEIDA, ALUÍSIO DE.
1944. A revolução liberal de 1842. Rio de Janeiro: José Olympio.
1945. Movimento liberal de 1842. *RAM*, CIV (Aug.-Sept.), 57-62.
1952. Notas para a história de São Paulo. *RAM*, CXLIX (July), 3-22.

ALMEIDA, GUILHERME DE.
1929. Cosmópolis. *O Estado de São Paulo* (March 10, 17, 24, and 31, April 7 and 21, May 5 and 19).

ALMEIDA, RAMIRO DE.
1929. A expansão vertical e latitudinal da cidade de S. Paulo. *Ilustração Brasileira*, X, No. 109 (Sept.), 91-94.

ALMEIDA, RENATO.
1942. História da música brasileira. 2nd ed. Rio de Janeiro: F. Briguiet.

ALMEIDA, TACITO DE.
1934. O movimento de 1887. São Paulo: Graphica.

ALMEIDA, VICENTE UNZER DE, and MENDES SOBRINHO, OTÁVIO TEIXEIRA.
1951. Migração rural-urbana — aspectos da convergência de população do interior e outras localidades para a capital do Estado de São Paulo. São Paulo: Secretaria da Agricultura.

ALMEIDA JUNIOR, A.
1940. Aspectos da nupcialidade paulista. *RAM*, LXVI (April-May), 97-106.
1945. Por que a Faculdade de Direito? *RAM*, CII (April-May), 7-25.

ALMEIDA JUNIOR, JOÃO MENDES DE.
1882. Monographia do municipio da cidade de S. Paulo. São Paulo: Jorge Seckler.

ALVARENGA, ONEYDA.
1942. A Discoteca Publica Municipal. *RAM*, LXXXVII (Dec.), 7-98.

1943. O movimento de consultos da Discoteca Publica Municipal durante 1941 e 1942. *RAM*, XCII (Aug.-Sept.), 53-72.

ALVES, ANTONIO DE CASTRO.
1938. Obras completas. 2 vols. São Paulo: Nacional.

ALVES, JOÃO TOMÁS DE MELO.
1882. Cinco anos numa Academia (1878-1882). São Paulo: Jorge Seckler.

ALVES SOBRINHO, RUFINO.
1932. São Paulo triunfante — depoimento e subsidio para a historia das Revoluções de 22, 24, 30 e 32, no Brasil. São Paulo: Author's edition.

AMADEI, JOSÉ.
1928. São Paulo e seu calçamento. *Revista Politecnica*, XXV, Nos. 87-88 (Aug.-Oct.), 297-306.

AMARAL, AMADEU.
1948. Tradições populares. São Paulo: IPÊ.

AMARAL, AZEVEDO.
1931. Alvares de Azevedo, o unico romántico brasileiro. *Revista Nova*, I, No. 3 (Sept. 15), 346-354.

AMARAL, F. POMPÊO DO.
1943. A alimentação da população paulistana. *RAM*, XC (May-June), 55-87.

AMARAL, LUIZ.
1940. O colono italiano e a libertação do negro. Anais do III Congresso Sul-Riograndense de História e Geografia, III, 1025-1035.

AMERICANO, JORGE.
1924. A lição dos factos — revolta de 5 de julho de 1924. São Paulo: Saraiva.
1947. A Universidade de São Paulo. São Paulo: Revista dos Tribunais.

AN (Arquivo Nacional).
1827-1828. Bishop of São Paulo to Pedro I, Nov. 9, 1827; José Arouche de Toledo Rendon to Lucio Soares de Gouvea, Jan. 1, 1828. Caixa 815.
1834. Director of the Law Academy of São Paulo to the minister of the empire, Feb. 15, and the reply, Feb. 28. Caixa 816.
1835-1839. Director of the Law Academy of São Paulo to the minister of the empire, April 11, Sept. 12, and Oct. 7, 1835, June 1, 1836, March 9, 1838, Aug. 13, 1839. Caixa 816.
1837. Julio Frank to the provincial president of São Paulo, Oct. 5. Caixa 817.
1842a. Dr. José Maria de Avelar Brotero to the provincial president of São Paulo, Feb. 15. Caixa 817.
1842b. Provincial president of São Paulo to José Clemente Pereira, May 30, June 2 and 25. Caixa 987, maço 1, pacote 1 (documento 6) and pacote 2 (documentos 1 and 13).
1843a. Joaquim José Luis de Souza to José Antonio da Silva Maia, June 20. Caixa 988, maço 2, pacote 7, documento 13.
1843b. Director pro tem of the Law Academy of São Paulo to the minister of the empire, Dec. 11. Caixa 817.
1843c. Thirty-two imprisoned São Paulo law students to Pedro II (undated). Caixa 817.

1867. Chief of police of São Paulo to the provincial president, April 8 and 12. Caixa 368, ano 1867.
1879. Director of the Law Academy of São Paulo to the minister of the empire, Dec. 23. Caixa 821.
ANCHIETA, JOSÉ DE.
1933. Cartas, informações, fragmentos historicos e sermões do Padre Joseph de Anchieta, S. J. (1554-1594). Rio de Janeiro: Civilização Brasileira.
ANDRADA, ANTÔNIO MANUEL BUENO DE.
1941. A abolição em São Paulo. RAM, LXXVII (June-July), 261-272.
ANDRADE, CELESTE SOUZA.
1952. Migrantes nacionais no Estado de São Paulo. Sociologia, XIV, No. 2 (May), 111-130.
ANDRADE, EUCLIDES, and CAMARA, HELY F. DA.
1931. A Força Publica de São Paulo. São Paulo: Impressora Paulista.
ANDRADE, HÓRACIO DE.
1932. Tudo por São Paulo! São Paulo: Author's edition.
ANDRADE, MÁRIO DE.
1934. Música, doce música. São Paulo: Miranda.
1935. O Aleijadinho e Alvares de Azevedo. Rio de Janeiro.
1936. Cultura musical. RAM, XXVI (Aug.), 75-86.
1942. O movimento modernista. Rio de Janeiro: Jornal do Comercio.
1943. Lasar Segall. Rio de Janeiro: Ministério da Educação.
1945. Padre Jesuíno do Monte Carmelo. Rio de Janeiro: Ministério da Educação.
ANDRADE, MARTINS DE.
1942. A Revolução de 1842. Rio de Janeiro: Vera Cruz.
ANDRADE FILHO, OSWALD DE.
1947. Desenvolvimento de arte moderna em São Paulo. São Paulo de Ontem, de Hoje e de Amanhã, VII, No. 23 (June), 4-6.
ANDREWS, C. C.
1887. Brazil — Its Conditions and Prospects. New York: Appleton.
Annaes da Assembléa Legislativa Provincial de S. Paulo (see AALPSP).
ANNAES DO 1.º CONGRESSO DE HABITAÇÃO.
1931. São Paulo: Liceu Coração de Jesus.
ARANHA, J. M. DE CAMARGO.
1937. A fundação d' "A Provincia de São Paulo." RAM, XXXI (Jan.), 9-26.
ARAUJO, OSCAR EGYDIO DE.
1935. Estatística predial. RAM, CI (March), 7-44.
1940a. Enquistamentos etnicos. RAM, LXV (March), 227-246.
1940b. A alimentação da classe obreira de São Paulo. RAM, LXIX (Aug.), 91-116.
1941a. Latinos e não latinos no município de São Paulo. RAM, LXXV (April), 65-98.
1941b. Padrão de vida de operários em São Paulo. O Observador Economico e Financeiro, VI, No. 69 (Oct.), 39-54.
1945. Habitações econômicas. RISP, II, No. 13 (Dec.), 55.
1947. Pesquisa entre motoristas, operários, contínuos e serventes da Prefeitura de São Paulo. RAM, CXIV (May-June), 7-136.
ARAXÁ, VISCONDE DE.
1883-1884. Reminiscencias e fantazias. 2 vols. Vassouras: Vassourense.
Arquivo do Estado de São Paulo (see AESP).

Arquivo Nacional (see AN).

ARROYO, LEONARDO.
1953. Igrejas de São Paulo. Rio de Janeiro: José Olympio.

ARRUDA, MARCOS.
1888. Boletim demographo-sanitario, especificando a mortalidade da cidade de S. Paulo em 1887. São Paulo: Martin Junior.

ASPECTOS SOCIAIS NO CONGESTIONAMENTO DO PÔRTO DE SANTOS.
1947. RISP, IV, No. 28 (March), 47-49.

(A) ASSIMILAÇÃO DO ELEMENTO ESTRANJEIRO EM SÃO PAULO (NOTAS ETNO-LÓGICAS SÔBRE OS ISRAELITAS).
1941. Planalto, I, No. 3 (June 15).

ASSIS, DILERMANDO DE.
1933. Abramos as portas – o plano rodoviario do Estado de S. Paulo. São Paulo: Liceu Coração de Jesus.

ATRI, A. D'.
1926. L'État de São Paulo et le renouvellement économique de l'Europe. Paris: Victor Allard, Chantelard.

AUBERTIN, J. J.
1862. Carta dirigida aos Srs. Habitantes da Provincia de S. Paulo. São Paulo: Literaria.

AUTOAÇÃO DAS COPIAS DOCUMENTOS. &. SOBRE A REBELLIÃO DA PROVINCIA DE S. PAULO.
1843. Rio de Janeiro: Nacional.

AZEVEDO, ANTÔNIO RODRIGUES DE.
1945. Combustíveis – lenha e reflorestamento aspectos economicos. RISP, I, No. 2 (Jan.), 26-33.

AZEVEDO, AROLDO EDGARD DE.
1943. Subúrbios de São Paulo. Separata from Anuário da Faculdade de Filosofia do Instituto "Sedes Sapientiae." São Paulo.
1944. Os subúrbios de São Paulo e suas funções. Boletim da Associação dos Geógrafos Brasileiros, IV, No. 4 (May), 59-69.
1945. Subúrbios orientais de São Paulo. São Paulo: Editora.

AZEVEDO, FERNANDO DE.
1937. A educação publica em São Paulo. São Paulo: Nacional.
1944. A cultura brasileira. 2nd ed. São Paulo: Nacional.
1948. Canaviais e engenhos na vida política do Brasil. Rio de Janeiro. Instituto do Açúcar e do Alcool.

AZEVEDO, MANUEL ANTÔNIO ALVARES DE.
1942. Obras completas. 8th ed., 2 vols. São Paulo: Nacional.

AZEVEDO, SALVIO DE ALMEIDA.
1941. Imigração e colonização no Estado de São Paulo. RAM, LXXV (April), 105-158.

AZEVEDO, VICENTE DE PAULO VICENTE DE.
1931. Alvares de Azevedo. São Paulo: Revista dos Tribunaes.

AZEVEDO FILHO, ROCHA.
1954. Um pioneiro em São Paulo: Joaquim Eugenio de Lima. São Paulo: Revista dos Tribunais.

BALDUS, HERBERT.
1954. Bibliografia crítica da etnologia brasileira. São Paulo: São Nicolau.

BANCO DO BRASIL.
1954. Estado de São Paulo. Rio de Janeiro: Giorgio.

BANDEIRA, MANUEL.
1946. Apresentação da poesia brasileira. Rio de Janeiro: Casa do Estudante do Brasil.
BANDEIRA JUNIOR, ANTONIO FRANCISCO.
1901. A industria no Estado de São Paulo. São Paulo: Diario Oficial.
BARATA, CANDIDO.
1875. Relatorio medico sobre o Hospital Publico da cidade de São Paulo durante a epidemia de variola de 1873 e 1874. São Paulo: Correio Paulistano.
BARBUY, HAROLDO.
1936. Beco da Cachaça (romance de costumes paulistas de 1860). São Paulo: J. Fagundes.
BARRETO, LUIS PEREIRA.
1874. As tres filosofias (1ª parte, Filosofia teologica). Rio de Janeiro.
1876. As tres filosofias (2ª parte, A filosofia metafisica). Jacareí.
1880. Positivismo e teologia – uma polemica. São Paulo: Marques.
1901. O seculo XX sob o ponto de vista brasileira. São Paulo: "O Estado de São Paulo."
BARRETO, PLÍNIO.
1933. Uma temerária aventura forense (a questão entre d. Amalia de Moreira Keating Fontaine de Laveleye e a City of San Paulo Improvements & Freehold Land Company, Limited). 2 vols. São Paulo: Revista dos Tribunaes.
BARROS, ERNANI THIMÓTEO DE.
1954. As migrações interiores no Brasil. Revista Brasileira de Estatística, XV, No. 58 (April-June), 77-84.
BARROS, LUCAS ANTONIO MONTEIRO DE (Visconde de Congonhas do Campo).
1946. Relatório da Província de São Paulo. Boletim do Departamento Estadual de Estatística, VIII, No. 3, 27-59.
BARROS, VALÊNCIO DE.
1945. São Paulo. RAM, CV (Oct.-Dec.), 25-39.
BARROSO, GUSTAVO.
1937-1938. Historia secreta do Brasil. 3 vols. São Paulo (Vol. I) and Rio de Janeiro (Vols. II and III).
BASTIDE, ROGER.
1943. Introdução ao estudo de alguns complexos afro-brasileiros. RAM, XC (May-June), 7-54.
n.d.(a). Os suicídios em São Paulo, segundo a côr. São Paulo: Faculdade de Filosofia, Ciências e Letras (Boletim CXXI), 1-49.
n.d.(b). A imprensa negra do Estado de S. Paulo. São Paulo: Faculdade de Filosofia, Ciências e Letras (Boletim CXXI), 50-78.
———, and FERNANDES, FLORESTAN.
1955. Relações raciais entre negros e brancos em São Paulo. São Paulo: Anhembi.
BASTOS, HUMBERTO.
1944. A marcha do capitalismo no Brasil. São Paulo: Martins.
BEALS, RALPH L.
1953. Social Stratification in Latin America. American Journal of Sociology, LVIII, No. 4 (Jan.), 327-339.
BELMONTE (Benedito Carneiro de Bastos Barreto).
1940. No tempo dos bandeirantes. 2nd ed. São Paulo: Departamento de Cultura.

BEYER, GUSTAVO.
1907. Ligeiras notas de viagem do Rio de Janeiro á Capitania de S. Paulo, no Brasil, no verão de 1813. *RIHGSP*, XII, 275-311.
BIALOSKORSKI, SEGISMUNDO.
1933a. Histórico da imigração polonêsa para o Brasil. *Boletim do Departamento Estadual do Trabalho* (May), 63-66.
1933b. As condições de vida e de trabalho do operario agricola no Estado de São Paulo. *Boletim do Departamento Estadual do Trabalho*, XXII, Nos. 78-79 (July), 65-67.
BICUDO, VIRGÍNIA LEONE.
1945. Estudo de atitudes raciais de pretos e mulatos em São Paulo. M.A. thesis (ms.), Escola Livre de Sociologia e Politica de São Paulo.
1947. Atitudes raciais de pretos e mulatos em São Paulo. *Sociologia*, IX, 3.
BIG TIME IN SÃO PAULO.
1950. *Fortune* (July), 65-71, 136-141.
BOJANO, CLEMENTE DE.
1940. O problema do pescado na cidade de São Paulo. *RAM*, LXVIII (July), 31-78.
BOURROUL, ESTEVÃO LEÃO.
1900. O Doutor Ricardo Gumbleton Daunt (1818-1893). São Paulo: Espindola Siqueira.
BRAGA, CINCINATO.
1921. Magnos problemas economicos de São Paulo. São Paulo: "O Estado de São Paulo."
BRAZIL'S CITY OF GO-GETTERS.
1957. *Business Week* (July 13), 58-64.
BRITO, F. SATURNINO RODRIGUES DE.
1911. Abastecimento d'agua de S. Paulo. São Paulo: Garraux.
BRITO, MÁRIO DA SILVA.
1954-1955. Notas para a história do modernismo brasileiro. *Anhembi*, XIV-XVII (March, 1954-Feb., 1955).
BROCA, BRITO.
1942. A aventura modernista. *A Gazeta Magazine* (Feb. 15 and 22).
BRUNO, ERNANI SILVA.
1944. Apontamentos sôbre a cidade e a casa de São Paulo no século dezenove. *Boletim Bibliográfico*, I, No. 3 (April-June), 99-104.
1947. Notas para a história da indústria paulistana. *RISP*, IV, No. 28 (March), 32-33.
1954. História e tradições da cidade de São Paulo. 2nd ed., 3 vols. Rio de Janeiro: José Olympio.
BUENO, FRANCISCO DE ASSIS VIEIRA.
1899. Auto-biographia. Campinas: Livro Azul.
1903. A cidade de São Paulo. *Revista do Centro de Ciencias, Letras e Artes de Campinas*, II, Nos. 1-3 (Jan.-July), 21-32, 79-84, 154-161.
BUSCH, REYNALDO KUNTZ.
1935. O ensino normal em S. Paulo. São Paulo: Record-Editora.
CALDEIRA, BRANCA DA CUNHA.
1935. A industria textil paulista. *Geografia*, I, No. 4, 50-66.
CALDEIRA, NELSON MENDES.
1939. Aspectos da evolução urbana de São Paulo. *Separata* from *Boletim do Departamento Estadual de Estatística*, No. 6 (June).

1940a. Economia urbana de São Paulo. *Economia*, II, No. 13 (June), 10-11.

1940b. O crescimento de São Paulo. *Economia*, II, No. 19 (Dec.), 11.

1940c. A propriedade urbana em São Paulo. São Paulo: Departamento Estadual de Estatística.

CALLAGE, FERNANDO.

1934. A imigração hungara para o Estado de São Paulo. *Boletim do Departamento Estadual do Trabalho*, XXIII, No. 80 (Jan.), 55-58.

CAMARGO, JOSÉ FRANCISCO DE.

1957. Exodo rural no Brasil: Ensaios sôbre suas formas, causas e conseqüências econômicas principais. São Paulo: Faculdade de Ciências Econômicas e Administrativas (Boletim No. 1).

CAMARGO, PAULO FLORÊNCIO DA SILVEIRA.

1941. Dom Antonio Joaquim de Melo e seu tempo. Ms. (loaned by the author).

1952-1953. A igreja na história de São Paulo. São Paulo: Instituto Paulista de História e Arte Religiosa.

CAMPOS, ERNESTO DE SOUZA.

1954. História da Universidade de São Paulo. São Paulo: Saraiva.

CAMPOS, FLAVIO DE.

1939. Planalto. Rio de Janeiro: José Olympio.

CAMPOS, PEDRO DIAS DE.

1908. O corpo de bombeiros de S. Paulo. *RIHGSP*, XIII, 137-157.

1909. A Força Publica. *RIHGSP*, XIV, 251-285.

CANNABRAVA, ALICE P.

1947. Tendências da bibliografia sôbre a história administrativa do município. *Revista de Administração*, I, No. 1 (March), 80-87.

1951. O desenvolvimento da cultura do algodão na Provincia de São Paulo (1861-1875). São Paulo.

CARDIM, FERNÃO.

1925. Tratados da terra e gente do Brasil. Rio de Janeiro: Leite.

CARDIM, MARIO.

1936. Ensaio de analise de factores economicos e financeiros do Estado de São Paulo e do Brasil no periodo de 1913-1934 pelo methodo de numeros indices. São Paulo: Secretaria da Agricultura, Industria e Comercio.

CARMELLO, JOAQUIM DO MONTE.

1873. O Arcipreste da Sé de S. Paulo, Joaquim Anselmo d'Oliveira, e o clero do Brasil. Rio de Janeiro.

CARMO, J. A. PINTO DO.

1948. Diretrizes partidárias. Rio de Janeiro: Pongetti.

CARNEIRO, EDISON.

1937. Castro Alves, ensaio de compreensão. Rio de Janeiro: José Olympio.

CARVALHO, AFONSO DE.

1933. Capacete de aço. Rio de Janeiro: Civilização Brasileira.

CARVALHO, AFONSO JOSÉ DE.

1942. São Paulo antigo (1882-1886). *RIHGSP*, XLI, 47-64.

CARVALHO, ANTONIO GONTIJO DE.

1946. Ruy Barbosa em São Paulo. *Jornal do Comércio* (April 28).

CARVALHO, C. M. DELGADO DE.

1910. Le Brésil méridional — étude économique sur les états du sud: S. Paulo, Paraná, Santa-Catharina et Rio-Grande-do-Sul. Rio de Janeiro.

CARVALHO, FERNANDO MIBIELLI DE.
1942a. População e imigração. *Revista Brasileira de Estatística*, III, No. 9 (Jan.-March), 111-124.
1942b. O êxodo rural. *Revista de Imigração e Colonização*, III, Nos. 3-4 (Dec.), 9-26.
CARVALHO, FLAVIO DE REZENDE.
1931. Experiencia N. 2. São Paulo: Ferraz.
CARVALHO, LAERTE RAMOS DE.
1946. A lógica de Monte Alverne. São Paulo: Faculdade de Filosofia, Ciências e Letras (Boletim LXVII).
CARVALHO, MENELICK DE.
1942. A Revolução de 30 e o município. Rio de Janeiro: Olimpica.
CARVALHO, ORLANDO M.
1937. Problemas fundamentaes do municipio. São Paulo: Nacional.
1946. Política do município (ensaio histórico). Rio de Janeiro: Agir.
CARVALHO, PAULO PINTO DE.
1943. Aspectos de nossa economia rural. São Paulo: Martins.
CARVALHO, PERICLES DE MELLO.
1940. A legislação imigratória do Brasil e sua evolução. *Revista de Imigração e Colonização*, I, No. 4 (Oct.), 719-739.
CASABONA, LOUIS.
1908. São Paulo du Brésil — notes d'un colon français. Paris: Librairie Orientale & Américaine.
CASAL, MANOEL AYRES DE.
1845. Corographia brasilica. 2nd ed., 2 vols. Rio de Janeiro: Laemmert.
CASTALDI, CARLO.
1957. Mobilidade ocupacional de um grupo primário de imigrantes italianos na cidade de São Paulo. *Educação e Ciências Sociais*, II, No. 4 (March).
CASTRO, SERTORIO DE.
1934. Diario de um combatente desarmado. São Paulo: José Olympio.
CATÁLOGO DOS DOCUMENTOS SÔBRE SÃO PAULO EXISTENTES NO ARQUIVO DO INSTITUTO HISTÓRICO E GEOGRÁFICO BRASILEIRO.
1954. São Paulo: Comissão do IV Centenário da Cidade de São Paulo.
CAVALHEIRO, EDGARD.
1940. Fagundes Varela. São Paulo: Martins.
1944. (ed.) Testamento de uma geração. Pôrto Alegre: Livraria do Globo.
1948. O livro em crise. *RISP*, IV, No. 41 (April), 20-24.
1955. Monteiro Lobato; vida e obra. 2 vols. São Paulo: Nacional.
CAXIAS, BARÃO DE (Luís Alves de Lima e Silva).
1931. Documentos sobre a Revolução de 1842. *Anais do Museu Paulista*, V (2nd part), 375-384.
CERQUERA, PAULO DE OLIVEIRA CASTRO.
1954. Um século de ópera em São Paulo. São Paulo: Guia Fiscal.
CHEMIN DE FER DE CEINTURE DE LA VILLE DE S. PAUL.
1904. São Paulo: Vanorden.
CIDADE, HERNANI.
1954. O bandeirismo paulista na expansão territorial do Brasil. Lisbon: Empresa Nacional de Publicidade.
CITY OF ENTERPRISE.
1952. *Time*, LIX, No. 3 (Jan. 21), 32-37.
CLEMENCEAU, GEORGES.
1911. South America To-day. London: T. Fisher Unwin.

COARACY, VIVALDO.
1931. O caso de São Paulo. São Paulo: Ferraz.
CODIGO DE POSTURAS
1875. . . . da Camara Municipal da Imperial Cidade de São Paulo approva-
do pela Assembléa Legislativa Provincial (lei n. 62 de 31 de maio
de 1875). São Paul: "Diario."
1886. . . . do municipio de São Paulo — 6 de outubro de 1886. São Paulo.
CODMAN, JOHN.
1870. Ten Months in Brazil: With Notes on the Paraguayan War. Edinburgh: R. Grant and Son.
COELHO, HENRIQUE.
1925. Ruy Barbosa em S. Paulo 1870-1886. Revista de Lingua Portuguesa,
VI, No. 33 (Jan.), 95-98.
COELHO, SALDANHA.
1954. Modernismo — Estudos criticos. Rio de Janeiro: Revista Branca.
COELHO, SALVADOR JOSÉ CORREIA.
1860. Passeio á minha terra. São Paulo: Lei.
COMISSÃO DO IV CENTENÁRIO DA CIDADE DE SÃO PAULO.
1954. São Paulo antigo — Plantas da cidade. São Paulo.
COMMISSÃO CENTRAL DE ESTATISTICA.
1888. Relatorio apresentado ao Exm. Sr. Presidente da Provincia de S.
Paulo. São Paulo: Bookwalter.
CORRÊA, A. A. MENDES.
1935. Cariocas e paulistas — Impressões do Brasil. Oporto: Machado.
COSTA, CYRO, and GÓES, EURICO DE.
1924. Sob a metralha . . . (histórico da revólta em São Paulo, de 5 de
julho de 1924). São Paulo: Monteiro Lobato.
COSTA, JOÃO CRUZ.
1956a. Contribuição à história das idéias no Brasil (o desenvolvimento da
filosofia no Brasil e a evolução histórica nacional). Rio de Janeiro:
José Olympio.
1956b. O positivismo na república — Notas sôbre a história do positivismo
do Brasil. São Paulo: Nacional.
CREVENNA, THEO R.
1950-1951. Materiales para el estudio de la clase media en la América
Latina. 6 vols. Washington: Pan American Union.
CRISSIUMA, EDDY DE F.
1935. Concentração japonesa em São Paulo. Geografia, I, No. 1, 110-114.
CRUZ, JOAQUIM LOUREIRO DA.
1948. O outro lado de Lobato. Folha da Manhã (Oct. 10).
CUNHA, MARIA L. MONTEIRO DA.
1947. Cultural Interests Stressed — São Paulo. Library Journal, LXXII, No.
9 (May 1), 690-691.
CUNHA, MÁRIO WAGNER VIEIRA DA.
1947. Características gerais da administração municipal no Estado de São
Paulo. Revista de Administração, I, No. 3 (Sept.), 3-44.
————, and SOUZA, MAY NUNES DE.
1947. As publicações oficiais no Estado de São Paulo. Revista de Administração, I, No. 1 (March), 16-29.
DANTAS, CHRISTOVAM.
1937. A lavoura paulista antes e depois da crise. Revista do Instituto de
Café, XII, No. 124 (June), 1087-1088.

DANTAS, GARIBALDI.
1938a. A crise do café e a expansão algodoeira paulista. *Revista do Instituto de Café*, XIII, No. 132 (Feb.), 170-176.
1938b. Novos aspectos da economia cafeeira de S. Paulo. *Revista do Instituto de Café*, XIII, No. 134 (April), 430-432.
DAUNT, RICARDO GUMBLETON.
1957. Diário da Princesa Isabel. São Paulo: Anhembi.
DAUNT NETO, RICARDO GUMBLETON.
1942. O Dr. Ricardo Gumbleton Daunt. *RIHGSP*, XLI, 65-104.
DAVATZ, THOMAS.
1941. Memórias de um colono no Brasil (1850). São Paulo: Martins.
DAVIS, HORACE B.
1935. Padrão de vida dos operarios da cidade de São Paulo. *RAM*, XIII (June), 113-166.
DEBENEDETTI, EMMA, and SALMONI, ANITA.
1953. Architettura italiana a San Paolo. São Paulo: Instituto Cultural Italo-Brasileiro.
DEFFONTAINES, PIERRE.
1935a. Regiões e paisagem do Estado de S. Paulo. *Geografia*, I, No. 2, 117-169.
1935b. As feiras de burros de Sorocaba. *Geografia*, I, No. 3, 263-270.
1936. Mascates ou pequenos negociantes ambulantes do Brasil. *Geografia*, II, No. 1, 26-29.
DENIS, JEAN FERDINAND.
1839. Brésil. Paris: Firmin Didot.
DENIS, PIERRE.
1928. Le Brésil au XXe siècle. 7th ed. Paris: Armand Colin.
DEPARTAMENTO DE CULTURA.
1936. Ensaio de um método de estudo da distribuição da nacionalidade dos pais dos grupos escolares da cidade de São Paulo. *RAM*, XXV (July), 197-237.
DEPARTAMENTO ESTADUAL DE ESTATÍSTICA.
1945a. Divisão judiciária e administrativa do Estado. São Paulo: Tipografia Brasil.
1945b. Ensáio de um quadro demonstrativo do desmembramento dos municípios. 4th ed. São Paulo: José Magalhães.
DEPARTAMENTO ESTADUAL DO TRABALHO (SECÇÃO DE INFORMAÇÕES).
1915. A immigração e as condições do trabalho em São Paulo. São Paulo: Rothschild.
1916. Dados para a historia da immigração e da colonisação em São Paulo: Rothschild.
DEURSEN, HENRI VAN.
1934. L'Émancipation industrielle du Brésil. Caractères et developpement de l'industrie dans l'État de São-Paulo. *Revue Économique Internationale*, 26, III, No. 2 (Aug.), 275-335.
DEUS, GASPAR DA MADRE DE.
1920. Memorias para a historia da Capitania de S. Vicente. São Paulo: Weiszflog.
DIAS, JORGE.
1953. Os elementos fundamentais da cultura portuguesa. Proceedings of the International Colloquium on Luso-Brazilian Studies (pp. 51-65). Nashville: Vanderbilt University Press.

DIHCSP (Documentos Interessantes para a Historia e Costumes de S. Paulo).
DIRETORIA DA SOCIEDADE PROMOTORA DE IMIGRAÇÃO EM S. PAULO.
    1887. Relatorio apresentado ao Illmo. e Exmo. Snr. Visconde do Parnaiba — 18 nov. 1887.
DISCURSO
    1848. . . . recitado pelo Exmo Senhor Doutor Domiciano Leite Ribeiro Presidente da Provincia de São Paulo. Na abertura da Assembléia Legislativa Provincial no dia 25 de junho de 1848. São Paulo: Tipografia do Governo.
    1852. . . . com que o Illustrissimo e Excellentissimo Senhor Dr. José Thomaz Nabuco d'Araujo, Presidente da Provincia de S. Paulo abrio a Assembléia Legislativa Provincial no dia 1º de maio de 1852. São Paulo: Tipografia do Governo.
    1858. . . . com que o Illustrissimo e Excellentissimo Senhor Senador José Joaquim Fernandes abrio a Assembléa Legislativa Provincial no anno de 1858. São Paulo: Dous de Dezembro.
    1859. . . . com que o Illustrissimo e Excellentissimo Senhor Senador José Joaquim Fernandes abrio a Assembléa Legislativa Provincial no anno de 1859. São Paulo: Imparcial.
Documentos Interessantes para a Historia e Costumes de S. Paulo (see DIHCSP).
DOMINGUEZ, LUIS L. (ed.).
    1891. The Conquest of the River Plate (1535-1555). London: Hakluyt Society.
DORNAS FILHO, JOÃO.
    1939. A ideia republicana em São Paulo. RAM, LXI (Sept.-Oct.), 7-22.
DUARTE, PAULO.
    1927. Agora nós! São Paulo.
    1938. Contra o vandalismo e o exterminio. São Paulo: Departamento de Cultura.
    1946a. Departamento de Cultura: vida e morte de Mário de Andrade. RAM, CVI (Jan.-Feb.), 75-86.
    1946b. Prisão, exílio, luta . . . Rio de Janeiro: Zelio Valverde.
    1947. Palmares pelo avêsso. São Paulo: IPÊ.
DUNCAN, JULIAN S.
    1955. Beef and Milk for Urban Brazil. Inter-American Economic Affairs, IX, No. 1 (Summer), 3-16.
EGAS, EUGENIO.
    1910. France et Brésil — de l'influence française sur le milieu brésilien. Paris: Aillaud.
    1925. Os municipios paulistas. 2 vols. São Paulo: "Estado de São Paulo."
    1926-1927. Galeria dos presidentes de São Paulo. 3 vols. São Paulo: "Estado de São Paulo."
    1935. Teatros e artistas. RAM, VIII (Jan.), 113-119.
EGYDIO, PAULO.
    1889. A Provincia de S. Paulo em 1888 (ensaio historico-politico). São Paulo: Louzada.
EIRAS, HEITOR A.
    1934. Uma série de sugestões para o novo código de obras. Record — Revista Mensal de Arquitetura e Decorações, I, Nos. 3-11 (March-Nov.).
ELLIS JUNIOR, ALFREDO.
    1937. A evolução da economia paulista e suas causas. São Paulo: Nacional.

1944. Capítulos da história social de S. Paulo. São Paulo: Nacional.
EPISCOPADO DA PROVÍNCIA ECLESIÁSTICA DE SÃO PAULO.
1942. Pastoral coletiva sôbre o jôgo, a dignidade da família e a defesa do Brasil. São Paulo: Ave Maria.
(AN) EVEN BILLION.
1952. Time, LX, No. 25 (Dec. 22), 31.
FARIA, ALBERTO DE.
1933. Mauá, Irenêo Evangelista de Souza, Barão e Visconde de Mauá 1813-1889. São Paulo: Nacional.
FEIJÓ, DIOGO ANTONIO
1830. Guia das camaras municipaes do Brazil no dezempenho de seus deveres. Rio de Janeiro: Astrea.
FERNANDES, FLORESTAN.
1944. Aspectos mágicos do folclore paulistano. Sociologia, VI, Nos. 2-3 (May-Aug.), 79-100, 175-196.
1947. As 'trocinhas' do Bom Retiro. Separata from RAM, CXIII.
1949a. A revolução constitucionalista e o estudo sociológico da guerra. RAM, CXXIII (March), 23-35.
1949b. A organização social dos Tupinambá. São Paulo: IPÊ.
1952. Contribuição para o estudo sociológico das adivinhas paulistanas. Revista de História, No. 9 (Jan.-March), 107-162.
n.d.(a) A economia paulista e a imigração — bibliografia. Ms. (loaned by the author).
n.d.(b) Aspectos da competição entre profissionais liberais descendentes de imigrantes. Ms. (loaned by the author).
FERRAZ, J. DE SAMPAIO.
1939. As garôas de S. Paulo. O Estado de São Paulo (April 26).
1940. Ligeiro esboço de alguns aspectos fundamentais da climatologia do Estado de São Paulo. Anais do IX Congresso Brasileiro de Geografia, II, 425-439.
FERREIRA, BARROS.
1954. Meio século de São Paulo. São Paulo: Melhoramentos.
FERREIRA, CLEMENTE.
1898. A febre typhoide em São Paulo (1897). São Paulo: Diario Oficial.
FERREIRA, TITO LIVIO.
1944. Gênese social da gente bandeirante. São Paulo: Nacional.
FERREIRA, TOLSTOI DE PAULA.
1940. Subsidios para a historia da assistencia social em São Paulo. RAM, LXVII (June), 5-76.
FLORENCE, AMADOR.
1937. Um prefeito vitorioso! RAM, XXXIII (March), 69-84.
FLORENCE, HERCULES.
n.d. De Porto Feliz a Cuyabá (1826-1827). Revista do Museu Paulista, XVI, 881-991.
FORJAZ, DJALMA.
1924. Senador Vergueiro, sua vida e sua época. São Paulo: Diario Oficial.
FRANCO, FRANCISCO DE ASSIS CARVALHO.
1944. Bandeiras e bandeirantes de São Paulo. São Paulo: Nacional.
1954. Dicionário de bandeirantes e sertanistas do Brasil. São Paulo: Siqueira.
FRANCO, JOÃO EVANGELISTA.
1944. O serviço de assistência aos menores no Estado de São Paulo. RAM, XCVIII (Sept.-Oct.), 7-44.

308 BIBLIOGRAPHY

FREIRE, J. J. DA SILVA.
1914. Influencia da viação ferrea na expansão economica de S. Paulo. Rio de Janeiro: Nacional.
FREIRE, VITOR DA SILVA.
1911. Melhoramentos de S. Paulo. *Revista Politecnica*, VI, No. 33 (Feb.-March), 91-145.
FREITAS, AFFONSO A. DE.
1914. A imprensa periodica de São Paulo desde os seus primordios em 1823 até 1914. *RIHGSP*, XIX, 321-1136.
1915. O "Correio paulistano" em 1831. *RIHGSP*, XX, 391-399.
1921. Tradições e reminiscencias paulistanas. São Paulo: Monteiro Lobato.
1922. São Paulo no dia 7 de setembro de 1822. *RIHGSP*, XXII, 1-35.
1924. Prospecto do Diccionario etymologico, historico, topographico, estatistico, biographico, bibliographico e ethnographico illustrado de São Paulo. São Paulo: J. Rossetti.
1927a. O primeiro centenario da fundação da imprensa paulista. *RIHGSP*, XXV, 5-42.
1927b. Notas á margem do estudo 'A imprensa periodica.' *RIHGSP*, XXV, 445-490.
1930. Diccionario historico, topographico, ethnographico illustrado do municipio de São Paulo (letra A). São Paulo: Gráphica Paulista.
FREITAS, BEZERRA DE.
1947. Forma e expressão no romance brasileiro. Rio de Janeiro: Pongetti.
FREYRE, GILBERTO.
1943. Problemas brasileiros de antropologia. Rio de Janeiro: Casa do Estudante do Brasil.
1944. O período republicano. *Boletim Bibliográfico*, I, No. 2 (Jan.-March), 61-72.
1946. The Masters and the Slaves. New York: Alfred A. Knopf, Inc.
1948. Ingleses no Brasil: aspectos da influência británica sôbre a vida, a paisagem e a cultura do Brasil. Rio de Janeiro: José Olympio.
1951. Sobrados e mucambos. 2nd ed., 3 vols. Rio de Janeiro: José Olympio.
1954. El IV centenario de São Paulo. *Cuadernos del Congreso por la Libertad de la Cultura*, 4 (Jan.-Feb.), 78-82.
FRONTINI, ROSA MARIA.
1957. São Paulo Landmarks. Américas (April), 22-25.
FUSCO, ROSÁRIO.
1940. Política e letras — sintese das atividades literárias brasileiras no decênio 1930-1940. Rio de Janeiro: José Olympio.
GAFFRÉ, L. A.
1912. Visions du Brésil. Paris: Aillaud, Alves & Cia.
GINSBERG, ANIELA MEYER.
1954. Relações raciais entre negros e brancos em São Paulo. *Anhembi*, XIII, No. 39 (Feb.), 443-464.
GODINHO, VITOR.
1898. A febre amarella — notas hygienicas. *Revista Medica de S. Paulo*, I, 8 (Sept. 15), 131-134.
GODOY, JOAQUIM FLORIANO DE.
1869. Ligação do valle do Parahyba á via ferrea de Santos. Rio de Janeiro: Villeneuve.
1875. A Provincia de S. Paulo, trabalho estatistico historico e noticioso. Rio de Janeiro: Diario do Rio de Janeiro.

GODOY, OSCAR DE.
1940. Factores de criminalidade na capital de São Paulo. *RAM*, LXIII (Jan.), 187-256.
GONÇALVES, CLOVIS.
1933. Carne para canhão! Rio de Janeiro: Renascença.
GOOD-NEIGHBOR SEARS.
1949. *Newsweek*, XXXIII, No. 13 (March 28), 70.
GOODWIN, PHILIP LIPPINCOTT.
1943. Brazil Builds; Architecture Old and New, 1652-1942. New York: The Museum of Modern Art.
GOUVEIA, PROENÇA DE.
1938. A situação atual do abastecimento de carnes a população de São Paulo. *RAM*, XLIV (Feb.), 391-400.
GROPP, DOROTHY M.
1940. Bibliotecas do Rio de Janeiro e de São Paulo e o movimento bibliotecário da capital paulista. *RAM*, LXVIII (July), 205-224.
HADDAD, JAMIL ALAMANSUR.
1945. O romantismo brasileiro e as sociedades secretas do tempo. São Paulo: Gráfica Siqueira.
HADFIELD, WILLIAM.
1869. Brazil and the River Plate in 1868. London: Bates, Hendy and Co.
1877. Brazil and the River Plate 1870-76. London: Sutton, Surrey.
HAMBURGER, ADELAIDE.
1954. A família numa pequena comunidade paulista. *Sociologia*, XVI, No. 3 (Aug.), 284-292.
HANDELMANN, HENRIQUE.
1931. Historia do Brasil. Rio de Janeiro: Nacional.
HELLER, FREDERICO.
1943. História natural de uma rua suburbana. *Sociologia*, V, No. 3 (Aug.), 199-216.
1944. História natural do Bairro Novo. *Sociologia*, VI, No. 2 (May), 101-110.
HERRMANN, LUCILA.
1943. Alterações da estrutura demográfica-profissional de São Paulo — da capital e do interior — num período de catorze anos — 1920-1934. *Separata* from *RAM*, LXXXIX.
1944. Estudo do desenvolvimento de S. Paulo através da análise de uma radial: — a estrada do café (1935). *RAM*, XCIX (Nov.-Dec.), 7-44.
1947. Características da evolução do parque industrial do Estado de São Paulo. *Revista de Administração*, I, No. 4 (Dec.), 87-114.
1948a. Flutução e mobilidade da mão-de-obra fabril em São Paulo. São Paulo: Instituto de Administração.
1948b. Evolução da estrutura social de Guaratinguetá num período de trezentos anos. *Revista de Administração*, II, Nos. 5-6 (March-June), 3-326.
1948c. Economia industrial e agrícola dó Estado de São Paulo. *Fundamentos*, I, No. 2 (July), 106-116.
n.d. Alteração do estrutura profissional da capital do Estado de São Paulo. Ms. (loaned by the author).
HOEHNE, EDUARDO.
1941. Cronologia dos presidentes, governadores e interventores de São Paulo 1822-1939. *RAM*, LXXIV (Feb.-March), 235-258.

HOLANDA, SÉRGIO BUARQUE DE.
1945. Monções. Rio de Janeiro: Casa do Estudante do Brasil.
1948. Raízes do Brasil. 2nd ed. Rio de Janeiro: José Olympio.
(A) HOSPEDARIA DE IMMIGRANTES.
1939. O Observador Economico e Financeiro, IV, No. 47 (Dec.), 53-66.
HOSTOS, EUGENIO MARÍA DE.
1939. Mi viaje al sur. Havana: Cultural, S.A.
HOUGH, JOHN.
1934. Reminiscences of Old São Paulo. Times of Brazil (Dec. 14).
HOUSSAY, FRÉDÉRIC.
1877. De Rio-de-Janeiro a S. Paulo. Paris: Gauthier-Villars.
HUMMEL, ALEXANDRE.
1901. São Paulo no limiar do novo seculo. Ms., located in the Museu
       Paulista.
HUTCHINSON, BERTRAM.
1957. Aspectos da educação universitária e status social em São Paulo.
       Educação e ciências sociais, II, No. 4 (March).
HYGIN-FURCY, C.
1888. L'Emigration ouvrière au Brésil, suite du Brésil actuel (guide de
       l'émigrant). Brussels: Rozez.
IDORT (Instituto de Organização Racional do Trabalho).
1940. Jornada contra o desperdício nos transportes. IDORT, IX, Nos. 97-
       100 (Jan.-April).
1941. Jornada sobre alimentação. IDORT, X, Nos. 116-120 (Aug.-Dec.).
1942. Jornada da habitação econômica. RAM, LXXXII (March-April).
1947. Anais da jornada de economia rural. São Paulo: Siqueira.
n.d.(a) Jornada da organização científica do trabalho na administração
       municipal. São Paulo.
n.d.(b) Jornada contra o desperdício. São Paulo.
IHGB (Instituto Histórico e Geográfico Brasileiro).
1855a. Provincia de São Paulo: descrição corografica e estatistica em 1855.
       Lata 45, ms. 871.
1855b. Mapa da divizão civil, judiciaria e ecleziastica da provincia de
       São Paulo com declaração do computo da população e do movi-
       mento no ultimo anno (1855). Lata 57, ms. 1081.
1856. Ricardo Gumbleton Daunt to Francisco Inácio Marcondes Homem
       de Melo, Aug. 4. Lata 8, ms. 148 B.
1891. Eduardo da Silva Prado to the viscount of Ourem, Oct. 27. Lata
       147, ms. 3436.
n.d. Comissão de Redação do Instituto Histórico. Imprensa em São Paulo
       — a primeira typographia. Lata 136, ms. 2362.
(O) INDUSTRIAL PAULISTANO — JORNAL DA SOCIEDADE AUXILIADORA DA AGRI-
       CULTURA, COMMERCIO E ARTES ESTABELECIDA NA CAPITAL DA PROVINCIA
       DE S. PAULO.
1854-1856. 2 vols. São Paulo: Literaria (Vol. I) and Dous de Dezembro
       (Vol. II).
INFORMAÇÕES SOBRE A ESCOLA LIVRE DE SOCIOLOGIA E POLITICA DE S. PAULO.
1935. RAM, XV (Aug.), 99-117.
IN MEMORIAM
1937. . . . Conde Francisco Matarazzo. São Paulo: Orlandi.
1944. . . . Martinho Prado Junior 1843-1943. São Paulo: Pocai.
INSTITUTO BRASILEIRO DE GEOGRAFIA E ESTATÍSTICA.
1946. Alfabetização e instrução no município de São Paulo. Boletim do
       Departamento Estadual de Estatística, VIII, No. 1, 27-47.

INSTITUTO CENTRAL DO CANCER, SÃO PAULO.
1950. *Architectural Record*, 107, No. 2 (Feb)., 108-111.
INSTITUTO DE ADMINISTRAÇÃO.
1948. Seminário de estudo das fontes primárias para a história de São Paulo no século XVI. *Publicações do Instituto de Administração*, 21-31 (May-July).
Instituto Histórico e Geográfico Brasileiro (see IHGB).
INSTITUTO DE PESQUISAS TECNOLÓGICAS.
1939. Instituto de Pesquisas Tecnológicas — histórico de sua evolução (1899-1939). São Paulo.
Instituto de Organização Racional do Trabalho (see IDORT).
INTERNATIONAL BASIC ECONOMY CORPORATION.
1950. São Paulo — Program of Public Improvements. New York: Steidinger.
INVENTARIOS E TESTAMENTOS.
JAGUARIBE, DOMINGOS.
1897. O municipio e a republica. 3 vols. São Paulo: Endrizzi.
JAMES, PRESTON E.
1933. Rio de Janeiro and São Paulo. *Geographical Review* (April), 271-298.
1946. Brazil. New York: Odyssey.
JARDIM, ANTONIO DA SILVA.
1879. A gente do mosteiro. São Paulo: Tribuna Liberal.
JARDIM, RENATO.
1932. A aventura de outubro e a invasão de São Paulo. Rio de Janeiro: Civilização Brasileira.
JORGE, J. DAVI.
1946. Esclarecendo datas do governo Oeynhausen. *Boletim do Arquivo do Estado*, V, 5-70.
JUNIUS (Antônio de Paula Ramos Junior).
1882. Notas de viagem. São Paulo: Jorge Seckler.
KIDDER, DANIEL P.
1845. Sketches of Residence and Travels in Brazil. 2 vols. London: Wiley & Putnam.
———, and FLETCHER, J. C.
1857. Brazil and the Brazilians. Philadelphia: Childs and Peterson.
KIDDER-SMITH, G. E.
1944. The Architects and the Modern Scene. *The Architectural Review*, XCV, No. 567 (March), 78-84.
KLINGER, BERTHOLDO.
1933. Nós e a dictadura. São Paulo.
KNOWLTON, CLARK S.
1955. Spatial and Social Mobility of the Syrians and Lebanese in São Paulo, Brazil. Ph.D. dissertation, Vanderbilt University.
KOSERITZ, CARL VON.
1943. Imagens do Brasil. São Paulo: Martins.
LAÈRNE, C. F. VAN DELDEN.
1885. Le Brésil et Java. Rapport sur la culture du café en Amérique, Asie et Afrique. The Hague: Nijhoff.
LALIÈRE, A.
1909. Le café dans l'Etat de Saint Paul (Brésil). Paris.
LANARI JUNIOR, AMARO.
1945. A laminação de ferro em S. Paulo. *RISP*, I, No. 6 (May), 35.
LAXE, JOÃO BATISTA CORTINES.
1885. Regimento das camaras municipaes — ou lei de 1º de outubro de 1828. 2nd ed. Rio de Janeiro: Garnier.

LEÃO, MÁRIO LOPES.
1945. O metropolitano em São Paulo. São Paulo: Prefeitura.
LEBRET, P. J. L.
1951. Sondagem preliminar a um estudo sôbre a habitação em São Paulo. *RAM*, CXXXIX (April-May), 7-52.
LECLERC, MAX.
1942. Cartas do Brasil. São Paulo: Nacional.
LEFEVRE, HENRIQUE NEVES.
n.d. Lineamentos gerais do zoneamento de S. Paulo e de sua região. Ms. (loaned by the author).
LEITE, AURELIANO.
1944. Ingleses no Estado de São Paulo. *Mensário do Jornal do Comércio,* XXV, No. 1 (Jan.), 209-213.
1954. História da civilização paulista. 3rd ed. São Paulo: Saraiva.
LEITE, NICOLÁO FRANÇA.
1874. Conferencia sobre o progresso material da Provincia de S. Paulo. Rio de Janeiro: Diario do Rio de Janeiro.
LEITE, SERAFIM.
1933-1934. A fundação de S. Paulo. *RIHGSP*, XXXI, 247-262.
1938-1950. Historia da Companhia de Jesus no Brasil. 10 vols. Lisbon and Rio de Janeiro.
1940. Novas cartas jesuíticas (de Nóbrega a Vieira). São Paulo: Nacional.
LEME, ERNESTO.
1949. Rui e São Paulo. Rio de Janeiro: Casa de Rui Barbosa.
LEME, PEDRO TAQUES DE ALMEIDA PAES.
1953. Nobiliarchia paulistana histórica e genealógica. 3 vols. São Paulo: Martins.
n.d. Historia da Capitania de S. Vicente. São Paulo: Melhoramentos.
LEMOS, MIGUEL.
1882. Resumo historico do movimento positivista no Brazil – anno de 93 (1881). Rio de Janeiro: Sociedade Positivista.
1884. L'Apostolat Positiviste au Brésil – rapport pour l'année 1882. Rio de Janeiro: Central.
1900. O Apostolado Positivista no Brasil, primeiro circular annual (anno de 1881). 2nd ed. Rio de Janeiro.
LEMOS, TÚLIO DE.
1941. O canto dos engraxates paulistanos. *Planalto*, I, No. 8 (Sept. 1), 7-8.
LÉONARD, ÉMILE-G.
1951-1952. O protestantismo brasileiro. Estudo de eclesiologia e de história social. *Revista de História*, Nos. 5-12 (Jan., 1951-Dec., 1952).
LEUENROTH, EDGARD.
n.d. A organização operaria de ação direta. Ms. (loaned by the author).
LE VOCI, ANTONIO.
1936. Transporte coletivo em São Paulo no ano de 1934. *RAM*, XXI (March), 99-107.
LEWIS, OSCAR.
1951. Life in a Mexican Village: Tepoztlán Restudied. Urbana: University of Illinois Press.
LIMA, HEITOR FERREIRA.
1954. Evolução industrial de São Paulo (esbôço histórico). São Paulo: Martins.

LIMA, MANOEL DE OLIVEIRA.
1907. O papel de José Bonifacio no movimento da independencia. *RIHGSP*, XII, 412-425.
LIMA SOBRINHO, BARBOSA.
1933. A verdade sobre a revolução de outubro. São Paulo: Unitas.
LOBO, T. DE SOUZA.
1924. São Paulo na federação. São Paulo.
LOEWENSTEIN, KARL.
1942. Brazil under Vargas. New York: The Macmillan Company.
LOURENÇO FILHO.
1940. Alguns aspectos da educação primária. *Revista Brasileira de Estatística*, I, No. 4 (Oct.-Dec.), 649-664.
LOWRIE, SAMUEL HARMAN.
1936. A assistência filantropica da cidade de S. Paulo. *RAM*, XXVII-XXIX (Sept.-Nov.), 193-238, 175-212, 23-49.
1938a. Origem da população da cidade de São Paulo e diferenciação das classes sociais. *RAM*, XLIII (Jan.), 195-212.
1938b. O elemento negro na população de São Paulo. *RAM*, XLVIII (June), 5-56.
1939a. Fontes bibliográficas das estatísticas de população no Estado de São Paulo. *RAM*, LIV (Feb.), 43-56.
1939b. Racial and National Intermarriage in a Brazilian City. *American Journal of Sociology*, XLIV, No. 5 (March), 684-707.
LUCROS E PERDAS NAS INDÚSTRIAS DE S. PAULO.
1948. *Conjuntura econômica*, II, No. 4 (April), 8-9.
MACHADO, ANTÔNIO DE ALCÂNTARA.
1940. Cavaquinho e saxofone (solos) 1926-1935. Rio de Janeiro: José Olympio.
MACHADO, JOSÉ DE ALCÂNTARA.
1905. Suicidios na capital de S. Paulo (1876-1904). São Paulo: Gerke.
1930. Vida e morte do bandeirante. 2nd ed. São Paulo: Revista dos Tribunaes.
MACHADO, LOURIVAL GOMES.
1948. Retrato da arte moderna no Brasil. São Paulo: Departamento de Cultura.
MACMILLEN, D. A.
1925. A solução do problema dos transportes de S. Paulo ao littoral. São Paulo: Monteiro Lobato.
MAGALHÃES, PAULO RIBEIRO.
1935. A fundação do Teatro Municipal S. Paulo. *RAM*, XVI (Aug.), 127-131.
MAIA, FRANCISCO PRESTES.
1930. Estudo de um plano de avenidas para a cidade de São Paulo. São Paulo: Melhoramentos.
1936. O zoneamento urbano. São Paulo: Sociedade "Amigos da Cidade."
1942. São Paulo metropole do século XX. São Paulo: Publicações Associadas.
1945. Os melhoramentos de São Paulo. São Paulo: Prefeitura Municipal de São Paulo.
——, and CINTRA, JOÃO FLORENCE D'ULHÔA.
1924-1926. Um problema actual — os grandes melhoramentos de São Paulo. *Boletim do Instituto de Engenharia*, VI, Nos. 26-29 and 31

314 BIBLIOGRAPHY

(Oct., 1924 – Oct., 1925, March-June, 1926), 56-60, 91-94, 121-132, 225-232.
MAIA, JOÃO DE AZEVEDO CARNEIRO.
1883. O municipio – estudos sobre administração local. Rio de Janeiro: Leuzinger.
MAJOR DIOGO ANTÔNIO DE BARROS, PIONEIRO DA INDÚSTRIA.
1945. RISP, I, No. 4 (March), 31.
MANGE, ROBERTO.
1944. O Senai. RISP, I, No. 1 (Dec.), 15-17.
MARIA, JULIO.
1900-1910. A religião, ordens religiosas, instituições pias e beneficentes no Brasil. In: Livro do centenario (1500-1900) (Vol. I). Rio de Janeiro: Nacional.
MARQUES, ABILIO A. S.
1881. Interesses da colonia portugueza na Provincia de S. Paulo (Brazil). São Paulo: Gazeta do Povo.
MARQUES, CICERO.
1942. Tempos passados. . . . São Paulo: Moema.
1944. De pastora a rainha. São Paulo: Cruzeiro do Sul.
MARQUES, JOSÉ CANDIDO DE AZEVEDO.
1874. Regulamentos expedidos pelo Exmo. Governo Provincial para execução de diversos leis provinciaes. São Paulo: Correio Paulistano.
MARQUES, MANOEL EUFRAZIO DE AZEVEDO.
1879. Apontamentos historicos, geographicos, biographicos, estatisticos e noticiosos da Provincia de S. Paulo. 2 vols. Rio de Janeiro: Laemmert.
MARTIN, HAROLD H.
1955. São Paulo. The Saturday Evening Post, 228, No. 5 (Oct. 8), 19-21, 102-106.
MARTINS, ANTONIO EGYDIO.
1911. S. Paulo antigo (1554 a 1910). 2 vols. São Paulo: Francisco Alves.
1912. Jornaes e jornalistas. RIHGSP, XVII, 113-138.
1915. Varias notas historicas. RIHGSP, XX, 343-362.
MARTINS, LUIS.
1953. O patriarca e o bacharel. São Paulo: Martins.
MARTUSCELLI, CAROLINA.
1950. Uma pesquisa sôbre a aceitação de grupos nacionais, grupos "raciais" e grupos regionais em São Paulo. São Paulo: Faculdade de Filosofia, Ciências e Letras (Boletim CXIX).
MATOS, ODILON NOGUEIRA.
1940. A evolução ferroviária de São Paulo. Anais do IX Congresso Brasileiro de Geografia, IV, 556-568.
1955. A cidade de São Paulo no século XIX. Revista de História, VI, Nos. 21-22 (Jan.-June), 89-125.
MATTHEWS, KENNETH.
1956. Brazilian Interior. London: Peter Davies.
MATTOS, J. N. BELFORT.
1925. O clima de S. Paulo. São Paulo: Rothschild.
MAURETTE, FERNAND.
1937. Alguns aspectos sociaes do desenvolvimento actual e futuro da economia brasileira. Geneva.

MAWE, JOHN.
1812. Travels in the Interior of Brazil. London: Longman, Hurst, Rees, Orme, and Brown.
MEDEIROS, OCÉLIO DE.
1946. Reorganização municipal. Rio de Janeiro: Pongetti.
MELLO, ROBESPIERRE DE.
1949. As democracias e a ditadura soviética. São Paulo.
MELO, ASTROGILDO RODRIGUES DE.
1935. Immigração e colonisação. Geografia, I, No. 4, 25-49.
MELO, RANDOLFO HOMEM DE.
1935. A agua em S. Paulo. RAM, XIV (July), 164-166.
MEMORIAL PAULISTANO PARA 1863.
1863. São Paulo: Imparcial.
MENDES, RENATO SILVEIRA.
1940. As estradas de rodagem do Estado de São Paulo. Anais do IX Congresso Brasileiro de Geografia, IV, 591-601.
MENDONÇA, LUCIO DE.
1901. Horas do bom tempo. Rio de Janeiro: Laemmert.
1930. Luiz Gama. RIHGSP, XXVIII, 433-444.
MENNUCCI, SUD.
1929. O vertiginoso crescimento de São Paulo. Educação, VIII, No. 2 (Aug.), 145-163.
1932. 100 annos de instrucção publica. São Paulo: Salles Oliveira, Rocha & Cia.
1938. O precursor do abolicionismo no Brasil (Luis Gama). São Paulo: Nacional.
1941. A guerra à zona rural. Revista Brasileira de Estatística, II, No. 8 (Oct.-Dec.), 1199-1214.
MENSAGEM APRESENTADA AO CONGRESSO LEGISLATIVO, EM 14 DE JULHO DE 1925, PELO DR. CARLOS DE CAMPOS, PRESIDENTE DO ESTADO DE SÃO PAULO.
1925. São Paulo.
MESQUITA, ALFREDO.
1951. Notas para a história do teatro em São Paulo. São Paulo.
MESQUITA FILHO, JULIO DE.
1925. A crise nacional — reflexões em torno de uma data. São Paulo: "O Estado de São Paulo."
MÉTRAUX, ALFRED.
1948. The Tupinamba. Handbook of South American Indians, III, 95-133. Washington: U.S. Government Printing Office.
MILLIET, SÉRGIO.
1938. Publicações da Sub-Divisão de Documentação Histórica e Social do Departamento de Cultura, São Paulo. Handbook of Latin American Studies (1937), 454-455. Cambridge: Harvard University Press.
1946a. Roteiro do café e outros ensaios. São Paulo: BIPA.
1946b. O poeta Mário de Andrade. RAM, CVI (Jan.-Feb.), 55-68.
MINDLIN, HENRIQUE E.
1956. Modern Architecture in Brazil. New York: Reinhold.
MINISTERIO DA AGRICULTURA, INDUSTRIA E COMERCIO.
1922-1929. Recenseamento do Brasil, realizado em 1 de setembro de 1920. 5 vols. Rio de Janeiro.

MIRANDA, ALCIBIADES.
1934. A rebellião de São Paulo. Curitiba.
MIRANDA, JOÃO PEDRO DA VEIGA.
1931a. Alvares de Azevedo. São Paulo: Revista dos Tribunaes.
1931b. Exhortações á classe dos fazendeiros. São Paulo: Revista dos Tribunaes.
MISSION BRÉSILIENNE D'EXPANSION ÉCONOMIQUE.
1909. Les progrès de São Paulo de 1887 à 1907. Paris: Aillaud.
MOACYR, PRIMITIVO.
1939-1940. A instrução e as províncias. 3 vols. São Paulo: Nacional.
1942. A instrução pública no Estado de São Paulo. 2 vols. São Paulo: Nacional.
MODERNIZING TRANSIT IN DIFFICULT TERRAIN.
1948. The American City, LXIII, No. 7 (July), 121.
MONBEIG, PIERRE.
1940. Ensaios de geografia humana brasileira. São Paulo: Martins.
1941. O estudo geográfico das cidades. RAM, LXXIII (Jan.), 5-38.
1952. Pionniers et planteurs de São Paulo. Paris: Armand Colin.
1953. La croissance de la ville de São Paulo. Grenoble: Allier.
1954. Aspectos geográficos do crescimento da cidade de São Paulo. Boletim Paulista de Geografia, No. 16 (March), 3-29.
MORAES, EUGENIO VILHENA DE.
1934. Caxias em São Paulo, a Revolução de Sorocaba. Rio de Janeiro: Briguiet.
MORAES, RAUL DE.
1947. Treinamento e aperfeiçoamento do pessoal das prefeituras de São Paulo. Revista de Administração, I, No. 3 (Sept.), 45-62.
MORAIS, ANTONIO EVARISTO DE.
1905. Apontamentos de direito operario. Rio de Janeiro: Nacional.
1924. A campanha abolicionista (1879-1888). Rio de Janeiro: Leite Ribeiro.
MORAIS, JOÃO BATISTA DE.
1907. Revolução de 1842. RIHGSP, XII, 441-617.
MORAIS, JOÃO PEDRO CARVALHO DE.
1870. Relatorio apresentado ao Ministerio da Agricultura, Comercio e Obras Publicas. Rio de Janeiro: Nacional.
MORAIS, RUBENS BORBA DE.
1935. Contribuições para a historia do povoamento em S. Paulo até fins do seculo XVIII. Geografia, I, No. 1, 69-87.
MOREIRA, GERALDO CAMPOS.
1947. O municipalismo. Revista de Administração, I, No. 1 (March), 88-94.
MORGAN, ARTHUR (Armando de Arruda Pereira).
1934. Os engenheiros de S. Paulo em 1932. São Paulo.
MORSE, RICHARD M.
1947. São Paulo — The Early Years. M. A. thesis (ms.), Columbia University.
1948. The Literary Life in Brazil: A Letter from São Paulo. The New York Times Book Review (May 16).
1949. O pesquisidor social e o historiador moderno. RAM, CXIII (March), 36-52.
1950a. São Paulo, raízes oitocentistas da metrópole. Anais do Museu Paulista, XIV, 453-487.

1950b. Brazilian Modernism. *The Hudson Review,* III, No. 3 (Autumn), 447-452.
1951a. São Paulo in the Nineteenth Century: Economic Roots of the Metropolis. *Inter-American Economic Affairs,* V, No. 3 (Winter), 3-39.
1951b. A cidade de São Paulo no período 1855-1870. *Sociologia,* XIII, Nos. 3-4, 230-251, 341-362.
1952a. A cidade de São Paulo no período de 1870 a 1890. *Sociologia,* XIV, Nos. 1-2, 17-42, 146-165.
1952b. São Paulo City under the Empire (1822-1889). Ph. D. dissertation (microfilm), Columbia University.
1953. The Negro in São Paulo, Brazil. *The Journal of Negro History,* XXXVIII, No. 3 (July), 290-306.
1954a. São Paulo in the Twentieth Century: Social and Economic Aspects. *Inter-American Economic Affairs,* VIII, No. 1 (Summer), 3-60.
1954b. São Paulo since Independence: A Cultural Interpretation. *Hispanic American Historical Review,* XXXIV, No. 4 (Nov.), 419-444. (Reprinted in: *Panorama,* III, No. 12, 5-29.)
MOURA, AMERICO BRASILIENSE ANTUNES DE.
1938. Govêrno do Morgado de Mateus no vice-reinado do Conde da Cunha. *RAM,* LII (Nov.), 5-155.
MOURA, PAULO CURSINO DE.
1943. São Paulo de outr'ora. 2nd ed. São Paulo: Martins.
MOURALIS, LOUIS.
1934. Un séjour aux Etats-Unis du Brésil. Paris: Presses Universitaires.
MÜLLER, DANIEL PEDRO.
1923. São Paulo em 1836 — ensaio d'um quadro estatistico da Provincia de S. Paulo ordenado pelas leis provinciaes de 11 de abril de 1836, e 10 de março de 1837. 2nd ed. São Paulo: "O Estado de São Paulo."
NABUCO, CAROLINA.
1950. The Life of Joaquim Nabuco. Stanford: Stanford University Press.
NABUCO, JOAQUIM.
1947. Minha formação. São Paulo: IPÊ.
1949. Um estadista do império. 4 vols. São Paulo: IPÊ.
NEME, MÁRIO (ed.).
1945. Plataforma da nova geração. Pôrto Alegre: Livraria do Globo.
NEMESIO, VITORINO.
1954. O campo de São Paulo. A Companhia de Jesus e o plano português de Brasil. 1528-1563. Lisbon: Comissão do IV Centenário da Fundação de São Paulo.
NERY, FERNANDO.
1932. Ruy Barbosa (ensaio bio-bibliografico). Rio de Janeiro: Guanabara.
NERY, M. F.-J. DE SANTA-ANNA.
1889. Le Brésil en 1889. Paris: Delagrave.
NETTO, GABRIEL AYRES.
1947. Código de obras "Arthur Saboya." São Paulo: LEP.
No. 1 BOOM CITY OF THE HEMISPHERE.
1951. *U. S. News & World Report,* XXXI, No. 6 (Aug. 10), 30-31.
NOBRE, JOSÉ FREITAS.
1950. História da imprensa de São Paulo. São Paulo: Leia.
NÓBREGA, MANUEL DA.
1931. Cartas do Brasil (1549-1560). Rio de Janeiro: Industrial Graphica.

Nóbrega, Melo.
1948. História de um rio (o Tietê). São Paulo: Martins.
Nogueira, Emília Costa.
1953. Alguns aspectos da influência francesa em São Paulo na segunda metade do século XIX. *Revista de História*, No. 16 (Oct.-Dec.), 317-342.
1954. O movimento republicano em Itú. Os fazendeiros do Oeste paulista e os pródromos do movimento republicano (notas prévias). *Revista de História*, V, No. 20 (Oct.-Dec.), 379-405.
Nogueira, J. L. de Almeida.
1907-1912. Tradições e reminiscencias. 9 vols. São Paulo: Vanorden (Vol. I) and A Editora (Vols. II-IX).
Nogueira, O. Pupo.
1935. A industria em face das leis do trabalho. São Paulo: Salesianas.
1945. A propósito da modernização de uma grande indústria. *RISP*, I, No. 6 (May), 16-18.
Nogueira, Oracy.
1942. Atitude desfavoravel de alguns anunciantes de São Paulo em relação aos empregados de côr. *Sociologia*, IV, No. 4 (Oct.), 328-358.
Noronha, Abilio de.
1924. Narrando a verdade. São Paulo: Monteiro Lobato.
1925. O resto da verdade. São Paulo: Rochéa.
Norton, C. McKim.
1953. Metropolitan Transportation. In: An Approach to Urban Planning (pp. 77-91). Princeton: Princeton University Press.
Novaes, José de Campos.
1905. Metropolitana paulista. Campinas: Livro Azul.
Nunes, José de Castro.
1920. Do estado federado e sua organização municipal. Rio de Janeiro: Ribeiro e Maurillo.
Nurses' School and Residence for São Paulo, Brazil.
1950. *Architectural Record,* 107, No. 2 (Feb.), 104-107.
Office Building for São Paulo, Brazil.
1952. *Architectural Record,* 111, No. 1 (Jan.), 154-158.
Oliveira, Antonio Rodrigues Vellozo de.
1822. Memoria sobre o melhoramento da Provincia de S. Paulo, applicavel em grande parte as outras provincias do Brasil. Rio de Janeiro: Nacional.
Oliveira, José da Veiga.
1950. Brazilian City Experiences Growth of Musical Interest. *Musical America*, LXX, No. 12 (Nov. 1), 9, 21.
1952. São Paulo Prefers Opera, but Other Music Flourishes. *Musical America*, LXXII, No. 6 (April 15), 10, 32.
Oliveira, José Feliciano de.
1898a. A propaganda positivista em S. Paulo. São Paulo.
1898b. O partidarismo positivista em São Paulo. São Paulo.
1932. O ensino em S. Paulo. São Paulo: Siqueira.
Oliveira, José Joaquim Machado d'.
1897. Quadro historico da Provincia de S. Paulo até o anno de 1822. 2nd ed. São Paulo: Gerke.
Ortigão, Ramalho.
1931. Carta a Eduardo Prado. *Revista Nova*, I, No. 1 (March 15), 5-14.

PACHECO, JOSÉ DE ASSIS.
1954. Revivendo 32. . . . Exumação de um diário de guerra. São Paulo.
PAIXÃO, MUCIO DE.
1936. O theatro no Brasil. Rio de Janeiro: Brasilia Editora.
PALMER, JR., THOMAS W.
1950. The Locomotive and Twenty Empty Freight Cars. *Inter-American Economic Affairs*, IV, No. 2 (Autumn), 53-94.
1951. São Paulo and the Republican Movement in Brazil. *The Americas*, VIII, No. 1 (July), 41-51.
PARTIDO REPUBLICANO.
1881. Programma dos candidatos — Eleição na Provincia de São Paulo. São Paulo. São Paulo.
PASCOALICK, ROMEU.
1941. Uma ferrovia paulista: — A Sorocabana. *RAM*, LXXVI (May), 183-196.
PAULA, E. SIMÕES DE.
1936. Contribuição monographica para o estudo da segunda fundação de São Paulo. São Paulo.
1954. Mensagem do Presidente João Teodoro Xavier à Assembléia Legislativa em 1873. *Revista de História*, V, No. 17 (Jan.-March), 233-242.
PENTEADO, A. A. BARROS.
1942. As represas da Light e a garôa em S. Paulo. *Engenharia*, I, No. 4 (Dec.), 128-129.
PEQUENO HISTÓRICO E PRONTUÁRIO DO DEPARTAMENTO DO ARQUIVO DO ESTADO.
1953. São Paulo: Departamento do Arquivo do Estado de São Paulo.
PEREIRA, JUVENAL PAIVA.
1938. O problema rural. *RAM*, XLVI, XLVIII (April, June), 325-346, 57-78.
PESTANA, PAULO R.
1923. A expansão economica do Estado de S. Paulo num seculo (1822-1922). São Paulo: Rothschild.
1927. O café em São Paulo. São Paulo: Levi.
PETRONE, PASQUALE.
1955. A cidade de São Paulo no século XX. *Revista de História*, VI, Nos. 21-22 (Jan.-June), 127-170.
PFEIFFER, IDA.
1880. Voyage d'une femme autour du monde. Paris: Hachette.
PICCAROLO, ANTONIO.
1908. Una rivoluzione economica — la proprietà fondiaria degli italiani nello Stato di San Paulo. Alessandria: Cooperativa.
1911. L'emigrazione italiana nello Stato di S. Paulo. São Paulo: Magalhães.
n.d. O socialismo no Brasil. 3rd ed. São Paulo: Piratininga.
———, and FINOCCHI, LINO.
1918. O desenvolvimento industrial de S. Paulo atravez da primeira exposição municipal. São Paulo: Pocai.
PIERSON, DONALD.
1942a. Habitações de São Paulo: estudo comparativo. *RAM*, LXXXI (Jan.-Feb.), 199-238.
1942b. Um estudo comparativo da habitação em São Paulo. *RAM*, LXXXII (March-April), 241-254.

320 BIBLIOGRAPHY

1942c. Negroes in Brazil, a Study of Race Contact at Bahia. Chicago: University of Chicago Press.

1944. Hábitos alimentares em São Paulo, estudo comparativo. *RAM*, XCVIII (Sept.-Oct.), 45-79.

1951. Cruz das Almas — A Brazilian Village. Washington: U.S. Government Printing Office.

PIMENTA, GELASIO.
1911. Alexandre Levy. São Paulo: Ronenhaim.

PINHO, WANDERLEY.
1942. Salões e damas do segundo reinado. São Paulo: Martins.

PINTO, ADOLFO AUGUSTO.
1902. Questões economicas. São Paulo: Vanorden.
1903. Historia da viação publica de S. Paulo (Brasil). São Paulo: Vanorden.
1916. As estradas de ferro de S. Paulo. São Paulo: Vanorden.

PINTO, ALFREDO MOREIRA.
1900. A cidade de S. Paulo em 1900. Rio de Janeiro: Nacional.

PINTO, L. A. COSTA.
1949. Lutas de familias no Brasil. São Paulo: Nacional.

PINTO JUNIOR, JOAQUIM ANTONIO.
1879. Movimento politico da Provincia de São Paulo em 1842. Santos: Diario de Santos.

PISANI, SALVATORE.
1937. Lo Stato di San Paolo. São Paulo: Napoli.

PIZA, ANTONIO.
1902. Considerações sobre o lugar onde, nos campos do Ypiranga, D. Pedro proclamou a independencia, em 7 de setembro de 1822. *RIHGSP*, VII, 458-469.

POLICIA DE SÃO PAULO.
1925. Movimento subversivo de julho. São Paulo: Garraux.

PONTES, ELOY.
1944. A vida exuberante de Olavo Bilac. 2 vols. Rio de Janeiro: José Olympio.

PRADO, EDUARDO DA SILVA.
1904-1906. Collectaneas. 4 vols. São Paulo: Salesiana.

PRADO, FÁBIO.
1936a. A administração Fabio Prado na prefeitura de São Paulo. São Paulo: Departamento de Cultura.
1936b. Mensagem do Prefeito Fabio Prado á Camara Municipal de S. Paulo. São Paulo: Departamento de Cultura.

PRADO, NAZARETH.
1929. Antonio Prado no imperio e na republica. Rio de Janeiro: F. Briguiet.

PRADO, PAULO.
1934. Paulistica — historia de São Paulo. Rio de Janeiro: Ariel.
1944. Retrato do Brasil — Ensaio sobre a tristeza brasileira. 5th ed. São Paulo: Brasiliense.

PRADO, YAN DE ALMEIDA.
1929. S. Paulo antigo e a sua arquitectura. *Ilustração Brasileira*, X, No. 109 (Sept.), 38-41.

PRADO JUNIOR, CAIO.
1935a. Destribuição da propriedade fundiaria rural no Estado de São Paulo. *Geografia*, I, No. 1, 52-68.

1935b.   O fator geographico na formação e no desenvolvimento da cidade de S. Paulo. *Geografia*, I, No. 3.
1941.   Nova contribuição para o estudo geografico da cidade de São Paulo. *Estudos Brasileiros*, III, 7, Nos. 19-21 (July-Dec.), 195-221.
1945a.   Formação do Brasil contemporâneo — colônia. 2nd ed. São Paulo: Brasiliense.
1945b.   História econômica do Brasil. São Paulo: Brasiliense.
PREFEITURA MUNICIPAL DE SÃO PAULO.
1911.   Melhoramentos do centro da cidade de S. Paulo. São Paulo: Rothschild.
1928.   O transporte collectivo no municipio de São Paulo. São Paulo.
1936.   Consolidação das disposições referentes aos serviços, repartições e funcionarios da prefeitura de São Paulo. São Paulo: Departamento de Cultura.
1947.   Repartições e funcionalismo da prefeitura do município de São Paulo — Atos, decretos, decretos-leis e leis de 5 de outubro de 1936 a 31 de dezembro de 1947. São Paulo: Departamento de Cultura.
PRIMEIRO CENTENARIO DO CONSELHEIRO ANTÓNIO DA SILVA PRADO.
1946.   São Paulo: Revista dos Tribunais.
PRODUÇÃO DE MÁQUINAS.
1947.   *RISP*, IV, No. 30 (May), 26-34.
PRODUÇÃO E CONSUMO DE LIVROS EM SÃO PAULO.
1947.   *RISP*, IV, No. 27 (Feb.), 27-33.
PUTTE, HUBERT VAN DE.
1890.   La Province de Sao Paulo du Brésil. Brussels: Vanderauwera.
QUEIROZ, MARIA ISAURA PEREIRA DE.
1950.   A estratificação e a mobilidade social nas comunidades agrárias do vale do Paraíba, entre 1850 e 1888. *Revista de História*, I, No. 2 (April-June), 195-218.
RAFFARD, HENRIQUE.
1892.   Alguns dias na Paulicéa. *Revista do Instituto Histórico e Geográfico Brasileiro*, LV (part 2), 159-258.
RAMOS, FRANCISCO FERREIRA.
1904.   Industries and Electricity in the State of São Paulo, Brazil. São Paulo: Vanorden.
RANGEL, ALBERTO.
1928.   Dom Pedro e a Marquesa de Santos. 2nd ed. Tours: Arrault.
RASM (Revista Anual do Salão de Maio, incorporando o catalogo do III Salão de Maio).
1939.   No. 1.
RECEPÇÃO DO SR. SENADOR RUY BARBOSA NA FACULDADE DE DIREITO NO DIA 18 DE DEZEMBRO DE 1909.
1909.   *Revista da Faculdade de Direito de São Paulo*, XVII, 137-178.
REDFIELD, ROBERT.
1930.   Tepoztlán: A Mexican Village. Chicago: University of Chicago Press.
1941.   The Folk Culture of Yucatan. Chicago: University of Chicago Press.
Registo Geral da Camara Municipal de S. Paulo (See RGCMSP).
REGO, JOSÉ PEREIRA.
1873.   Memoria historica das epidemias da febre amarella e cholera-morbo que têm reinado no Brasil. Rio de Janeiro: Nacional.
REGULAMENTO PARA OS CEMITERIOS DA CIDADE DE S. PAULO.
1858.   São Paulo: Lei.

REIS, MOREL MARCONDES.
   1945. A evolução do ensino técnico em São Paulo. São Paulo: Departamento do Serviço Público.
REIS JUNIOR, JOSÉ MARIA DOS.
   1944. História da pintura no Brasil. São Paulo: Leia.
RELATÓRIO
   1865. . . . da Comissão encarregada pelo Governo Imperial por avisos do 1º de outubro e 28 de dezembro de 1864 de proceder a um inquerito sobre as causas principais e acidentais da crise do mes de setembro de 1864. Rio de Janeiro: Nacional.
   1886. . . . apresentado á Assembléa Legislativa Provincial de São Paulo pelo Presidente da Provincia João Alfredo Corrêa de Oliveira no dia 15 de fevereiro de 1886. São Paulo: Jorge Seckler.
   1891. . . . dos estudos para o saneamento e aformoseamento das varzeas adjacentes á cidade de S. Paulo, apresentado ao Presidente do Estado Dr. Americo Brasiliense de Almeida Mello, pela Commissão para esse fim nomeada em 1890 pelo então governador Dr. Prudente José de Moraes e Barros. Ms., located in the Biblioteca Municipal de São Paulo.
   1894. . . . apresentado á Camara Municipal de São Paulo pelo Intendente Municipal Cesario Ramalho da Silva — 1893. São Paulo: Espindola Siqueira.
   1906. . . . nº 57 da Companhia Paulista de Vias Ferreas e Fluviaes para a sessão de assembléa geral em 30 de junho de 1906. São Paulo: Vanorden.
   1940. . . . das Commissões de Direcção e Executiva da Campanha de Ouro e da Commissão da Campanha do Ouro da Santa Casa de Misericordia de São Paulo. 2 vols. São Paulo: Revista dos Tribunais.
RENDON, JOSÉ AROUCHE DE TOLEDO.
   1851. Pequena memoria da plantação e cultura do chá (1833). In: Collecção das tres principaes memorias sobre a plantaçam, cultura e fabrico do chá. São Paulo: Liberal.
REQUERIMENTOS, CONTRACTOS E MAIS DOCUMENTOS RELATIVOS À ESTRADA DE FERRO CIRCULAR EM S. PAULO.
   1911. São Paulo: Weiszflog.
Revista Anual do Salão de Maio (see RASM).
REZENDE, CARLOS PENTEADO DE.
   1948. O ano de 1859 na vida de Carlos Gomes. O Estado de São Paulo (June 23).
REZENDE, FRANCISCO DE PAULA FERREIRA DE.
   1944. Minhas recordações. Rio de Janeiro: José Olympio.
REZENDE, JOSÉ SEVERIANO DE.
   1890. Cartas paulistas. Santos: Diario de Santos.
REZENDE, NELSON DE.
   1933. Prefeito technico ou prefeito politico? Revista Polytechnica, 107 (Jan.-Feb.), 453-473.
RGCMSP (Registo Geral da Camara Municipal de S. Paulo).
RIBEIRO, ABRAÃO.
   1946. Remodelação do serviço de transporte coletivo da cidade de São Paulo. São Paulo: Prefeitura Municipal.

RIBEIRO, ALVARO.
1927. Falsa democracia – A revolta de São Paulo em 1924. Rio de Janeiro: De Piro.
RIBEIRO, JOSÉ JACINTHO.
1899-1901. Chronologia paulista. 2 vols. (2nd in two parts). São Paulo: Diario Official.
1907. Indice alphabetico da lei nº 1038 de 19 de dezembro de 1906 que deu nova organização municipal no Estado de S. Paulo. São Paulo: Maré e Monti.
RIBEIRO, JOSÉ QUERINO.
1945. A memória de Martim Francisco sobre a reforma dos estudos na Capitania de São Paulo. São Paulo: Faculdade de Filosofia, Ciências e Letras (Boletim LIII).
RIBEIRO, JULIO.
1908. Cartas sertanejas. 2nd ed. Lisbon: Teixeira.
1946. A carne. 20th ed. Rio de Janeiro: Francisco Alves.
RICARDO, CASSIANO.
1942. Marcha para oeste. 2 vols. Rio de Janeiro: José Olympio.
RICARDO JUNIOR, GASPAR.
1933. A linha de Mayrink a Santos. Revista Polytechnica, 107 (Jan.-Feb.), 438-443.
RICCIARDI, ADELINO R.
1938. Parnaíba, o pioneiro da imigração. RAM, XLIV (Feb.), 137-184.
RODRIGUES, JOÃO L.
1930. Um retrospecto. São Paulo: Instituto D. Anna Rosa.
RODRIGUES, JOSÉ CARLOS.
1900-1910. Religiões acatholicas. In: Livro do centenario (1500-1900) (Vol. II). Rio de Janeiro: Nacional.
ROMERO, SÍLVIO.
1943. História da literatura brasileira. 3rd ed., 5 vols. Rio de Janeiro: José Olympio.
RUDOLFER, BRUNO, and LE VOCI, ANTONIO.
1943. O transporte coletivo na cidade de São Paulo. 2 vols. São Paulo: Prefeitura do Município.
RUGENDAS, JOÃO MAURÍCIO.
1940. Viagem pitoresca através do Brasil. São Paulo: Martins.
SÁ, MANUEL ALVARO DE SOUZA.
1880. Esboços criticos da Faculdade de Direito de São Paulo em 1879. Rio de Janeiro: Brasil Católico.
SABOIA, EDITH.
1939. Francisco Rangel Pestana. RAM, LXI (Sept.-Oct.), 23-42.
SAIA, LUÍS.
1938. Carapicuiba. Ms. (loaned by the author).
1944. Notas sôbre a arquitetura rural paulista do segundo século. Revista do Serviço do Patrimônio Histórico e Artístico Nacional, No. 8, 211-275.
SAINT-HILAIRE, AUGUSTE DE.
1851. Voyage dans les provinces de Saint-Paul. 2 vols. Paris: Bertrand.
1887. Voyage à Rio-Grande do Sul. Orléans: Herluison.
SAITO, HIROSHI.
1954-1955. O cooperativismo na região de Cotia: Estudo de transplantação

cultural. *Sociologia*, XVI, No. 3 (Aug., 1954), 248-283; XVII (March-Oct., 1955), Nos. 1-4, 56-71, 163-195, 254-268, 355-370.

SAMPAIO, THEODORO.
1900-1901. S. Paulo no seculo XIX. *RIHGSP*, VI, 159-205.
1904. Restauração historica da villa de Santo André da Borda do Campo. *RIHGSP*, IX, 1-19.

SANT'ANNA, NUTO.
1937-1944. São Paulo historico. 6 vols. São Paulo: Departamento de Cultura.
1939. O Jardim da Luz. *RAM*, LXI (Sept.-Oct.), 43-52.

SANTOS, JOSÉ MARIA DOS.
1930. A politica geral do Brasil. São Paulo: Magalhães.
1942. Os republicanos paulistas e a abolição. São Paulo: Martins.

SÃO PAULO E A SUA EVOLUÇÃO — CONFERENCIAS REALISADAS NO CENTRO PAULISTA EM 1926.
1927. Rio de Janeiro: Gazeta da Bolsa.

SÃO PAULO HÁ QUARENTA ANOS.
1928. *O Estado de São Paulo* (April 17, 19, 22, and 27, May 3, 9, 16, and 17, June 7, 12, 13, 17, 19, 22, and 27, July 1 and 11).

SARMIENTO, DOMINGO FAUSTINO.
1916. Recuerdos de provincia. Buenos Aires: La Cultura Argentina.

SCHMIDT, AFONSO.
1940. A vida de Paulo Eiró. São Paulo: Nacional.
1942. A sombra de Julio Frank. São Paulo: Anchieta.
1947. Sombras inquietas. Ms. (loaned by the author).

SCHOMPRÉ, EMILE QUONIAM DE.
1911. La bourse de São Paulo. São Paulo: Garraux.

SCULLY, MICHAEL.
1955. São Paulo's Mackenzie U. *Américas* (Feb.), 18-23.

SCULLY, WILLIAM.
1866. Brazil; Its Provinces and Chief Cities; the Manners and Customs of the People. London.

SEARS, ROEBUCK IN RIO.
1950. *Fortune* (Feb.), 78-80, 151-156.

SECRETARIA DA AGRICULTURA, INDÚSTRIA E COMÉRCIO DO ESTADO DE SÃO PAULO.
1940a. O vale do Paraíba. São Paulo: Tipografia Brasil.
1940b. Aspectos do padrão de vida do operário industrial da capital de São Paulo. São Paulo.

SECRETARIA DA EDUCAÇÃO E SAUDE PUBLICA DO ESTADO DE SÃO PAULO.
1937. Alguns problemas da educação technico profissional em São Paulo. São Paulo.

SEVERO, ARCHIBALDO.
1946. O moderno município brasileiro. Pôrto Alegre: Thurmann.

SEVERO, RICARDO.
1917. A arte tradicional no Brasil. *Revista do Brasil* (April), 394-424.

SHAW, PAUL VANORDEN.
1938. The Subdivision of Historical Documentation of the Department of Culture of the Municipality of São Paulo, Brazil. *Handbook of Latin American Studies* (1937), 450-454. Cambridge: Harvard University Press.

SILVA, CLODOMIRO PEREIRA DA.
1913. Plano de viação. São Paulo: Levi.

SILVA, FLORENTINO BARBOSA E.
1954. São Paulo Art Center. *Américas*, VI, No. 10 (Oct.), 20-23.
SILVA, HERCULANO DE CARVALHO E.
1932. A revolução constitucionalista. Rio de Janeiro: Civilização Brasileira.
SILVA, IVAN.
1941-1942. O linguajar paulistano. *Planalto*, I-II, Nos. 4, 6, and 18 (July
1 and Aug. 1, 1941, Feb. 1, 1942).
SILVA, JOÃO PINTO DA.
1922. Fisionomias dos novos. São Paulo: Monteiro Lobato.
SILVA, NESTOR DUARTE.
1930. Libero Badaró. *RIHGSP*, XXVIII, 463-577.
SILVA, OLIVEIRA E.
1940. O município no Estado Novo. Rio de Janeiro: Borsoi.
SILVA, RAUL DE ANDRADA E.
1941. A cidade de Santo André e sua função industrial. *RAM*, LXXIX
(Oct.), 201-216.
1955. São Paulo nos tempos coloniais. *Revista de História*, VI, Nos. 21-22
(Jan.-June), 55-88.
SILVEIRA, ARGIMIRO DA.
1890. Alguns apontamentos biographicos de Libero Badaró e chronica do
seu assassinato perpetrado na cidade de São-Paulo em 20 de
novembro de 1830. *Revista Trimensal do Instituto Histórico e
Geográfico Brasileiro*, LIII (2nd part), 309-384.
SILVEIRA, HORACIO A.
1935. O ensino technico-profissional e domestico em São Paulo. São Paulo:
Revista dos Tribunaes.
SILVEIRA, J. F. BARBOSA DA.
1941. Ramos de Azevedo e sua actividade. São Paulo: Riachuelo.
SILVEIRA, JOEL.
1946. Grã-finos em S. Paulo e outras notícias do Brasil. São Paulo:
Cruzeiro do Sul.
SIMÕES, CARLOS QUIRINO.
1940a. Rêde rodoviária do Estado de São Paulo. Anais do IX Congresso
Brasileiro de Geografia, IV, 89-112.
1940b. Historico e situação da rêde rodoviaria do Estado de São Paulo.
São Paulo: Salesianas.
SIMONSEN, ROBERTO C.
1939. Brazil's Industrial Evolution. São Paulo: Escola Livre de Sociologia
e Política.
1940. Aspectos da história econômica do café. *RAM*, LXV (March),
149-226.
1947. As atividades do Serviço Social da Indústria no Estado de São
Paulo. São Paulo: Siqueira.
SITWELL, SACHEVERELL.
1944. The Brazilian Style. *The Architectural Review*, XCV, No. 567
(March), 65-77.
SMITH, T. LYNN.
1944. The Locality Group Structure of Brazil. *American Sociological
Review*, IX, No. 1 (Feb.), 41-49.
————, and MARCHANT, ALEXANDER.
1951. Brazil, Portrait of Half a Continent. New York: The Dryden Press,
Inc.

SOARES, JOSÉ CARLOS DE MACEDO.
1925. Justiça – a revolta militar em São Paulo. Paris: Dupont.
SOARES, SEBASTIÃO FERREIRA.
1865. Esboço ou primeiros traços da crise commercial da cidade do Rio de
Janeiro em 10 de setembro de 1864. Rio de Janeiro: Laemmert.
SOCIEDADE PROMOTORA DE IMIGRAÇÃO.
1892. Relatorio ao Vice Presidente do Estado de São Paulo – 1892. São
Paulo.
SODRÉ, ALCINDO DE AZEVEDO.
1945. Primeira visita de Pedro II a São Paulo. RIHGSP, XLV, 124-143.
SODRÉ, NELSON WERNECK.
1947-1948. História da indústria em São Paulo. O Observador Econômico
e Financeiro, XII, Nos. 141-144 (Oct., 1947-Jan., 1948).
1948. O problema da distribuição. RISP, IV, No. 40 (March), 26-28.
1950. A pequena imprensa na regência e no império, RAM, CXXXIV
(July-Aug.), 69-86.
SODRÉ, RUY DE AZEVEDO.
1944. A crise da advocacia. Arquivos do Instituto de Direito Social, 4,
III (Dec.), 131-162.
SOUSA, EVERARDO VALLIM PEREIRA DE.
1946. A Paulicéia há 60 anos. RAM, CXI (Nov.-Dec.), 53-65.
1948. Reminiscências acadêmicas, 1887-1891. RIHGSP, XLIV (1st part),
55-75.
SOUSA, GABRIEL SOARES DE.
1938. Tratado descriptivo do Brasil em 1587. São Paulo: Nacional.
SOUSA, OCTAVIO TARQUINIO DE.
1942. Diogo Antônio Feijó (1784-1843). Rio de Janeiro: José Olympio.
SOUSA, PERO LOPES DE.
1861. Diario de navegação. Revista Trimensal do Instituto Histórico, Geográfico e Etnográfico do Brasil, XXIV (1st trimester), 9-96.
SOUSA, WASHINGTON LUIS PEREIRA DE.
1938. Capitania de São Paulo. 2nd ed. São Paulo: Nacional.
SOUZA, PAULINO JOSÉ SOARES DE (Visconde do Uruguay).
1865. Estudos praticos sobre a administração das provincias no Brasil.
2 vols. Rio de Janeiro: Garnier.
SPENGLER, OSWALD.
1939. The Decline of the West. 2 vols. New York: Alfred A. Knopf, Inc.
SPIX, JOH. BAPT. VON, and MARTIUS, C. F. PHIL. VON.
1824. Travels in Brazil, in the Years 1817-1820. London: Longman, Hurst,
Rees, Orme, Brown, and Green.
STEIN, STANLEY J.
1957a. Vassouras, a Brazilian Coffee County, 1850-1900. Cambridge:
Harvard University Press.
1957b. The Brazilian Cotton Manufacture; Textile Enterprise in an Under-
developed Area, 1850-1950. Cambridge: Harvard University
Press.
STRAIN, W. L.
1899. A febre amarella – Seu modo de propagação. Revista Medica de S.
Paulo, II, No. 8 (Aug. 15), 232-237.
SYLOS, HONORIO DE.
1936. São Paulo e a immigração italiana. Revista do Instituto de Café,
XI, No. 109 (Feb.), 168-171.

TACITO, HILARIO (José Maria de Toledo Malta).
  1919. Madame Pommery. São Paulo: Monteiro Lobato.
TAPAJÓZ, TORQUATO.
  1894. Saneamento de S. Paulo. São Paulo: Cia. Industrial.
TATE, ALLEN.
  1948. On the Limits of Poetry: Selected Essays. Denver: The Swallow
    Press.
TAUNAY, AFONSO D'ESCRAGNOLLE.
  1920. S. Paulo nos primeiros annos (1554-1601). Tours: Arrault.
  1921. S. Paulo no seculo XVI. Tours: Arrault.
  1922. Na era das bandeiras. São Paulo: Melhoramentos.
  1923. Sob El Rey nosso senhor — aspectos da vida setecentista brasileira,
    sobretudo em S. Paulo. São Paulo: Diario Official.
  1924-1950. Historia geral das bandeiras paulistas. 11 vols. São Paulo.
  1926-1929. Historia seiscentista da villa de São Paulo. 4 vols. São Paulo.
  1927-1937. Historia do café no Brasil. 15 vols. Rio de Janeiro: Departa-
    mento Nacional do Café.
  1937. O café e as rendas municipaes (1836-1872). Revista do Instituto
    de Café, XII, No. 126 (Aug.), 1439-1447.
  1945. Pequena história do café no Brasil. Rio de Janeiro: Departamento
    Nacional do Café.
  1946. Impressões de São Paulo (1886). São Paulo de Ontem, de Hoje e
    de Amanhã, VI, No. 21 (Jan.-June), 5-6, 61-62.
  1949. História da cidade de São Paulo no século XVIII. 2 vols. São Paulo.
  1953a. Relatos sertanistas. São Paulo: Martins.
  1953b. Relatos monçoeiros. São Paulo: Martins.
  1954a. História da cidade de São Paulo. São Paulo: Melhoramentos.
  1954b. História das bandeiras paulistas. 2 vols. São Paulo: Melhoramentos.
TAUNAY, ALFREDO D'ESCRAGNOLLE.
  1914. João Carlos Augusto d'Oeynhausen Grevenberg. RIHGSP, XIX, 217-
    225.
  1944. Cartas da campanha de Matto Grosso (1865 a 1866). Rio de
    Janeiro: Perfecta.
TAUNAY, HIPPOLYTE, and DENIS, JEAN.
  1822. Le Brésil, ou histoire, moeurs, usages et coutumes des habitans de
    ce royaume. 6 vols. Paris: Nepveu.
TEATRO CULTURA ARTISTICA.
  1950. Architectural Record, 108, No. 1 (July), 85-90.
TELES, GUIOMAR URBINA.
  1940-1941. O problema do cortiço. Serviço Social, II-III, Nos. 23-27
    (Nov., 1940-March, 1941).
TOLEDO, LAFAYETTE DE.
  1898. Imprensa paulista. RIHGSP, III, 303-521.
TORRES, JOÃO CAMILO DE OLIVEIRA.
  1943. O positivismo no Brasil. Rio de Janeiro: Vozes.
TSCHUDI, JOHANN JAKOB VON.
  1953. Viagem às províncias do Rio de Janeiro e São Paulo. São Paulo:
    Martins.
UNITED NATIONS (DEPARTMENT OF ECONOMIC AFFAIRS).
  1951. Labour Productivity of the Cotton Textile Industry in Five Latin
    American Countries. New York.

VALE, FREITAS.
1924. O ensino publico no governo Washington Luis. São Paulo: Garraux.
VAMPRÉ, SPENCER.
1924. Memorias para a historia da Academia de São Paulo. 2 vols. São
    Paulo: Saraiva.
1936. São Paulo em 1827. Revista da Faculdade de Direito, XXXII (fasc.
    2) (May-Aug.), 301-314.
VARNHAGEN, FRANCISCO ADOLFO DE.
1938. Historia da independência do Brasil. Revista do Instituto Histórico
    e Geográfico Brasileiro, 173, iii-lx, 5-634.
VASCONCELLOS, SIMÃO DE.
1865. Chronica da Companhia de Jesu. 2nd ed., 2 vols. Lisbon: A. J.
    Fernandes Lopes.
VASCONCELOS, HENRIQUE DORIA DE.
1941. Alguns aspectos da imigração no Brasil. Boletim do Serviço de
    Imigração e Colonisação, 3 (March), 5-36.
VEIGA FILHO, JOÃO PEDRO DA.
1896. Estudo economico e financeiro sobre o Estado de S. Paulo. São
    Paulo: Diario Official.
VIANNA, FRANCISCO JOSÉ DE OLIVEIRA.
1949. Instituições políticas brasileiras. 2 vols. Rio de Janeiro: José Olympio.
(A) VIDA E OBRA DE PAULA SOUZA.
1945. RISP, I, No. 8 (July), 24-25.
VIEIRA, DORIVAL TEIXEIRA.
1947. A evolução do sistema monetário brasileiro. Revista de Adminis-
    tração, I, No. 2 (June), 3-385.
VIEIRA, HERMES, and SILVA, OSWALDO.
1955. História da polícia civil de São Paulo. São Paulo: Nacional.
VILARES, HENRIQUE DUMONT.
1946. Urbanismo e indústria em São Paulo. São Paulo: Revista dos
    Tribunais.
1948. Urbanismo e problemas de São Paulo. São Paulo: Cruzeiro do Sul.
VILLAS-BÔAS, A.
1947. Santos – Suas ligações com o planalto e o hinterland. RISP, IV,
    No. 28 (March), 45-46.
VIOLICH, FRANCIS.
1944. Cities of Latin America. New York: Reinhold.
WEAVER, BLANCHE HENRY CLARK.
1952. Confederate Immigrants and Evangelical Churches in Brazil. The
    Journal of Southern History, XVIII, No. 4 (Nov.), 446-468.
WERNECK, ANTONIO LUIS DOS SANTOS.
1880. O positivismo republicano na Academia. São Paulo: Jorge Seckler.
WHITAKER, EDMUNDO DE AGUIAR.
1940. O espiritismo em São Paulo. Arquivos de Polícia e Identificação,
    II, No. 2, 553-560.
WHITAKER, PLÍNIO PENTEADO.
1946. Abastecimento de agua da cidade de São Paulo. Engenharia, V,
    No. 50 (Oct.), 65-83.
WILLEMS, EMÍLIO.
1944. O problema rural brasileiro do ponto de vista antropológico. São
    Paulo: Secretaria da Agricultura, Indústria e Comércio.
1946. A aculteração dos alemães no Brasil. São Paulo: Nacional.

1948. Aspectos da aculteração dos japoneses no Estado de São Paulo. São Paulo: Universidade de São Paulo.
1953. The Structure of the Brazilian Family. *Social Forces*, XXXI, No. 4 (May), 339-345.
n.d. Mobilidade e flutuação das profissões no Brasil e o problema educacional. São Paulo: Salesianas.

WILSON, BETTY.
1954. De misión a metrópoli. *Américas* (July), 9-12.

WYTHE, GEORGE.
1949. Industry in Latin America. 2nd ed. New York: Columbia University Press.

ZALECKI, GUSTAVO.
1938a. O problema da carestia do pão em São Paulo. *RAM*, XLIV (Feb.), 5-113.
1938b. O problema da carne. *RAM*, XLIV (April), 257-324.

ZALUAR, AUGUSTO-EMILIO.
n.d. Peregrinação pela Provincia de S. Paulo 1860-1861. Rio de Janeiro: Garnier.

ZANOTTI, ISIDORO.
1946. Migração dos campos para as cidades. *Revista de Imigração e Colonização*, VII, No. 4 (Dec.), 628-648.

ZENHA, EDMUNDO.
1950. A colônia alemã de Santo Amaro − Sua instalação em 1829. *RAM*, CXXXII (March), 47-142.

Part V — Beyond Metropolis (1955-1970)

*T*HIS BOOK, researched in the late 1940s and written in the early 1950s, betrays its own age and the youth of its author. If it were to be rewritten many details would need to be retouched, certain judgments reconsidered, certain perspectives deepened. The book has not been rewritten, however, nor has this new section been composed with a remedial or apologetic purpose. It simply seemed a dereliction to let the volume go forth again with no acknowledgment of São Paulo's protean growth and change, which have continued unabated since the 1950s, or of the increasingly sophisticated and voluminous research devoted to the city and its region. Some may find the similarities between this section and those which precede to be somewhat coincidental. Be that as it may, the writer feels no overmastering compulsion to highlight the discrepancies.

At the outset two historical issues receive attention: first, the question of how the city's history is to be periodized; second, the perennially intriguing question of why the city grew so fast and so suddenly. Subsequent sections deal with city planning, the city's regional role, entrepreneurship, social classes and mobility, political and religious mobilization, race relations, culture and social change, and the city in literature.

Chapter 22

THE CITY IN TIME AND SPACE

Periodization

𝓔VEN IF agreement were reached on a schema for periodizing the history of a nation, determining the phases of development of each of its cities would remain a challenge. Urban history, while responsive to events and trends of national importance, may lead or trail those trends and take sharper definition from localized occurrences such as economic or technological change, immigration, regimes of benign or nefarious political bosses, cultural or intellectual movements, or an occasional natural disaster such as earthquake or fire. The histories of São Paulo dealt with here illustrate two pairs of criteria for periodization: concern with manifest versus concern with subsurface phenomena of change, and an internal versus an external view of the city in its regional setting.

The criterion of Silva Bruno's three-volume history (1954) may be called impressionistic. He characterizes historical periods by seizing on a manifest distinguishing feature: "campsite for path-finders" (1554-1828), "student town" (1828-1872), "coffee metropolis" (1872-1918), and loosely, "contemporary São Paulo" to suggest modernization and explosive growth (1918-1954). This account, rich in narrative detail, makes little attempt to detect and interlink subsurface agents of historical process.

Leite de Barros (1967), whose study terminates at 1889, uses a pluralistic criterion to identify successive configurations of features: economic activities, customs and social structure, bureaucrati-

333

zation, rationalization, physical change, regional ecology. He starts with periods of consolidation (1554-1600) and of *bandeirismo* and impoverished agriculture (1600-1765). The balance of his account may be outlined as follows:

1765-1822: Stabilization of life; routinized trade and farming; city becomes trade and transport hub; new public services.
Mule trade creates capital for sugar and coffee cycles.
More complex social, economic, political organization.
Firmer urban control over surrounding nuclei and hinterland.

1822-1850: Bureaucratization of city as provincial capital; rationalization of public life; physical improvements.
Class distinctions sharpened.
Exodus of entrepreneurs to coffee lands.

1850-1875: Coffee boom brings trade, capital accrual, commercial credit.
Coffee plantations lose autarky, become dependent on city.
Urban professions multiply; family system loosens; liberalizing influence of law students; Europeanization of life.

1875-1889: Beginnings of a "metropolitan" economy; local capital accumulation; industrialization; city becomes a rail center.
European immigration; population and spatial growth; sweeping physical change.

This treatment pays attention to subsurface change—rationalization, bureaucratization—that created habits, outlooks, and institutions receptive to eventual possibilities for economic expansion and capital accrual. In particular the years 1765 to 1822, which Silva Bruno dismisses as an interlude of lethargy and impoverishment,[1] Leite de Barros considers a pivotal period of routinization of public

1. Similarly Taunay (1954), whose diffuse history of the city defies skeletonization, calls the years 1701 to 1821 a time of "stagnation and decadence."

and commercial life. This interpretation finds support in M. T. Schorer Petrone's conclusion (1968) that after 1790 the Paulista sugar cycle contributed to modernize the economic and social outlook of the regional elite and to create infrastructure (transport system, dock facilities, investment capital, commercial mechanisms, new towns) that later served the coffee trade.

My own treatment, while in some ways congruent with Leite de Barros', is perhaps impressionistic in its attempt to re-create the tone or ethos of city life in successive ten- to twenty-year periods of the nineteenth century.[2] This effort implies a generational criterion, an assumption that change takes hold only after it finds purchase in the outlook and mindset of a coming generation. Pushed too far, this view runs the risk of intellectual determinism; it may misgauge the forces of long-term cultural commitment and historical process; in Mumfordian fashion it may overestimate the capacity of bold and devoted leadership to re-create the legendary polis.

Unlike the vantage points so far mentioned, those of geographer Langenbuch (1971) and architect-planner Luiz Saia (1963; 1967) are external to the city and offer a spatial, ecological perspective. Langenbuch's study of the city and its close environs traces the processes by which the metropolis appropriated adjacent space. (For historical studies of individual *bairros* and suburbs see Penteado, 1962; Petrone, 1963; São Paulo, 1969-71.) A late-colonial trend was the appearance of a belt of well-to-do country estates (*chácaras*) around the urban nucleus and, beyond it, a belt of small-plot *caboclo* or *caipira* farming which replaced the town's satellite Indian missions. The decisive "premetropolitan" period was 1875-1915 when the *chácara* belt was subdivided and urbanized; lands of the *caipira* belt appreciated in value and were put to diverse uses for supplying the city; colonies of immigrant farmers were created; and construction of railroads and of the hydroelectric system determined subsequent patterns of urban expansion and land use. The period of early "metropolitanization," 1915-1940, witnessed the displacement of population growth from center to periphery; feverish

---

2. I did not try to periodize the twentieth century save in the cultural realm, where the Modernist movement yields divisions at about 1920 and 1945. These dates might be of use for industrialization and sociopolitical trends (cf. Dean, 1969; Pereira, 1967; Fernandes, 1964), but the case would have to be made with all its cross-linkages, and it seems to require another benchmark between 1929 and 1932 (cf. Simão, 1966; Rodrigues, 1966).

speculation in suburban lands; urbanization of interstitial land, though without integration of existing *bairros;* differentiation of industrial and bourgeois-residential zones; the growing importance of the bus and automobile in articulating spatial expansion. Finally, full-scale "metropolitanization" since 1940 has intensified these processes, producing steady territorial growth and annexation of outlying nuclei, accompanied by politico-administrative fragmentation; build-up of vacant lots hitherto held for speculation; explosive vertical growth in large zones of the urban center; new axes of expansion determined by interurban expressways.

The ecological unit analyzed by Luiz Saia is not the immediate metropolitan area but the whole interior hinterland of São Paulo. From the city's founding to the present he looks for periods of urban-rural polarity or "binary" (i.e., when the city functions as a self-contained outpost, sanctum, geometric enclave, or bastion of privilege) and periods of urban-rural interpenetration and accommodation. Saia's approach is appealing because he organizes the whole of São Paulo's history around a few key questions; he suggests cyclical as well as developmental trends; his concept of "city" has no artificial spatial limits; he is boldly normative in keeping the health of city and hinterland (social, institutional, economic, technological) constantly in focus. His schema may be outlined as follows:

1554-1600: Garrison of seaborne empire and utopian Jesuit sanctum; urban-rural polarity.

1600-1727: *first phase*
Colonist-Jesuit conflict over secularization of the urban nucleus.
second phase
Bandeirismo causes depopulation and impoverishment. Negation of urban-rural polarity and of geometric planning.

1727-1848: No clear expression of the individuality of city as it falls prey to circumstance and bureaucratic fiat.

1848-1929: *central theses:*
Colonial-type coffee monoculture; fan-shaped rail system centering on capital.
subtheses:
Predatory pioneering of coffee zones; linear spacing of towns along interfluvial ridges; new urban-

rural polarity; abstract, reticulated management of urban and rural lands; São Paulo functionally absorbs port of Santos.

1929-1945: Metropolitanization; region acquires energy potential sufficient to overcome underdevelopment; radical shift in regional planning needs unperceived by elites and professionals.

1945-   :   *central thesis:*
Regional industrial system erodes urban-rural polarity.

subtheses:
Reinterpretation of original urban site; integration of reticulated settlement pattern; reformulation of problems of public services, transport, electric power.

Saia's focus on the external relations of the city leads him to discount the development of urban institutions in the late-eighteenth century, emphasized by Leite de Barros. Nor does he indicate a watershed at the 1870s, when the city began its rapid growth. One also finds discrepancies in the use of the term "metropolis." Silva Bruno and Leite de Barros apply it to the city of the 1870s; I use it for the post-1890 period; Langenbuch dates "metropolitanization" from 1915 and Saia from 1929. Thus the term serves variously to signify rapid population growth and prosperity, cosmopolitan life style, power over a tributary region, centrifugal expansion of the urban area, or for Saia, the evaporation of "city limits" when urban technology and industrial patterns erupt across the hinterland.

Causes for metropolitan growth

The causes for São Paulo's breakaway growth continue to arouse speculation. Table 1 tells the story statistically. For recent years the demographic weight of the state capital looms even more formidable if one expands the *município* of São Paulo, used in the table, to include the thirty-three *municípios* officially constituted as Greater São Paulo in 1967. (São Paulo, 1967) This metropolitan area had a population of 8,137,401 in 1970. Projections give it 13,245,000 by 1985 and 21,026,000 by 2000. (Souza, 1968: 100)

Historians are specifically challenged, first, to explain the city's

TABLE 1

POPULATION GROWTH OF SÃO PAULO

Year	Population of São Paulo state (earlier province or captaincy)	State's annual growth rate (%)	Population of São Paulo City	City's annual growth rate (%)	City's population as % of state's
1772	100,537	—	21,272	—	21.2
1803	188,379	2.1	24,311	0.4	12.9
1816	219,867	1.2	25,486	0.4	11.6
1836	326,902	2.0	21,933	−0.7	6.7
1872	837,354	2.6	31,385	1.0	3.7
1890	1,384,753	2.7	64,934	4.1	4.7
1900	2,282,279	5.4	239,820	14.0	10.5
1920	4,592,188	3.6	579,033	4.5	12.6
1934	6,433,327	2.4	1,074,877	4.5	16.7
1940	7,180,316	1.8	1,326,261	3.6	18.5
1950	9,134,423	2.4	2,198,096	5.2	24.1
1960	12,974,699	3.6	3,825,351	5.7	29.5
1970	17,775,889	3.2	5,921,796	4.5	33.3

Sources: Nogueira, 1964: 35; Ikeda-Bueno, 1967; Marcílio, 1968: 119; Souza, 1968: 26; Fundação IBGE, 1971.

decades of stability after national independence despite its new functions (Barros, 1967: II, 347-68) and the rising population and prosperity of the province; second, to trace the concatenation of causes for the city's sudden growth in the late 1880s and 1890s; third, to explain both the continued high growth rate of the twentieth century and short-term fluctuations in that rate.

In accounting for the apparent stagnancy of the capital in the century before 1872, Marcílio (1968: 118-22) notes the reduction of the city's census area with the amputation of Santo Amaro in 1832 and of Cotia in 1836 (see above, p. 122) and the deployment of population into agriculture. In 1765 the captaincy had only 19 small towns. By 1803, owing in part to officially sponsored town-founding, these had become 35; by 1836 they were 46. This urbanizing process accompanied the expansion and commercialization of agriculture, notably sugar (Petrone, 1968: 9-23), which drew population from older settlement zones of São Paulo, including the capital and its environs, attracted migrants from decadent mining areas, and required importation of slaves. The relative stability of the capital during these decades therefore signifies regional economic development rather than a condition of stasis. Even when coffee invaded the Campinas area in the 1850s, eclipsing the sugar cycle and creating new fortunes, the impact on the growth of the capital remained gentle for a quarter of a century.

Standard explanations for the rocket-like growth of the capital starting in the late 1880s advance four interrelated sets of factors (e.g., Pereira, 1967: 15-16; also above, pp. 225-27): (1) temperate climate, favorable site, transportation linkages; (2) the coffee boom, which created capital for industry and attracted foreign immigration; (3) industrialization, facilitated by immigrant workers and entrepreneurs, availability of raw materials and hydroelectric power, and a regional market for manufactures; (4) a spirit of enterprise variously identified with the *bandeirante* mystique, the economic rationalism of Paulista coffee planters, and the pluck and skills of European immigrants.

Attempting to focus more sharply on the sequence and efficacy of diverse causes, Momsen (1964: 143-71) asks why São Paulo and not Santos experienced runaway growth. He makes three central points. First, the single route-zone between the two cities prevents regional transportation arteries from interconnecting at the port. Second, the routes converging on São Paulo serve a highly productive hinterland. Inasmuch as agricultural exports alone could not trigger the main growth of the capital, a final ingredient was industrial development based on local raw materials. This obviated the double crossing of the coastal escarpment, required so long as raw materials were exchanged for foreign manufactures. Thus the critical moment when the capital outstripped its port came when the value and volume of traffic between São Paulo and its hinterland exceeded those of its overseas traffic via Santos. This formula suggests comparisons with other "coupled nuclei" (Curitiba-Paranaguá in Paraná, Barra Mansa-Angra dos Reis in the state of Rio, Caracas-La Guaira in Venezuela, Santiago-Valparaiso in Chile) and has possible predictive value for the recent case of Governador Valadares (Minas Gerais) and Vitória (Espírito Santo).

The geographer's explanation, while enlightening, fails to consider the possibility raised by Cardoso (1960b; 1961) and Singer (1968: 57) that coffee profits might have been invested elsewhere in Brazil rather than in local industry. Given the coffee boom and the emergence of Santos as Brazil's leading coffee port (Araújo, 1969), Cardoso attributes industrialization to (1) the existence of a consumer market in the towns of the Paulista interior and (2) the impetus coffee planting gave to the profit motive and to rationalization of entrepreneurship (a point requiring qualifications supplied by Cardoso's research on the industrial elite, discussed later).

Other accounts emphasize the creation of infrastructure. Not only did coffee expand the money economy and the demand for basic manufactures, Dean (1969: 4-9) points out, but it also was the cause for railway construction, enlargement of Santos port facilities, and the new urbanites' demand for electric power to provide illumination and trolleys. These ingredients, combined with a work force disciplined by coffee and a cadre of foremen and technicians trained to tend plantations and build railroads, Dean takes as an interacting complex causing industrialization.

Singer (1968: 30-37), concerned more specifically with the growth of São Paulo city, groups his leading causes under two headings, capital and labor, and links both to coffee. Although the value of coffee exported through São Paulo-Santos in the late decades of the century far exceeded that of sugar in the early ones, the capital was a necessary stopping place for mule-borne sugar, while train-borne coffee could proceed from Campinas or Jundiaí directly to Santos. Santos therefore became the coffee mart. In 1873 the capital had only thirteen brokerage houses compared to Rio's two thousand. However, the banks required to finance new plantations and sustain planters during market fluctuations were another matter. These were drawn to the seat of political decisions, given the dependence of business on provincial policy. The second factor, labor, was provided by immigrants, originally destined for plantations. The construction of the Immigrants' Lodge in the 1880s helped transform the city into a labor market, and the growing number of planters' families who moved to the city created urban employment with their demand for shops, manufactures, and services. To his "principal" factors Singer adds the railway net and provincial revenues, which rose from 489 contos (1851) to 1,420 (1871) to 5,700 (1886) and paid for public services and utilities in the capital. Unlike Dean, Singer (1968: 56) considers electric power installations more consequence than cause of the industrial surge.

Finally the question remains, how was São Paulo's growth sustained after the early crisis of coffee overproduction? Marcílio (1965: 113) holds that these shocks caused certain leaders to "understand the urgent need to break with the colonial structure of Brazilian production and to envision the creation of an industrial center." Singer (1968: 40) similarly believes that coffee's long-term developmental effects are usually exaggerated and differs from Dean (1969: 86) in maintaining that industry replaced coffee as the propulsive force of urbanization. Coffee alone, he feels, could have supported modest urban growth until 1930, but that year's crisis and the crop's subsequent advance into Paraná would have left São Paulo a "dead city."

Sidestepping the question as to why, when, and how industry came to Brazil, on which much ink has been spilt, one must further ask why São Paulo replaced Rio as Brazil's industrial leader. One might have expected Rio—seaport, national capital, and Brazil's most populous city—to have stretched its comparative advantage. Yet in about 1910 industrial production in São Paulo state overtook that of Rio, and soon after 1920 the state capital followed suit. Singer (1968: 50-56) finds the explanation in these circumstances: that the spread of coffee created for São Paulo a larger tributary market for manufactures than was accessible from Rio; that the Paulista hinterland supplied more abundant raw materials for the characteristic light industry of 1890-1920 (textiles, food processing);

that the political and fiscal decentralization of 1891 favored a rich state like São Paulo which could finance its own development needs (subsidized immigration, railway construction). To this list can be added the fact that Rio's greater dependence on imports allowed São Paulo to invade its consumer market when World War I interrupted the inflow of foreign manufactures. (Dean, 1969: 97) Once São Paulo pulled ahead, new sets of reinforcing factors were set in motion (population concentration, industrial modernization) which preserve its primacy despite the spread of coffee into Paraná.

A point on which further controversy flickers is the impact of international shocks (war, depression) on Paulista industrialization. Dean (1969: 87-104) questions the opinion widely held by economists—and indeed by a contemporary observer like Walle (1921: 120)—that World War I sharply stimulated the growth and diversification of infant industry by cutting off manufactured imports. He claims that Paulista plants increased production only of traditional foodstuffs and textiles for export and that since the inflow of capital goods and raw materials was cut as well as of manufactures, home industry conducted largely a holding operation. Dean's intimation that Paulista industrialization might have progressed more swiftly without the war thus challenges the hallowed "external jolt" thesis of regional industrial growth. Straddling the canonical and revisionist positions, Fishlow (1970) ascribes substantial though not landmark importance to the war as an industrial accelerator, noting that the wartime rate of increase in cotton cloth production for the São Paulo region was twice the national average. (See also Baer-Villela, 1973.)

What "caused" São Paulo's expansion in this earlier period can scarcely be answered definitively. The question becomes hopelessly complex, however, as one advances into the twentieth century, and city growth, nourished by self-reinforcing causes, becomes increasingly entwined with interregional patterns of internal migration and economic development and with political action and policy formation at the national level.

Bases for city planning

São Paulo's growth has posed monumental problems for planners. Many have been met ineffectively if at all. Wilheim (1965) echoes the despair of Saia (1963) over this fact, yet he attributes the *paulistanos'* lack of civic concern (in contrast to the *cariocas'* pride in Rio) to the same historical legacy—erosion of the urban-rural dichotomy—which Saia finds appealing. The long era when the urban patriciate was dispersed and ruralized, Wilheim claims, created a tradition of alienation from municipal affairs, reflected in the weak and intermittent action of the town council. The nineteenth-century afflux of population to the city was composed of floating groups (students, traveling venders, freed slaves, immigrant workers) who carried weak traditions of civic loyalty. After 1870 the release of city lands to real-estate speculation minimized the possibilities for organic, concentric growth. Expansion was a disorderly process of filling in empty spaces and connecting up those peripheral settlements which, in Saia's analysis, had once been a healthy hallmark of rural-urban interpenetration.

Wilheim's recommendations are addressed not to Saia's broad hinterland but to the immediate São Paulo-Santos zone of conurbation which will contain more than twenty million inhabitants by the end of this century. In particular he stresses the need to revolutionize the city's circulation system, constricted by the unicentric loop-and-spoke plan imposed in the 1920s. Wilheim suggests: (1) A spacious parking ring around the inner city designed as a circular terminus for the radial arteries. Inner-city transportation would then be handled by buses, microtaxis, moving sidewalks, and the subway now under construction. (2) Depollution and channelization of the waterways (Tietê, Pinheiros) to allow incorporation of the river basins into the urban system as residential-recreation areas and as transportation arteries. Elsewhere Wilheim (1969: 185-93) elaborates a plan to rehabilitate the Tietê sector as a series of *bairros* nucleated at points where bridges cross the river-basin artery. (3) Replanning of the city's traffic pattern so that it no longer converges on the ancient "triangle" but takes advantage of the city's "most important topographic accident," the long, curving massif or *espigão central* (Azevedo, 1958: I, 183-95) which divides the Tietê and Pinheiros basins. Developed as an eight-mile elevated artery, the massif would become a distribution axis for many *bairros*, supplanting the unicentric radials-perimeter plan with a vertebrate, pluricentric one. (Campos Filho, 1972, elaborates and extends some of Wilheim's ideas.)

Cultural features are as important to Wilheim's diagnosis as those of urban topography. His emphasis, for example, on a well-knit transport system reflects a conviction that the city cannot be reconstructed on the basis of work-residence neighborhood units. São Paulo's case is not that of Lima, Peru, where 600,000 people, a quarter of the 1968 city population, live in shanty towns. Industrial site-planning might permit the Lima *barriadas* to become self-contained neighborhoods for residence, work, commerce, schooling, and recreation. Only a small fraction of the *paulistanos*, however, inhabit *favelas*, the Brazilian equivalent for *barriadas*. In 1967 nearly half the population of Greater São Paulo lived in substandard dwellings distributed as follows: 362,000 persons (5% of the population) in 72,500 *favela* units; 1,195,000 persons (16.5%) in 239,000 *cortiço* units; and 1,811,000 persons (25%) in 362,000 units of "precarious" housing. (Souza, 1968:59)[3] Why the *cortiço* continues to prevail in São Paulo rather than Rio's characteristic *favela* can be attributed to many factors: topography, ecology of urban growth, the urban transport system, social control mechanisms, the industrial labor market, availability of credit. (Leeds, 1969: 64-65) The modern *cortiço*, generally located in the inner city, takes three typical forms: the humid, unventilated *porão* (basement), the *meia-agua* (U-shaped cluster of ten or fifteen one-room dwellings around a narrow court), and the *andar superior* (rented room in a converted mansion). (Lagenest, 1962) Such dwellings are clearly less suited than *favelas* for planning territorial neighborhoods.[4] And certainly São Paulo's middle-class zones are no better adaptable as work-residence communities, given that the high cost of land for home-buyers and, until 1964, rent control have caused residential mobility to lag far behind job mobility. (Wilheim, 1969:55) Neighborhood communities, formerly widespread, are now limited to

3. In that year 55% of the city's residences had no private indoor toilets, 49% were without sewage connections, 21% lacked piped water, but only 5% were without electric light. The city had but 350,000 telephones, one for twenty inhabitants; the daily average of calls per phone was 46, one of the world's highest. It was estimated that 72,000 new dwellings a year were needed to keep pace with population growth, and hundreds of thousands to replace substandard units. However, building starts had dropped to 11,000 in 1966 from a peak of 21,000 a few years earlier, and new dwelling units provided by public agencies were averaging only 1,400 a year. São Paulo (1970: III, 219-80) surveys housing problems and makes recommendations; Conn (1968) canvases the *favelados'* legal rights as squatters in Rio and São Paulo.

4. Moreover, while a Lima *barriada* is often formed by an invasion of inner-city slum dwellers acquainted with city ways, the São Paulo *favela* tends to be a reception camp for rural and semirural migrants. (Goldman, 1965: 526)

favelas, to occasional old-time *bairros*, and to dwelling clusters beyond easy reach of public transportation. (Goldman, 1965: 535; also Singer, 1973: 15-60)

These conditions pose obstacles to schemes like that of Delorenzo (1967:124) and the late Father Lebret (Resumo, 1958) to reorganize the city's administration into a six-level pyramid based on neighborhood units of 500 meters' radius, combined in larger units of one-, two-, and four-kilometers' radius, culminating in "urban units" and a supreme "supra-urban unit." In almost Durkheimian language Wilheim suggests that we conceive São Paulo neighborhoods in terms not of physical but of social distance: "Social cohesion no longer arises as a product of community sentiments but through free *association of interests*." Planners, he feels, should give priority not to the territorial neighborhood but to functional gathering points that already exist: places of work, education, and recreation, markets and shopping centers, meeting-places for speeches, rallies, plays, and worship, and embarkation points for public transportation. The final item has special importance. For if one accepts the city as it is and abjures the herculean task of replanning it on a basis of territorial neighborhoods, then transportation assumes high priority as a factor of urban integration, perhaps even higher than housing. This consideration was not neglected in the São Paulo master plan initiated in 1967 by the vigorous mayor, José Vicente de Faria Lima (Lowe, 1969), although the piecemeal, sectoral orientation of current planning efforts impairs their viability. (Loeb, 1970: 148)

The regional impact of urbanization

In 1962 the Interstate Commission of the Paraná-Uruguay Basin produced a report on economic development, urbanization, and urban systems in a vast area comprising seven states of southern Brazil: Minas Gerais, São Paulo, Paraná, Santa Catarina, Rio Grande do Sul, Mato Grosso, and Goiás. (Costa-Kowarick, 1963) The Basin was found to gravitate around two urban poles, the São Paulo complex in the north and the Pôrto Alegre complex in the south. A secondary complex centers on Belo Horizonte and an incipient one on Curitiba. The Paulista system is "the dynamic center of the whole region." Containing six of the state's seven cities of over 100,000 inhabitants (as of 1960), it extends along four axes from the state capital, three of them penetrating the neighboring states of Minas, Mato Grosso, and Paraná. It produces 90% of the manufactures of the state and 67% of those of the whole Basin; it employs 85% of the state's industrial workers and 57% of the Basin's; it contains 68% of the state's urban population and 36% of the Basin's.

The report finds that settlement density in the area is quite uneven and the infrastructures for urban systems restricted in number and regional influence. It indicates the desirability of two complementary systems along an axis from Curitiba into the coffee zone of Londrina, with southern extensions into Santa Catarina, and along an axis joining Belo Horizonte to the agricultural zone of Governador Valadares and Teófilo Otoni along the River Doce. The latter would offset the polarization of that zone by Rio de Janeiro.

The isolation and self-containment of the chief urban systems raise questions about their internal structure. Is the morphology of the whole Basin, that is, replicated within single urban systems? Even the impressive Paulista system exhibits weak dispersion of urban functions.[5] Of the state's 17,776,000 inhabitants in 1970, 8,137,000 lived in Greater São Paulo. The three next-largest cities dropped off to populations of 376,000 (Campinas), 346,000 (Santos), and 212,000 (Ribeirão Prêto). If higher education and certain sectors of public administration have been decentralized, commercial and most administrative functions are still heavily concentrated in the state capital. Industry has expanded into the interior, but along continuous zones radiating from the metropolis and favoring the routes toward Rio (Müller, 1969), Santos, and Ribeirão Prêto. Although São Paulo city's share of the state's industrial labor force declined from 59.1% (1947) to 56.4% (1957) to 54.8% (1964), this in part signifies a spillover of factories, especially large ones, into neighboring municipalities where land is cheaper and less congested. (Rodrigues, 1959: 55; Singer, 1968: 69) The share of the state's industrial workers employed in the Greater São Paulo region did not begin to shrink till the 1960s. (Table 2; also Rattner, 1972)

The Interstate Commission proposes a strategy of decentralized urban development to counteract the hegemonic influence of the state capital: "The question here is not the lack of cities sufficiently

5. This system is described in IBGE (1957-64: XI, 136-84), Geiger (1963:249-73), and Azevedo (1967).

TABLE 2

INDUSTRIAL EMPLOYMENT IN SÃO PAULO STATE AND THE
GREATER SÃO PAULO METROPOLITAN AREA

	São Paulo State		Greater São Paulo		
Year	Industrial employees (000's)	Average annual growth (%)	Industrial employees (000's)	Average annual growth (%)	% of state's industrial employees
1939	329	–	200	–	60.8
1949	517	4.6	363	6.9	70.2
1959	825	4.8	580	4.8	70.3
1965	1,071	4.4	737	4.1	68.8

SOURCE: São Paulo, 1969: I, 36-37.

large to assume the role of regional centers but the powerful dominance exercised by the agglomeration of the capital. . . . Despite the great density of urbanization in the system, Ribeirão Prêto is the only city beyond the direct influence of the capital with a population of over 100,000 and a substantial development of industry and regional services, or the minimum conditions for a real regional center. Other cities like Bauru, Presidente Prudente, or Araçatuba will acquire these characteristics in rounded, balanced form only when an appropriate strategy can be defined." (Costa-Kowarick, 1963: 395)

The state's industrial park can be seen as a series of concentric circles radiating from the capital with an inner periphery transecting the regions of Sorocaba, Campinas, and the Paraíba valley. At the center, "traditional" industries (textiles, food-processing) tend to stagnate, or at most keep pace with their growth on the periphery, while complex "modern" industries (electrical, communications, chemical, mechanical, automobile) expand briskly. In outlying Ribeirão Prêto the traditional sector flourishes and the modern is still incipient. (Rocca, 1968: 84-99) Further evidence for the preemptive role of the capital in regional development is found in Gauthier's analysis (1968) of transportation growth and urbanization in the state from 1940 to 1960. He finds the two processes in "unbalanced" relationship, with highway accessibility (created by decisions and resources at the center) acting as a "lead" factor for regional industrialization and, to a less extent, urban population growth. This finding is consistent with the fact that the efficiency with which markets for consumer goods are exploited decreases as one moves out from centers of production. (Oliveira, 1966) Forces of demographic change have anticipated the planners in shaking out the lumpy distribution of the state's population. During the 1940s urban dwellers in Greater São Paulo increased by 68% and the rest of the state's urban population by only 39%. During the next decade the metropolitan rate edged up to 72% while in the rest of the state it jumped to 68%. (Ikeda-Bueno, 1967: 13) The distribution tilts heavily toward larger cities. Medium-sized centers have held their own, while the share of the state's urban population in small towns has dropped sharply. Although Table 3 includes

TABLE 3

DISTRIBUTION OF URBAN POPULATION IN SÃO PAULO STATE

Size of urban center	% of State's Urban Population			
	1940	1950	1960	1970 (est.)
Small (less than 10,000)	29.1	23.8	16.0	11.4
Medium (10,000-100,000)	26.2	30.0	32.8	27.2
Large (100,000-500,000)	4.9	4.1	12.4	28.0
São Paulo city	39.7	42.0	38.8	33.4
	99.9	99.9	100.0	100.0

SOURCE: Ikeda-Bueno, 1967: 14.

some municipalities of Greater São Paulo under the "large" category, a significant drift to larger centers outside the metropolitan area is underway. From a study of four urban zones in the state Berlinck (1968) hypothesizes that developmentally significant thresholds of division of labor ("structural complexity") and communications activity may here require a critical urban mass of perhaps 10,000 people. In other words, "the precondition for the socioeconomic development of sparsely settled areas is population increase." Given prevailing demographic trends in São Paulo, the conjecture is heartening.

Analysis of the urban hierarchy should extend to include the consequences of urbanization for the 37% of the state's population classified as "rural" in 1960. The number of rural dwellers increased by only 7.9% in the 1940s and 11.4% in the 1950s. If one excludes "rural" residents of Greater São Paulo, many of them doubtless "suburbanites," the percentages reverse to 4.5 and 0.7 respectively. (Ikeda-Bueno, 1967: 12-13) This trend is linked with a regional agricultural revolution. Until the mid-1950s São Paulo and its neighboring states supported a "colonial" agriculture. The cash crop, coffee, was destined for world markets, and farming for local consumption employed extensive methods causing heavy soil erosion: land rotation, rapid clearing of new lands, little use of fertilizers. Only in Rio Grande do Sul, traditional supplier of the south-central zone since the eighteenth century, had intensive "capitalist" agriculture developed (cattle, rice, wheat) to meet the soaring consumer demand of São Paulo-Rio. After the coffee glut of the early 1950s, however, the export crop found a more appropriate habitat in Paraná and, secondarily, in Goiás and Mato Grosso. São Paulo state and neighboring zones then turned to intensive farming, edging out the southern states, Rio Grande and Santa Catarina, as suppliers for the central metropolitan market. (Singer, 1963)

What economic and social implications the rationalization of agriculture holds for rural Paulista communities are open to question. Analyzing the effects of industrial-urban development on rural zones in São Paulo, Nicholls (1969) finds that the expansion of credit and consumer demand in cities benefits adjacent agriculture by facilitating investments in land improvement, more profitable capital-intensive enterprises, and an increased scale of farm. Proximity to cities also gives the countryside access to better public utilities and social services, and it provides job alternatives for excess farm labor. In short, the presence of industrial centers improves rural productivity, public services, and per capita income.[6] Although he draws on Nicholls' data, different conclusions emerge from Souza Martins' study (1969) of agriculture along the Paraíba valley on the São Paulo-Rio axis. Here he finds the rural world victimized by the city's "colonial" conception of it. The city requires that the country submit to programs of credit and modernization, absorb urban wares and attitudes, and yet continue supplying oligopsonistic urban middlemen at low prices. (See Comissão, 1967; Stilman, 1962.) Figures for the Paraíba region are adduced to show that under these conditions the most profitable units are not modern,

6. Singer (1963:162), however, holds that workers on modern farms lack bargaining power to raise their incomes because their companions who move to cities are replaced by the demographic overflow from areas of "colonial" agriculture.

technified but traditional, *caipira*-based farms whose marketable surplus flows from utilization of production factors that are not used for subsistence and would otherwise stand idle. This conclusion is supported by Paiva's finding (1969:230) that mechanization on Paulista farms greatly increases the yield of corn and potatoes, both per acre and per worker, but also raises the unit cost of production by 12 to 48%.

Two other studies examine the quality of life in rural zones. Haller (1967) uses quantitative methods to test the Marxist hypothesis that urban economies have deleterious effects on adjacent rural populations—namely, proletarization of the labor force, decrease in real incomes, and polarization of social strata.[7] Having surveyed sample households in four kinds of farm community located 35 to 75 miles from the metropolis, he finds that between 1953 and 1962: (1) rapid proletarization occurred, not primarily because independent farm operators lost status but because many workers rose "from a subproletariat stratum of sharecroppers" to the stratum of wage earners; (2) monetary income and land ownership showed little change up or down, while non-monetary income (radio listening, education) showed substantial increase; (3) there was little evidence for either polarization or equalization of the social strata.

Without questioning the accuracy of Haller's data, one can challenge the meliorist implications of his finding that the "relative impoverishment" hypothesis is untenable for rural populations of the Rio hinterland. For his analysis is silent on the cultural and psychological stress which looms so important in the qualitative field study of Antonio Candido (1964). From the latter's chapter, "The *caipira* confronting urban civilization," one surmises that even if Haller's indicators hold true for the Paulista zone they fail to illuminate the central fact of rural society change: "The *caipira* no longer lives in a precarious balance determined by the resources of the immediate environment and the sociability of isolated groups. He lives in clear economic disequilibirum vis-à-vis the resources provided by modern technology." A social revolution is suddenly occurring. Rural and urban types, subsistence farmers and *fazen-*

---

7. Although Haller claims no universal validity for his findings, which apply to the rural zone of Rio, his methods would presumably yield similar results for the São Paulo hinterland.

deiros, farm and factory wage earners find themselves "brusquely colliding in geographic and social space, sharing a universe which lays economic and cultural discrepancies painfully bare." In this new cacaphonous dialogue the weakest, most neglected voice "is beyond doubt the *caipira's.*"

What Haller perceives as a situation partly of equilibrium, partly of "relative enrichment," Antonio Candido designates a "crisis situation" in which traditional culture traits vanish more swiftly than they can be replaced because the *caipira* has no means to acquire new ones. This encroachment of urban culture forces persons and families into dramatic decisions which undermine the solidarity of social groups that have traditionally yielded consolation and support. Obliged to abandon "material and social techniques elaborated for a bygone way of life," the *caipira* may even exhibit "regressive adaptation" and fall back on archaic social patterns "incompatible with fully developed cultural life."

In recent years the Paulista metropolis has been viewed not simply in relation to its adjacent hinterland but also (as part of the Rio-São Paulo metropolitan axis) in a dominant relation to centers of production throughout the nation. This frame of reference introduces national-level economic and political factors and removes one somewhat from a consideration of the city *qua* city. On the national as on the regional stage a central issue, explored more fully elsewhere (Morse, 1971: 2, 36-55), is whether the metropolis is to be conceived as a point of diffusion for innovation and development or as a bastion for "colonial" control. The ambiguities of the question are apparent when we reflect that Paulista financing and know-how can stimulate industrialization with all its side-effects in Brazil's depressed Northeast while decisions about production and disposition of profits continue to emanate from São Paulo.

An appraisal of this situation by Frank (1969: 190-201) suggests conspiratorial elements. Without lingering to explain why the Paulista zone industrialized in the late nineteenth-century, he purports to expose a metropolis-satellite chain of exploitation that links the São Paulo bourgeoisie to world capitalist centers, the Northeast landlords and merchants to São Paulo, and in turn subjects Northeast workers and consumers to this last group. Singer (1968), while recognizing interregional alliances of elites that make for "internal colonialism," attributes the rise of São Paulo to its economic resources and to the free play of market forces. For him, investment concentration is neither an original conspiracy nor an ultimate explanation of regional imbalances but a natural outcome of the development process. As interregional transport, marketing, and financial systems became integrated after 1920, São Paulo extended its hegemony, ploughed profits into an infrastructure which other states could not afford, and thus consolidated its natural advantages. At this point, Singer concludes, decisive intervention by the national government might begin to rectify accumulated imbalances.

Chapter 23

PRESSURES AND PROCESS IN URBAN SOCIETY

Entrepreneurship

IN THE city reputed to be the hub of South America's largest industrial park, the question of entrepreneurship holds a priority claim on our attention. Ever since the late-nineteenth-century travelers who admired the drive and modernity of Paulista businessmen, observers have referred to a regional Paulista or *bandeirante* mystique in explaining the emergence of this Brazilian Chicago or Milan. Here are two recent formulations of the theme.

Warren Dean (1969: 34-48) asks whether the regional culture has indeed been more congenial to the capitalist spirit than others in Latin America. His conclusion is negative; he finds it more plausible to assume that entrepreneurial talent was distributed more or less evenly throughout Brazil. The success of Paulista planters who turned to urban enterprise he attributes not to psychocultural but to historical and economic factors, such as the nature of coffee cultivation (which favored "capitalistic" planters who reinvested profits), prior capital accumulation, a profitable market economy, and a free labor market. Despite the importance he ascribes to the market economy, Dean paradoxically adds to his explanatory list those "factors discouraging competition from other groups."

Dean's argument tends to be circular. He considers entrepreneurial spirit to be a ubiquitous reservoir of energy, releasable by happy conjunctions of transcultural factors. Yet he accounts for Paulista entrepreneurship by commercial and institutional preconditions that seem as much result as cause of a "rational" economic outlook. The primacy Dean attributes to "situational processes" is certainly convincing—one would scarcely have expected an industrial explosion along the Amazon in 1890. But once he dismisses the restraining effect of "cultural process" on the "capitalist" market economy, culture makes a backdoor reappearance in his admission that the planters' entrepreneurial spirit was conditioned by a "thoroughly politicized view of economic development," a preference for government clientage arrangements, and the cooptation and neutralization of immigrant elites.

In his studies of Brazilian entrepreneurship, which rely heavily on the Paulista case, Cardoso (1961; 1964; 1965) formulates the problem differently. He is not interested in the causal role of either psychocultural or circumstantial factors in São Paulo's industrial revolution. Nor does he conceive of entrepreneurial spirit as a standard unit of psychic energy. His premise is that entrepreneurship in Brazil can be studied only as a function of the institutional context which sustains it. "I was less concerned with the innovative capacity of a talented entrepreneur than with the social conditions that permit the deployment of entrepreneurial skills under the form of industrial capitalism" (1964: 8). São Paulo therefore ceases to be an idiosyncratic case of industrial progressivism and antitraditionalism, and becomes an exemplary case of the complex forms of industrialism in the Ibero-American cultural world.

From this perspective Cardoso (1964: 80-92, 159-66) interprets the "frames of reference" of Paulista industrialists as having been "relatively restricted" until as late as the 1950s, when technological change and expansion of the modern sector took a quantum jump. Till then the choice of manufactures was traditional; business practices were routine; and political pressures generated by industrialists were weak. Cardoso therefore challenges the familiar thesis that "private initiative—or, the entrepreneurial bourgeoisie—constitutes the original motive force for development and modernization in Brazil."[8] Rather than calling entrepreneurship an engine of modern-

8. In his study of Matarazzo, Souza Martins (1967) traces the Count's slow and cautious, if highly profitable, entry into industry via importing and shows how both the management of his vast firm and Matarazzo's own self-image reflected an unresolved tension between "São Paulo's No. 1 Worker" and the Italian nobleman, between the cult of "success" and the cult of hierarchical station.

ization, he suggests that only recently has the institutional, political, and cultural climate supported industrial innovation. Frequently, in fact, this public climate encounters resistances to change precisely from family-controlled entrepreneurial groups with "pioneering" traditions—a fact well documented in subsequent parts of Dean's analysis. The industrial elite is so heterogeneous that it fails to exert coherent political pressure on national leadership; its members perceive themselves primarily in the light of private status criteria and only secondarily as an entrepreneurial group; their view of the social order inhibits them from construing their personal or class situation in terms of economic interest; and their response to market requirements is the "minimum necessary for enterprises to survive as economic organizations with a profit-making objective." (See also Cordeiro, 1966.) In short, Cardoso finds Paulista entrepreneurship to be less innovative than accommodative with respect to economic attitudes and social change.

Social mobility

Just as Cardoso's study alerts us against exaggerating the "dynamism" of Paulista industry, so the Hutchinson studies (1960: 97-229) warn us not to overestimate the social change caused by industrialization, immigration, and education. In comparison even to English schools those of São Paulo, particularly the traditional primary and secondary systems, tend to maintain *status quo* and discourage social mobility. "That is, available resources for education do not correspond to the requirements for economic development." The seeming antitraditionalism of São Paulo society is therefore explained by a distinction between "structural" mobility, resulting from the creation of new middle- and upper-level positions by an expanding economy, and "exchange" or "replacement" mobility, resulting from promotion and demotion up and down the occupational ladder on a merit basis. (Hutchinson, 1958a) São Paulo obviously offers considerable mobility of the first or structural type but much less of the second than one might expect. A survey of six Brazilian cities including São Paulo showed that 44% of the cases of social mobility were made possible by structural change, as contrasted with only 12% in a similar survey conducted in Great Britain some years earlier. Cityward migration in Brazil appears stimulated less by a prospect of breakdown in the rigidity of the social hierarchy than by the new mobility paths opened by industrialization. (Hutchinson, 1963: 56-57)

Studies of the earlier foreign immigrants to São Paulo show that their background and motivations advantaged them for upward mobility in comparison to native Brazilians. (Hutchinson, 1960: 281-359; Foracchi, 1963)[9] The new environment, however, encouraged them to abandon the very ethic of work which had assured their survival and early advancement and to adopt its prevailing status orientations. Cultural reality worked against economic to stigmatize physical labor and petty commerce. (Durham, 1966) The new middle class, composed largely of immigrants, contributes to "an artificial overpopulation of the traditional professions, which continue to retain social prestige if not economic predominance." (Hutchinson, 1960: 358) Since many immigrants achieved success without much education, the schooling received by their children has a largely symbolic value. This implies that there is weak correlation between a person's intelligence and his chances for improving his position, that "personality" rather than capacity is the critical motive force for upward mobility, and that schools and family conventions tend to produce an average individual who would rather preserve status than accept the risks inherent in mobility.

These conclusions are reinforced by Leeds' research (1965), conducted in six cities including São Paulo, on how informal primary groups function to establish and sustain careers in Brazilian urban society. Such a group, or *panelinha* (saucepan), characteristically contains a customs official, an insurance broker, a lawyer, a businessman, an accountant, a local or federal deputy, and a banker. It serves "both status and contractual ends" to provide linkage, horizontal and vertical, among the otherwise weakly interrelated institutions and formal organizations of Brazilian society. The *panelinha* places a premium on the talent for ingratiation, for perception of cues relating to career possibilities, for energetic cultivation of "connections," and for mobilizing *igrejinhas* (little churches) of loyal supporters. By excluding the poor from access to "cue-transmitted information" the system perpetuates institutionalized poverty and the dichotomy between "masses" and "classes."

9. Foreign immigrants in late-nineteenth-century Atlanta, Georgia, were about as mobile as native whites and much more so than Negroes. (Hopkins, 1968) In São Paulo immigrants were generally advantaged over natives of all races, which gives special bite to the phrase "racial democracy" often applied to Brazil.

"Furthermore, the great degree of control exercised over the masses tends to force them to look to the classes for support, thus reinforcing the system structurally and ideologically through institutions generally described as 'paternalistic.'"

Conventional family ties also bolster the position of privileged groups. Not only does a family's involvement with the extended kinship system increase at higher socioeconomic levels, but lower-class kinship systems are inadequate to urban demands for counsel and support, and are largely occupied with "tension management." (Berlinck, 1969: 79-100) The complexity of urban society, moreover, may even strengthen rather than weaken the upper-class family, "since the multiplication of mobility channels may lessen the number of disputes over the control of previously existing ones, decreasing, as a consequence, the possibilities of social conflict that tends to endanger existing structures." (Rosen-Berlinck, 1968: 94)

By calling the barrier between "classes" and "masses" virtually impermeable, Leeds reverses the conclusion of Beals (see above, p. 217), who found only "mild" breaching of barriers between middle and upper classes in urban Brazil and increasing mobility from lower to middle. Goldman (1965: 530) confirms Leeds in finding greater social distance between the upper-middle and lower-middle classes in São Paulo than between the lower-middle and the "urban popular" classes; in effect, he claims, there are only two "clearly visible" classes, the upper-middle and the "popular." These impressions receive empirical support from Hutchinson's mobility study (1963:58), from data on the class origins of São Paulo university students (Table 4), and from a family survey in São Paulo which

TABLE 4

CLASS DISTRIBUTION OF STUDENTS IN TWO UNIVERSITIES
IN THE 1950s (%)

Social class	University of São Paulo	University of Wisconsin
Upper	38	15
Upper middle	36	25
Lower middle	16	30
Upper working	8	25
Lower working	2	5
	100	100

SOURCE: Havighurst, 1958: 178.

concludes that intragenerational mobility correlates positively with social class and that lower- or lower-middle-class persons tend to skid or stay put. (Berlinck-Cohen, 1970) São Paulo, then, seems a prime example of class "polarization" in its Latin American version. (Morse, 1965: 63; Soares, 1967: 41)

The proletariat

Like entrepreneurial and middle-class groups, São Paulo's "popular" classes have received increasing attention. Many who study urban workers in Latin America or the Third World emphasize that in these areas urbanization has outrun or been only loosely linked to industrialization. This leads to the inference that the new urbanization merely transfers poverty from rural to urban areas, inflating the urban work force (particularly the tertiary or "services" sector) with unskilled and irregularly employed laborers, street venders, and disguised mendicants. Cardoso (1969: 104-39) cautions against a simplistic interpretation of the "inflated tertiary," pointing out that the capacity of privileged strata for control and selective absorption of those below raises doubts as to the extent to which lower classes are "marginalized." (Also Morse, 1971)

The tertiarization argument seems especially inapplicable to cities of southern Brazil during the 1940s, where employment in the secondary sector (industry, construction, public services) tended to keep pace with rates of urbanization and employment in services. (Bazzanella, 1963) In 1950 São Paulo had only 16% of its work force unemployed, or "underemployed" in such activities as personal or domestic service and street-vending, compared with 27% in Belo Horizonte and 32% in Salvador (Table 5). The same year Greater São Paulo had 55% of its population in tertiary employment while Rio had 71%. Camargo (1968: 68-71) calls the former's occupational structure "more solid," with a larger secondary sector, more favorable distribution of the tertiary, and fewer persons in unremunerated activities.

If the secondary sector virtually kept abreast of the tertiary in the 1940s, however, its share of the work force dropped by almost 9% in the 1950s while that of the tertiary rose by 10%. During the twenty-year period the income share of the tertiary dropped by 12%. (Table 6.) Both employment and income trends for industry in the 1950s reflect a qualitative change in the industrial park

TABLE 5

UNEMPLOYMENT AND "UNDEREMPLOYMENT" IN THREE BRAZILIAN CITIES, 1950

	Men		Women		Total	
	Number	%	Number	%	Number	%
Work force	769,608	100.0	279,521	100.0	1,049,129	100.0
Unemployed	73,894	9.6	25,791	9.2	99,685	9.5 } 16.1
"Underemployed"	25,262	3.3	44,433	15.9	69,695	6.6

São Paulo

	Men		Women		Total	
Work force	102,472	100.0	48,199	100.0	150,671	100.0
Unemployed	13,676	13.3	5,789	12.0	19,465	12.9 } 27.4
"Underemployed"	3,752	3.7	18,153	37.6	21,905	14.5

Belo Horizonte

	Men		Women		Total	
Work force	123,277	100.0	53,492	100.0	176,769	100.0
Unemployed	17,489	14.2	8,280	15.5	25,769	14.6 } 32.1
"Underemployed"	9,106	7.4	21,795	40.7	30,901	17.5

Salvador

SOURCE: Lopes, 1968: 23.

TABLE 6
DISTRIBUTION OF EMPLOYMENT AND INCOME BY SECTORS IN GREATER SÃO PAULO

Year	Primary Sector			Secondary Sector			Tertiary Sector		
	Persons employed (000's)	% of work force	% of income*	Persons employed (000's)	% of work force	% of income*	Persons employed (000's)	% of work force	% of income*
1940	46.4	7.8	0.8	269.5	45.5	37.4	275.9	46.6	61.8
1950	48.5	4.3	1.0	514.5	46.0	44.2	554.6	49.6	54.8
1960	58.2	3.2	1.3	680.2	37.3	48.8	1087.3	59.5	49.9

*Income percentages for 1939, 1949, and 1959
SOURCE: São Paulo, 1969: I, 41, 43.

marked by mechanization, renovation, heavy capitalization, and a shift from traditional manufactures to electrical, communications, and transportation equipment—notably São Paulo's famous automobile industry. (Pereira, 1967: 16-32; Almeida, 1972) Industrial indices for this decade show a commensurate jump in per capita production. (Table 7) Because the time span of this surge of in-

TABLE 7

INDUSTRIAL INDICES FOR SÃO PAULO STATE (1939/40 = 100)

Year	Number of workers	Value of production (adjusted for inflation)
1939/40	100.0	100.0
1949/50	179.0	176.9
1959/60	237.2	372.1

SOURCE: Pereira, 1967: 31.

dustrial growth and modernization was from 1955 to 1962, its full impact is not registered in Table 6. After 1962 came three years of relative stagnation, following which the growth of the secondary sector recovered its momentum, indicating that "the pace of the 1955-62 expansion will be resumed even though the process of import substitution may have reached the limits of saturation." (São Paulo, 1969: I, 171)

The longer-term, rather unpredictable effects of industrial modernization on tertiary "inflation" in São Paulo constitute an interesting bellwether case for Latin America. One consequence may be a lower occupational ceiling for in-migrants from rural places and small towns. At present disagreement exists as to the comparative advantage enjoyed by native urbanites. Balán (1969: 14) feels that the credentials required to enter São Paulo's occupational structure already militate against migrants, although the rate of increase of jobs in high-productivity sectors eventually absorbs them or their children. Berlinck-Cohen (1970: 60), on the other hand, find that within each socioeconomic stratum no appreciable difference exists between the mobility rates of migrants and those of persons with extended urban residence.[10]

10. Silva (1967) describes typical occupational paths leading the migrant and his children toward absorption into the urban work force. An atypical path

Migration studies raise questions of psychological adaptation as well as those of training and economic opportunity. Touraine (1961) addresses this topic by contrasting the proletarian self-image in contemporary São Paulo with that in pre-World War I Europe. In Europe, he points out, the urban worker felt himself partly *outside* the national society. The era of mass consumption had not yet arrived, and the worker could not aspire to a comfortable middle-class style of life. This motivated him to organize as a proletarian class and sensitized him to appeals and ideologies of international communism, socialism, and anarchosyndicalism. As late as the eve of World War I European socialists wavered between patriotic allegiance to nation and class allegiance to an international proletariat. The European worker won his social democracy only gradually. The achievement of a mass-consumption society is only the recent end-product of a long history of industrialization and political reform. Workers' movements never separated problems of economic policy from the goals of social change, and never faltered in the objective of placing the forces of production under control.

The Brazilian migrant to São Paulo, on the other hand, soon feels himself part of a national society in transition and eligible to consume its products.[11] The appeal of nationalism strikes more deeply than that of class solidarity. What in fact attracted him to the city was not so much the prospect of occupational training and lifelong identification with a single career and social class as vague promises of the urban environment, exemplified in the middle- or upper-class style of life. In this situation Touraine finds that São Paulo's industrial workers adopt three different forms of socialization: (1) The individual search for opportunities, which diminishes worker solidarity in the factory. (2) Solidarity with small primary groups, uninformed by ideology or class consciousness. This camaraderie is kindled in time of crisis and in the face of concrete issues,

is that of Carolina M. de Jesus, an *ex-favelada* whose now-classic diary (1960) relates how she kept her family alive by collecting old newspapers in the streets; once her book became a best seller she moved into a brick house and wrote the sequel (1961). Sarno (1967) and Kowarick *et al.* (1973) present some more conventional life histories. Ferrari (1959) describes cultural adaptations of migrants from northeast Brazil.

11. Rodrigues (1966:101-211) establishes 1930 as the watershed between an ideologically anticapitalist Brazilian labor movement controlled by European workers and a subsequent movement that is elitist, state-dominated, and composed of native workers who harbor "developmentalist" hopes. For the history of strikes and labor problems in São Paulo see Marcílio (1965), Simão (1966), and Rodrigues (1966: 49-100).

but does not outlast the provocation. (3) Acceptance of a vague, generalized image of the society at large. This outlook recognizes the opposition between the weak, disinherited majority and the powerful minority, but without calling into question the appropriateness of existing economic institutions or the social role of capital. It is concerned more with assessing the moral behavior of the elite than with discovering a leverage point for social revolution. The state-supported labor syndicate to which workers appeal for defense functions more as a sovereign granting relief from oppression than as an agent for sociopolitical change created by its members.

These three orientations are not mutually exclusive and may be found in combination, but none is compatible with the grand tradition of proletarian class solidarity. They reflect the fact that the behavior of a worker who comes to São Paulo from a rural or small-town background is guided by personal criteria rather than by requirements of a system, whether a factory routine or class ideology. The most notorious aspect of this complex of personalism is a quest for a dependency or clientage relationship, the search for a *bom patrão*. The natural complement to dependency, however, is personal independence. Touraine finds that Brazilian workers tend more than their French counterparts to resist "the social organization of firms; they do not want masters and they wish to preserve a freedom which is at once reminiscent of bygone working conditions and a sign of nonintegration into the industrial scene." This conclusion is confirmed by Brandão Lopes (1964: 22-95; see also Ferrari 1962), who found that the usual goal of migrants to São Paulo is to work independently as a taxi driver, shopkeeper, or artisan. His explanation is that migrants have already internalized rural norms linked to independent economic activities, including a sense of "obligation." Their lack of experience with urban forms of impersonal, "rational" association together with their knowledge that workers exercise little control in such organizations causes them to redefine their interests on a highly individual basis. The lack of group consciousness which Cardoso notes among industrialists is therefore replicated among workers.

Populism

The political corollary to the situation just described is the politics of populism. As a general Latin American phenomenon, populism has been said to require three ingredients: upper- and middle-level elite groups who harbor anti-*status quo* motivations (that is, "counterelites"); a mass which has become available or mobilized because of a revolution of expectations; and an ideology or widespread emotional state which fosters direct communication between leaders and followers, creating collective enthusiasm. (Di Tella, 1965) Among the first to identify the Brazilian version was Morazé (1954: 135), who interpreted what was later called "populism" as an urban mutation of the traditional politics of the old rural bosses, the *coronéis*. He claimed that a hybrid, new-style politics could first be glimpsed in São Paulo's 1932 revolt against the Vargas regime, when *coronelismo* became allied to urban reformism. "By 1945 one witnesses throughout Brazil a curious amalgam of rejuvenated republican *coronelismo* and new urban political structures which, adapted to the patterns of traditional Brazilian functions, deserves the name 'urban *coronelismo*.'"

"A whole mass of voters is detached from the old colonels; they become partisans of the reforms of the New State and, even before elections take place, they display steadfast confidence in Getúlio Vargas."

There are undoubtedly analogies between *coronelismo* and populism insofar as the latter is institutionalized in local clientage systems whose key figures (*patrão, pistolão, cabo eleitoral, pelego*) have rural counterparts. It is misleading, however, to say that large Brazilian cities are becoming "ruralized" by the influx of rural and small-town migrants; it is rather that country and city share a common but differentiated set of national institutions. Trujillo Ferrari (1962: 171) shows that the *cabo eleitoral* whom migrants from the Northeast encounter in São Paulo differs significantly from the rural version in that he not only delivers votes for a candidate but must also pursue a wide range of activities to politicize constituents and recruit them to party affiliation. The contrast between rural *coronelismo* and urban populism can be drawn as follows (Weffort, 1965a, 1965b; Lopes, 1968: 83-93):

coronelismo	*populism*
1. Social and economic contacts of the populace are restricted to single rural localities.	Adherence of the urban mass to a leader presupposes freedom from local constraints.
2. Political relation between leader and voter is merely one dimension of a broader social dependency.	Political relation between leader and voter is frequently their only relation.
3. Reflects a compromise between public and private power.	Exalts the power of the state, placing it in direct relation with the people.

Weffort and Trujillo Ferrari (1962: 178-79) analyze two divergent styles of populist leadership emanating from São Paulo: the "politics of love" of Ademar de Barros with its benign, conservative, patriarchal appeal to marginal and threatened sectors of the petty bourgeoisie who felt themselves impotent to seize and direct the historical process; and the "politics of hate" of Jânio Quadros with its ascetic, moralistic appeal to proletariat groups who had made their peace with the industrial order but resented the injustices of a society ridden with privilege and favoritism.

In two early interpretations of populist nationalism, Weffort saw it to be of petty-bourgeois inspiration and aimed at radical incorporation of the masses into the national polity, while Ianni (1963) saw it to serve the needs of urban industrialists by soothing the political conscience of the proletariat and restraining the process of politicization. (Debrun, 1964: 236-44) Writing after the military coup of 1964, Cardoso (1969: 154-85) finds that the "developmentalist alliance" which linked industrial-financial groups and "urban-popular" sectors as uneasy partners brought only intermittent benefits to "popular" elements outside the modern industrial sector. The alliance snapped when, at a moment of economic crisis, there was a threat that these least privileged groups might be recruited into its populist wing. Ianni (1968) assumes that the "collapse of populism" closes the chapter of populist democracy in Brazilian history. But whether the long-term outcome of the present situation will be class struggle leading to socialism, as he suggests, or whether, as Cardoso intimates, it will be the "rearticulation of the statist-developmentalist axis," the grass-roots political mechanisms for mobilizing the urban populace that date from the first Vargas period have probably not outlived their usefulness. Nor will they so long as the potential appeal of charismatic leaders for the popular classes is unmediated by agenda tailored to groups and localities, and so long as patronage structures are opportunistic, imposed from above, and inadequate in their rewards.

Revitalized primary groups

City dwellers who despair of finding accommodation within "the system" may be expected to find ways to "secede" from it, psychologically and in some measure organizationally. The prime example in Brazil are non-Catholic religious movements, which may have long-run implications for political action that are now only dimly discernible. Such movements prominently include Pentecostalism, which increased its share of Brazil's Protestant population from less than 10% in 1932 to 60% in 1960, and the mediumistic cults that fall in a spectrum from typically upper-class spiritism or *kardecismo* to typically lower-class *umbanda* and *quimbanda* having syncretic African features.

The sects thrive in areas of rapid change such as rural frontier zones and large cities, and hold special attractions for the least privileged groups. In São Paulo, where mass pilgrimages by bus to attend seaside ceremonies for the goddess Iemanjá were unheard of before the 1950s, the cults have won adherents at a prodigious rate. (Souza, 1969; Camargo, 1961a, 1961b.) In varying styles these movements symbolically subvert the existing power structure, reject upper-class paternalism, and offer the initiate a chance to rebuild his personal community. The convert feels needed and relied on as a "brother." If he possesses "powers" he is accorded the recognition of personal capacity denied by the outer world. The cults provide therapy for anxieties and personality disorder. They aim toward radical reorganization of society and of the personal habits of converts. Some sponsor programs of social assistance through hospitals, asylums, shelters, and schools. (Willems, 1966.)

Because their vitality comes from primary groups, the sects are not effectively organized into regional or citywide associations. Nonetheless they are now recognized to comprise an important sector of the electorate. More important, their accomplishments in reorienting personalities and energizing small groups may be contributing to more effective political mobilization of the urban lower classes. The sects are analogous to populist political structures in that their support and resources supplement the inadequate information exchange available from the lower-class *parentela,* or extended family. (Berlinck, 1969: 45, 89-94) Willems (1967: 259) feels "the organizational schism" of the Pentecostal sects to be "a more adequate means of expressing rebellion against the traditional social order than the doctrinal schism." Although radical Pentecostal groups in São Paulo like the "Christian Congregation of Brazil" condemn political ambitions of their leaders, others like "Brazil for Christ" have provided solid constituencies for designated aspirants or have launched their own candidates, notably in the elections of 1966. (Souza, 1969: 45-46)

Protestant evangelical movements in contemporary Brazil represent an age-old form of protest and renovation within the Catholic order. Though some might see them as outposts of northern industrial civilization, sociologically they seem more akin to the radical sects or congregations of pre-Protestant Europe. The parallel is suggested by a passage in which Troeltsch (1960: I, 343) notes that the reappearance of sects in medieval Europe "was connected with the social transformation, and the new developments of city-civilization in the central period of the Middle Ages and in its period of decline—with the growth of individualism and the gathering of masses of people in the towns themselves— and with the reflex effect of this city formation upon the rural population." Souza (1969: 77-85) employs the ideal types of Troeltsch (1960: I, 331-43) and Weber (1964) to array São Paulo's Pentecostal groups on a gradient from "sect"-type to "church"-type organization. Those with petty-bourgeois adherents and bureaucratized leadership move toward the "church" form and toward accommodation with the larger society. Certain lower-class groups, however, seem able to maintain their emotional fervor and radical nonconformism for indefinite periods.

Like religious cults and squatter communities, guerrilla movements too are rehabilitating anonymous persons and families to assert their force in the metropolitan mass societies of Latin America. After the death of Che Guevara in Bolivia and the collapse of the rural guerrilla strategy publicized by Regis Debray, Brazilian groups in revolt against the military regime initiated urban guerrilla actions in 1968 along lines already familiar in Uruguay (see Guillén, 1966). As stated by the Communist-turned-*guerrilheiro* Carlos Marighela (1971: 78-79), the prime objective of the movement recalled the strategy of General Isidoro Dias Lopes in the 1924 revolt. It was:

> To shake the basis upon which both the State and the domination of North America depend. That basis consists of the Rio-São Paulo-Belo Horizonte triangle, a triangle whose base is the line from Rio to São Paulo. It is there that the country's vast industrial, financial, economic, political, cultural and military power is concentrated—in other words the centre of national decision.

In São Paulo the guerrillas took more than $600,000 from fifty banks in one year and gave impetus to strong outbreaks of student protest.

The hoped-for solidarity of the lower classes, however, did not and could not materialize. The increasingly repressive national government killed or captured many guerrilla leaders in late 1969 and early 1970, leaving it for a possible future to reveal the full potential of guerrillas in urban Brazil. (Quartim, 1971)

Race and class

The most sustained and penetrating sociological study of São Paulo yet written is probably Florestan Fernandes' analysis (1964) of the incorporation of the Negro into urban society. Fernandes conclusively demonstrates the presence of color prejudice in São Paulo, bringing to light its origins, functions, effects, and resultant dilemmas. He does less to disprove earlier scholars who linked color prejudice to social prejudice than to show that they failed to take account of developments since 1930 in Brazil's leading industrial metropolis. Here, appreciable numbers of Negroes have achieved socioeconomic mobility without corresponding relief from pressures of color prejudice. In other words, the parallelism between racial and social attitudes has been broken. Fernandes explodes the myth of "racial democracy," showing how the reality of prejudice is camouflaged by the "external cordiality" and "mask of civility" which, in his clinical view, reflect a cultural paucity of "social techniques for manipulating tensions."

Two special strengths of Fernandes' presentation are: (1) his generous temporal perspective, which allows one to perceive discriminatory patterns as a form of inertial traditionalism rather than an innovative defense mechanism, and thus to gauge their historical logic and momentum; (2) his unmasking of the color-related psychological stress experienced by both whites and Negroes, a feature which escapes many other analyses. If there is oversimplification in his otherwise elaborate treatment of color prejudice it may lie in his failure to contrast the position of blacks with that of mulattoes. There are only occasional hints as to whether he accepts the distinction between "prejudice of origin" and "prejudice of mark," or between "genealogical" and "phenotypical" color. (Bastide-van den Berghe [1957] detect both attitudes in São Paulo.)

As the book's title indicates, however, the author is concerned not simply with clarifying the forms and prevalence of color prejudice but also with identifying obstacles to the incorporation of

Negroes into urban society at various periods since the abolition of slavery in 1888. It is a study in sociology as well as social psychology. The key proposition is that a "bourgeois revolution" has transformed São Paulo society into one that is competitive and class-based for increasing numbers of white citizens, yet subjects Negroes and mulattoes to archaic forms of domination inherited from the "society of estates and castes" of the nineteenth century.[12] The challenging part of this proposition is the assertion that whites themselves participate in an open, competitive class society, for it is at odds with the fact the many sociologists cited earlier deny Marxian class identity to the proletariat, to middle groups, and to entrepreneurial elites. Indeed, Queiroz (1965) generalizes the thesis of weak class identifications to Brazilian society as a whole. It is no surprise that Fernandes' description of how Negroes achieve mobility by ingratiating white protectors echoes the Hutchinson finding that white immigrants' children often get ahead by virtue of "personality," not capacity;[13] or that his analysis of the "acephalization" of the Negro community, which occurs as successful members infiltrate the "world of the whites" and lose identification with the "mass of the colored," recalls Touraine's finding that workers who obtain steady jobs and syndical protection abrogate their allegiance to the subproletariat. It is even the case that Fernandes' three forms of Negro personality adjustment to white dominance (1964: 508-18) are virtually identical to the three ways in which Touraine (1961: 84) finds workers adapting to urban society at large:

Forms of Negro personality adjustment (Fernandes)	Forms of worker personality adjustment (Touraine)
1. passivity and conformism	apathetic adaptation a. *conscience segmentée* b. *conscience éclatée*
2. complex of fear which causes the Negro to make ineffective use of opportunities for upward mobility	utopian nonconformism; submissiveness combined with hopes for own or children's advancement
3. reactive mechanism permitting a dynamic response to concrete possibilities	reinterpretation of present situation leading to integration of attitudes

12. Elsewhere Fernandes (1968: 107-99) expands his analysis of a two-stage "bourgeois revolution" (1875-1930, 1930–).
13. From a study of São Paulo families Rosen (1962: 623) concludes that "submission in the form of ingratiation and obedience is the dominant adjustment to authority in Brazil."

If São Paulo's population is less than 10% black, then great numbers of whites as well as most Negroes are denied access to significant opportunity. Leeds' guess (1965: 397) that the larger urban societies of Brazil are composed 40% of privileged "classes" (used here without connotations of "integration" or "self-consciousness") and 60% of underprivileged "masses" roughly corresponds to the 1968 income figures for Greater São Paulo, which show 54% of the population earning less than 500 new cruzeiros a month per family. (Table 8) Within the "classes," Leeds observes, ascent

TABLE 8

FAMILY INCOMES IN GREATER SÃO PAULO (1968)

Group	Monthly income (N Cr)	% of population
Lower	less than 200	16.6
Lower middle	200-500	37.4
Middle	500-1000	25.6
Upper middle	1000-2000	13.4
Upper	more than 2000	7.0

In mid-1968 3.6 new cruzeiros (N Cr) were worth one dollar.

Source: São Paulo, 1970: III, 222.

from lower strata is selectively controlled at the top. Aspirants must therefore secure favor and protection, utilizing the small-group support and connections afforded by the *panelinha*. Again, the similarity to Fernandes' description of mobility patterns for Negroes is evident. One is therefore led to question the assertion that "the 'white' stocks of the São Paulo population soon acquired the psychological and sociocultural traits which characterize class formation." (Fernandes, 1964: 253) For advancement in São Paulo society seems to depend less on the strength and militancy of class identifications than on a capacity to organize primary-group coteries and *trampolins* ("springboards").[14] Fernandes (1964: 495) in effect recognizes this when he attributes "the failure of the 'Negro' vis-à-

14. The immigrant-led labor movement of the early twentieth century, notably São Paulo's 1917 general strike, forced the nation to heed the oppression of the proletariat, but the workers' "importance as a social force was practically nil." (Marcílio, 1965: 129) The early labor leaders had no more success in creating permanent "class" ideology and militancy than did the Negro protest movements of 1927-1945 that sought the "Second Abolition."

vis the Italian, the 'Turk' and especially the Japanese" to the superior capacity of the latter groups to generate mutual aid and cooperativism—precisely the forms of solidarity which, in Marxist literature, are *antecedent* to the formation of class consciousness. The point is also implicit when he observes that many Negroes now appreciate the importance of establishing the "integrated Negro family" as a firm, small-group basis for socializing the child and supporting the ambitions of the young. (1964: 524) Other small-group organizations available to Negroes, which may well have greater significance than their potential for "class" militancy, are the spiritist and Pentecostal sects; it is revealing that he pays them no attention.

In short, Fernandes claims that the historical and cultural imperatives of the "society of estates" of the nineteenth century no longer govern relations among urban whites but continue to govern those between whites and urban Negroes. Evidence from other sociologists and from Fernandes' own research, however, lays the first part of this proposition under question. It seems more accurate to say that the whole of urban society is permeated with vigorous survivals from the agro-commercial regime of the past (status ascription, hierarchical patterns of deference, masks of etiquette, clientage systems, primary-group organization) which have been reworked in answer to structural and psychological requirements of industrialism and urbanization. The Negro is severely disadvantaged in his quest for opportunities because: (1) he has not inherited a position of prestige and authority, such as that long monopolized by the "traditional-whites"; (2) he has been handicapped vis-à-vis immigrant groups because of their focused motivations and their cultural resources for family and mutual-assistance organization; (3) he is victimized by color prejudice. Negroes are a negatively privileged but not an outcast group. Their hopes for the future would seem to depend less on their ability to develop "class consciousness" or a "racial self-image" than on their success at discovering and revitalizing forms of action consistent with the traditions of the culture which they share.

Cultural tradition and social change

None of the sociological studies that have been cited endorses the simplistic notion that the Paulista industrial region is merely recapitulating the historic socioeconomic stages of the northern industrial countries. They emphasize configurations of tradition and innovation, linkages between political and economic change, attitudes toward work, authority, and social action that are largely without precedent in nineteenth-century industrial societies. Analysts of social change in contemporary Brazil recognize what Brandão Lopes (1964) calls the "juxtaposition of epochs."

By virtue of their primary focus on change or process, however, most of these descriptions of urban society make it appear that present configurations are "transitional" toward a more standard or universal ethos of industrialism. The idiosyncrasy or "asymmetries" of prevailing patterns are attributed to alterations of the phasing and sequences associated with nineteenth-century industrialization. Little attention is paid to the enduring belief system which not only influences "transitional" patterns but may significantly determine the features of the more completely industrialized society of the future. Thus, for example, Cardoso (1964: 159-187) is concerned with how the "industrial bourgeoisie" is to attain ideological consistency in a society en route from "irrational" to "rational" patterns of economic action, from "traditional" forms of behavior to "collective modernizing aspirations."[15] Hutchinson (1958b: 19) observes that a unilinear process of "disintegration of the immigrant primary group, and of the consanguine family pattern, follows closely in São Paulo the lines suggested by Talcott Parsons' analysis of the rise of western society." Leeds (1965: 379-382) describes his research as a case study for a broader inquiry into "regularities of developmental sequences" from "static-agrarian" to "expansive-industrial" societies. Goldman (1965: 539) predicts that the Paulista worker may acquire class consciousness "following patterns like those of Europe," while Fernandes (1964) defines the problem of the Negro as one of integrating to a society which has *already* moved from a basis of castes or estates to one of classes.[16]

No one would deny the appropriateness of this concern with change to a study of São Paulo society. Moreover, the versions of

15. Cardoso (1961: 163) does however hint that "rationality" requires contextual definition, and he criticizes simplistic dual or polar modes of analysis (1969: 135-9).

16. Soares (1967) criticizes "unilinear" frameworks for Latin American development but emphasizes structural and international factors, while my discussion emphasizes psychocultural ones.

development theory just cited all fit respectably within Durkheim's classic paradigm for the transformation of societies from regimes of mechanical to those of organic solidarity in response to the requirements of division of labor. What must be remembered, however, is that Durkheim's model is transcultural. It attempts to identify generic, universal requirements for complex industrial societies. As he made clear in his preface to the second edition of the *Division of Labor,* he himself was uncertain as to specific institutional arrangements that industrial division of labor might dictate in any particular society. He was also aware that unpropitious conditions might generate "abnormal forms." Contemporary analysts of São Paulo society tend to identify such conditions as temporary rigidities caused by the "juxtaposition of epochs." Few give serious attention to long-term cultural imperatives that will leave their mark on institutions of that eventual society variously described as rational (Cardoso), individualistic (Hutchinson), expansive-industrial (Leeds), and open-competitive (Fernandes).

What must be made explicit in the study of Brazilian urban society is that social attitudes and social action continue to be informed by the pervasive Catholic ethic, however lax or heterodox Brazilian church-goers may be. Language and ideologies of belief may change from one decade to the next; but the premises of belief—the often unspoken assumptions about how people are to enter a state of grace, singly or collectively—are far more durable. A primary task in analyzing the industrialization and urbanization of Brazil is therefore to chart present and foreseeable patterns of accommodation between the foundations of a Catholic society and Durkheim's requirements for organic solidarity produced by division of labor.

What partly accounts for neglect of this point is the fact that Max Weber so persuasively identified the Protestant ethic with "rational" economic organization and capital accumulation. To emphasize the tenacity of the Catholic ethic in Brazil might seem—to any but a staunch Catholic ideologue—to condemn its society to penury, atrophy, and tumult.[17] Societies, however, do not abrogate spiritual commitments easily. The secret of an effective educational

---

17. Fernandes (1964: 629), for example, finds that Catholic morality is more suited to coating the pill of prejudice with artifices and rationalizations than to effecting reform of attitudes and social organization.

reform or a successful "revolution" is that it returns to and reinterprets such commitments. As suggested above, the radical Protestant sects of contemporary urban Brazil might be construed as an archetypal form of protest and renovation within a Catholic civilization. Whatever resistances the Catholic ethic may offer to Weberian requirements for "rational" economic and organizational behavior, one must recognize its historic traditions of protest and "revolution" as well as its therapeutic promise for pathological conditions of depersonalization, cut-throat competitiveness, and anomie.

The role of the religious ethic in Brazil's social and economic development becomes clearer when we call to mind the Japanese case. In his study of Japanese city life, Dore (1965) shows how private ambition, or "getting on," was legitimized during the early Meiji period in the framework of a morality oriented toward the collectivity.[18] The leaders of the Meiji Restoration were mostly samurai of lower grades who rose to positions of power by virtue of ability. They had no vested interest in the existing feudal hierarchy and were concerned "to dismantle the class structure from the top" and to design egalitarian reforms. "A unified nondiscriminatory school system was established and has persisted to the present day with, at the primary and secondary level, only a very limited development of private-school alternatives." Channels of mobility were opened—bureaucratic, military, entrepreneurial; and although patronage continued to lubricate the advancement of talent, bureaucratic status became ascribed to persons rather than families, and individual enterprise was encouraged as necessary to the state.

In São Paulo, according to the Hutchinson studies, the situation was almost the reverse. Social ascension certainly took place, but as a by-product of economic change, not as the fruit of systematic promotion of ability. Successful climbers tended to adopt an elitist outlook, and the educational process functioned more to validate privilege than to recruit talent. The merits of individual enterprise were publicized, but its exercise was enjoyed principally by elite groups and foreign concessionaires; its contributions to national welfare or to strengthening the state were fortuitous.

18. Dore (1964) has perceptively developed the Japanese-Latin American comparison.

Urban Japan and urban Brazil of the late nineteenth and early twentieth centuries both exhibit preindustrial survivals: familialism, paternalism, patron-client relations, hierarchical attitudes of deference, weak class identifications. But in Japan these features were accommodated to a state-supported system which required identification and release of talent from lower social strata. "The masses, in short, had minds, not simply souls, to be saved." (Dore 1964: 235.) In Brazil the wellborn and most foreigners were immensely advantaged for careers, and the state was not erected into an engine for social reorganization and economic development.

The contrast between these two industrializing societies can be related to a difference in social ethic. In Japan the reformulation of Shinto and Confucian ideals promoted the mystique of a strong, integrated, imperial nation while encouraging social attitudes that served the needs of personal self-development, among them consideration for others, loyalty to principles, frank expression of opinion, equality before the law, equality of the sexes, the duty of personal accomplishment, and the right to self-fulfillment. Except for its failure to include liberation of private conscience, this list corresponds to conventionally cited moral requirements for an industrial society, or to features of Durkheim's organic solidarity.

Catholicism, unlike Shinto, is a universal faith and therefore a less reliable source of mystique for nation-building. Furthermore, although the resources of Catholicism for personal consolation are impressive, it is not a faith which conspicuously motivates and rewards personal accomplishment. The Catholic community, as Weber (1964: 186-190) analyzes it, is one in which grace is institutionally dispensed. In such a society the personal qualifications of those seeking "salvation" are a matter of indifference to the institution distributing grace. Salvation is universal and therefore accessible to other than "virtuosi"; in fact, the virtuoso falls under suspicion if he seeks to attain grace by his unaided power. The expectation of personal accomplishment is modestly defined, for the conduct of life is largely patterned by distributions of grace by institutions and charismatic persons. The vouchsafing of grace facilitates the individual's capacity to bear guilt and "largely spares him the necessity of developing an individual planned pattern of life based on ethical foundations. . . . Hence, value is attached to concrete individual acts rather than to the total personality pattern which has been produced by asceticism, contemplation, or eternally vigilant self-control." This typology is consistent with recent socio-logical findings for São Paulo and helps to place them in historical and cultural perspective.

Juxtaposing Durkheim's transcultural moral requirements for in-dustrialization with Weber's paradigm for the ethos of Catholicism has important advantages for the study of urbanization in Brazil, assuming that idiosyncratic historical circumstances are not lost sight of. This approach draws attention to psychological commit-ments and to the morphology and logic of institutions rather than to artificial stages and dynamisms. It leads us to construe urban change in Brazil as the transactions between an enduring social ethic and the flexible preconditions, both moral and organizational, for any industrial society—and not as an extraneous ethic impinging on an "archaic" social system, or as the collision of two closed and alien systems. For all its apparent resistance to the "rationalism" of an industrial market society, the ethic in question has historically demonstrated considerable resilience and innovative potential. It may in the long run help to preserve certain affective modes of fellowship and moral bases for action which in other technified Western societies seem lost beyond retrieve.

The mirror of literature

Turning from social science to literature refreshes one's sense of the immediacies of a city. São Paulo is often a setting for prose fiction (Antônio 1966), but in this case one finds the city's person-ality projected less forcefully in the genre of the novel than in periodic bursts of creativity in the several literary and art forms. Antonio Candido (1965: 167-199) identifies five historical "mo-ments" since 1750 when groups of writers and artists, each in a different relationship to the urban community, have imaginatively rendered its "social and spiritual life." The two most vigorous were the Romantics of 1845 and the Modernists who rallied at Modern Art Week in 1922. The Romantics were law students—marginated by their society, given to amorous idealism, melancholia, sarcasm, satanism, and necrophilia—who contributed a "Paulista tonality" to the whole of Brazilian romantic literature. The style of the Modernists has an equally strong regional accent. Their mission, however, was not to secede from urban society, which was by now complex and dynamic enough to accommodate them, but to defy academicism and cultural snobbery and to break the artistic monopoly of the elite.

Both Silva Brito (1964) in his exhaustive study of the origins of Modern Art Week and Wilson Martins (1965) in his conspectus of the whole movement agree on the urban, Paulista inspiration of Modernism. Its early phase reflected the impudence and iconoclasm and experimentalism of a generation born in the 1890s, the first to be formed in the ethos of bustling commercialism and dynamic change. If, however, the preceding sociological analysis holds true —if the dynamism of the present has reworked without effacing the patriarchal heritage from the past—we would expect the post-Modernist writer to come to grips with this theme. Such is the case with São Paulo's foremost contemporary playwright, Jorge Andrade, whose theater documents a personal quest for the vitalities and meanings of the old patriarchal order and their implications for the fragmented, anonymous world of today. In this sense his plays recapitulate the dominant motif of Gilberto Freyre's work; but whereas Freyre's sentimental and psychological ambivalences remain largely subliminal, Jorge Andrade persistently objectifies his in dramatic form.

Jorge Andrade's theater is pertinent to our concerns precisely because he is not an "urban" playwright but takes a whole society as his subject. He perceives city energies as fermenting and eroding the old agrarian order, yet also as being dampened, deflected, or turned on themselves in a setting vaguely hostile to them. An "urban" play such as *A Escada* (The Staircase) must therefore be considered in a context with: *Pedreira das Almas* (Quarry of Souls), which turns back in history to render the archetypal ancestral family with epic, sculptural strength; *A Moratória* (The Moratorium), which catches the plantocracy at its moment of collapse, weaving an ironic temporal counterpoint between the threshold and aftermath of disaster; and *O Telescópio* (The Telescope), which shows the ideals and accomplishments of a coffee planter's family being undermined by the hedonism, slovenliness, and city-bred acquisitiveness of the young generation.

A Escada transports the generational conflict to the urban setting. Whereas *O Telescópio* measures children against the norms of their parents in the domain of the *fazenda*, the aging father and mother in *A Escada* dwell in the city, where they appear as living ghosts through the eyes of their married children. The children have made their respective adjustments to city life—save for the perplexity, guilt, and exasperation created by the sentimental burden of the past in the form of their anachronistic parents. Condescendingly, the children allow the parents their "illusions" and freedom, take turns caring for them, explain away their idiosyncrasies to outsiders. Yet the presence of the senile couple becomes cumulatively more oppressive. Their recollections and remarks and actions continually interfere with the domestic routine, personal relations, and business affairs of the children's families. Oblivious to the human dramas about them, they live unreachably in a fantasy world of the past. ("The past is a monster!" one son finally cries out.) Filial duty prevents the children from following their separate interests and moving to homes of their choice. Just as the staircase linking their four adjoining apartments symbolizes the forced solidarity of the young generation, so, ironically, does it afford the parents free access to the city, where their business schemes and acts of hauteur create repeated family embarrassments. At length the children prove incapable of handling the burden of the past; they send their parents to an institution and in "great anguish" watch them depart as the curtain falls.

The tension of Jorge Andrade's theater derives not from the universal theme of generational conflict but from his unrelenting quest to locate the "reality" of his own world, and from his honest struggle with the suspicion that it may reside irrecoverably in the more solid, rounded lives of tradition and memory. This is the question, the ambivalence, the fear expressed by the son in *A Escada* who tells why he likes his parents to live with him.

> It's as though a whole world were caught in my hands! A completely different world that we alone possess! no one else! They stay inside there, locked in . . . you only hear a murmur! And I always having the feeling that if I open this door I'll find the answer to so much that torments me . . . and I don't know just what it is! But I don't want to open it! I don't know what holds me back!

Who then inhabits the world of fantasy? The old couple lost in reveries of the Empire? Or their children who dare not acknowledge the force and consistency of those dreams? Only the Italian *nouveau riche* in Jorge Andrade's comedy, *Os Ossos do Barão* (The Bones of the Baron), can relate fearlessly, generously, comprehendingly to those who "carry the caravel of Martim Afonso de Sousa on their backs." But he is an immigrant, born of another "reality." This play provides a palliative but no resolution for the tension of the playwright. His most intimate drama, *Rasto atrás* (Backtracking), suggests in fact that this resolution must be pursued on a very personal plane.

If Jorge Andrade has explored the nostalgia and ambivalences of the *haute bourgeoisie*, then—as we recall Leeds' classes and masses, or Goldman's upper and "popular" classes—it is Plínio Marcos who renders the desperate, elemental world of the *Lumpenproletariat*. His *Navalha na carne* (Razor in the Flesh) has been called a poor man's *Huis-Clos*. The single scene is a shabby hotel room where three characters—a prostitute, her pimp, and a male homosexual—are trapped in a primitive drama of self-preservation. Obscenity, braggadocio, selfishness, duplicity, threats, and sadomasochism are the coin of their personal relations. When the prostitute relents for an instant she forfeits her money and her brief interlude of sexual release with the pimp. What cripples their life is not economic deprivation but moral infantilism. "Sometimes I even wonder," sighs the prostitute, "*pôxa*, am I really a person? Are you and I and Veludo people? I almost doubt it!"

The plays of Plínio Marcos are neither militant proletarian theater nor a theater of the absurd in a morally anarchic world. He gives us a "pre-morality play." Like the razor that flashes between pimp and whore as a surrogate for the mutuality they can never attain, so the play itself is a blade against the flesh of the larger society. Beyond even this, it bares the stubborn core of yearning, fright, and egotism that lies beneath the masks of Everyman.[19]

A literary reconstruction of the city should compose such strokes of the private imagination against a generalized, anonymous image from its popular culture. Mário de Andrade referred to the latter in explaining why Modernism exploded in São Paulo rather than the nation's capital. São Paulo, he wrote in *O movimento Modernista*, was the highland *caipira* who had preserved a servile, provincial

---

19. Jorge Andrade's one "proletarian" play (*Vereda da salvação*, Path of Salvation) deals with rural workers. Although more deprived and, in the conventional sense, exploited than the threesome in *Navalha* (indeed, they are finally massacred), their tiny community still has reference points in the social order and in the cosmos. Political, moral, and religious options are available and must be exercised.

spirit yet who, because of his commercialism and industrialism, lived in closer "spiritual and technical contact with the realities of the world." In São Paulo there was a classic bourgeoisie to be shocked. Rio had the cosmopolitanism and "vibrant malice" of a port and capital, fused with folkloric exoticism and "a traditional, arrested character"—a blend less conducive to cultural revolution.

The folklore studies of Florestan Fernandes (1961: 9-35) confirm this characterization of São Paulo. He finds that the style of urban life developed "in a convergence of cultural legacies somewhat alien to the old rural tradition that had dominated the city." There was less continuity here than in Rio, Salvador, or Recife between inherited and imported cultural forms. Disparaged for its rusticity and provincialism, Paulista folklore could not accompany the evolution of the city to become a true "urban folklore." Research yields only "residues of the old inherited traditions which managed to survive the general liquidation of the disdained rural past." Fernandes predicts not the eventual emergence of a coherent body of urban folklore, but a pluralistic reworking of traditional themes, assisted by technology and mass media (newspapers, recordings, radio, television) and serving diverse functional uses in such areas as recreation, relations with the supernatural, or ethical and esthetic guidance.

The confluence of folk and highbrow currents which produced the São Paulo school of samba in the 1960s sharpens our image of the cultural personality of the city. According to Regis (1966) the internationalism and technical sophistication of bossa nova created problems for self-trained composers and led in 1964 to the appearance of three distinct schools of samba in Salvador, Rio, and São Paulo. Although there is continual exchange among these schools, their local inspiration differs. The Bahian samba reflects systematic research into folkloric traditions. It is a samba "forged close to the roots," liberated from classical forms, bringing freshness and originality to the national musical scene. The Rio samba (*samba de morro, samba de carnaval*) is also of popular inspiration but has explored social and agrarian themes at an ideological level. Folk and highbrow music had not found their synthesis here as of 1966, partly because of the composers' immaturity, partly because of the city's limited facilities for reaching a mass audience. Consumption of good popular music tended still to be an upper-class privilege.

São Paulo possesses more fully developed mass media than Rio (television, press, promotional organizations) and more ample facilities for bringing performances direct to a democratic public of workers and students. The environment encourages dialogue between an intellectual composer and his mass audience. Chico Buarque de Holanda is the prototype of the contemporary Paulista musician; the fact that he composes from a narrower base of folkloric research than the Bahian group is compensated "by the depth of his general vision of the diverse cultures of Brazil." Regis (1966) ascribes his success to his ability to blend an educated middle-class outlook with the culture of the university intelligentsia and produce a music which is popular in fact as well as in name, "which can be and is sung by the people in their daily life and has possibilities for pleasing and illuminating that people."[20]

With Kubler (1964), then, we can give the term "metropolis" cultural as well as ecological definition. It is a city having a distinctive ethos which imbues without circumscribing its cultural expression. It originates styles, ideas, and expressive forms because as a window both to a regional culture and to the world it performs a task of innovative mediation. São Paulo is assuming such a role, and one may expect its cultural self-definition to affect and be affected by the perception of problems in the political, economic, and social orders. This indeed is the burden of the "confession" of Mário de Andrade, high priest of São Paulo's Modernist movement: "I feel that the modernists of Modern Art Week should serve as an example to no one. But we can provide a lesson. Man is passing through an integrally political phase of humanity. . . . And despite our contemporaneity, our nationalism, our universalism, there is one thing we didn't take part in: the politico-social betterment of man. And this is the very meaning of our times." *(O movimento Modernista)*

In retrospect the self-criticism seems unduly harsh, for the achievement of the Modernists was to democratize language and the arts and to revitalize their cultural roots—a *sine qua non,* surely, for "the politico-social betterment of man."

---

20. Galvão (1968) criticizes the lack of ideological content of the contemporary samba, especially Chico Buarque's compositions. They offer consolation and fraternity, she observes, only for the duration of the song; the message is one of fatalism and scepticism.

References

ALMEIDA, JOSÉ.
  1972. A implantação da indústria automobilística no Brasil. Rio de Janeiro, Fundação Getúlio Vargas.
ANDRADE, JORGE.
  1970. Marta, a árvore e o relógio. São Paulo, Editôra Perspectiva.
ANTÔNIO, JOÃO.
  1966. Inquérito: o romance urbano. Revista Civilização Brasileira 1, 7: 190-220.
ARÁUJO FILHO, JOSÉ RIBEIRO DE.
  1969. Santos, o pôrto do café. Rio de Janeiro, Instituto Brasileiro de Geografia.
AZEVEDO, AROLDO DE, ed.
  1958. A cidade de São Paulo, estudos de geografia urbana. 4 vols. São Paulo, Nacional.
———. 1967. A rêde urbana paulista. In: Ernani Silva Bruno, ed. São Paulo terra e povo. Pôrto Alegre, Editôra Globo. Pp. 65-75.
BAER, WERNER and ANNIBAL V. VILLELA.
  1973. Industrial growth and industrialization: revisions in the stages of Brazil's economic development. Journal of Developing Areas 7, 2: 217-234.
BALÁN, JORGE.
  1969. Migrant-native socioeconomic differences in Latin American cities: a structural analysis. Latin American Research Review 4, 1: 3-51.
BARROS, GILBERTO LEITE DE.
  1967. A cidade e o planalto, processo de dominância da cidade de São Paulo. 2 vols. São Paulo, Martins.
BASTIDE, ROGER and PIERRE VAN DEN BERGHE.
  1957. Stereotypes, norms and interracial behavior in São Paulo, Brazil. American Sociological Review 22, 6: 689-694.
BAZZANELLA, WALDEMIRO.
  1963. Industrialização e urbanização no Brasil. América Latina 6, 1: 3-27.
BERLINCK, MANOEL TOSTA.
  1968. População, centralidade relativa e morfogênese sistêmica em áreas

urbanas do Estado de São Paulo. Revista de Administração de Emprêsas 29: 61-79.

———. 1969. The Structure of the Brazilian Family in the City of São Paulo. Ithaca, New York, Cornell University Latin American Studies Program Dissertation Series.

BERLINCK, MANOEL TOSTA and YOUSSEF COHEN.

1970. Desenvolvimento econômico, crescimento econômico e modernização na cidade de São Paulo. Revista de Administração de Emprêsas 10, 1: 45-64.

BRITO, MÁRIO DA SILVA.

1964. História do modernismo brasileiro: I, Antecedentes da Semana de Arte Moderna. 2nd ed. Rio de Janeiro, Civilização Brasileira.

BRUNO, ERNANI SILVA.

1954. História e tradições da cidade de São Paulo. 2nd ed. 3 vols. Rio de Janeiro, José Olympio.

CAMARGO, CÂNDIDO PROCÓPIO FERREIRA DE.

1961a. Aspectos sociológicos del espiritismo en São Paulo. Freiburg and Bogotá, FERES.

———. 1961b. Kardecismo e Umbanda, uma interpretação sociológica. São Paulo, Pioneira.

CAMARGO, JOSÉ FRANCISCO DE.

1968. A cidade e o campo, o êxodo rural no Brasil. Rio de Janeiro, Ao Livro Técnico.

CAMPOS FILHO, CÂNDIDO MALTA.

1972. Um desenho para São Paulo: o corredor metropolitano como estrutura urbana aberta para a Grande São Paulo. São Paulo, Universidade de São Paulo, Faculdade de Arquitetura e Urbanismo.

CANDIDO, ANTONIO.

1964. Os parceiros do Rio Bonito, estudo sôbre o caipira paulista e a transformação dos seus meios de vida. Rio de Janeiro, José Olympio. (2nd ed., São Paulo, Duas Cidades, 1971.)

———. 1965. Literatura e sociedade. São Paulo, Nacional.

CARDOSO, FERNANDO HENRIQUE.

1960a. Proletariado e mudança social em São Paulo. Sociologia 22, 1: 3-11.

———. 1960b. O café e a industrialização da cidade de São Paulo. Revista de História 20, 42: 471-475.

———. 1961 Condições e fatôres sociais da industrialização de São Paulo. Revista Brasileira de Estudos Políticos 11: 148-163.

———. 1964. Empresário industrial e desenvolvimento econômico. São Paulo, Difusão Européia do Livro.

———. 1965. The structure and evolution of industry in São Paulo: 1930-1960. Studies in Comparative International Development 1, 5: 43-47.

———. 1969. Mudanças sociais na América Latina. São Paulo, Difusão Européia do Livro.

COMISSÃO INTERESTADUAL DA BACIA PARANÁ-URUGUAI.

1967. Aspectos do abastecimento na cidade de São Paulo. São Paulo.

CONN, STEPHEN.

1968. The squatters' rights of favelados. Ciências Econômicas e Sociais (Osasco, São Paulo) 3, 2: 50-142.

CORDEIRO, LAERTE LEITE.

1966. O empresário paulista perante os problemas administrativos atuais. Revista de Administração de Emprêsas 6, 20: 21-40.

COSTA, LUIZ CARLOS and LÚCIO FREDERICO KOWARICK.
  1963. Estudos da Bacia Paraná-Uruguai: aspectos demográficos e desen-
    volvimento. Sociologia 25, 4:345-397.
DEAN, WARREN.
  1969. The Industrialization of São Paulo 1880-1945. Austin, University of
    Texas Press.
DEBRUN, MICHEL.
  1964. Nationalisme et politiques du développement au Brésil. Sociologie
    du Travail 6, 3-4: 235-257, 351-380.
DELORENZO NETO, A.
  1967. O município da capital de São Paulo e a região metropolitana.
    Osasco, Faculdade Municipal de Ciências Econômicas e Admin-
    istrativas de Osasco.
DI TELLA, TORCUATO S.
  1965. Populism and reform in Latin America. In: Claudio Véliz, ed. Ob-
    stacles to Change in Latin America. London, Oxford University
    Press. Pp. 47-74.
DORE, R. P.
  1964. Latin America and Japan compared. In: John J. Johnson, ed. Con-
    tinuity and Change in Latin America. Stanford, Stanford Uni-
    versity Press. Pp. 227-249.
———. 1965. City Life in Japan. Berkeley, University of California Press.
DURHAM, EUNICE RIBEIRO.
  1966. Assimilação e mobilidade, a história do imigrante italiano num
    munícipio paulista. São Paulo, Instituto de Estudos Brasileiros.
DURKHEIM, ÉMILE.
  1933. Division of Labor in Society. New York, Macmillan.
FERNANDES, FLORESTAN.
  1961. Folclore e mudança social na cidade de São Paulo. São Paulo,
    Anhambi.
———. 1964. A integração do negro à sociedade de classes. São Paulo, Uni-
    versidade de São Paulo, Faculdade de Filosofia, Ciências e Letras.
    (English translation: The Negro in Brazilian Society. New York,
    Columbia University Press, 1969.)
———. 1968. Sociedade de classes e subdesenvolvimento. Rio de Janeiro,
    Zahar.
FERRARI, ALFONSO TRUJILLO.
  1959. Movimientos migratorios internos y problemas de acomodación del
    inmigrante nacional en São Paulo (Brasil). UN document GEN-
    ERAL E/CN.12/URB/12.
———. 1962. Atitude e comportamento político do imigrante nordestino em
    São Paulo. Sociologia 24, 3: 159-180.
FISHLOW, ALBERT.
  1970. The rise of Brazilian industrialization before the Second World War.
    Unpublished paper.
FORACCHI, MARIALICE M.
  1963. A valorização do trabalho na ascensão social dos imigrantes. Revista
    do Museu Paulista, nova série 14: 311-319.
FRANK, ANDRÉ GUNDER.
  1969. Capitalism and Underdevelopment in Latin America. 2nd ed. New
    York, Monthly Review.
FUNDAÇÃO IBGE.
  1971. Anuário estatístico do Brasil—1971. Rio de Janeiro.

GALVÃO, WALNICE NOGUEIRA.
    1968. MMPB: uma análise ideológica. aParte 2: 18-31.
GAUTHIER, HOWARD L.
    1968. Transportation and the growth of the São Paulo economy. Journal of
        Regional Science 8, 1: 77-94.
GEIGER, PEDRO PINCHAS.
    1963. Evolução da rêde urbana brasileira. Rio de Janeiro, Centro Brasileiro
        de Pesquisas Educacionais.
GOLDMAN, FRANK PERRY.
    1965. Big metrópole, América do Sul. Journal of Inter-American Studies
        7, 4: 519-540.
GUILLÉN, ABRAHAM.
    1966. Estrategia de la guerrilla urbana. Montevideo, Manuales del Pueblo.
HALLER, ARCHIBALD O.
    1967. Urban economic growth and changes in rural stratification: Rio de
        Janeiro 1953-1962. América Latina 10, 4: 48-67.
HAVIGHURST, ROBERT J.
    1958. Education, social mobility and social change in four societies. Inter-
        national Review of Education 4, 2: 167-185.
HOPKINS, RICHARD J.
    1968. Occupational and social mobility in Atlanta, 1870-1896. Journal of
        Southern History 34, 2: 200-213.
HUTCHINSON, BERTRAM.
    1958a. Structural and exchange mobility in the assimilation of immigrants
        to Brazil. Population Studies 13, 2: 111-120.
    ———. 1958b. Conditions of immigrant assimilation in urban Brazil. UN
        document GENERAL E/CN.12/URB/13.
    ———. 1960. Mobilidade e trabalho, um estudo na cidade de São Paulo. Rio
        de Janeiro, Ministério da Educação e Cultura.
    ———. 1963. Urban social mobility rates in Brazil related to migration and
        changing occupational structure. América Latina 6, 3: 47-61.
IANNI, OCTÁVIO.
    1963. Industrialização e desenvolvimento social no Brasil. Rio de Janeiro,
        Civilização Brasileira.
    ———. 1968. O colapso do populismo no Brasil. Rio de Janeiro, Civilização
        Brasileira. (English translation: Crisis in Brazil. New York,
        Columbia University Press, 1970.)
IBGE (Instituto Brasileiro de Geografia e Estatística).
    1957-64. Enciclopédia dos municípios brasileiros. 32 vols. Rio de Janeiro.
IKEDA, AKIHIRO and LUIZ DE FREITAS BUENO.
    1967. Análise demográfica do Estado de São Paulo. São Paulo, Associação
        Nacional de Programação Econômica e Social.
JESUS, CAROLINA MARIA DE.
    1960. Quarto de despejo, diário de uma favelada. 8th ed. São Paulo, F.
        Alves. (English translation: Child of the Dark, the Diary of
        Carolina Maria de Jesus. New York, Dutton, 1962.)
    ———. 1961. Casa de alvenaria, diário de uma ex-favelada. Rio de Janeiro,
        P. de Azevedo.
KOWARICK, LÚCIO et al.
    1973. Os cidadãos da marginal. Argumento 1, 1: 112-131.
KUBLER, GEORGE A.
    1964. Cities and culture in the colonial period in Latin America. Diogenes
        47: 53-62.

LAGENEST, H.-D. BARRUEL DE.
1962. Os cortiços de São Paulo. Anhembi 12, 139: 5-17.
LANGENBUCH, JUERGEN RICHARD.
1971. A estruturação da Grande São Paulo, estudo de geografia urbana. Rio de Janeiro, Instituto Brasileiro de Geografia.
LEEDS, ANTHONY.
1965. Brazilian careers and social structure, a case history and model. In: D. B. Heath and R. N. Adams, eds. Contemporary Cultures and Societies of Latin America. New York, Random House, Pp. 379-404.
————. 1969. The significant variables determining the character of squatter settlements. América Latina 12, 3: 44-86.
LOEB, ROBERTO.
1970. Aspectos do planejamento territorial urbano no Brasil. In: Betty Mindlin Lafer, ed. Planejamento no Brasil. São Paulo, Editôra Perspectiva. Pp. 139-160.
LOPES, JUAREZ RUBENS BRANDÃO.
1964. Sociedade industrial no Brasil. São Paulo, Difusão Européia do Livro.
————. 1968 Desenvolvimento e mudança social, formação da sociedade urbano-industrial no Brasil. São Paulo, Nacional.
LOWE, ARBON JACK.
1969. São Paulo 1990. Américas 21, 1: 28-31.
MARCÍLIO, MARIA LUIZA.
1965. Industrialisation et mouvement ouvrier à Sao-Paulo au début du XXe siècle. Le Mouvement Social 53: 111-129.
————. 1968. La ville de São Paulo, peuplement et population 1750-1850. Rouen, Université de Rouen.
MARCOS, PLÍNIO.
1968. A navalha na carne. São Paulo, Editôra Senzala.
MARIGHELA, CARLOS.
1971. For the Liberation of Brazil. London, Penguin Books.
MARTINS, JOSÉ DE SOUZA.
1967. Empresário e emprêsa na biografia do Conde Matarazzo. Rio de Janeiro, Universidade Federal do Rio de Janeiro, Instituto de Ciências Sociais.
————. 1969. Modernização agrária e industrialização no Brasil. América Latina 12, 2: 3-14.
MARTINS, WILSON.
1965. O modernismo. São Paulo, Cultrix.
MOMSEN, RICHARD P., JR.
1964. Routes over the Serra do Mar, the Evolution of Transportation in the Highlands of Rio de Janeiro and São Paulo. Rio de Janeiro.
MORAZÉ, CHARLES.
1954. Les trois âges du Brésil, essai de politique. Paris, Armand Colin.
MORSE, RICHARD M.
1965. Recent research on Latin American urbanization: a selective survey with commentary. Latin American Research Review 1, 1: 35-74.
————. 1971. Trends and issues in Latin America urban research, 1965-1970. Latin American Research Review 6, 1: 3-52, and 2: 19-75.
MÜLLER, NICE LECOCQ.
1969. O fato urbano na bacia do Rio Paraíba, Estado de São Paulo. Rio de Janeiro, Instituto Brasileiro de Geografia.

NICHOLLS, WILLIAM H.
1969. The transformation of agriculture in a semi-industrialized country: the case of Brazil. In: Erik Thorbecke, ed. The Role of Agriculture in Economic Development. New York, Columbia University Press. Pp. 311-378.

NOGUEIRA, ORACY.
1964. O desenvolvimento de São Paulo: imigração estrangeira e nacional e índices demográficos, demógrafo-sanitários e educacionais. São Paulo, Comissão Interestadual da Bacia Paraná-Uruguai.

OLIVEIRA, ALCIDES CASADO D'.
1966. Um método para a determinação do potencial econômico do Estado de São Paulo. Revista de Administração de Emprêsas 6, 20: 59-88.

PAIVA, RUY MILLER.
1969. Bases de uma política para a melhoria técnica da agricultura brasileira. In: Caio Prado Jr. et al. A agricultura subdesenvolvida. Petrópolis, Editôra Vozes Limitada. Pp. 204-261.

PENTEADO, JACOB.
1962. Belenzinho, 1910. São Paulo, Martins.

PEREIRA, JOSÉ CARLOS.
1967. Estrutura e expansão da indústria em São Paulo. São Paulo, Nacional.

PETRONE, MARIA THEREZA SCHORER.
1968. A lavoura canavieira em São Paulo, expansão e declínio (1765-1851). São Paulo, Difusão Européia do Livro.

PETRONE, PASQUALE, ED.
1963. Pinheiros, aspectos geográficos de um bairro paulistano. São Paulo, Editôra da Universidade de São Paulo.

QUARTIM, JOÃO.
1971. Dictatorship and armed struggle in Brazil. New York. Monthly Review.

QUEIROZ, MARIA ISAURA PEREIRA DE.
1965. Les classes sociales dans le Brésil actuel. Cahiers Internationaux de Sociologie 39: 137-169.

RATTNER, HENRIQUE.
1972. Industrialização e concentração econômica em São Paulo. Rio de Janeiro, Fundação Getúlio Vargas.

REGIS, FLÁVIO EDUARDO DE MACEDO SOARES.
1966. A nova geração do samba. Revista Civilização Brasileira 1, 7: 364-374.

RESUMO DO ESTUDO DA ESTRUTURA URBANA DE SÃO PAULO.
1958. Cuadernos Latinoamericanos de Economia Humana 1, 3: 268-295.

ROCCA, CARLOS ANTÔNIO et al.
1968. A indústria paulista. São Paulo, Associação Nacional de Programação Econômica e Social.

RODRIGUES, JOSÉ ALBERTINO.
1959. Condições econômico sociais da mão de obra em São Paulo. Anhembi 35, 103: 44-63.

RODRIGUES, LEONCIO MARTINS.
1966. Conflito industrial e sindicalismo no Brasil. São Paulo, Difusão Européia do Livro.

ROSEN, BERNARD C.
1962. Socialization and achievement motivation in Brazil. American Sociological Review 27, 5: 612-624.

Rosen, Bernard C. and Manoel T. Berlinck.
1968. Modernization and family structure in the region of São Paulo, Brazil. América Latina 11, 3: 75-96.
Saia, Luiz.
1963. Notas para a teorização de São Paulo. Acrópole 25, 295/6: 209-221. Reprinted in: Morada paulista. São Paulo, Perspectiva, 1972. Pp. 223-257.
————. 1967. A arquitetura em São Paulo. In: Ernani Silva Bruno, ed. São Paulo terra e povo. Pôrte Alegre, Editôra Globo. Pp. 229-251.
São Paulo City (Grupo Executivo do Planejamento).
1970. Plan urbanístico básico. 6 vols. São Paulo, Prefeitura do Município de São Paulo.
São Paulo City (Prefeitura Municipal, Departamento de Cultura).
1969-71. Historia dos bairros de São Paulo. 7 vols. São Paulo, Gráfica Municipal.
São Paulo State (Departamento de Estatística).
1967. A Grande São Paulo. São Paulo, Secretaria de Economia e Planejamento.
São Paulo State (Grupo Executivo da Grande São Paulo).
1969. Diagnóstico definitivo, análise macroeconômica da região da Grande São Paulo. 3 vols. São Paulo, Secretaria da Economia e Planejamento.
Sarno, Geraldo.
1967. Três emigrantes em São Paulo. Teoria e Prática 1: 121-130.
Silva, Armando Corrêa da.
1967. Estrutura e mobilidade social do proletariado urbano em São Paulo. Revista Civilização Brasileira 3, 13: 57-90.
Simão, Azis.
1966. Sindicato e estado, suas relacôes na formação do proletariado de São Paulo. São Paulo, Dominus.
Singer, Paul.
1963. A agricultura na Bacia Paraná-Uruguai. Revista Brasileira de Ciências Sociais 3, 2: 31-171.
————. 1968. Desenvolvimento econômico e evolução urbana. São Paulo, Nacional.
————(ed.). 1973. Urbanización y recursos humanos, el caso de San Pablo. Buenos Aires, Ediciones SIAP.
Soares, Glaucio Ary Dillon.
1967. A nova industrialização e o sistema político brasileiro. Dados 2/3: 32-50.
Souza, Beatriz Muniz de.
1969. A experiência da salvação, Pentecostais em São Paulo. São Paulo, Duas Cidades.
Souza, Heitor Ferreira de.
1968. Área metropolitana de São Paulo. São Paulo, Grupo de Planejamento Integrado.
Stilman, Meyer.
1962. O comércio varejista e os supermercados na cidade de São Paulo. 2 vols. São Paulo, Universidade de São Paulo, Faculdade de Ciências Econômicas e Administrativas.
Taunay, Afonso d'E.
1954. História da cidade de São Paulo. São Paulo, Melhoramentos.

TOURAINE, ALAIN.
    1961. Industrialisation et conscience ouvrière à São-Paulo. Sociologie du
        Travail 3, 4: 77-95.
TROELTSCH, ERNST.
    1960. The Social Teachings of the Christian Churches. 2 vols. New York,
        Harper and Brothers.
WALLE, PAUL.
    1921. Au pays de l'or rouge, l'État de São Paulo (Brésil). Paris, Augustin
        Challamel.
WEBER, MAX.
    1964. The Sociology of Religion. Boston, Beacon.
WEFFORT, FRANCISCO.
    1965a. Raízes sociais do populismo em São Paulo. Revista Civilização
        Brasileira 1, 2: 39-60.
————. 1965b. Política de massas. In: Octávio Ianni et al. Política e revo-
        lução social no Brasil. Rio de Janeiro, Civilização Brasileira. Pp.
        159-198.
————. 1966. State and mass in Brazil. Studies in Comparative International
        Development 2, 12: 187-196.
WILHEIM, JORGE.
    1965. São Paulo metrópole 65. São Paulo, Difusão Européia do Livro.
————. 1969. Urbanismo no subdesenvolvimento. Rio de Janeiro, Editôra
        Saga.
WILLEMS, EMÍLIO.
    1966. Religious movements and social change in Brazil. In: E. N. Baklanoff,
        ed. New Perspectives of Brazil. Nashville, Vanderbilt University
        Press. Pp. 205-232.
————. 1967. Followers of the New Faith, Culture Change and the Rise of
        Protestantism in Brazil and Chile. Nashville, Vanderbilt Uni-
        versity Press.

This index does not include the material in Part V

INDEX

Grande R.

Turvo R.

ARARAQUARA R.R.

BAR

SÃO JOSÉ
RIO PRET

Tietê R.

MATO GROSSO

Aguapei R.

ARAÇATUBA

NOROESTE DO BRASIL R.R.

Peixe R.

ADAMANTINA

PAULISTA R.R.

Paraná R.

PRESIDENTE
PRUDENTE

POMPÉIA

BAU

Paranapanema R.

SOROCABANA R.R.

BO

PARANÁ

SOUTH AMERICA

BRAZIL

BRASÍLIA

SOROC

ITARARÉ

RIO DE JANEIRO
SÃO PAULO

R